Kabbalah and the Spiritual Quest

Recent Titles in
Religion, Health, and Healing

Among the Healers: Stories of Spiritual and Ritual Healing around the World
Edith Turner

Kabbalah and the Spiritual Quest

The Kabbalah Centre in America

Jody Myers

RELIGION, HEALTH, AND HEALING
Susan Starr Sered and Linda L. Barnes, Series Editors

Westport, Connecticut
London

Library of Congress Cataloging-in-Publication Data

Myers, Jody Elizabeth, 1954–
    Kabbalah and the spiritual quest : the Kabbalah Centre in America / Jody Myers.
        p. cm. — (Religion, health, and healing, ISSN 1556–262X)
    Includes bibliographical references and index.
    ISBN-13: 978–0–275–98940–8 (alk. paper)
    ISBN-10: 0–275–98940–2 (alk. paper)
    1. Kabbalah Centre International. 2. Cabala—History. I. Title.
    BM526.M94 2007
    296.8'33—dc22   2007016067

British Library Cataloguing in Publication Data is available.

Library of Congress Catalog Card Number: 2007016067
ISBN-13: 978–0–275–98940–8
ISBN-10: 0–275–98940–2
ISSN: 1556–262X

First published in 2007

Praeger Publishers, 88 Post Road West, Westport, CT 06881
An imprint of Greenwood Publishing Group, Inc.
www.praeger.com

Printed in the United States of America

The paper used in this book complies with the
Permanent Paper Standard issued by the National
Information Standards Organization (Z39.48–1984).

10 9 8 7 6 5 4 3 2 1

Contents

Series Foreword

The Religion, Health and Healing series brings together authors from a variety of academic disciplines and cultural settings in order to foster understandings of the ways in which religious traditions, concepts, and practices frame health and healing experiences in diverse historical and social contexts.

The present volume provides the first thorough examination of the popular phenomenon known as the Kabbalah Centre. Through interviews with Centre leaders and participants and analysis of Centre literature, Jody Myers documents how the Centre uses a vocabulary drawn from ancient and esoteric Jewish texts to offer modern Jews and non-Jews a ritual community, coherent symbol system, and locus for healing.

In this volume, as in other books in this series, we see that the word "healing" in and of itself is multidimensional and multifunctional, especially in religious settings. It can mean the direct, unequivocal, and scientifically measurable cure of physical illnesses. It can mean the alleviation of pain or other symptoms. It can also mean coping, coming to terms with, or learning to live with that which one cannot change (including physical illness and emotional trauma). Healing can mean integration and connection among all the elements of one's being, reestablishment of self-worth, connection with one's tradition, or personal empowerment. Healing can be about repairing one's relationships with friends, relations, ancestors, the community, the world, the Earth, or God. It can refer to developing a sense of well-being or wholeness, whether emotional, social, spiritual, physical, or in relation to other aspects of being that are valued by a particular group. Healing can be about purification, repenting from sin, the cleaning up of one's negative karma, entry into a path of "purer," abstinent, or more moral daily living, eternal salvation, or submission to God's will.

Perhaps the most common theme in religious accounts of healing is the enactment of change, whether understood as restoration to an earlier state or as transformation to a new one.[1] The transformation that comes about in the healing process implies movement from one less desirable state to another, more desirable state. Thus, the study of religion and healing includes looking at how individuals, communities, and religious traditions diagnose and interpret causes of illness and misfortune, as well as at practices aimed at addressing affliction both ideally and pragmatically. In the case of the Kabbalah Centre, this theme is developed in relationship both to the individual in terms of healing from physical and spiritual illness and more broadly to healing the world from communal catastrophes such as the Chernobyl nuclear disaster.

This volume, together with other books in this series, grapples with a core challenge faced by all religious healers: religious healing is not only about belief or ideology, but more importantly about transforming real, tangible suffering. In his classic work on Brazilian religion, Roger Bastide coined the term "law of accumulation." By this he meant the different efforts made by ritual experts to maximize the effectiveness of their healing work by accumulating a wide repertoire of ritual techniques.[2] Bastide's "law" aptly describes contemporary spiritual seekers making their way through the complexities of international, globalized, mixed religious cultures. Indeed, the Kabbalah Centre's repertoire of doctrines and practices mix elements from Judaism, Christianity, and Hinduism and psychoanalytic theory and self-help psychology. At the same time, recognizing the limited potency of healing practices that feel artificial or cobbled together, the Kabbalah Centre casts itself as a movement with authentically ancient roots.

We hope that through facilitating the publication of studies of diverse healers, healing communities, and healing practices, we will offer readers tools to uncover both the common and the uncommon, the traditional and the innovative, and the individual and the communal ways in which Americans engage with, find meaning in, and seek to embrace, transcend, or overcome affliction and suffering.

Susan Starr Sered and Linda L. Barnes

March 2007

NOTES

1. For more on this, see Linda Barnes and Susan Sered, eds., *Religion and Healing in America* (New York: Oxford University Press, 2005).

2. Roger Bastide, *African Civilisations in the New World* (New York: Harper and Row, 1971).

Preface

Dressing entirely in white is normal practice on a five-block stretch of Robertson Boulevard in Los Angeles. Western men and women, garbed in white from their turbans to their Keds, traverse the busy streets surrounding the Sikh Temple. Further north, you have to wait until Friday afternoon to see white clad young men in yarmulkes gathering outside the Kabbalah Centre greeting each other with hugs, the spaces around them filled with women and children wearing multicolored garments. As a professor of religious studies, I was familiar with the new purity rituals of twentieth-century American converts to Sikhism; my doctorate in Jewish history, however, did not explain the white-garbed Kabbalists. I was curious to learn how medieval Jewish Kabbalah, its purity concerns expressed in doctrines, such as the demonic power of women's menstrual blood or the soulless bodies of Gentiles, had been made palatable for what looked like a hip, ethnically mixed, contemporary audience in my neighborhood. Friends and associates warned me not to set foot in the place: two women acquaintances confided that their husbands' involvement in the Kabbalah Centre had hastened the end of their marriages, rabbis alerted me to the strange teachings they had heard from troubled congregants, and therapists recounted tales of vulnerable women lured into servitude and debasement by charismatic teachers. My academic colleagues, including those trained in Kabbalah—who, unlike me, could assess the historical authenticity of the Centre's teachings—adamantly refused to walk through the sculpted wooden doors of the Centre and investigate the offerings within. Being the intrepid and resolute sort, I decided to research the organization anyway, and the need to fill an upcoming semester of sabbatical leave made the prospect irresistible. I began attending the Los Angeles Kabbalah Centre in the fall of 1999. This book presents my experience and my findings.

There are lots of ways to attend the Kabbalah Centre, and I cannot pretend that mine were entirely typical. For several years, I looked ostensibly like many of the "on again, off again" students at the Los Angeles Centre who check out the place through the free introductory lecture and then sign up for the 10-week (90 minutes per session) Kabbalah I course. When that was completed, I enrolled in two more courses. Over the next few years, I attended occasional special lectures and Sabbath activities, listened to audio tapes, and read the latest publications. I visited the Centres in Israel, London, and New York. Unlike most people who made such efforts, however, I did not engage in the recommended daily meditations or change any aspects of my customary religious practice. In addition, during the first few years, I made sure that no one would really notice me. I never chose someone to be my teacher, I did not try to make friends, and I refused all suggestions to volunteer or attend special study sessions outside of class.

When, in early 2005, I finally decided to write a book on the Kabbalah Centre, I abandoned this "fly on the wall" approach. I employed a methodology of "disciplined empathy," the term used in the field of religious studies to describe a scientific and objective approach that incorporates an insider's view of the religious phenomenon under study. Although I did not adopt the spiritual practices of the Centre, I became a more engaged listener and observer. I informed the directors and teachers of my project and received their assistance in interviewing teachers and staff. I went to additional classes and events, including an international Rosh Hashanah retreat. I sought out interviews with "unofficial" men and women from a variety of backgrounds, ages, and levels of involvement. This was a somewhat random process of looking for friendly-looking people or those who seemed easy to approach. If we hit it off, I disclosed my intentions and arranged an interview. "How did you first get involved?" "How do you apply the teachings?" "How has your involvement changed your life?" were a few of the questions I asked. Kabbalah Centre books, documents, and Web communications, in addition to popular articles and research in the history and sociology of religion, became my reading of choice. I also interviewed ex-members and opponents of the Centre and examined a prodigious number of popular media articles, accusatory reports, and editorials.

Had I relied only on written sources for my study of the Kabbalah Centre, I would have remained ignorant about much of what is contained in this book. Trained as a historian, I learned a number of methods of researching contemporary religion when I was hired in an academic department of religious studies. Yet, it was only when I added ethnography to the tools with which I study religion that I was able to grasp fundamental aspects of Kabbalah Centre teachings. Hearing the participants' own account of their experiences and the teachings enabled me to see beyond the disdain aroused by any group that promotes an alternative perspective on older religious doctrines and beyond the sensationalist reporting generated by the Kabbalah Centre's celebrity followers. I realized that the Kabbalah Centre's method of outreach, a clever type of marketing that is very successful at bringing people through its doors, tends to conceal the core components of its teachings.

Despite my immersion, the portrait of the Kabbalah Centre in this book should be regarded as one educated observer's view of a new religious community in evolution. Sociologists explain that new religions will form during a time of change when older understandings of the world do not seem to apply anymore. A leader arises who makes sense of the new reality and explains and models better ways to behave. He or she connects these new interpretations and behaviors to existing ones, so that it appears that the new path is not really new, but a purer form of an existing religion or spiritual outlook. With the right skills and a favorable environment, a community of like-minded and enthusiastic people can grow. Only by undergoing rapid change will a small religious community become a sizable, established one. My own observation of the Kabbalah Centre began when it had already arrived on a firm footing. During the seven years I was involved, I witnessed the original founders increasingly pass on greater responsibility to the next generation. Before my eyes, I saw greater professionalization and standardization in the operations and curriculum, and I watched the organization expand and grow more influential. In this book, however, I have kept my attention on what it means to be a practicing and believing member of the community.

Figuring this out has been quite a challenge. Because of its connection to Kabbalah, an elite expression of Jewish mysticism, Kabbalah Centre social relations and communal structure resemble that of an esoteric religion. In accordance with the definition offered by historian of religion Olav Hammer, the Kabbalah Centre is an example of an esoteric religion that has internalized the democratic values of its environment. In such a case, the leader—Rabbi Philip Berg—receives knowledge as privileged information, and he is the prime exegete, but he in turn passes it on to the multitudes. The criteria for ascending the hierarchy are in accordance with democratic values: ascension is open to those who wish to do and practice more.[1] This, ostensibly, is what the Kabbalah Centre promises: the more you do, the more you learn, the more powerful and enlightened you will be. If you do not want to do more, there need be no guilt, for there is no obligation. You simply will not receive the benefit.

Followers eventually filter out into concentric circles: the largest is the peripheral group of supporters and spiritual seekers who have accepted kabbalistic "philosophy." These tend to be individualistic spiritual seekers of a wide variety of ethnic and religious backgrounds. To them, Kabbalah is a purely intellectual resource that answers questions about the origins of the cosmos and the purpose of human existence. It makes few practical demands; it is a spiritual outlook. Moving inward, the next concentric circle contains people who accept Kabbalah Centre doctrines and engage in a few rituals such as meditating on Hebrew letters, drinking water infused with the power of Kabbalah, and wearing a red string bracelet. Moving inward, there is an inner core of followers who have absorbed Kabbalah Centre doctrines and perform the above rituals as well as many *mitzvot*—the "commandments" practiced by devout Jews. They are, essentially, practitioners of a singular type of Judaism. With few exceptions, the members of the inner core are ethnically Jewish with a high proportion of Israelis.

The Kabbalah Centre is an excellent vehicle for illustrating the international, globalized, hybrid nature of today's religious culture. Living in an environment characterized by religious pluralism and resistance to religious authority, individuals searching for a nurturing spiritual life filter through diverse traditions, especially exotic ones, to find those that fit. Not only do they have access to foreign religions rooted in distant lands, but the thousands of immigrants in American cities also make it far easier to move freely between religious worlds by walking through nearby neighborhoods, or by way of television, reading, public lectures, and the media. There is an expanded menu of teachings, images, rituals, and techniques available for perusal and adaptation. Secular outlooks are also an option. Spiritual seekers select from these sometimes theoretically incompatible ingredients to create a sustaining spiritual practice. The Kabbalah Centre's doctrines, rituals, and outreach techniques conspicuously illustrate this phenomenon, mixing together elements from Judaism, New Age, psychotherapy, physics, medicine, and popular culture. Kabbalah Centre teachers and top staff have shaped a movement that appeals to upwardly mobile Western urbanites, disappointed by organized religion yet looking for a spiritual and ethical outlook with ancient roots.

The Los Angeles Kabbalah Centre after the conclusion of Shabbat (Sabbath) morning prayers. Photo by Timothy Williams.

Acknowledgments

Studying Kabbalah and its expression within the Kabbalah Centre constituted, in many ways, a new direction for my academic work and a challenge
to my assumptions. I am most appreciative to all those who have assisted me
in this book and joined me on the adventure that it represents.

Through this project, I became acquainted with the fascinating scholarship and diverse methodologies used by academic scholars of Kabbalah and
anthropology. Of these, Boaz Huss, Pinchas Giller, Jonatan Meir, Susan
Sered, and Matt Goldish deserve special mention for their knowledge, in-
sight, constructive criticisms, and unfailing encouragement. The support of
my colleagues at California State University, Northridge, has been indispens-
able: Phyllis K. Herman and Crerar Douglas of the Department of Religious
Studies daily cheered me on and provided expert counsel; Elizabeth Say, dean
of the College of Humanities, unstintingly supported my investigations and
writing; and student assistants Dov Isaac—who helped construct this book's
index—and Nicole Durso were a tremendous help. Chanoch Ben Yaakov,
Ron Csillag, Vince Gonzalez, Aaron Katz, Martin Lockshin, Michael Rosen,
and Jayna Zimmelman generously extended me the fruits of their own experience and research. I have been fortunate to have had the assistance of
librarians Fred Bogin, Rick Burke, and Haim Gottschalk; their enthusiasm for
my research was inspiring, and their able assistance in tracking down elusive
literary sources saved me hours of work.

This book was written with the cooperation and knowledge of many of
the people associated with the Kabbalah Centre. Michael Berg, Billy Phillips,
and especially Shaul Youdkevitch were generous with their time and explanations, tolerant of my intrusiveness, and helpful in introducing me to others.
Nicholas Linindoll and Osnat Youdkevitch searched through the Kabbalah
Centre Archives for the photographs. The Kabbalah Centre supplied these
and other materials for my research with no conditions attached and without

prior review of this book. Dozens of individuals, former and current members of the Kabbalah Centre community, shared their private experiences and feelings with me; their voices and convictions are fundamental to this book. Aside from those of the senior teachers, all names have been changed or kept anonymous in these pages. I have done my best to convey the statements and sentiments of the members of the Kabbalah Centre community accurately and fairly within the framework of my academic methodology, which they do not share. In the end, this work is my own interpretation for which I bear full responsibility.

For the preparation, production, and publication of this book I have been fortunate to have had the support and guidance of Praeger editor Suzanne Staszak-Silva, the careful copyediting of the team at Apex Publishing, and the artistic talents of Kathryn de Boer for the illustrations.

Friends and family have been utterly splendid for their encouragement, advice, suggestions for revision, and sustaining loyalty. These include David Ackerman, Cornelis de Boer, Jon and Julie Drucker, Karen Fox, Sally Goodis, Erin Johnson, Jeffrey Pomeranz (of blessed memory) and Ellen Blumenthal, Michele Porjes, Lucia Robles, John Sears, and those who do not wish to be recognized. I owe special thanks to my children Adina, Benjamin, and Aaron, who have borne my stories and dedication to research with loving and bemused tolerance. Finally, I could not do without the enduring affection of my siblings Jane Myers, Kathryn de Boer, Paulo Cohen-Myers, and Amy Sabrina, to whom I dedicate this book.

CHAPTER 1

———— ✠ ————

Kabbalah, from Origins
to Popularization in America

Kabbalah is the collective name for Jewish mystical writings produced in the medieval era and afterward, as well as the term for the spiritual engagement with these writings.

It is a new and rather sudden phenomenon that Kabbalah has today become one of the many options available to Western spiritual seekers of all backgrounds. From the twelfth century onward, Jewish men who were engaged at the highest levels of religious education would be exposed to kabbalistic doctrines and texts, and religious authorities who promulgated Jewish religious law incorporated kabbalistic concerns into their decisions. However, when modern political and intellectual pressures to create a more rational religious outlook became the norm in Europe and America, Kabbalah was not only removed from the curriculum, but was furthermore generally scorned as superstitious medievalism that had no place in Jewish life. Among Jews living in North African and Middle Eastern—generally, Muslim—societies, the study of Kabbalah and the honor paid to kabbalistic sages survived into the twentieth century before these societies, too, scorned Kabbalah. Just a few decades ago, Kabbalah seemed bound for extinction. Kabbalistic literature as a relic of the past was becoming the object of study in universities, but very few devout Jews sought to engage in it as a religious expression. In the mid 1960s, teachers of Kabbalah could be found primarily among a few circles of Jews in Jerusalem. They limited themselves to select students; they sought adult male Jews possessing extensive education in classical rabbinic literature, whose personal behavior was strictly circumscribed by the observance of Jewish ritual laws and who could invest significant blocks of time in the isolating regimen of kabbalistic study and meditation. Today, there are many opportunities to study Kabbalah in religious seminaries or by engaging a private teacher. Bookstores, libraries, and the Internet make kabbalistic teachings available to anyone, regardless of religion or gender. Kabbalah has been brought back to life, but in a distinctly different form.

Kabbalah has always been caught in a dynamic in which its admirers alternatively zealously guarded its secrecy or exposed it to broader circles. At its inception in the Middle Ages, Kabbalah was considered an essential part of God's revelation, but it was "hidden wisdom" that was not meant to become known outside of a small circle of men. It was considered too precious to be widely revealed. He who learned Kabbalah was privy to special, intimate knowledge of God and might even be able to influence God. Kabbalah required such a subtle and refined understanding and sensibility that it was regarded as potentially dangerous for those who were not up to its demands. This tantalizing combination was so alluring that it invariably resulted in people yearning to learn it or to share it with others. Secrecy is inextricably bound up with dissemination. Yet the cryptic, veiled style of kabbalistic writing inevitably resulted in diverse ways of explaining the doctrines, and these multiplied in complexity as adepts lovingly elaborated on earlier teachings or tried to reconcile differing interpretations. There were numerous schools of kabbalistic teaching within Jewish society. One strain of Kabbalah became known to Christians, was shaped by them into a Christian theology, and eventually branched out into occult spiritualities that presented themselves as alternatives to Christianity. The proliferation of approaches to Kabbalah did not diminish the conviction by most Jews that the subject was, strictly speaking, supposed to be esoteric, and certainly it was not to be tampered with by those outside of the Jewish faith. Today, at the beginning of the twenty-first century, we are living in a period of dissemination and expansion of kabbalistic teachings. Beginning in the 1960s, small circles of college-aged Jews seeking an alternative to their parents' form of Judaism turned to Kabbalah as a source of religious wisdom that would revive and invigorate their spiritual lives. By the end of the twentieth century, the popularization of Kabbalah reached a new level when the Kabbalah Centre interpreted and shaped Kabbalah to attract a large, multicultural, and international following.

The first part of this chapter recounts the dynamic history of Kabbalah in broad strokes and answers the basic questions necessary for understanding popular Kabbalah today. What exactly is this kind of mysticism, and what is its connection to the more normative Judaism? What are its basic doctrines and practices? How did Kabbalah become known outside of the Jewish community and take on different forms within Jewish society? Special attention is given to the question of hierarchy and boundaries—that is, the ways that Kabbalah provided a way of dividing and layering all of reality (spiritual and earthly) and society (Jews and non-Jews) into an ordered system of sacred values, roles, and behaviors. Through Kabbalah, the masters of "hidden wisdom" were explaining why God behaved as he did and why Jewish practices and the Jewish fate were different from the rest of humanity.

The second part of this chapter focuses on the version of Kabbalah developed by Yehuda Ashlag in the early twentieth century. More than any previous version of Kabbalah, Ashlag's was most suited to be spread to a wide audience. Ashlag's disciple, Levi Isaac Krakovsky, was the first to attempt disseminating it in America. Although Krakovsky did not achieve a following, he laid the groundwork for others. During a later, more congenial era, his student, Shraga Feival Gruberger—later named Philip Berg—would build on Krakovsky's achievements to create his own mass movement of popular Kabbalah.

WHAT IS MYSTICISM?

There are dozens of definitions of mysticism, and scholars have struggled to arrive at a single definition that includes all the manifestations commonly regarded as mystical rituals, experiences, and activities. Most define mysticism as an experience in a religious context in which a person feels he or she is directly encountering God. People who do not accept the existence of a personal deity, but who are convinced of the reality of ultimate divinity or spiritual consciousness (or any number of other terms for the sacred, transcendent dimension of life), may also be said to have had a mystical experience when they encounter that sacred dimension. The mystic's enlightenment or awareness is not the product of rational thinking or sensual perception, it is claimed, but is the result of a unique and extraordinary mode of apprehension. The connection to the divine may be expressed in a number of ways: for example, a person may feel completely filled and suffused by a sacred force; or experience one's self dissolving into God; or sense that one is being embraced by God or that one is at one with the entire cosmos. This definition of mysticism was coined at the end of the nineteenth century by academic scholars who were describing, first and foremost, Christian mysticism. In Christianity, it was understood that God, through grace, might gift an individual with his presence in the form of an exulting and immense joy and infusion of divine love. This ecstatic encounter was considered the ultimate height of Christian religiosity. Scholars assumed that people of all religions encouraged much the same experience and that there was a pure mystical experience at the heart of all such encounters, even though people expressed it in different ways.[1]

Yet in recent decades, scholars of religion have criticized the universalistic claims of this definition of mysticism. They have pointed out that mysticism described in this manner does not adequately or accurately explain the activities and subjective feelings of people of other cultures. This is certainly the case for Jewish society.[2] Most men whom researchers have labeled "Jewish mystics" have not had as their chief goal the achievement of an ecstatic connection with God. Instead, their primary focus has been to attain *knowledge* of God and to learn the ways in which God is connected to the material world. They were seekers of normally inaccessible divine wisdom—the term for this is "theosophy," meaning knowledge of the inner mysteries of God. Although some Jewish communities generously supported Jewish mystics and credited them with fulfilling the highest religious ideal, for the most part, it was the scholars of Jewish law whose religious accomplishments were the most celebrated. Examining Jewish mysticism on its own terms, then, is more helpful than focusing on what it might have in common with a "universal" mysticism. This is the same for other mysticisms, too, because there was no independent mysticism that stood apart from established religions. People who claimed to have a mystical experience of God expressed themselves in the language of their religion, whatever it was.

JUDAISM AND KABBALAH

The primary focus of Kabbalah has been the acquisition of the concealed knowledge of God and God's designs of and plans for the world. The authors of these writings gave answers to questions that were left unresolved in other Jewish writings, or that had not been answered to their satisfaction. The Kabbalists affirmed a new cultural outlook different than the prevailing ones, yet the Kabbalists generally remained part of the larger Jewish community and in intimate connection with people who were not Kabbalists. In order to understand Kabbalah, it is helpful to have a sense of those Jewish beliefs and practices that Kabbalists sought to interpret.

Jews have believed that God relates to humanity as a personal deity. They have often used human, usually male, images to describe God. Jewish sages suggested that one could attempt to understand God by observing life on earth, which was the consequence of God's will. One could also gain knowledge of God through the study of the Bible and other sacred writings, sincere and regular prayer, and the performance of religious rituals and ethical behavior. Jewish philosophers struggled to find ways to define God without limiting his transcendence and omnipotence. They sought to explain how the profane, decaying, material world—including human society—had its source in eternal, perfect divinity.[3]

Jews did agree that one aspect of God's character was his desire that human beings live virtuous lives. They thought that God endowed each individual with free will, an impulse toward good and an impulse toward evil, and the capacity to choose good. Society at large is enjoined to encourage righteous behavior through rewards and punishments. God's high expectations for humanity are not uniform, however, because from the Jewish perspective, humanity is not uniform. Humanity was divided into two groups: Jews and non-Jews. Jews defined themselves as descendants of common ancestors and of voluntary adherents (converts). They believed that God gave them hundreds of laws to follow, intricate ceremonies and forms of worship, and the general rule to keep themselves holy and distinctive from the rest of humanity. The label "the chosen people" originally referred to the notion that God chose the Jews for a greater burden of responsibility. It casts in positive terms the extra burden placed on Jews, the more exacting requirements for achieving God's approval, and the greater consequences for failure to perform to God's expectations. Jews maintained that God gave them so many laws because he loved them and desired their service.

People who are not Jewish—in Jewish literature they are called "the nations of the world"—are judged by a different measure. The nations of the world, according to Jewish sages, were given seven basic laws after the great flood. Called the Seven Commandments for the Children of Noah (or the Noahide commandments), these consist of the obligation to respect society's judicial system and the prohibitions against murder, idolatry, blasphemy, theft, sexual immorality, and cruelty to animals. Theoretically, the nations of the world do not need to follow Jewish laws in order to merit God's favorable reception. Those non-Jews who were drawn to Judaism would be increasing their obligations to God and consequently the likelihood that they would fall short of fulfilling their religious obligations. At times, Jewish people were active and successful proselytizers—certainly this was the case in the Hellenistic era. However, Jewish proselytism ceased when Christianity became the official religion of the Roman Empire in the fourth century of the Common Era and Islam became the official religion of the Moslem Empire in the seventh century. Imperial rulers decreed that Jewish proselytism was punishable by death.

Jews developed a more closed, insular attitude towards non-Jews during the Middle Ages. The persistence of Jews and Judaism posed a dilemma for Christians and Muslims, who believed that their religions were the perfection of Judaism and were meant to be the universal religion of humanity. Christian and Muslim governments imposed discriminatory laws against Jews, and clerics taught that Judaism was false and Jews were not to be trusted. Suspicion between the followers of the three religions was common. Each considered its own co-religionists to be endowed with a higher spiritual capacity and moral potential than the others. Under these conditions, most Jews considered it pointless, unwise, and risky to discuss Jewish religious beliefs, texts, and practices with non-Jews. They regarded Judaism—and this included Judaism's sacred and mystical texts—to be of relevance only to themselves. Although there were certainly times and regions in which religious tolerance and cultural exchange comfortably occurred, Jews understood that such favorable conditions were not permanent, and it was best to be cautious.

Of course, there were Jews who raised serious questions about the division of humanity and the troubling relations between the peoples of the world. Why had God not created human beings with the capacity to agree with one another on matters of religion and the social order? Why had God not established one, uniform set of rules that people could easily obey? Why was humanity torn apart by religious competition and hostility, and would this situation ever improve?

In response to these questions, Jewish authors produced speculative and consolatory writings. For example, the prophets of the Hebrew Bible insisted fairly regularly that the current disharmony was a result of people not recognizing the one God and not fulfilling their obligations to him. The prophets promised that if the Jews as a whole fulfilled their obligations, God would reward them with fertility, great progeny, prosperity, and peace in their promised land. Near the end of the biblical era and afterward, Jews extrapolated on this earthly reward by anticipating rewards and punishments for individuals after death. Furthermore, in light of the fact that the earthly rewards promised by the biblical prophets had not been entirely fulfilled, they began to anticipate a future era in which matters would be set entirely right. This upcoming golden age, or *geula*, meaning redemption, was earthly and temporal. It would be heralded by a messiah, a human being designated and empowered by God. He would lead all dispersed Jews back to their land and establish a theocratic state ruled by a sovereign king from the Davidic dynasty. Jewish speculations about this messianic era invariably included the expectation that the system of worship described in the Bible would be restored; that is, there would once again be worship of God through sacrificial offerings at a temple in Jerusalem. (With the destruction of the Jerusalem Temple in 70 C.E. by the Romans, who consequently forbade the Temple's reconstruction, sacrificial worship ceased to be part of Judaism.) They imagined that evil people would be punished, world peace would ensue, and hostility between Jews and the nations of the world would cease. Although these scenarios provided some comfort, they also produced additional questions. Really, no one knew just when and how the redemption would occur, or what really happens after death. Jewish religious authorities, when addressing their communities, were inclined to stress that it was best to ignore all these speculations and to concentrate on behaving well.

Jews located the source of religious teachings in God's revelation to Moses. This was partially contained in the first five books of the Hebrew Bible, known collectively as the Written Torah (the Hebrew word for "teaching" or "law"). The rest of the Hebrew Bible was very important, and it too contained prophetic revelation, but it did not carry the same status as the Written Torah. Not all of God's revelation was recorded, however. Some was kept in oral form, as were many explanations and details of the revelation. The oral teachings were called collectively the Oral Torah, even after being set in writing. Over the generations, the Oral Torah became a vast library that included the Talmud (a collection of discussions of religious law as well as legends, religious speculation, and prayers completed in the seventh century C.E.), commentaries on the Bible and Talmud, law codes, philosophy, and liturgy. Most of this literature was written in Hebrew and Aramaic. It was part of the formal curriculum for male Jews; girls and women, in contrast, were generally denied such book learning, although they were taught to live as Jews and to recite some prayers. Generally, the more specialized and highly esteemed the sacred literature, the less likely it was that women would have direct access to it.

Quite a bit of Jewish religious literature focuses on the behaviors obligatory for Jews: worship, Sabbath and holiday observances, life cycle rituals, and the hundreds of obligations and prohibitions relating to general ethical conduct, diet, dress, and sex. These are called *mitzvot*—literally commandments, sometimes translated as "good deeds." They were understood to be divine law, binding and obligatory. Jews believed they were enjoined by God to fulfill the commandments as an act of obedience and love. No little fear was present, either, for the Torah made it clear that God judges the Jews on their performance of the mitzvot. One's life on earth would be affected, and after death, each individual would be rewarded or punished in accordance with his or her deeds. The Written Torah and the oral teachings that accompanied it were less explicit about *why:* why were the Jews commanded and not others or everyone? Why were these specific rituals mandated, and these foods and sexual relations prohibited? Explanations were proffered for the thousands of details of the hundreds of commandments, but most of the explanations were considered mere speculation. That is, the many rationales for the mitzvot were never confirmed by religious leaders as dogma; the subject remained available for each generation's creative minds to address.

In short, Judaism has many tenets of religious belief, but these appear in general doctrines. There were quite a few legal scholars and philosophers who insisted that their scenarios for the future and rationales for the apparently inexplicable commandments were the absolutely correct ones. However, religious leaders generally insisted on *not* deciding the intricate details of doctrinal questions once and for all. They accepted the limits of human understanding and believed that God had clearly stated his intent to keep some things secret. To them, Deuteronomy 29:28 summarized both the problem and the solution: "The hidden things are for God, but the revealed things are for us and for our children forever, to carry out all the words of this teaching."

The men who were later called Kabbalists described themselves as engaging in *hochmat ha-nistar,* wisdom of secret matters, or *razei ha-torah,* the hints of the Torah. They taught that God's revelation contained elements that were to be kept secret and disclosed only to a few. The link to the Torah, to God's revelation to Moses, was central to their activities. Kabbalists denied their originality and insisted that their knowledge had its source in God; they explained that God himself had communicated the details of his reality to select individuals (for example, Adam, Abraham, and Moses) who had passed them down over the ages. The word *kabbalah* actually means "something handed down by tradition." Individual authors tried to demonstrate the legitimacy of their explanations of mystical texts by insisting that they did not add a single original element to the teachings they had received, but had merely translated their teachers' lessons into the idiom of their time so that they could be understood.[4]

Academic researchers cannot accept faith claims such as the divine origin of the Kabbalah at face value; they investigate mystical literature using the tools of various academic disciplines. They have shown that Jewish mysticism was a very complex, evolving matrix of ideas and practices, and new elements were added over time. The conclusions of academic scholarship do not sit easily with traditional Jewish mystics. For example, historians maintain that *Sefer Ha-Yetzirah*, a book traditionally ascribed to Abraham, is likely a post-biblical work. Traditional Jews and many devout Kabbalists, however, are unaware of this finding, give no credence to it, or assert that it is utterly irrelevant to the sanctity and authenticity of the revelatory truths contained in the book. Such a religious conviction deserves respect. Most people who have constructed meaningful and spiritually satisfying religious lives have done so without the help of academic scholarship.

HOW MUCH SECRECY, AND WHY?

Kabbalah, it is often explained, is special knowledge of holy matters that is secret or, minimally, reserved for an elite. There is an old teaching that only devout married men above the age of 40 who are fully conversant in Talmud and Jewish law are allowed to study Kabbalah.[5] The reality was more complex than this simple dictum suggests. Kabbalah study was not circumscribed by universally agreed-upon rules, but the general preference was to keep it limited. Formal schooling for boys in Jewish society was devoted primarily to the study of the Bible and Talmud. The curriculum for older and more advanced students—these schools were called *yeshivot*—provided greater depth and breadth in Talmudic commentaries and law codes; the highest and most promising of these students might, if their teachers considered them worthy, receive training in Jewish philosophy or Kabbalah. Thus, men under 40 certainly studied Kabbalah, and some of the most illustrious Kabbalists were men in their twenties and thirties. Outside of the school setting, men could study Kabbalah from manuscripts, books, or directly from a Kabbalist. There were Kabbalists who believed that Kabbalah should be widely taught, and there were communities, such as the Galilean town of Safed during the sixteenth century, in which the study of Kabbalah and engagement in mystical practices (by men only, it has been presumed) was encouraged and supported. There were eminent Kabbalists who firmly believed that Kabbalah should be taught widely to many Jews, and there were even some Kabbalists who shared their learning with non-Jews. Indeed, within a few decades after the emergence of kabbalistic teachings in the thirteenth century, small circles of Christians incorporated them into Christian theology. More uniform strictness with regard to Kabbalah study became the norm in the eighteenth century, when rabbinic assemblies and widely respected Kabbalists emphatically prohibited premature and unsupervised access to Kabbalistic writings.

Generally, most Jews did not approve of a widespread dissemination of Kabbalah. Furthermore, getting access to kabbalistic texts was not easy; manuscripts were rare and highly expensive. When the invention of the printing press made possible the mass distribution of kabbalistic writings, many rabbis tried to keep Jewish mystical writings in handwritten form. They were unsuccessful, and multiple editions began to appear, as well as new translations and permutations. Some of the core kabbalistic texts were deliberately obscure, cryptic, and worded in codes, and even with the help of commentaries, one could not really gain any mastery by studying in isolation. Generally, one could only learn Kabbalah by finding a teacher who would give private instruction, and it was not easy to find someone knowledgeable in the texts and special devotional practices. Women, children, and unlearned men would not have been given formal training in the subject, although kabbalistic ideas may have entered their worldview.

Kabbalah was kept from widespread dissemination because it dealt with matters that had not been explicitly revealed in the Written or Oral Torah, especially teachings about God. Pre-kabbalistic Jewish mystical literature featured visions of God's "exterior" from afar. The biblical prophet Ezekiel described himself gazing at God sitting on a throne mounted on a fiery chariot propelled by huge creatures. Writings from the first few centuries of the Common Era indicate that religious enthusiasts would induce ecstatic visions in which they felt themselves ascending through the layers of heaven, palaces, phalanxes of angels and across dangerous barriers until finally gazing at God on his heavenly throne. Beginning in the last quarter of the twelfth century, however, a new approach was evident: the focus turned to the *inner* aspects of God. In Provence (southern France), a book titled *Sefer Ha-Bahir* appeared that described God as a being composed of 10 powers.[6] These internal powers are dynamic and always in flux: at various times, some dominate the others, some join together in harmony, and some are pitted against each other. These theosophical ideas, later called Kabbalah, marked a new type of cultural activity in which the objective was to discover the inner workings of God, influence these inner dynamics, or cling to God.

THE IDEAS AND PRACTICES OF KABBALAH

The core document of Kabbalah was the Zohar. The Zohar is commonly described as a single book written by a single author, Rabbi Shimon Bar Yohai, who lived in the second century C.E. Tradition teaches that his teachings were lost or hidden and then rediscovered at the end of the thirteenth century in Castile (Spain). Academic scholars, however, recognize that the Zohar is actually a composite term for about two dozen compositions issued and revised by a number of authors in Spain from about 1280 and continuing for a few more decades.[7] Most parts of the Zohar were written in Aramaic, a language similar to Hebrew and sharing the same alphabet. In the medieval era, Aramaic was a spoken language only for small communities of Jews in remote parts of Mesopotamia, but Jewish men schooled in the Talmud (which was written in Aramaic) could understand the Zohar. The Zohar was a comprehensive commentary on many sections of the Written Torah, and it was eventually accepted as canonical—that is, it was considered utterly holy at the same level as the Written Torah.[8]

The Zohar and the Kabbalists teach that God's essence is unknowable and beyond human comprehension. The unknowable essence of God is called *Ein sof*, meaning infinite or limitless. It is like an impersonal First Cause. The Ein sof emanated divinity downward, progressively revealing itself in greater clarity so that it could be known by and relate to humanity. When human beings feel God's presence, it is not Ein sof, but the realm of revealed divinity whom they contact and address. In short, God consists of an unknowable essence and knowable aspects of God's being, and it is the latter that are the focus of Kabbalists' attention.

The knowable God is manifested in 10 stages. Called *sefirot*, these 10 sefirot (singular form is *sefirah*) are not separate entities, and they are not intermediaries between God and the world, even though they are often described as separate powers or as a vessel that contains divinity. These 10 sefirot are emanated from Ein sof. Divine energy flows from the Ein sof into these 10 sefirot and between each sefirah. Each represents a greater degree of distance from Ein sof and consequently a greater capacity to be known by human beings.[9] The highest are so elevated that they can be perceived by only the most highly spiritual mystics. Far less spiritually endowed people may learn the sketchy outlines of these heights by studying the Zohar. The lowest sefirah serves as the channel between the divine realm and the physical world, and it is the most accessible to human beings.

Kabbalah gives these 10 aspects of divinity full-fledged characteristics. The sefirot are named and ascribed functions, and the dynamic between them and the created world is elaborated. The most commonly used names of the sefirot sound like divine attributes or elements of God's authority: (1) *Keter* (crown), (2) *Chochmah* (wisdom), (3) *Binah* (understanding), (4) *Chesed* (grace or mercy)

Figure 1.1 The Emanation of the Sefirot (Revealed Divinity) from Ein Sof (Limitless, Unknowable Divinity)

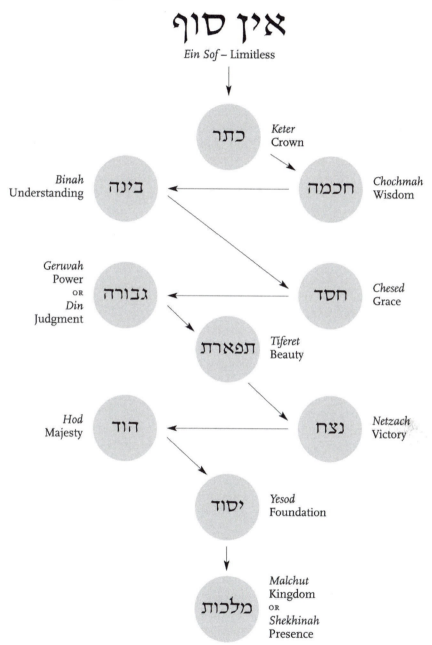

Diagram: Kathryn de Boer.

or *Gedullah* (greatness), (5) *Gevurah* (power) or *Din* (judgment), (6) *Tiferet* (beauty), (7) *Netzach* (victory), (8) *Hod* (majesty), (9) *Yesod* (foundation), and (10) *Malchut* (kingdom). The highest three sefirot constitute the intellectual level within God. The tenth and lowest sefirah (the link to the physical world) is that aspect of revealed divinity that receives and responds to human prayers. It is often called *Shekhinah,* the Hebrew term for God's divine presence, and it is described as the feminine aspect of divinity. The system of the sefirot enables the Jew to affirm the existence of one God while also affirming that God appears to act differently at different times. The 10 sefirot with their separate individualities makes order and sense out of God's apparent complexity.

In kabbalistic teachings, the 10 sefirot are arranged and grouped in multiple ways. One way of depicting the sefirot is as a tree: the roots of the tree are formed by the three sefirot most connected to Ein sof, and the trunk and branches are formed by the arrangement of the lower seven sefirot. Another image representing the overall structure of the sefirot is that of a man, with the top nine sefirot placed at the man's head, trunk, arms, legs, and genitals, and the tenth sefirah at the base of the entire figure. It later became common to describe the third through the ninth sefirot as an active masculine unit meant to be coupled with the tenth, feminine sefirah. Each of these metaphors for God's dynamic being provides a different explanation for God's actions. For example, the Zohar taught that God acts stern and judgmental when the feminine powers are dominant over the masculine.

Kabbalah teaches about the connection between divinity and the tangible, physical universe. The world as we know it is the result of emanations originating from Ein sof that moved progressively toward greater manifestation. The manifestation of the 10 sefirot and the creation of the physical world occurred simultaneously in the same process of emanation. The lower realm is parallel to and mirrors the upper world. There would have been perfect harmony between the upper and lower worlds, and within each world, except for the sin of Adam. Consequently, our physical world is flawed and characterized by separation and division. Nevertheless, the two realms are intimately connected. Divine energy continuously flows from the upper realm and nourishes the lower one. Human beings can behave in such a way so as to restore divine harmony.

Academic scholars typically discuss the kabbalistic doctrine of the human soul and its connection to the realm of the sefirot without reference to the fact that Kabbalists attributed a lower metaphysical quality to non-Jewish souls. The Zohar, for example, described the origin of Jewish souls in the sefirah Binah (understanding). From there they were conveyed to the male sefirah Yesod (foundation), then born out of the coupling with the female tenth sefirah before being released into the world. Because they had an existence in the sefirot prior to the creation of material world, Jewish souls have a direct connection to the divine world and can influence its dynamic. The souls of the "nations of the world," however, originate in "the other side"—the evil realm visualized outside and to the left of the sefirot. Because of their origins, non-Jews can have fear of God and wisdom and be meritorious, but they cannot perceive God in any intimate sense or have a reparative effect on the sefirot. Those who convert to Judaism, however, undergo an elevation in their souls. Their souls are described as moving to a place of honor in the realm of the sefirot, although not at the same level as the Jew until generations later.[10] The distinction between Jews and non-Jews and proselytes articulated in the Zohar remains fundamental in later kabbalistic literature and thought. In the premodern era, the notion that people from one's own religion were metaphysically superior to outsiders was normative. Only with the rise of modernity and its ideal of human equality did the Zohar's hierarchy of souls become problematic and the source of dismay. This book later discusses how in contemporary popular Kabbalah, particularly for the Kabbalah Centre, erasing distinctions between Jews and non-Jews became a central issue.

Because of the link between Jewish souls and the sefirot, the Kabbalist can take actions on earth that will affect God; when the dynamic within God changes, the situation on earth will change as a result. This type of religious behavior is called theurgy, a compound derived from the Greek words for God and work. In the kabbalistic context, it refers to the ability to "work an effect" on God. For Kabbalists, Jewish practice was insufficient if it involved merely the dutiful performance of God's commandments. Instead, they taught that speech, gestures, and religious observances may be enhanced and shaped so as to restore the sefirot to harmony. The Kabbalists lived their lives within the framework of Judaism, engaging in worship, rituals, and Torah study; yet they performed these in a manner and with a special consciousness that, in their views, connected them to the divine realm and influenced it. In addition, they added practices unique to themselves: meditations, chanting, midnight study sessions, pilgrimages to the tombs of holy men, ritual ablutions, and ascetic exercises such as fasting and self-mortification.[11]

In short, medieval Kabbalah presented a distinctive theology and promoted a distinctive spiritual practice. The brief summary of the kabbalistic understanding of God should make apparent that these ideas differed from the basic contours of Judaism described earlier, and it may be obvious why it was considered best to keep them hidden. How could a common person understand the visual images of divinity used in Jewish mystical texts, the images of God depicted in bodily form, the male and female sides of God's inner self, or the divine realm described as a sexual coupling? Such information would likely be perceived as blasphemy, be considered confusing or misleading, and perhaps lead to a loss of faith. Mystical *practices*, however, were less noticeably different than the norm. Indeed, Kabbalists generally were more careful and exacting in their performance of the mitzvot. They did not allow their mystical additions to prayers and innovative new rituals to violate the laws of the Torah, for they believed that the Torah was the vehicle that connected the lower to the upper world. The Jewish community would likely not have been aware of Kabbalists' radical religious ideas, but they would have been aware of their behavior. Perhaps it was the Kabbalists' loyalty to the system of Jewish law that enabled the Jewish community to tolerate their theological deviance.

Although the Zohar was designed by and for Jews, its ideas spread to the Christian world within a few decades. Latin translations and commentaries designed to reinforce Christian doctrines were produced by Jewish converts to Christianity in Spain and Italy. From the late fifteenth century onward, small circles of Christians had a deep interest in Kabbalah and incorporated it into Christian theology. Kabbalistic teachings spread by Christians were not the same as those taught in Jewish communities. Christian Kabbalists saw in the Kabbalah's conception of God as a unity of multiple powers an affirmation of their understanding of God as Father, Son, and Holy Spirit. The Catholic Church, for its part, was alarmed by Christian interest in the Kabbalah. Church officials protested that it was impossible that divine wisdom would have been given to Jews and not Christians. They believed that orthodox Christian belief was endangered by the claim that there were authentic sources of divine knowledge outside of those traditionally confirmed by the Church.[12]

Kabbalistic writings were also attractive to Christians (and Jews, as well) for seeming to provide the power to control the physical world. The late fifteenth century was a time when a number of Hellenistic magical systems were revived and reconfigured. Magic was then not a term of disparagement; it meant ancient wisdom and arts that had been suppressed or kept secret and that enabled one to manipulate the course of nature by controlling the supernatural forces through ritual and spell. Some western European Christians exposed to Christian Kabbalah regarded Kabbalah as an early—perhaps even the earliest—form of magic. Over the course of the next few centuries, kabbalistic theosophy and meditations were synthesized with other occult systems.

KABBALAH UP TO THE TWENTIETH CENTURY

From the thirteenth to the end of the eighteenth century, Kabbalah expanded and penetrated more deeply into Jewish practice and religious beliefs. Centers of Kabbalah study were established where mystical writings were produced in abundance. It has been suggested that from about 1500 to 1800, the kabbalistic theology described was accepted by the elite as well as on the popular level in Jewish communities in Europe and the Muslim world. Others disagree that Kabbalah penetrated so far into Jewish culture, but there is no doubt that it influenced Jewish ethics, prayer, customs, and Sabbath and holiday observances.[13] Distinctive doctrines of sin, evil, and the transmigrations of the soul—ideas that first entered Jewish thought through Kabbalah—became widely accepted and integrated into legend, popular books of ethics, and song. In the 1660s, Jews in all communities were convinced by the messianic claims of a Turkish Jew, Shabbatai Zevi. Widespread disappointment set in when Shabbatai Zevi converted to Islam, but scandal ensued when it became apparent that there were Kabbalists who continued to revere the man and to shape kabbalistic teachings in defense of his apostasy. Religious leaders consequently called for more restrictions on access to Kabbalah.[14]

Yet interest in Kabbalah persisted. In late eighteenth-century Eastern Europe, a new religious movement called Hasidism began to convey kabbalistic teachings to a broad audience. The Hasidic practice, however, was not to teach kabbalistic texts like the Zohar or its commentaries; instead, kabbalistic concepts were taught without the use of kabbalistic terminology and through stories, aphorisms, songs, and sermons. Hasidic Judaism, which started in Austrian Galicia in the 1760s, spread to Russian Poland, Ukraine, and Lithuania; until the mid-twentieth century, it was restricted to those regions (except for the few Hasidim that moved to Palestine). In the Mediterranean and Muslim lands after the Shabbatai Zevi debacle, Kabbalah study persisted. A new kind of kabbalistic prayer was developed in Jerusalem by the Yemen-born Kabbalist Shalom Shar'abi (1720–1780). In his lifetime, Shar'abi was recognized as among the great teachers of Kabbalah. He composed *kavvanot*, meditations on sequences of Hebrew letters and divine names, which were thought to contribute to the harmonious dynamic of the sefirot. The use of Shar'abi's kavvanot in mystical prayer was adopted by Kabbalists in Middle Eastern Jewish communities. The veneration of Kabbalists (living and dead), the ritualized reading of the Zohar, and other kabbalistic practices remained a part of Jewish life in these lands into the twentieth century.[15]

A noticeable diminution of interest in Kabbalah began with the onset of modernization. The multifaceted elements of modernization and its deleterious effects on religion first became evident in western Europe in the late eighteenth century and then spread east and south. Intellectually, modernity means that people increasingly believe that is possible to seek a rational explanation of all phenomenon and that such rational explanations are the most accurate apprehension of reality. Religious faith—including belief in miracles and the divine origin of scripture, neither of which can be empirically verified—was undermined and rendered somewhat irrelevant to many aspects of life. The primary political change has been the increasing centralization of the administrative organs of the state, and modernizing states diminished the power of religious authorities standing between the state and its subjects. The effect of modernization involved the greater integration of Jews into non-Jewish society and the loss of Jewish communal autonomy. Jews who accepted modern principles came to regard many Jewish teachings, and kabbalistic ones in particular, as unacceptably irrational and out of step with the rationalistic theologies advanced by European intellectuals, and they compared Jewish religious practices unfavorably with those of European Christians. Political leaders who were instituting centralized nation-states consisting of relatively equal citizens did their best to weaken the Jewish community's ability to govern and perpetuate distinctive religious beliefs and practices.

Consequently, even Jews who rejected modern ideas were deeply affected by them. By the late nineteenth century, in Europe, Kabbalah remained a living tradition only in the eastern and south-central regions. In a strange twist of history, the weakening of Christian belief and religious governance enabled European Christians to more freely explore the occult and spiritual traditions that had been frowned on by Christian authorities. A number of philosophies and spiritual practices arose out of Western esoteric traditions, such as Transcendentalism, Spiritualism, New Thought, and Theosophy. These spiritual philosophies presented themselves as alternatives to the established forms of Christianity, and kabbalistic concepts and symbols drawn from the writings of Christian Kabbalists figured in their writings. Alternative religious thinkers argued against a literal reading of the Bible, but taught that it should be understood as a code that establishes correspondences between the divine realm and the earthly realm that had been created in the divine realm's image. They held that divine energy was diffused throughout the physical world, and individuals could be taught to draw it into their minds and bodies and channel it toward the common good. These alternative spiritual movements remained small in size, however. They were marginal to the dominant Christian outlook and to the growing rational and scientific perspectives.

In North Africa and the Middle East, societies that were being modernized more erratically and at a slower rate, traditional religious beliefs and practices increasingly were being abandoned by the young, but Jewish people accorded Kabbalah study and Kabbalists more respect than in Europe. In fact, Jerusalem at the beginning of the twentieth century was experiencing a rebirth as a center of Kabbalah study, with Kabbalists from Europe and different parts of the Middle East gathering there to pursue their studies.[16]

YEHUDA ASHLAG

And so it is not surprising that a young Polish man, an ambitious Kabbalist, decided in 1921 that his future lay in Palestine. The biography of Yehuda Ashlag, woven through with the legends spun by his family and followers, is the story of a man with deep intellectual interests and a strong passion for Kabbalah.[17] Born in Warsaw in 1885, Ashlag was raised in a Hasidic family and received the traditional Talmud-centered education typical of the elite of religious Jewish society. He was ordained as a rabbi at the young age of 19 and appointed to a teaching post in the Jewish community. His interest in

Kabbalah was precocious, according to his recollection, for he began secretly studying it when he was a young boy. He also explored non-Jewish philosophical literature that was considered "foreign" to his pious Polish Hasidic community and its sensibilities. Nonetheless, Ashlag was firmly committed to a Jewish religious outlook, and he rejected those elements of modern European culture that did not accord with his Torah-centered outlook. For example, he accepted Marx's critique of capitalism and was an avid socialist throughout his life, but he was convinced that Marx's atheism blinded him to religion's positive role in the betterment of society. These convictions eventually led to Ashlag's "calling" in 1921. According to his wife's later account, when Ashlag was 36 years old, he informed her that his work in Europe was completed. He told her he would die if he did not leave immediately for Palestine, and despite her advanced pregnancy, he stuck to his word. Except for the years 1926–1928, when he was given financial support to live in England and write, he spent the rest of his life residing in Jerusalem or Tel Aviv and devoted himself to writing, publishing, studying, and teaching Kabbalah.

Ashlag's approach to Kabbalah was built upon the theosophy of Isaac Luria, the sixteenth-century kabbalistic master.[18] Luria's teachings were so respected by subsequent generations that he was commonly referred to as "Ari ha-kadosh," the holy lion, and Ashlag agreed that Luria's grasp of the "hidden wisdom" was unblemished. The images and concepts in Luria's teaching became the common vocabulary of virtually all Kabbalists who came after him. Luria modified the cosmogonic narrative in the Zohar and imbued it with tremendous drama. According to Luria's narrative, in the beginning there was only Ein sof, endless and undivided divinity. The first act of Ein sof was not emanation, but a contraction inward (tsimtsum) that left an empty space in its midst. Into this empty space Ein sof emanated light into Adam kadmon, primordial man, a spiritual figure who contained all human souls. Following this, rays of light emanated out from Adam kadmon into vessels that were designed to contain them. The power of the light proved too much for the vessels, however, and they exploded into pieces. Some of the sparks of divine light adhered to the fragments of vessels, known as kelippot (shells), evil forces. The unified human soul of Adam kadmon dropped down into the lowest world containing the kelippot, and it splintered into individual souls that entered human bodies. Material existence as we know it began.

According to this narrative, the sad, troubled history of humanity is the consequence of souls cut off from their divine origin, separated from each other, and trapped in a broken world. The upper, spiritual realm is fragmented and out of order, and the lower, earthly realm mirrors this disorder it in its wickedness and in the Jews' dispersed and humiliated condition. Luria taught that the purpose of human existence was to enact a tikkun (repair) of the divine realm by returning all scattered sparks of divinity to their source. More precisely, this theurgical task could be accomplished by Kabbalists: Jewish men performing the Torah laws in a most meticulous manner and through special kabbalistic rituals and meditations would posses a disproportionate power to restore sparks and hasten the achievement of final and total Redemption.

Until the achievement of the universal tikkun, the task of each soul was to extricate itself from material existence and return to its divine source. Only the perfectly righteous could, in one lifetime, achieve that. Others—that is, most everyone—would not succeed, and upon death, their souls would be reborn, perhaps many times and in many different forms of life, until they had reached individual tikkun. (The idea of reincarnation had appeared in kabbalistic literature centuries before Luria, but Luria's version ties it to an individual's responsibility and fate in life.)[19]

Ashlag accepted Luria's teachings and believed that he was explaining them exactly as the master had intended. In fact, Ashlag was convinced that Luria's soul had entered his own and that Ashlag had been designated by God to accurately convey Luria's understanding of Kabbalah to others.[20] Yet, living in the twentieth century, Ashlag produced a distinctive kabbalistic philosophy that reflected the concerns and assumptions of his own era.

In his version of the cosmogonic narrative, Ashlag describes the cosmos governed by two fundamental impulses, the Desire to Give and the Desire to Receive. God is defined as the infinite Desire to Give, an entirely positive force. In the "beginning" when all reality is undivided divinity (Ein sof), there is no Other to whom God could give, and so God created vessels—the sefirot—imprinted with the Desire to Receive. The sefirot were part of divinity, and from the first (Keter) to the tenth (Malchut), they were imbued with greater capacity to contain divine light. Receiving divine light without giving any in response, the vessels of Malchut were ashamed. In order to give, Malchut stopped receiving the divine light. This caused *tsimtsum* (contraction), and the vessels shattered and produced entities differentiated from God—the universe and human beings as we know them.[21] Human beings are imprinted with the Desire to Receive. At the most unenlightened, immature level, each human is endowed with a selfish, urgent Desire to Receive for the Self Alone. For this reason, human society is often cruel and unjust, and history is a series of violent conflicts and imperialism. The beneficent God who created and presides over this world, and whose light is diffused through it, has a purpose for humanity, and that is to purify humanity's Desire to Receive. Through conscious and rigorous discipline motivated by love for God, an individual's self-centered Desire may gradually be elevated to higher and higher levels of holiness until it is transformed into a Desire to Receive for the Sake of Sharing. The person then achieves *devekut*, equality of form, with God. Individual transformation and inner bliss, however, cannot take place within a vacuum. Tikkun is not completed with the "repair" of an individual. A person who has ascended in holiness would necessarily dedicate him or herself to ensuring that other people have been given what they need. A society in which there is economic justice and political responsibility can give rise to many people who are altruistic and moral, and they in turn influence the rest of humankind to elevate itself. At the highest level, the Days of the Messiah, the earthly realm would ultimately dissolve and all matter would be returned to its source in God. Ashlag's cosmogonic narrative shifts the focus of energy onto human ethics.[22]

Ashlag described how this transformation occurs within the framework of Judaism. He explained that God in his loving beneficence designed Jewish religious precepts as vehicles of transformation. Even if they are performed in a rote manner and the person may be motivated to fulfill them for a selfish benefit, the mitzvot may eventually be performed out of the motive of bringing pleasure to others, including God. The conscious striving to connect oneself to God is facilitated by the study of Kabbalah. Through Kabbalah, one learns how the precepts connect the devotee to divinity, and a person learns of God's great love for humanity and the wisdom of his Torah. This realization induces love and gratitude. The person's Desire to Receive is stimulated to give back, and it becomes transformed into a Desire to Receive for the Sake of Bringing Pleasure to God. This transformation brings a person as close as is humanly possible to the divine Desire to Give.

Ashlag departed from medieval Kabbalah in his focus on the human dimension and in his advance toward egalitarianism, two values characteristic of modern thought. Certainly, his Hasidic heritage contributed to this shift. Hasidic leaders accepted Luria's system, but they largely ignored its imperative to "work on God" to repair him and, indirectly, the world. Instead, Hasidic teachers turned the focus onto the inner life of the devout Jew with the objective to connect the individual's soul to God. Some counseled the individual to use prayer to eliminate the sense of self and the sense of material reality in order to achieve devekut (literally, adhering) with the omnipresent God. Others were less exacting and taught that even distracting thoughts and evil impulses during prayer contained divine sparks; by bringing them to consciousness, one could "release" the divine sparks from them, just as divine sparks might be released from kelippot. Whatever their particular teachings, Hasidic Kabbalists rejected the elitist tradition that had limited the teaching of Kabbalah. They believed it their task to teach mystical concepts to all Jews, even the uneducated ones. Ashlag shared and expanded both of these innovations, although he departed from Hasidic thought in a number of ways. He, too, disregarded the theurgical repair of the heavenly realm and turned his attention to tikkun on the individual and social level. He understood the cataclysmic "breaking of the vessels" in social terms, as an event that resulted in the creation of self-centered, destructive human beings. For Ashlag, tikkun moves forward when individuals become altruistic, promote economic justice, and reshape human society to be just and peaceful.[23]

Ashlag affirmed the importance of spreading kabbalistic knowledge outside of a select elite. In contrast to the Hasidic mode of teaching through stories and through a relationship with one's *rebbe* (the Hasidic term for leader), Ashlag's approach was highly intellectual. He was not known as a teacher who raised many disciples; he had a circle of students around him, but he registered his organization as a publishing house, and his students and sons helped him publish his writings.[24] To this end he wrote a voluminous commentary on the writings of Isaac Luria called *Talmud Eser Ha-Sefirot* (Teachings on the Ten Sefirot). This work was quite complex, however, and despite Ashlag's declaration in its preface that all should study it, it was written for a reader who already possessed extensive kabbalistic knowledge. A more successful example of dissemination was *Ha-Sulam*, Ashlag's translation of almost the entire Zohar into modern Hebrew with a full commentary. It made the Zohar intelligible to the non-specialist reader, and it presented a step-by-step guide (*Ha-Sulam* means "the ladder") for the individual to ascend to the highest levels of ethical behavior and spirituality. Ashlag's later followers, such as the Kabbalah Centre, put great stock in the precedent of Ashlag's belief in widespread propagation of Kabbalah. Yet the historical record shows a more complex reality. Only later in his life did Ashlag advocate teaching Kabbalah broadly; beginning in the 1930s he argued that the Messianic Age was at hand, and this was evidenced by the ability of his generation to comprehend the Zohar. Through *Ha-Sulam* and other writings, Ashlag sought to spread knowledge of Kabbalah to many; but it is clear that even then, he meant this to apply to Jewish men who had a serious commitment to Jewish religious law.[25] Nonetheless, this constituted a very liberal stance in its time.

Ashlag also sought to address the public through essays that addressed topics of general interest. He wrote these in a philosophical and analytical style and avoided kabbalistic terminology.[26] One theme that he developed was science. He was quite aware of the tremendous scientific discoveries and new theories that were daily transforming life and challenging older religious outlooks. Yet Ashlag insisted that Kabbalah and science were in harmony. The existence of a supremely intelligent creator was demonstrated by the scientific studies that showed the complex internal construction of even the tiniest of living creatures. The universality of the Desire to Receive was evident in the fact that forms of life had been engineered in order to receive sustenance and perpetuate themselves. Another theme Ashlag addressed was modern politics. Ashlag's optimistic conviction that humanity's Desire to Receive could and would be elevated was in accord with the assumption of many modern intellectuals that human society was gradually increasing in understanding and progressing toward greater awareness of itself. Socialism was for him the ideal economic-political system and the most compatible with kabbalistic principles. He adapted Marx's dialectical materialism to explain his own kabbalistic dialectical theory: the self-interested individual and chauvinistic society would be confronted by the opposing needs of others, and the clash would cause tremendous suffering and pain for all. This clash would inevitably spawn an awareness of the need for a higher system of ethics. A new level of development would be reached, until another confrontation of opposites would ensue, and a higher system would be achieved. The final stage was a utopia.[27]

This political vision matched Ashlag's kabbalistic theory. More so than his predecessors, he highlighted God's desire to give pleasure to all his creations and the potential of every soul to cleave to God. He de-emphasized the stark contrast between Jews and non-Jews that is assumed or expressed in most kabbalistic writings, although he believed that Jews had a pivotal role to play in the refinement of humanity's Desire to Receive. Through their study of Torah and observance of the mitzvot, motivated entirely by the desire to connect to God, the Jews would purify themselves and guide the rest of humanity toward God as well. But this separate Jewish mission would not persist through the end. The final stage of history and human development was one in which there would be no distinctions whatsoever between humans—not religious, racial, or national. This universal earthly realm would give way to a fully spiritual one, as all reached an affinity with God.[28]

Although many elements suggest that Ashlag's Kabbalah had the potential to win a large following, he could not find many followers in his lifetime. From the time of his arrival in Jerusalem, he openly expressed his disdain for other Kabbalists, and they in turn scorned him and his singular teachings. Nor did Ashlag have success in attracting students. Palestine was modernizing rapidly under the rule of the British, and the Jewish community there was increasingly focused on state building and absorbing immigrants. Although Jerusalem at the beginning of the twentieth century had been a gathering place for Kabbalists, it could no longer boast of such vibrancy in the 1940s and beyond. From 1943 until his death in 1955, Ashlag dedicated himself to making the Zohar accessible to the public by translating it into modern Hebrew, but the publication of Ha-Sulam seems to have attracted only the attention of his few devoted disciples.[29] With barely any demand for his writings, Ashlag had to pay for the printing out of his own resources, and with few students and no other means of earning a livelihood, he had no resources. His son Baruch, like virtually all other Kabbalists at that time, was unable to muster a vibrant group of students with whom to transmit kabbalistic teachings.[30] It took one more generation for Ashlag's writings to catch on, and when they attracted a following, it was primarily outside of his family line.

Perhaps this is because Ashlag's passionate commitment to improving the world wreaked havoc on his family life. When Ashlag decided to leave Warsaw for Palestine in 1921, his wife insisted on joining him. The versions of the story differ: some say she gave birth at sea en route; others say she was delayed in Czechoslovakia, and he went ahead without her. All agree that some of the children were temporarily left in Poland with relatives, and two of them died before they could be reunited with their parents. The family's life in Palestine was quite difficult. Ashlag continued to move seven more times after his arrival in Palestine in 1921. The author of the sole biography on Ashlag, written by a devoted follower, describes Ashlag's life as one in which in which he and his students engaged in manual labor by day and studied Kabbalah only in the middle of the night.[31] Others tell a starkly different tale.[32] According to the son of his disciple Levi Krakovsky, Ashlag and students studied all the time, huddled around the kitchen table furtively whispering words of Kabbalah. Only one of them, Rabbi Yehuda Brandwein, held a regular job during the day. Mrs. Ashlag and the other wives worked, and their children accompanied them in a weekly routine of hustling donations from the moneyed new immigrants in their neighborhood. The disciples handed over what meager

Figure 1.2 The Chain of Transmission of Kabbalah from Yehuda Ashlag to the Bergs

Shimon Bar Yohai
2ND CENTURY OF THE COMMON ERA

Isaac Luria "The ARI"
1534–1572

Yehuda Ashlag
1885–1955

Levi Isaac Krakovsky   Yehuda Zvi Brandwein
1891–1966   1903–1969

other disciples

Shraga Feival (Philip) Gruberger (Berg)
1929–

Yehuda Berg   Michael Berg
1972–   1973–

other disciples in the
Kabbalah Centre

Yehuda Ashlag's teachers trace their learning back to Isaac Luria and Shimon bar Yohai. Diagram: Kathryn de Boer.

earnings they earned to their teacher. Ashlag and his large family were terribly poor, however, and available funds had to be stretched to support them and the publishing costs. The women were by no means content with this arrangement; they complained bitterly that they had entered their marriages under false pretenses. Ashlag's sons, who helped typeset and print their father's manuscripts when they were young, eventually moved out and established their own families. Ashlag became increasingly dependent on his few disciples; Yehuda Brandwein was the most important among them. After Ashlag's death, relatives and disciples fought in and out of court over the rights to his manuscripts and the right to claim title as kabbalistic master after him. Brandwein eventually took control of publishing the last volumes of *Ha-Sulam*, and Ashlag's son Baruch retained most of his father's unpublished manuscripts.[33]

LEVI KRAKOVSKY AND THE ARRIVAL OF ASHLAGIAN KABBALAH IN AMERICA

Rabbi Levi Krakovsky, one of Yehuda Ashlag's disciples, was the first to bring Ashlag's teachings to the United States. Beginning in 1937 and for the next 30 years, Krakovsky published books and pamphlets, traveled to different cities where he thought there might be a receptive audience, and taught students privately. It is important to insert Krakovsky into the historical record. Years before late twentieth-century kabbalistic charismatic teachers crafted their messages and followings, he pioneered a popular version of Ashlag's Kabbalah and attempted to disseminate it in America. Examining his experience shows the crucial differences between the mid-twentieth-century American religious environment and that of the end of the century and between an unsuccessful adaptation of traditional ideas and a successful one.

Levi Isaac Krakovsky was born in 1891 in Romny, a town in Polish Russia, and after his father died and left the family impoverished, Krakovsky moved to the United States. The year was 1906, and he was 15 years old and the youngest of several siblings. In the years following, Krakovsky's siblings and mother also immigrated to the United States and established themselves in business. Levi Krakovsky had an intellectual bent, and departing from the family's lukewarm religious heritage, he enrolled in a rabbinic seminary, adopted the strict obedience to Jewish law characteristic of American Orthodox Judaism, and received rabbinic ordination. Excited by his learning and wanting more, and still a bachelor at the age of 30, he moved to Palestine in 1922.

Shortly after Krakovsky's arrival in Palestine, he joined the circle of students around Yehuda Ashlag.[34] Ashlag was also Polish-born, just five years Krakovsky's senior, and they established an intense teacher-disciple relationship. Krakovsky's family, like Ashlag's, suffered from his involvement with Kabbalah. Krakovsky married a young Jerusalem-born woman named Tzippora who was chagrined to learn that her husband was unreservedly devoted to the study of Kabbalah and the support of his teacher. Krakovsky's mother in New York regularly sent her son a check, which he handed over to Ashlag. Tzippora was responsible for the financial support of the family. Within weeks of giving birth to their fifth child in 1931, Tzippora died. With the approval of Ashlag, Krakovsky put the children into Jerusalem orphanages and continued his studies. But the loss of a breadwinner became a serious obstacle, and in 1937 Ashlag suggested that his disciple return to New York alone. The Krakovsky children were to grow up in the orphanages, looking after each other with the help of their mother's relatives and an occasional visit from Mrs. Ashlag.[35]

Ashlag's letter of recommendation that Krakovsky carried with him indicates that both men regarded his return to the United States as the beginning of an important mission. The disciple would spread kabbalistic wisdom in America by publishing in English. He already had one manuscript ready. It was a massive concordance of kabbalistic wisdom—the fruit of 10 years' labor— containing and explaining distinctive concepts and terminology, arranged in an orderly and easy-to-use fashion, in clear English. Ashlag requested in his letter that the reader donate funds or aid to Krakovsky so that he could publish the concordance:

> We have here a matter of revealing wisdom for the good of all Israel, for I am certain that when this composition is published, the heavenly channels will become unblocked and streams from this wisdom will be revealed to the eyes of every enlightened person, so that every Jew will be able to drink from its well. As it is written in the Zohar, at the end of days even the Jewish children will understand, discern, and reveal the secrets of the Torah.[36]

These remarks make clear that Ashlag intended Levi Krakovsky to direct his efforts toward Jews.

Shortly after arriving in New York, Krakovsky embarked on his mission. He settled in Brooklyn, lived modestly, and found another wife to support him. He was not successful with his concordance. It may have been transformed into the volume he later described as an English popular textbook of the Kabbalah, over which he toiled 15 years; this, like the concordance, was never published. Nevertheless, Krakovsky managed to publish two books of his own composition, an English translation of a work by Ashlag, and two Hebrew editions of kabbalistic commentary by others. He also printed three pamphlets in English (one was in Yiddish as well as English) that explained the permissibility and benefits of studying Kabbalah. He had dreams of founding a Kabbalah academy, an institution that would acquaint the general public in America with "the profound wisdom of the Kabbalah." In one of his books, he described himself as the head of a yeshiva devoted to the teaching of Kabbalah,[37] but in actuality he instructed young Orthodox Jewish men on a one-on-one basis. He offered them an introduction to Kabbalah in English before moving on to a study of kabbalistic texts in the original Hebrew and Aramaic.[38] He was a man of great energy. He would go door-to-door to find students, readers, and publishers, and he even drove across the country to peddle his books and pitch his manuscripts to publishers. He continued to write his own works and translate Ashlag's works into Hebrew, and when he died in 1966, he left behind at least 10 sizable unpublished manuscripts.[39]

In America from 1937 until 1966, Levi Krakovsky faced a readership strikingly different than that faced by his teacher. In Palestine, where there was virtually no common culture between the Jews and the Arab Muslims and Christians, Ashlag was addressing a narrow, Jewish readership. In America, Krakovsky was writing to Jews primarily and non-Jews secondarily. Unlike the Jews of Palestine, very few American Jews possessed knowledge of Hebrew, and an even smaller percentage of the community had facility with the religious texts upon which Kabbalah was dependent. American Jews and non-Jews shared, to a great extent, a common culture. Jews were a minority that was somewhat self-conscious and embarrassed about the elements of its religion that diverged from Christianity.

Furthermore, Kabbalah was entirely foreign to American Jewish culture. Kabbalists and Hasidic Jews who may have possessed knowledge of Kabbalah typically did not immigrate to the United States until after World War II. When they did, they were singular, isolated men who were not likely to find a disciple who would pass on their teachings. American Jews shaped their synagogue, home rituals, and Jewish school curricula to promote a rational, ethical, elevating, and staid religion. This applied to Orthodox Jews as well. They generally did not share Krakovsky's enthusiasm for the Kabbalah and did not find it an appropriate subject for study. Orthodox Jews may have followed Jewish law with relative strictness, but they did not display much passion for Torah study.[40] Jewish mysticism was regarded a part of Ashkenazic culture that was—not so unfortunately—lost with the arrival of modernity. In 1938, a year after Krakovsky's return to New York, Gershom Scholem, the Hebrew University professor who was one of the creators of the academic study of Kabbalah, was brought to the city by the Jewish Institute of Religion to deliver a series of lectures on Jewish mysticism. His research was an object of curiosity, not spiritual seeking. Krakovsky was acutely aware that America was not an environment friendly to the Kabbalah.

There was, however, a small portion of the population that was open to and interested in Kabbalah. These were the Americans who had heard of it through the new spiritual and occult-metaphysical movements. The Theosophical Society's free public lectures and gifts of books to public libraries had explained kabbalistic symbols in conjunction with others from Hinduism, Buddhism, Christianity, and Hellenistic occult systems. American businessmen in Masonic lodges had been exposed to kabbalistic symbols as well. These people were a natural audience for Krakovsky's teachings, even though they were generally not Jewish. It seems likely that they helped fund the publication of Krakovsky's first book, in 1939, titled *The Omnipotent Light Revealed: The Luminous Tegument to Unite Mankind into One Loving Brotherhood*.[41]

The influence of the new spiritual movements is evident in Krakovsky's references to them as well as his tactic of identifying Kabbalah as science. Ashlag had crafted an argument that appealed to people's admiration of science, and certainly his disciple learned it from him. However, Krakovsky translated it into an American idiom. Whereas Ashlag had highlighted the harmony between Kabbalah and the findings of scientific research, Krakovsky described Kabbalah as a scientific tool for material advancement. Americans, he pointed out, had aspirations for improving the conditions of life, and they had initiated inventions in electricity and transportation. Their interest in technology and scientific knowledge would be served by learning from Kabbalah. "Kabbalah is based on scientific fact, its laboratory the human organism" is the epigraph on the title page of *The Omnipotent Light Revealed*. Yet it is clear that by "science," Krakovsky did not mean scientific method and research, but a spiritual outlook that concerned itself with the concrete, day-to-day conditions of life on earth. He declared that Kabbalah is the source of "everything scientific and grand" in the teachings of eighteenth-century spiritualists such as Jacob Boehme and Emanuel Swedenborg, and Freemasons, he wrote, knew that it contained all their secrets. Similarly, he wrote, "The Kabbalah has developed a profound, scientific system wherein we are taught that our small and insignificant earth is the true aim and purpose of the Creator."[42] By attuning one's will to that of God, he insisted, one could improve the physical conditions of life as well as social relations. In short, he presented Kabbalah as a means for achieving pragmatic goals. Krakovsky did not expand the science theme beyond the major emphasis it received in *The Omnipotent Light Revealed*, and in his later writings, he began to be critical of scientific knowledge as a "false god." He pointed out that science was failing in its promise to bring human fulfillment. Although science improved life materially, World War II had demonstrated that humanity had regressed spiritually. Therefore, "man can no longer postpone his quest of the eternal spiritual values" that govern life.[43] Decades later, the Kabbalah Centre shaped these themes for its own audience.

Krakovsky explained the human situation as a function of divine processes that had occurred prior to the creation of the earthly realm: Ein sof, emanation of light, sefirot, and so on. Krakovsky described the development methodically, and his achievement should not be minimized. He was synthesizing information from a variety of sources and crafting it for the nonspecialist, inventing an English lexicon of kabbalistic terms. For example, the kabbalistic term *nehama dekisufa*—Krakovsky translated it "bread of shame"—explains why God made this world one in which humans have to work hard, and in which achievement often requires suffering and sacrifice.

Were one to receive one's sustenance without working for it, one would be ashamed. Here is Krakovsky's summary of this concept:

> Since the Supreme Being is all-goodness and His will is to bestow His ineffable bounty of light; to accomplish this end He has created souls to whom He can bestow His bounty. The Supreme Being also desired that the souls receive their bounty through merit and not charity for this brings embarrassment and shame to the soul. Therefore, He placed them in bodies and put them into the mundane world where they can toil in Torah and fulfill the precepts, and consequently merit the bestowal of His Light. Thus in order that man earn the bestowal and not eat the "bread of shame," the Supreme Being left unfinished the channels through which light could be transmitted so that by his efforts man can adjust and complete them.[44]

The principle of earning the bestowal of divine light was central to Ashlag and previous Kabbalists, but it was Krakovsky who concisely summarized it in English. In this form it passed into the literature of the Kabbalah Centre, where it assumed major importance.

What was the purpose of informing non-Jews about Kabbalah? The question arises because Krakovsky made it so clear that Jews played the most important role in raising the divine sparks sunk into the realm of evil, the kelippot, which had tainted all human souls since the time of Adam's fall. He believed that humanity's efforts to extricate itself from evil was doomed to fail unless the Jews achieved their particular task. In other words, the Jews' responsibility "to be a light unto the nations" did not mean that they served as a model for the rest of humanity; rather, they "raised light" on behalf of humanity in the spiritual realm.[45] All humanity would benefit, for the final stage of history would "bring peace and complete redemption to Israel and to all races and peoples."[46] He believed that in the last phase of history, the Messianic Age, all peoples would come to learn Kabbalah—and Krakovsky declared in several of his works that he believed he was living in the Messianic Age. Yet there is no evidence showing that Krakovsky had as a goal a "mission to the nations." He did not suggest that non-Jews perform mitzvot or join Jews in prayer. It was permissible to teach them Kabbalah, Krakovsky wrote, and they could benefit from learning the secret dynamics of the universe, the reasons for the existence of evil, and the means that God had instituted for removing evil. They could be corrected in their misguided notion that the source of Kabbalah is in non-Jewish traditions "such as the Hindu philosophy, the Yoga, Egyptian teachings, and others"—in fact, it was the other way around.[47] In short, non-Jews were relegated to the roles of onlookers and supporters. It is not surprising that Krakovsky did not attract many of them to his cause.

Because of his objective to broadcast the truth widely, Krakovsky took pains to make his writings easy to understand. He could not write as most Kabbalists did, in cryptic and abbreviated language that assumed a great deal of knowledge on the part of the reader. The best demonstration of his style is in his major work, *Kabbalah: The Light of Redemption*, a book he published privately in 1950. It is addressed to the intelligent Jewish lay person, and the language is erudite but not densely technical. It is organized by topic, and these topics are arranged logically in book sections and chapters. Generally, the book presents multiple, overlapping, and sometimes contradictory arguments promoting an understanding of life through the symbols and concepts found in kabbalistic texts. Much of the book consists of Ashlagian Kabbalah explained in plain English and a few drawings. Krakovsky does not differentiate between previous kabbalistic schools of thought and does not name the originators of distinctive kabbalistic concepts. He was writing for non-specialists, and they did not care about such matters. Krakovsky's other book and his unpublished manuscripts were similar in style. Today, there are dozens of books of this sort available; then, it was an utter novelty. Gershom Scholem came across the book and was quite puzzled by it. In his review of the book, he mentioned that it was a genre he had never before seen, and he called it a form of "kabbalistic propaganda."[48]

Krakovsky was more consistent than his teacher Ashlag in insisting that it was imperative to teach Kabbalah to all Jews, and he certainly acted on this conviction more than Ashlag had. Throughout his writings, he responded to those who would keep Kabbalah esoteric. He granted that there were some aspects of Kabbalah known as *sitrei Torah*, the secrets of the Torah, which must be reserved for an elect. However, contained within Kabbalah were the underlying reasons for the commandments (*taaimei ha-mitzvot*), and with this knowledge one would love the commandment and from there ascend to love God and to worship God out of pure motives.[49] Was it not apparent that religious indifference and spiritlessness was a problem among American Jews? Krakovsky asked. Only the study of Kabbalah could rectify the situation; only the study of Kabbalah could generate adherence to a life of the mitzvot and impassioned love of God.

He added to this a kabbalistic explanation. Kabbalah was meant to be popularized in this era, Krakovsky explained, *because* there were so very few select, superior souls. There will be three 2,000-year eras of human history, according to the Talmud; the first two thousand years occurred when the Torah was not manifest, the second were the years of the Torah, and the final two thousand constitute the period of the advent of the Messiah. In this last era, the souls of the crudest of the divine substance have come into being and are required to raise the sparks.[50] Krakovsky believed the truth of this teaching was apparent in the unprecedented extent of evil in the present era. This is how he explained it, writing in 1950:

> However, God foresaw that at the end of time, that is, in our day and age which is actually the dawn of the coming of the Messiah; at that time, lust, greed and

self-centeredness will prevail over humanity to an unbridled degree, submerging our thoughts and spiritual aspirations into the oblivion of our corporeal instincts. Because such evil forces are rampant in our world, we have become spiritually sick....Therefore, the need of unveiling the most powerful antidote of Torah, the wisdom of Kabbalah, by which we could subdue our bitter enemy, the "Yetzer" [evil impulse], is absolutely a matter of survival.[51]

When evil forces are the most rampant, it is actually be the dawn of redemption, and that is when the study of Kabbalah is the most urgent and a matter of survival.

Needless to say, Krakovsky found his subject to be a rather hard sell. His Kabbalah was embedded into a form of Judaism that was then on the wane. Many American Jews probably agreed that they were living during a time when evil was rampant. The spread of Nazism, the genocide of European Jews, the tremendous toll of World War II, the atomic bomb, and the Cold War were frightful and horrific events. Yet few Americans, including American Jews, would have found Krakovsky's prescription healing. In their minds, evil would be vanquished by strong armies, the rule of law, and the spread of democratic values. It was not likely that they could be convinced that evil could be vanquished by Jews who observed mitzvot out of selfless devotion to God, who were unmindful of material acquisitions and worldly success, and who acted ethically purely out of love for God. In praise of these righteous ones, Krakovsky wrote,

> The highest attainment possible for a human being is to enlist himself in the army of those valiant ones who pass sleepless nights and days of struggle in order to become ripe for a great burst of Light and Life. Thus, the man of valor for the sake of this should make up his mind to reject with disdain temporal pleasures; to encounter for it afflicting penury; to search for it through obscurity...and sorrow, and derision as our Patriarchs, the Prophets and all the Tsaddikim [righteous ones] have done throughout the generations of bygone years and at all times.[52]

These behaviors and ideals were not greeted with enthusiasm by mid-century American Jews, nor would they be embraced by many later in the century either. They bring to mind the impoverished dedication of Krakovsky's years in Ashlag's home, and perhaps they have within them the echo of the socialist pioneers of Palestine. Although Krakovsky's way of thinking was modern, it was unfashionable in America, and there was no sizable cohort of American Jews or non-Jews who embraced it enthusiastically.

For the full length of his life, however, Levi Krakovsky continued to promote the study of Kabbalah. When his second wife died in 1947, he returned to Palestine with the intention of resuming his study of Kabbalah. At that time, he became friendly with Ashlag's disciple Yehuda Brandwein. However, once more, Krakovsky could not make ends meet, and he returned to Brooklyn and eventually married a third time. None of the Krakovsky children carried on their father's interest in the Kabbalah. His son Shlomo explained it simply: "Kabbalah destroys families."[53] Nevertheless, several of them immigrated to the United States and reestablished relationships with their father and his third wife. They saw that, even in his seventies, until shortly before his death in 1966, their father would pack his satchel with copies of *Kabbalah: The Light of Redemption* and drive to distant cities or nearby neighborhoods seeking interested buyers. While in Brooklyn, he taught a number of students, usually young Orthodox men who knew little about Kabbalah. One of them was Eugene Semel, who would in later years emulate his teacher by devoting his spare time to teaching Ashlagian Kabbalah one-on-one to Orthodox rabbis and untrained young men.[54] Another was Shraga Feival Gruberger (Philip Berg). Gruberger solicited Krakovsky's help in incorporating the National Institute for Research in Kabbalah, which later became the Kabbalah Centre.[55] Krakovsky did not plan to stay in America to see the fruits of his students' labors. He sent money to his daughter in Israel in anticipation of his own return there, at some point in the future. However, he died in New York after a brief illness. His children fulfilled the dictates of his will and arranged for Yehuda Brandwein to bury him in Jerusalem alongside Ashlag.[56]

As we have seen in the brief history of Kabbalah, the matter of transmission is a deeply important one. Kabbalah means "received tradition," and every human link in the chain of transmission must establish that he received it from an exemplary and highly reputed source. Philip Berg of the Kabbalah Centre regards his teacher to be Yehuda Brandwein, and in his account of his reception of Kabbalah, there is no mention of Krakovsky.[57] Instead, Berg refers to an unfortunate, unworthy, and unnamed Ashlag disciple who lived in New York. Brandwein warned him to never work with this man, but Berg ignored Brandwein's advice and collaborated with this man in translating kabbalistic texts. According to Berg, this man had been abandoned by his family and lived in poverty. His attempt to teach Kabbalah had never succeeded, and it was clear to Berg that it simply was not yet time for the Kabbalah to be widely disseminated. This man died alone and penniless, and no one from his family even attended the funeral, Berg writes, just himself and Brandwein, who arranged and paid for the funeral plot. Years later, according to Berg, this man's son falsely accused Berg of stealing his father's books. To Berg, the accusation was proof of Brandwein's prescience as well as the heroic forbearance necessary for those who wish to spread Kabbalah in the world.[58]

There is no doubt that Berg benefited a great deal from his experience with Levi Krakovsky. Although Berg's contacts with Brandwein were far more extensive, Krakovsky's translations, original compositions, and mode of expression laid the groundwork for Berg's later activities. Krakovsky's manuscripts and his book *Kabbalah: The Light of Redemption*, which Berg acquired from Krakovsky's widow after the funeral, launched his publishing career.[59] Perhaps most crucial, in Krakovsky Berg saw a model of a new type of Kabbalist: a devout, venerable Jewish sage who revealed formerly hidden wisdom to Jews as well as to the wider world, prompted by God's desire to benefit humanity. Like Ashlag and Krakovsky before him, Berg emphasizes the universal relevance of Kabbalah, Kabbalah's value as a source of science, and the social ills that will be solved through the spread of its teachings. Yet Berg did it differently. By the 1970s, he was adding elements that would be attractive to a wide audience, and he eliminated or suppressed the aspects of Ashlagian Kabbalah that would be considered unappealing. Perhaps most important, Berg was active in a later era than his two predecessors. His audience, in Israel as well as America, was hungry for Kabbalah and eager to bask in "the light of Redemption."

CHAPTER 2

———— ✻ ————

Kabbalah and New Religious Movements in America, 1960s–1980s

This chapter describes the dissemination and transformation of Yehuda Ashlag's teachings from the 1960s until the 1990s, when they moved from their setting within Orthodox Jewish society to outside of it. When Shraga Feival Gruberger first studied Kabbalah in the 1960s under the disciples of Ashlag, teachers and students alike were situated within Orthodox Judaism. The study of Kabbalah was limited to men generally knowledgeable in rabbinic texts, and practitioners of Kabbalah felt incumbent to obey Jewish ritual and ceremonial law to its fullest. Beginning in the 1970s, Gruberger presented the kabbalistic teachings of Ashlag in a manner that would appeal to Americans and Israelis who were seeking religious understanding and practices outside of the conventional modes available. During the first phase of the religious movement that Gruberger fostered, Kabbalah was described as an ancient spiritual tradition that would enhance the Judaism of its Jewish adherents and have tremendous spiritual value for all of humanity. Gruberger expanded access to Kabbalah to an audience that included secular Jews as well as non-Jews and women as well as men; and he removed Kabbalah from its association with strict religious law. His willingness to modify the delivery of kabbalistic teachings so as to fit the level of his students and to be responsive to their concerns, as well as his openness to empowering his talented students to help promote Kabbalah, led to quick growth of his followers in North America. By the late 1990s, the Kabbalah Centre had become an international movement, and its leaders exerted themselves to disassociate Kabbalah from Judaism and from Jews. This chapter recounts the birth, growth, and transformation of this phenomenon.

THE KABBALAH OF ASHLAG AND ITS PROMOTERS IN THE 1960s

Shraga Feival Gruberger was born in 1929 in Brooklyn, New York. His father, Max Gruberger, was an immigrant from a town in what is now Ukraine.[1]

The family lived in the Williamsburg neighborhood, which was home to a heavy concentration of Orthodox and Hasidic Jews. The young Gruberger was sent to Orthodox Jewish elementary and high schools that stressed acquisition of Talmudic learning, good morals, a life of sober practice of Jewish ritual commandments, and obedience to rabbinic authority. He then studied at Beth Medrash Govoha, a yeshiva (school of advanced Talmudic education) in Lakewood, New Jersey. He returned to Williamsburg and attended another yeshiva, Torah VaDaat, from which he received ordination in 1951, when he was 22 years old.[2] Gruberger did not attend college or another nonreligious postsecondary school, despite his later claim that he received a doctorate in comparative religion. Secular subjects were included in the curriculum of his high school, but they were considered of secondary importance to religious studies. No students in the schools he attended would have been instructed in Kabbalah, and it is likely that the Orthodox men who served as teachers were entirely ignorant and uninterested in the subject.

Rabbinic ordination did not necessarily mean embarking on a career as a teacher or pastoral leader; it was more common to enter the world of business, and it was expected that one would marry and have many children. Gruberger went into business and worked as an insurance agent for New York Life. Through this and his involvement in real estate, he became a very wealthy man.[3] It is likely that in that business environment, Gruberger was called by the English name Philip. Using an English equivalent was (and still is) not an unusual practice among Jews who have Yiddish or Hebrew names; it is more comfortable in a secular or non-Jewish environment and is not considered evidence of deception. He married Rivka Brandwein in 1953; they lived within the Orthodox community in Brooklyn, and together they had eight children.[4]

Gruberger, like Ashlag and Krakovsky before him, did not let family ties hamper his interest in Kabbalah and his desire for independence. It was a very difficult life for Gruberger's wife and children. They were plagued by serious illness: one child died in infancy, and one struggled with cancer many years before succumbing. There were kabbalistic scholars living in Brooklyn during the 1950s and 1960s with whom Gruberger could study privately, and it is certain that he studied with at least one of them, Levi Krakovsky, up to the time of Krakovsky's death in 1966. Yet Gruberger spent considerable time in Israel during the 1960s, and as early as 1964, he was studying Kabbalah with Rabbi Yehuda Brandwein of Tel Aviv. Gruberger's connection to Brandwein was probably facilitated by the fact that Rivka Brandwein Gruberger was Brandwein's niece.[5] Brandwein was a Hasidic rabbi and had been a student in the kabbalistic circle around Yehuda Ashlag. He earned an income as a builder, and after 1957, he also served as the head of the Department for the Provision of Religious Requirements for the Israeli national workers union, Histadrut. Like Ashlag's other students, Brandwein aspired to spread his master's teachings. His position with the Histadrut allowed him access to a wide range of people and the frequent opportunity to teach. Although Brandwein also received funds from the Histadrut, he seems to have needed other resources for his plan to publish Ashlag's manuscripts and sell them in Israel and beyond. Gruberger became Brandwein's book distributor and U.S. fund-raiser. Probably under Brandwein's guidance, Gruberger established the National Institute for Research in Kabbalah in New York in 1965. There were four stated purposes for the corporation: to support research in Kabbalah, to publish books and periodicals reflecting that research, to establish scholarships for "Orthodox Jewish Scholars" to do research in Kabbalah, and to finance transportation costs by scholars to the Vatican and other libraries for their Kabbalah research. Gruberger was the presiding officer of the corporation, and Krakovsky was one of the corporation subscribers.[6]

About three dozen letters written from Brandwein to Gruberger from 1965 to 1969 give a glimpse of what it was like for the two men to promote Kabbalah to a relatively uninterested audience. (The letters appear in a three-volume Hebrew set published by the Kabbalah Centre titled *Sefer Yedid Nafshi*, in their original, mostly handwritten form as well as in an abridged, transcribed version.) Brandwein had established a yeshiva called Kol Yehuda (*Voice of Yehuda*), named after his teacher Yehuda Ashlag. He regarded it as a continuation of Ashlag's yeshiva-publishing house. Kol Yehuda was like many other yeshivot in that it was a room where students would study together and listen to a daily lecture from the head of the yeshiva; its uniqueness was that kabbalistic texts were the focus of study. The students received a stipend to cover their living expenses so that they could dedicate themselves to learning.[7] Brandwein had difficulty finding funds for even such a modest operation and for his publishing goals.

Gruberger served a crucial role in New York, where money could be raised more easily than in Israel, and it is clear that the National Institute for Research in Kabbalah was set up for these purposes. Apparently, Krakovsky asked that his book be included among those Gruberger was promoting or arranging to publish. Gruberger asked Brandwein, and Brandwein's response illustrates the relationship between these three men and the partnership between Brandwein and Gruberger:

> Which books of Rabbi Krakovsky do you want to purchase. I have a principle that the yeshiva should not publish books that have already been published. The book Or Ne'erav [by the Kabbalist Moses Cordovero] I will [re-]publish simply because it is a small book which awakens interest in Kabbalah and there will not entail much expense, for we must be careful of every cent we spend on our sacred goal, for which we received it. For example there is the book Talmud Eser Ha-Sefirot, which is still unpublished from volume 8 and following...we must

Rabbis Phillip Berg (l.) and Yehuda Brandwein
(r.) in front of the Western Wall in Jerusalem during 1967–1969. Copyright © The Kabbalah Centre International/Kabbalah University Archives/
university@kabbalah.com/www.kabbalah.com.

seek all kinds of means in order to publicize and publish it. *And regarding the
books of Rabbi Krakovsky that are published, he should be the one concerned about
distributing them, what business is it of the yeshiva. With all due respect, my wish is
to come to his help, but not through crooked ways. The publisher of the Zohar in the
Diaspora is named Yosef Weinstock. He wrote me that he already sent you 100 sets,
and they should have already arrived. He wants 15 dollars for every set. You can
arrange with him that you sell them for a higher price than that, and the profit will go*

toward the yeshiva. [Italicized words are in the original and are omitted from the transcribed letter][8]

Here is it obvious that Brandwein respected Krakovsky, but regarded their goals as distinct. Indeed, the men were competitors for the same audience. Brandwein's concern about proper expenditure of funds is found in many of the letters, as is his lament about his shortage of money, and he came to rely on Gruberger's financial resources. The two men had a number of joint ventures in Israel, some of which involved the purchase of real estate in Israel and investments in potentially lucrative medical technology, and the profits were to be used for the yeshiva-publishing company. In 1965, the National Institute for Research in Kabbalah published Brandwein's edition of *Or Ne'erav,* and in the book's preface, Gruberger is identified as the Institute's president, and Brandwein holds the title of dean.[9]

Because Gruberger's letters are not preserved, his personal goals are not obvious, but there is no doubt from Brandwein's writings that the "mission to spread Kabbalah" was understood by the latter as occurring entirely within Jewish society. Brandwein lived in Israel, where there was a firm religious boundary separating Jews, Muslims, and Christians; the books he published and distributed (even outside Israel) were written in Hebrew, which only Jews were likely to understand. To Brandwein, Kabbalah had always been the preserve of a few Jewish men, and he praised Ashlag for calling for larger numbers of Jewish men to be taught it. In Israel, large numbers of young Jews were simply uninterested in a life circumscribed by Jewish laws and rituals, and these men (this was not an option for women) could not be induced to adopt a discipline of Torah study. Coming on the heels of the murder of millions of Jews during the Holocaust, the situation was alarming. In Brandwein's preface to *Or Ne'erav,* he echoed the words of Ashlag in attributing the Holocaust as well as the loss of Jewish religiosity to the absence of Kabbalah from the curriculum. The singular focus on the revealed Torah (Bible, Talmud, law codes) was too dry and uninspiring for the current generation of Jews, he wrote; they required the lessons of the secret Torah for inspiration. In addition, Brandwein endorsed Ashlag's belief that, because it was currently the brink of the Messianic Era, the widespread teaching of Kabbalah was mandated. Brandwein explained that he had established two branches of a kabbalistic yeshiva in Israel "to give the possibility to all who want to penetrate the depth of this wisdom." The preface ends with a rousing call for those who wish "to elevate Israel's light, the light of Torah and Judaism and to bring an end to the Exile." Those who could not commit to a regimen of study were invited to contribute financially instead.[10] He does not specify exactly to whom he is addressing this invitation to study. Brandwein did not explicitly call for the formal teaching of Kabbalah to women or non-Orthodox Jews. Such a move would have been anathema in his community and would have imperiled his sources of support in Israel.

Brandwein had deep reservations about including non-Jews even in the financial support of his Kabbalistic enterprise, according to his letters to Gruberger. In the summer of 1965, Gruberger informed Brandwein that Cardinal Spellman (of the archdiocese of New York) had agreed to help raise funds for the yeshiva. Brandwein found this disturbing, "for the contributors would certainly be non-Jews," and they would know that they were contributing to a Jewish cause. Brandwein was referring to an old Jewish teaching that should be understood as an outgrowth of the hostile relations between Jews and non-Jews. Accepting charitable funds from non-Jews was problematic because historically Jews had been ridiculed and persecuted by non-Jews (that is, Christians and Muslims) for their religion. Jews' poverty or their inability to take care of each other was often held up as evidence that they had been rejected by God and that they were contemptible. Therefore, if Jews accepted funds from non-Jews, it would reflect badly on Jews and desecrate God's name. Consequently, Jewish law differentiated between aid given publicly and aid given in quietness (the latter was preferred) and between aid offered in normal times and aid offered in times of grave emergency (the former was discouraged and the latter was permitted). Some religious authorities, in particular those who were Kabbalists, included an additional objection: charity would expiate sins, and Jews should not facilitate the expiation of non-Jews' sins. This opinion grows out of the kabbalistic teaching that non-Jews' souls originated in the realm of evil.[11] Brandwein, a student of Kabbalah, took the restrictive position on all these matters:

> If the Cardinal perhaps prints an announcement calling for people to contribute to the Kol Yehudah yeshiva, that will be prohibited by Jewish law, for it desecrates God's name, and thus it is written in the *Shulhan Arukh, Yoreh Deah,* sec. 254 that the people of Israel may not accept charity [*tzedaka*] given publically by idolaters. One can distinguish between donations [*nedarim* and *nedavot*] and charity [*tzedaka*]; for one is permitted to accept donations from them, for these are like the sacrifices accepted from idolaters which were accepted [in the ancient Jerusalem Temple], but this was not the same as charity, which expiates sin. And if you allow them to donate items to a synagogue, the principle violated here is that it is public and publicized. If you need to give public recognition to the donors and what they gave, it is not worthwhile and may even be prohibited. However, if it is merely a donation and is given secretly [i.e., with no public recognition], it may be possible to receive from them. And if—may it be God's will—that we build housing [for the yeshiva] and the like, it may be possible to apply their monetary contributions toward building the bathrooms and also other expenses like travel and the like. The non-Jews should not be able to specify for what their money is spent. One must be careful so as not to desecrate God's name, God forbid.[12]

According to Brandwein, then, one should accept funds from non-Jews under the following conditions: the funds must be given privately, the donor's name must not be publicized, the funds must be understood as donations and not charity, and the funds are spent on profane matters only. Three weeks later, Brandwein reiterated his position with regard to funds from Spellman.[13] Given this position, one could also conclude that he did not want to teach Kabbalah to non-Jews, an opinion in stark contrast to the universalism of the future Kabbalah Centre.

The original letters indicate that Brandwein regarded Gruberger with warm but mixed feelings. Brandwein expressed affection toward his student and partner, especially in the openings of his letters. He looked forward to Gruberger's visits to Israel.[14] Often he scolded Gruberger for his carelessness in business dealings, for not following through on matters they had decided together, and for inadequate communication.[15] Gruberger appears as a neo-phyte, a person starting his learning, and Brandwein usually included some teaching in each letter and advised him where to read further. "Read the pas-sage three times before you tell it to anybody," he instructed him, although later that year, he gave permission for Gruberger to take on a single pupil.[16] Yet, in 1966 Brandwein conferred upon him an ordination additional to the one he had received from the rabbinical seminary, one that acknowledged mastery of Kabbalah. In addition to testifying to Gruberger's Kabbalistic ex-pertise, it conferred the highest rabbinical rank possible.[17]

Nevertheless, Gruberger's role in the yeshiva is unclear. Although he had been president of the National Research Institute in Kabbalah since at least 1965, it is not clear what the role entailed; certainly it was not equivalent to being the head of the yeshiva and did not include the responsibility for teaching the students. In 1968, when Brandwein wrote Gruberger a let-ter acknowledging his new position as president of the yeshiva, Brandwein took pains to tell the new president basic information about the institution: "Since you have accepted the burden of the presidency of the Kol Yehuda Yeshiva ... it is of urgent necessity to inform you of its purpose and establish-ment in holiness, which it has followed continuously these past forty years."[18] Clearly, Brandwein was desirous that his publishing work and yeshiva would be continued after his death. However, when he died in 1969, he left no obvious successor in Israel. Years later, Gruberger claimed that he had been designated for those roles.[19]

RELIGIOUS REBELLION AND SEEKING DURING THE 1960s

The religious culture that prevailed among the Americans to whom Gru-berger would later promote Kabbalah was quite different than the culture in the close-knit Orthodox community of his youth. When he was young, dur-ing the 1940s and 1950s, Americans' religious behavior was linked to ethnic and familial bonds, to sacred spaces within the local community, and to the conviction that religious truth could usually be found by looking into the heritage left by one's ancestors. Already in the mid-1950s, a number of new developments seemed to be weakening the foundation upon which American religious culture was based. A vast cohort of people was establishing households and raising children to carry on inherited family traditions. For many, local and intimate work settings gave way to bureaucratic offices, large-scale enterprises, and new places of employment in response to economic change. People moved away from communities in which they had attended church and synagogues, where they had engaged in religious worship and acknowledged life transitions, and where their dead were buried. The growing anonymity within expanding cities, and the social isolation and dislocation characteristic of suburban life, gave people the feeling of being unanchored and less restrained. The numbers of religious institutions increased to meet the demands of the growing population, but observers of American religious life predicted that religious enthusiasm and commitment would diminish over the next decade.[20]

American Jews shared in the postwar religious revival and expansion in a distinctive manner. They experienced residential change more than most Americans. In large numbers they moved to the suburbs, where they built new synagogues and community centers for worship, social life, and religious education for children. Among Jews there was also an internal migration from the urban centers in the Northeast and Midwest to Florida and California, and new synagogues and schools were established there as well. However, much of Jewish life was social rather than spiritual. Jews who strictly obeyed Jewish religious law were a small minority of the whole. Although an influx of strictly observant Jewish refugees came to the United States after the war, and new Orthodox and Hasidic synagogues and schools were established, the absolute number of Jews who identified themselves as Orthodox continued to decline. Many synagogues that were traditional in their practices during the 1940s shifted toward more lenient and liberal Jewish denominations in the 1950s. Consistent with the general trend of American religious institutions in mid-century, American Jews avoided extreme liberal or extreme conservative postures. Most American Jews regarded it as a priority to integrate into American society, and although they regarded religious affiliation as an element of Americanization, they felt that conspicuous Jewish religious practices were eccentric and isolating. Studying Kabbalah was out of the question. It was in this environment (and earlier, during the war era) that Krakovsky had tried and failed to spread kabbalistic teachings. Many Jews did not affiliate with synagogues at all or did so only when they had children living in their homes. Jewish weekly synagogue attendance was about one-third the rate of Catholics and one-half the rate of Protestants.[21] It was commonly acknowledged that American Jews lacked religious passion. Their ethnic identity was relatively strong, but they did not demonstrate much depth of religious commitment or hunger for a deep, intense relationship with God.

This changed during the 1960s for many of the younger generation. By 1963, the West was entering a period of tremendous social and religious turmoil. Presuppositions about patriotic ideals and traditional morality were under attack. Religion did not diminish in importance, as observers had predicted. Rather, it underwent significant transformations, and new permutations appeared. The political protest movements of the 1960s played an important role in transforming religious culture. The civil rights struggle, the antiwar movement, and agitation for women's equality involved very public questioning of middle-class white society's assumptions about justice, law, and God's will. The challengers accused religious leaders and institutions of being unresponsive to social ills and acquiescent toward evil. Religious leaders disagreed about the roles they were to play in these conflicts and the proper position to take on the issues. It became more difficult to know the right way to think and behave. In a stable and homogeneous community, it is obvious what it means to follow one's conscience. In the complex, unstable new settings, however, a single individual lives amid multiple groups: within a family, a work setting, a religious community, a gender cohort, and a racial or ethnic group. The individual faces many and changing notions of the truth, and it becomes far more difficult to know what to do. It is no longer a simple matter of right and wrong; instead, one has an array of options, some of which are considered better than others.

Added to the new complexity in matters of conscience in the 1960s was the greater pressure to be tolerant of diversity and nonconformity. It became easier for people to adopt different lifestyles and outlooks than their parents and communities. The young, especially, encouraged experimentation and exploration of religions and perspectives outside of the norm. This was particularly the case at colleges and universities, where students often lived at a distance from their families.

Consequently, during the 1960s, American religious life became transformed in ways that were not anticipated by academics and community leaders. A sizable number of young people voiced dissatisfaction with their parents' religious lives and with conventional modes of practicing established religions. Those who did not reject religion entirely brought religion into the battles. Some attempted to take the lead within established churches and synagogues, forging alliances with members of the older generation who shared their concerns. Some established religious communities of their own with others of like minds. Some chose to become involved with the variety of seemingly new religious options that appeared in the West in the 1960s. Eastern religions such as Buddhism and Hinduism, revivals of nature-centered and Native American religions, New Age spirituality, and all types of meditation and mysticism gained followers.

A high percentage of graduating Jewish high school students attended colleges and universities, and consequently, a great number were deeply influenced by the political, social, and religious movements percolating on American campuses. Like other young Americans during the 1960s and 1970s, college-aged Jews were dismissive of their parents' religious lives and of conventional modes of practicing Judaism. Jewish students complained that synagogues and Jewish communal institutions were not addressing larger questions of meaning and were not conducive to spiritual experiences and religious devotion. They maintained that religious rituals were performed only out of a sense of duty or loyalty to the past.[22] Those with a thirst for mysticism and meditation did not find either option in the Judaism to which they had been exposed. A great many young Jews came from Jewish homes in which Judaism was not considered a value, and so they had not been given a religious education at all.

Consequently, young Jews intent on engaging in intense religious experiences were likely to look outside of Judaism. Around them were many exciting and exotic choices. One could seek "out-of-body" experiences and elevated consciousness through the use of drugs, in or out of a religious context. Various types of Buddhism, Hinduism, and new religious movements associated with them provided opportunities for expanding one's horizons and engaging in ecstatic worship, meditation, and spiritual exercises. Jews joined these groups at a proportion noticeably higher than their percentage in the larger population. Approximately 2 to 3 percent of Americans identified themselves as Jews, yet Jews constituted between 6 and 20 percent of the membership of radical new religious groups, especially those connected to Eastern religions.[23] Most of those Jewish recruits described the Jewishness of their families as ethnic or cultural, but not religious.[24]

CULTS, SECTS, AND BRAINWASHING

The proliferation of radical, separatist religious groups produced a great deal of alarm among the white, middle-class, educated segment of American society whose young formed the great majority of new members. They were choosing a life path greatly at odds with their families of origin. Furthermore, in modern American society, where self-interested individualism is the norm, people who elect to subsume their individuality in order to belong to an unconventional, highly demanding group are regarded as peculiar. The clergy, the popular media, ex-members and their families, and outside observers regarded the new communities as dangerous false religions. They accused the leaders of exploiting emotionally vulnerable and ideologically confused people and offering them the option of no longer having to make decisions for themselves. The new religious communities were labeled "cults." The popular understanding of a cult had (and still has) the following components: it is a group whose members are under the hypnotic-like control of a charismatic, autocratic leader; the leader demands rigid conformity to his or her demands and prompts his or her followers to reject their pasts and their families; the members commit themselves to communal living in an impoverished manner, donate large sums of money to the religious group or leader, or both; and furthermore, the group engages in strange rituals, radical political behaviors, or illegal and violent activities.

Historians have shown that in Western society, past and contemporary allegations of coercive persuasion at the hands of powerful and subversive forces crop up during periods of high sociocultural tension. During unsettled periods, clashing social groups compete to win individual and group loyalty. When unfamiliar elements are successful at winning support, they are likely to be accused of operating from unfair advantages and by way of conspiracies.[25] Widespread acceptance of brainwashing theories in mid-twentieth century can be explained by two particular historical factors. The first was the background of the Cold War: among Americans during the 1950s–1980s, the world was perceived as being divided into two opposing and inherently antagonistic blocs, the Communists and the free world. Instances of collaboration with or conversion over to the Communist side were especially disquieting. Sociologists Edgar Schein and Robert Lifton, in separate studies of Korean and Chinese Communist influence on American prisoners-of-war, identified specific techniques exercised by captors that resulted in their prisoners' cooperation and sympathy.[26] Even though both studies showed that virtually all of the prisoners-of-war rejected their newly adopted beliefs when they were freed from captivity and returned home, the vocabulary and imagery of these case studies left a great impression.

The second factor was the validation of brainwashing theories by psychologists who had studied former members of radical religious groups. Psychologist Margaret Singer identified six tactics that are used to recruit members: deceiving the individual about the group's goal and extent of control, controlling the environment so as to limit the individual's access to information, inducing a sense of fear and helplessness within the individual, uprooting and then replacing older attitudes and behaviors, and presenting a logical but closed worldview that interprets all information so as to reinforce the group's perspective.[27] There were other psychological theories as well, but Singer's theories were the most influential and gained the support of other academics, and they are still widely accepted by anti-cult activists today.

Religious organizations with a long history of opposing Christian sectarian and non-Christian religious groups tended to argue that the cause lay in the bad education and false information disseminated by the new religious groups. However, there were many people, including secular opponents of the new religious groups, who favored Singer's theories of mind-control. "Cult de-programmers" began to offer their services to rescue the supposed victims. Friends, family members, or others would kidnap or persuade the new devotee to engage with de-programmers who would counsel, persuade, or badger him or her to disassociate from the cult. This strategy was controversial. De-programming was not a professional, trained activity, and de-programmers often employed the same tactics as the stereotypic demagogic leaders. The de-programmers were not always successful, especially with long-term affiliates of the group, and they occasionally caused damage to the people they were supposed to be helping. In addition, the objects of de-programming who were legal adults could and did object that their civil liberties were being violated. They insisted that they had converted willingly, and some brought de-programmers and those who had hired them to the state courts. Judges and juries were asked to differentiate between false cults and legitimate churches, and between the experts who regarded the group members as brainwashed or as converts. Religious studies scholars were generally among those who believed that the members had been converted. In the 1970s and early 1980s, the courts generally agreed with the academics and other experts who insisted that the cults were using "coercive persuasion" and other mind-control techniques. They allowed parents to become guardians and conservators of their adult children and engage the services of cult de-programmers. By the mid-1980s, however, the courts began to make decisions in favor of the research and arguments of civil libertarians and religious studies academics.[28] This tolerant approach has remained the norm.

Religious studies scholars depart from popular opinion and the psychological approach mentioned previously on three grounds. First, they reject the claim that religious groups gain members through "brainwashing" or "mind control." Scientific standards require that one examine behaviors by isolating and measuring them and establishing a control group, but it is considered unethical to do this with potential converts to a religious group. In the absence of any evidence of threats of bodily harm or financial intimidation, religious studies scholars had to conclude that new adepts were persuaded and joined voluntarily as converts or affiliates. The "unreasonableness" or unconventional nature of the religion does not controvert this conclusion. In addition, researchers found a high rate of membership turnover in the religious groups, about 30 percent per year, a figure that does not comport with the brainwashing model. Second, empirical studies of the new religious movement showed a much more complex picture of them than had been initially described. The power of the charismatic leaders had been exaggerated, and other elements in the definition of a cult did not fit one group or the other, or could be applied to describe a feature of an established, mainstream religious group.

Third, it is fundamental to the methodology of religious studies to avoid judgments about a religion's legitimacy or illegitimacy. One does not label a religion false because it is based on unverifiable truth claims—all religions contain purely subjective and empirically unverifiable convictions. There is no way to logically prove the central belief in Western religions that there is a sacred dimension of existence that is beyond the physical world, superior to the physical world, or coexisting within it but of a different value. Scholars of religion do, however, investigate the factual claims made by adherents of religion, the integrity and vested interests of religious leaders, the religion's beneficial or destructive effect on society, and so on. Yet, if evidence is uncovered showing that, for example, the group's claims cannot be historically verified or they appear to be false, or that its members are hypocrites, this evidence is not utilized to prove that the religion is inauthentic. No religion could survive such a standard. Furthermore, human beings are social animals, desirous of acceptance and approval, and they are not always rational. Although there is a great range of degrees of human susceptibility to persuasion, there is considerable evidence—in politics, economics, sexual behavior, religion, and so on—that people believe unsubstantiated claims and promises. Historians of religion know that when new religious movements are formed, they are often regarded by the rest of society as heretical, revolutionary, lunatic, and so on. The devotees of these groups are often judged harshly and with strong emotions. A more dispassionate observer would notice the neophytes' search for a new symbolic identity and a new community, their effort to find meaning in their lives, their exploration of a new role for themselves, and so on. Religious studies scholars who approach the issue this way reject the term "cult" as an emotionally laden, pejorative label and one that conveys an inaccurate picture of the leaders, groups, and individuals under discussion. They prefer to use the neutral term "new religious movement" (NRM).[29]

There have been a number of helpful advances toward understanding these groups. In the 1970s, historian of religion J. Gordon Melton attempted to find a single or set of characteristics that differentiated NRMs from established religions. After years of research and proposed theories, he finally concluded that new religious movements that are called cults share only what they lack: they are not a part of the religious establishment; their status is contested (that is, are they a new denomination of an existing religion, or an entirely new entity? Are they a "real" religion or a sham?); they are feared, disliked, and hated by outsiders; and they are perceived as being "out of step with the general religious environment."[30] These standards are subjective, and they vary between societies and even within a single society. In short, he argues that NRMs have in common only their nonconformity to generally accepted standards of religious rectitude.

In explaining this last point, Melton suggests that we regard religious groups in society along a continuum that stretches from established religions to those that are labeled cults. Established religions are those that dominate a society or a significant portion of a society; or, an established religion may be an ethnic tradition (such as Judaism or Greek Orthodoxy in America) that is considered legitimate and unthreatening as long as its keeps its activity relegated to its own ethnic community. These established religions are sometimes called "churches." Slightly more troubling to society are groups that have broken off from established religions. They have dissented on matters of doctrine, ritual, or organization. Their dissent, however, falls within acceptable limits to most people. These groups are commonly called "sects." Beyond these, however, are groups whose differences go beyond what their host societies regard as acceptable limits. These are the ones that people label as cults or regard as new, aberrant creations.

Yet, even these, Melton observes, are not necessarily new. It is quite unusual for a new religious movement to appear that has no connection to an existing religion. Some of the mid-century religious groups that were perceived as new had actually been in existence in America for quite some time, marginal and unnoticed until revived by a young generation of religious seekers. Some of the NRMs are hybrid constructs, combining elements from a number of religious traditions. Many are variations on established religions, dissenting in ways that place them outside of acceptable limits.[31] New religious movements generally do not help outsiders place them into familiar categories. They typically do not announce themselves as church, sect, or cult or as variants of established religions.

Eileen Barker, a sociologist of religion, points out that although the NRMs may not be new in their doctrines, their differentness from established religions lies in the fact that they are made up entirely of first-generation converts.[32] A sociologist who focuses on the NRM believers' actions and lifestyles and on the group's leadership patterns and organizations will discern many common features. For example, because NRM members are new converts, they are more enthusiastic and impassioned than people who are born and raised within a religion, and they are more eager to proselytize others. Because their religious faith is new to them, they are likely to feel more vulnerable to outsiders' criticisms. In response, the NRM erects barriers to prevent nonbelievers from planting doubts that might undermine the members' faith. It establishes an "us versus them" attitude or a concern for unambiguous doctrinal, or behavioral standards may prevail. Furthermore, whereas established religions consist of a wide range of followers, new religious groups often attract people of like background and age, education, or other characteristics, and these produce a different dynamic. For example, a group that attracts economically privileged middle-aged people will have different concerns and activities than a group that attracts economically disadvantaged young adults. Barker points out that charismatic authority is common in NRMs simply because new religious doctrines and practices are not likely to be produced by an elected or appointed committee or a democratically organized group. Finally, the group tends to change more rapidly and radically than established religions because it is attempting to define itself and find a form that will enable it to survive. Its changes may also be connected to the aging of the charismatic leader and the founding members or to external events. After the first generation, NRMs that survive tend to become less divergent from the larger society, more flexible, and more internally diversified.

Both Melton's and Barker's theories are helpful in understanding the emergence and evolution of the Kabbalah Centre movement, as well as the representation of the Kabbalah Centre as a "cult" and its members as "brainwashed." Yet, ironically, Gruberger shared the Jewish community's desire to keep young Jews out of groups that were strange, foreign, dogmatic and controlling. When he began to teach and publish Kabbalah in the late 1960s, he intended that in doing so he would show alienated and spiritually hungry Jews that their own religious heritage contained everything they needed for fulfillment. His focus on Kabbalah as a vehicle for outreach was unusual, but it was not unique in its time.

PATHS TO KABBALAH IN MID-TWENTIETH CENTURY AMERICA

The 1960s and 1970s were a period of tremendous expansion of colleges and universities in the United States, and courses in all areas of Jewish studies—history, literature and languages, philosophy, sociology—began to be offered by seasoned or newly hired instructors. In addition to publishing works for academic readers that advanced research, faculty also produced anthologies of primary source documents, many of them religious texts, for their courses. However, American universities and colleges could not provide Jewish students with much in the way of resources on Jewish mysticism. The academic study of Jewish mysticism began in the late nineteenth century, when men trained in history and philology examined mystical texts in order to reach an objective, scientific view of their meaning, function, and authors. Although he was not the first such scholar, Gershom Scholem is regarded as one of the founders of the field. Born in Germany in 1897, he moved to Palestine in the 1920s and was appointed professor at the Hebrew University of Jerusalem. He identified and described thousands of manuscripts, and he published extensive, reasoned studies (many in German and Hebrew) that were the foundation for future academic study of Jewish mysticism. In 1938 the Jewish Institute of Religion brought him to New York to deliver a series of lectures on Jewish mysticism. These were published as the book *Major Trends in Jewish Mysticism,* a volume that served for decades as the basic textbook on Jewish mysticism for Americans. Scholem described different mystical philosophies and practices in their historical contexts, comparing them to one another as examples of a creative spiritual outpouring of the past. Very little on Jewish mysticism in English was available beyond Scholem's *Major Trends in Jewish Mysticism.* Beginning in the 1960s, ambitious graduate students could study the subject more intensively at Brandeis University under

Figure 2.1 Sources of Contemporary Kabbalah

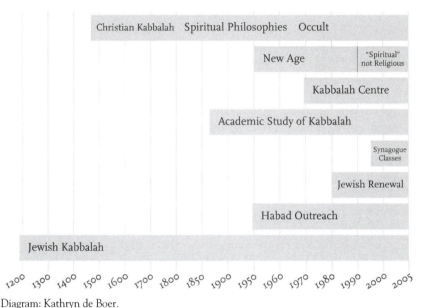

Diagram: Kathryn de Boer.

the rubric of Jewish philosophy. Serious training, however, required travel to Jerusalem to study with the scholars at the Hebrew University. Scholem, and most of the academic scholars who followed him, paid virtually no attention to living Kabbalists in their midst and did not regard Kabbalah as a sacred text for their own or anybody else's religious lives.[33]

One option that presented itself in the 1960s and 1970s was Hasidism, which, according to Scholem, was the latest phase of Jewish mysticism. Hasidic groups came to the United States amid the refugee immigrants arriving after World War II. They lived in strict adherence to Jewish religious law, characteristic of other Orthodox Jews, but they were tight-knit communities uninterested in integrating with other Americans (including American Jews). The exception among them was the Hasidic group known as Habad, or Lubavitcher, Hasidism. Although Lubavitcher rabbis did not actually teach explicitly kabbalistic texts, they regarded themselves as recipients of authentic mystical teachings, and their prayer services used the liturgy established by the Kabbalist Isaac Luria. More than other Hasidic groups, Habad was welcoming of new members who had not been raised from birth within the community. In the aftermath of the Holocaust, the chief Lubavitcher rabbi taught that the Messianic Era was at hand and would be hastened by an outreach effort to unaffiliated and irreligious Jews throughout the world. He and his successor extended the outreach effort to American Jewish college students. Habad sent emissaries to the campuses who offered counseling and teaching for young

American Jews. They were attractive to young Jews because they presented a form of Judaism that stressed God's love and the joy of worship through music, storytelling, dance, and community celebration of the Sabbath and holidays. Young people reported that it was warmer and seemingly more spontaneous and heartfelt than the other—their parents'—forms of Judaism. Yet settling down into a Hasidic community was different than one's experience of it on campus. Living within the Habad community entailed accepting rabbinic authority over one's personal life, marrying young and producing many children, and rejecting the intellectually free-spirited principles of the youth culture.[34]

A more flexible, open, and tolerant variation of Habad Hasidism grew out of the efforts of two of the first Habad college emissaries, Rabbis Shlomo Carlebach and Zalman Schachter. Carlebach (who was a student with Gruberger at the Beth Medrash Govoha yeshiva) grew prominent for his songwriting and performances as singer and storyteller, and Schachter was known for encouraging the creative exploration of Judaism alongside Eastern religious traditions. During the 1950s and 1960s, they made inroads into and were influenced by the beatniks and the youth counterculture. To some extent, they adopted egalitarian ideals and permissive approaches to sexuality as well as tolerance for the use of recreational drugs. The unorthodox practices and ideas of these men led to the severance of their ties to Lubavitch Hasidism. However, Carlebach and Schachter remained "outreach rabbis" intent on showcasing the spiritual and ecstatic elements within Jewish tradition and keeping Jews from flocking to the NRMs. They guided the outreach center established in San Francisco in 1967 known as the House of Love and Prayer, and they had small circles of devoted followers in various cities in North America. Both men were careful not to rule authoritatively or insist that their followers observe Jewish law. However, Carlebach remained within the realm of Orthodox Judaism, whereas Schachter, by the mid-1970s, was establishing his own non-Orthodox form of Judaism that contributed to the founding of the Havurah movement.[35]

Havurah (friendship circles) was the name given to a type of alternative religious community that college-aged Jewish men and women established in the 1960s. Away from their families of birth, Havurah members attempted to live together in a spiritual, Jewish, egalitarian manner. They practiced Sabbath and Jewish holiday rituals, prayers, dietary laws, and other religious behaviors in a joyful manner. Regular Torah study was made part of the routine so that religion would continue to be a matter of exploration and discovery. Members made an effort to make decisions on these and other communal matters in a democratic nonhierarchical spirit, as much as possible living naturally and "making it themselves," showing a concern for the environment and feminism. Although text study was an important part of the Havurah routine, kabbalistic texts were not routinely studied; they were too difficult for most people, even for those who could read Hebrew and Aramaic, and the complex kabbalistic symbolism obscured the understanding of the concepts and their applicability to peoples' lives.[36] Years later, in the 1980s, key figures from these Havurah centers became leaders of the Jewish Renewal movement, in which Kabbalah as interpreted by Rabbi Zalman Schachter played and still plays an important role.

Unconnected from Habad Hasidism and the Havurah centers was a circle of individuals who sifted through the dry, dispassionate studies of Jewish mysticism to find the nuggets that had literary and artistic value. A number of American Jewish men living in Los Angeles and San Francisco Bay in the late 1950s through the 1970s became enthralled with the use of the Hebrew alphabet and other kabbalistic images described by Scholem in *Major Trends in Jewish Mysticism*.[37] Poets David Meltzer, Jack Hirschman, and Nathaniel Tarn and the artist Wallace Berman shared with earlier writers and artists of the "beat generation" an interest in Eastern religions, jazz, and intense experiences; in addition, they integrated kabbalistic concepts and symbols into their works. For them, kabbalistic symbols—the sefirot, charts of letters, visions of the layers of divinity—were vehicles for fostering awareness of the mystery at the center of life. Meltzer published a kabbalistic journal in the early 1970s called *Tree* (after the tree image of the sefirot). Each volume was an anthology of poetry, essays, translations of religious writings, and drawings by diverse poets and artists that were arranged according to kabbalistic themes. The collaborative efforts of these men faded away in the mid-1970s when Meltzer found the work of publishing too dispiriting. He and his fellow writers were rebels, and they regarded true spirituality as subversive and resisting of power and conformity. They were highly critical of the materialistic values and commercialism that they felt dominated American society, and they disagreed with the conventional boundaries set between religions as well as the elevation of established religion over magical and occult traditions. Consequently, they remained unaffiliated with Jewish institutions—even alternative ones such as the House of Love and Prayer—and uninterested in developing religious rituals or an alternative liturgical system for any organized religious community. There was no link between them and the later Kabbalah Centre movement that set down roots in California in the 1990s.

THE BEGINNING OF THE INDEPENDENT
KABBALAH CENTRE

It was in this setting of general religious transformation—in which there was much searching for spiritual philosophies and behavioral guides outside of the established organized religions and a hunger for mystical encounter—that Philip Gruberger decided to exert himself. There were very few resources on mysticism from within Judaism available for young Jewish seekers. Gruberger realized that he had the resources to fill the vacuum, and he also had the independence. Brandwein died in the spring of 1969. Gruberger had extricated himself from his first wife and children and had married a woman named Tova (she later changed her name to Karen). She was eager to partner with him in shaping kabbalistic teachings into a meaningful religious practice and healthy social experience for young Jews. According to Kabbalah Centre lore, it was Karen's idea to teach Kabbalah to everybody—that is, women as well as men, nonreligious as well as religious Jews. The two made every decision together, although they possessed unique perspectives and skills. Within two years, they moved to Israel. At that point, the Grubergers changed their surname to Berg. (The practice of shortening European-origin Jewish surnames upon moving to Israel is a common one.) To their students, they were "the Rav" and "Karen."[38]

It was obvious from Berg's writings and activities in the first two decades of his independent activity that he was responding to a widespread spiritual crisis and that he was particularly disturbed about its manifestation among Jews. He had his own diagnosis for the crisis, one that echoed the complaints of alienated young Jews. He believed that Judaism was being presented dogmatically, and the mitzvot were taught as deeds that must be done through rote obedience. Young Jews, in particular, were not being exposed to a Judaism that included contemplation and inner feelings.[39] Consequently, one can see "the disappearance of the large majority of Jews from the ranks of Judaism," Berg wrote, "either to atheism or to foreign spiritual teachings."[40] Berg was convinced that the lack of a spiritual content to the religion led to the "degeneration of Judaism into a marginal social activity, and in the flight of young people away from Judaism to the more mystically-inclined eastern religions."[41] This deadening presentation of Judaism could not withstand the prevailing rationalism of modern thought, Berg observed. Many people were persuaded by reason and science to be skeptical of religion entirely. At the same time, they were aware that science cannot "make sense of a world in which chaos and injustice abound and the innocent suffer."[42] Berg noted the very negative repercussions for Jewish life that this situation produced in the ancient period:

> At times when the children of Israel have lacked leaders to keep them on their proper path, and to ensure that the precepts and commandments of Torah were understood and kept, they are susceptible to attack from other countries which exploited the enormous potential metaphysical energy of the Jewish people for their own ends.[43]

It was to avoid these problems that Berg taught, published, and wrote books on Kabbalah. He was determined to show that Judaism was *not* without answers:

> Yet there exists within Judaism, within Torah, a full, complete and intellectually satisfying consideration of all such questions. Indeed, it is one of our chief aims in publishing these volumes of commentary on the works of Kabbalah to

reveal to all Jews the richness and extent of the Jewish heritage of knowledge and wisdom which are so relevant and vital to our time.[44]

It appears that his unabashed love for Judaism and concern for Jews inspired Berg's adoption of his new role.

The most noticeable aspect of the independent Kabbalah Centre movement was the publishing house. Berg had acquired Krakovsky's unpublished writings and books after his death in 1966, and with those he was able to quickly launch himself as a publisher of English works of Kabbalah. In 1970 he legally changed the name of the National Institute for Research in Kabbalah to the Research Centre of Kabbalah.[45] The Research Centre of Kabbalah published five books from 1970 to 1973. The first was *Ten Luminous Emanations*, volume 1. This was a small part of Yehuda Ashlag's *Talmud Eser Ha-Sefirot*, and in this printing, Berg credited Krakovsky as translator. In 1970 he published Krakovsky's translation of a book by the eighteenth-century Kabbalist Moses Hayyim Luzzatto called *General Principles of Kabbalah*.[46] In that same year, he reissued Krakovsky's *Kabbalah: The Light of Redemption*. In two of these volumes, Berg gave his title as President of the Research Centre of Kabbalah, and he described it as an institution with an academy in Jerusalem and, in the United States, a publishing house offering lecture series and seminars. Yet, because he was the only teacher in the organization, and he resided during 1969 and 1970 in the United States, his educational work manifested itself primarily in publishing.

Although Berg's target audience was Jews, the publishing enterprise in which he was engaged could not be sustained on their patronage alone. Without the restraining arm of Brandwein, Berg was free to approach non-Jews for financial support for the Research Centre of Kabbalah. Evidence of his overtures is in the acknowledgments included in the books. Most supporters appear to be Jewish people, and some were able to have the books dedicated to the honor or memory of their loved ones. However, the list of contributors who enabled the publication of *An Entrance to the Zohar* included obvious non-Jewish names such as Fitzpatrick, Christianson, and Farmer.[47] Prominently mentioned as the sole supporter of the 1970 edition of Luzzatto's *General Principles of Kabbalah* was the Sangreal Foundation of Dallas, Texas. *Sangreal* is the medieval term for Jesus's "holy grail," and the Sangreal Foundation generally funded the publication of spiritual-metaphysical literature, including the occult, spurned by established churches.[48] The attempt to appeal to both a Jewish and a broader audience is explicitly acknowledged in the book prefaces written by Berg's friend and sometimes editor, Kenneth R. Clark. Clark, who was not Jewish, believed that knowledge of the Kabbalah could provide a solution to the younger generation's abandonment of synagogues and churches. The young "increasingly turn to Eastern religions and to weird and often repressive cults in their search for fulfillment," Clark lamented. According to him, "Kabbalah is not a religion and Rabbi Berg does not teach it as such.... With study of its principles, a Jew becomes a better Jew, a Christian a better Christian and an agnostic a doubter no more."[49]

In the English volumes published by the Research Centre of Kabbalah, Berg sought credibility by highlighting the skills and expertise that were important to non-Jewish society and to nonreligious people. The phrase "Compiled and Edited by Dr. Philip S. Gruberger" appears on the title pages of the first books. No explanation for the "Dr." title appeared during the 1970s; in his 1980s publications, Berg explained that he held a doctorate in comparative religion, but he later dropped this claim as well as the title.[50] He did not refer to himself as a rabbi on the cover of his books. In 1973 he produced a second volume of *Ten Luminous Emanations*, with no reference to the translator, but with his own name as compiler and editor. In 1974 he published a collection of Ashlag's essays called *An Entrance to the Zohar*, with an acknowledgment to Rabbi Mordechai Klein "for his assistance in the translation." Here, too, he referred to himself as compiler and editor.[51]

It took some time for Berg to produce his own book-length compositions. During the 1970s, his published writing was limited to the prefaces of the previously mentioned five books. Several more books in English were announced in the end pages of these books, but they did not actually appear in print until the 1980s. Berg was not trained in writing, and the only model he had for writing about Ashlagian Kabbalah for an English-reading general audience was Krakovsky. He sought assistance from others, but there were few people with experience in this type of popular writing. The following unedited request, written by the secretary of the Research Centre of Kabbalah (probably Berg's wife) to a book collector and independent scholar of Christian Kabbalah, shows the organization's wide reach for help:

> Do you know anyone that might be able to edit a new book by Dr. Berg, the Dean of the Centre and one of the only living Kabbalists? This would be tremendously appreciated. Also we are preparing a cover the Tree of Life. Would you be willing to give us an idea as to what you would design for this volume.... P.S. Dr. Berg, is a Kabbalist and as such he has a thorough knowledge of all our text and would be willing to help you on any question you might have. However, he is not an English major and his work needs someone who knows style as well as grammar. Any help you can offer would be great.[52]

With outside assistance, during the 1980s, the Research Centre of Kabbalah began publishing Berg's books. They include acknowledgments to colleagues and friends who reviewed and edited his manuscripts. The titles issued during the 1980s lay down the fundamental principles of Kabbalah Centre teachings, and the books include *Kabbalah for the Layman* (volume 1 in 1982 and volumes 2 and 3 in 1988), *The Kabbalah Connection: Jewish Festivals as a Path to Pure Awareness* (1983), *Wheels of a Soul* (1984), and *Astrology: The Star Connection* (1986).

The instructional effort of the Research Centre of Kabbalah is harder to chart than the publications. Berg moved to Israel in 1971 with his new wife and her two daughters from a previous marriage. Two sons, Yehuda and Michael, were born in 1972 and 1973, and the family resided in Tel Aviv (and for a period in Jerusalem) until 1981. They moved back to the United States in 1981, but returned to Israel for short visits and for a longer stay in 1983–84. Although Berg kept a base of operations in Queens and returned as necessary to arrange the English publications of the Research Centre of Kabbalah, in Israel he was teaching in Hebrew to an entirely Jewish audience. Both he and his wife held classes and gathered around themselves a community of young Israelis.[53] The Research Centre of Kabbalah did not have to seek out translators for Israeli readers, and the publishing house produced its own editions of Hebrew and Aramaic kabbalistic texts written by the Kabbalists Isaac Luria and Yehuda Ashlag, which served as reading material for the classes. Berg himself wrote in English. Berg was immersed in Israeli society, he and his wife had roots in the United States, and they were addressing themselves to Israeli and American students and readers. Kabbalah Centre teachings cannot be understood outside of this mixed Israeli and American context.

RELIGION WITHOUT COMPULSION

Berg's teachings and writings were shaped by his outreach to a young audience of Israelis and Americans who were highly resistant to organized religion. A central tenet of Kabbalah Centre teaching is the principle that the Torah's directives—the mitzvot—are not mandates, but suggestions. This was quite unorthodox: for centuries Jewish people had understood God's directives in the Hebrew Bible literally, as commandments. Berg disagreed. According to him, the literal meaning of the Bible's words is not the real meaning. He insisted that Kabbalah understands the "commandments" of the Torah as gifts from a loving God that one may accept or refuse. They are tools given to humans by God, somewhat like cables, enabling connection to God's cosmic energy. One is not commanded by God to behave or think in a particular way. On the contrary, God has no expectations or demands of humans, nor does God desire specific human responses. Rather, God gives, and God is always giving—following Ashlag's formulation, God is pure Desire to Share—with no expectation of receiving anything in return. If a person accepts the gift of the mitzvah, performing it with the right consciousness, he or she will connect to God and benefit tremendously. If a person refuses to do the mitzvah, he or she will not receive the benefit. There is no need to feel guilty or to expect a punishment from God. Despite what people commonly think, Berg taught, Kabbalah teaches that a meaningful spiritual life cannot include any element of duty, coercion, or guilt. Kabbalah does not value the performance of rituals in and of themselves. Without meaning and spirituality, prayer and rituals "are like straw—the epitome of lifelessness."[54]

Berg's principles matched the spirit of American youth culture in the 1970s and 1980s. He elevated love to the highest ideal, considering it the only justification for curtailing one's freedom. Kabbalah was all the more attractive because it had been secret and suppressed by the religious establishment for centuries. Young Jewish spiritual seekers found in Berg's writings an echo of their own dissatisfaction with American synagogue services and family religious practices that enshrined tradition, conformity, communal and familial unity, sentimentality, and membership in a group. Berg was presenting an alternative Jewish spirituality in which the highest praise was reserved for those who worshiped out of love alone. As its starting point, it affirmed a central truth about these young peoples' state of mind: they did not feel commanded. They did not feel obliged to follow the traditions of the past, and the previous reasons for compliance (for example, the belief that God demanded religious rituals) had lost credibility. Indeed, this reaction is still common today among people who grow up in families in which religious behavior is expected; when they become fully independent, they realize that they are free to do as they choose, and they conclude that God will not punish or reward them for their religious behavior. People who feel liberated from the idea of a commanding God, and from an environment that demands conformity, will not be convinced to follow religious rules by the older arguments based on obligation. They will adopt religious rules because they feel it enhances their lives.

Furthermore, Berg's stance confirmed the distrust of religious authority that emerged in the 1960s and that persists to this day. American culture harbors antiauthoritarianism: there is the high regard for individualism, personal independence, and the separation of church and state. Berg taught that God was not a lawgiver, and no human being should arrogate that power either. Berg did not operate with his followers in such a manner. He described himself as a recipient of his teacher's wisdom, charged by him and his teacher before him with the mission to reveal it to the public. That is, he received knowledge as privileged information, but he in turn shares it with the multitudes. This, according to historian of religion Olav Hammer, is a modified form of esotericism. Olav Hammer defines esotericism as "a form of religion that embraces the idea that access to salvific knowledge and to ritual competence is a multitiered construction." The most powerful possess secret knowledge (and this includes secret rituals); they are the in-group, and there is an out-group of people who do not have access to it. The criteria for ascending the hierarchy reflect what is important for that group: it may be gender, genealogy, money, skills mastered, or other considerations. This controlled, hierarchical structure is not compatible with modern and New Age ideals of democracy and equal access. This does not mean the end of esotericism, but a transformation of it in accordance with modern ideals. This is what occurred within Berg's community. Kabbalah (except for the most arcane elements within it) was no longer considered to be esoteric and strictly limited. People who sought knowledge of kabbalistic ideas and practices were given it, and it was understood that the more one knew and practiced, the higher one was. Berg remained at the highest level, and his interpretation of Kabbalah was the prevailing one. This was a type of democratized esotericism.[55]

In an era in which people were wary of "cults" led by charismatic leaders exercising control over adoring followers, Berg's alternative spirituality struck a very different tone. His was the opposite of a "cult." With his principles, he could not encourage his followers to conform for the sake of group cohesiveness. Naturally, this principle, which was shared by many New Age teachers, would inhibit the growth of a cohesive movement. Historian J. Gordon Melton points out that New Age practitioners did not coalesce into larger groups because the "organizational phobia operated as a built-in self-limiting mechanism."[56] Berg eventually figured out how to build an organized national movement while remaining consistent with this principle of nonconformity.

The principle of noncoercive spirituality was strikingly at odds with many elements of the Israeli ethos. The state of Israel was founded in the aftermath of the Holocaust, and the continuing hostility of the surrounding Arab nations necessitated the forfeiture of many individual comforts and freedom. Duty to the state is manifested in the obligation of young men and women to enter the military and serve in the army reserves well into middle age. During the 1960s and 1970s, the economy was for the most part socialist, and this too added to the sense of collective responsibility. The sense of duty and conformity to a law higher than the individual permeated religious life as well. In Israel, the term "religious" was understood as Orthodox. This refers to Hasidism as well as religious practices that stemmed from European, Middle Eastern, and North African traditions, and these practices were associated with the strict observance of Jewish religious law. Israeli synagogue practices were conducted according to Jewish law, although there were many different variations among them. Also unlike the North American model, Israel did not affirm the separation of church and state. The Israeli state was a secular entity, but key areas of law and policy were given over to the state-sponsored rabbinate and rabbinical organizations. Marriage, divorce, and individual Jewish status, for example, were determined by the Israeli rabbinate's rulings on the basis of religious law. The state rabbinical body officially recognized only those rabbis who conformed to its standards. The state paid salaries to rabbis, funded a religious school system alongside nonreligious school systems, and granted licenses and operating expenses to synagogues. The only religious institutions to receive funds and sanction were those that were approved by the rabbinate and that conformed to its dictates. Those rabbis and religious institutions that were not recognized by the Israeli rabbinate had a very poor chance of success: they were denied funds, permits, and legitimacy, and they were often subjected to harassment.

Yet despite the dominance of the Orthodox in Israel, approximately 80 percent of Israelis self-identified as "not religious." This was somewhat of a misnomer because the national calendar and culture include the Sabbath and Jewish holidays, and family traditions even among the nonreligious typically included Sabbath and holiday meals. However, the vast majority of Israelis did not attend synagogues more than once or twice a year, send their children to religious schools, or express loyalty to the religious tradition. The necessity of bowing to rabbinical decisions and conforming to religious law, such as in the cases of marriage and burial, was often resented or regarded as an irritant. More than half of the immigrants to the new state in the early 1950s—from North Africa and the Middle East, and Holocaust survivors—had roots in cultures that were deeply religious and that included belief in the power of the sacred, but they were firmly pressured by Israeli society to cast off old ways of thinking and behavior. The Israeli ethos embraced secular, modern, rational thinking. Israeli public culture celebrated the new values that had led to Israel's military victories, its scientific achievements, and its establishment of a socialist democratic state. Israeli schools and the influential agents of the Israeli social welfare system inculcated modern Hebrew language and national pride.

As in the United States, in Israel in the mid-1960s, there was a growing counterculture. Artists and writers voiced dissatisfaction with a life of dutiful conformity to the demands of the state and expressed a desire to escape from the stultifying pressures of Israeli life. They criticized secular and rational thinking and preferred images of natural wilderness and the untamed desert to those of the civilized, restricted spaces of urban and familial life. During the 1960s, the first Hebrew translations of the writings of Sigmund Freud and Carl Jung appeared, stressing the tremendous power of the irrational and subconscious. Elements of U.S. and European revolutionary movements filtered into the country: rock and roll music, psychedelic drugs, and the accompanying ideals of anarchy and sexual freedom. Relative to American young people, disaffected Israelis were compliant; the very obvious threat of destruction under which all Israelis lived tended to curb rebellious political behavior. Rebelliousness found a more acceptable outlet in a search for spirituality. Texts from Buddhist and Hindu traditions appeared in Hebrew, and people began to explore the works of European and American occultists, Theosophists, and other metaphysical-spiritual thinkers. By the early 1970s, young Israelis were making treks to the United States and India to engage in the religious devotions offered by new religious movement leaders. Within a few years, Israelis found resources within their own country to enable them to design their own alternative spiritual practices outside of Judaism.[57] As in the United States, Jewish mysticism did not present itself as an option. Israelis knew well the tradition that Kabbalah was supposed to be kept secret and that it could be taught only to males over 40 years old, fully conversant in the Torah and observant of all the commandments. One could study Jewish mysticism in the university, where it was presented by academics who used philological and historical methodologies and described it as an element of past culture. Actual religious study of Kabbalah was buried within Orthodoxy. It was part of a Judaism that seemed to lack all spirituality and promised only "obligation" and the loss of individual choice.

Consequently, Berg's teaching of Kabbalah in Israel was a welcome novelty that filled a gaping hole in the religious options available to spiritual seekers. His preference for a young, secular audience that included women was an even greater mark of his independence and defiance of the religious establishment. This was a definite point in Berg's favor for young nonreligious Israelis. Seeking them out, Berg placed his school in Tel Aviv, the center of secular Israeli culture. Describing the classes and communal meals organized by Berg and his wife Karen, an Israeli reporter noted the unconventional explanations the couple offered for the observance of the dietary laws: the foods and blessings were surrounded by meditations and explained with reference to astrology and reincarnation. "You would think you're hanging around some Indian guru or Krishna sect, but actually it's one of our own," she writes. Berg's followers explained that his teachings answered questions of ultimate meaning, provided them with elevated consciousness, and gave them the knowledge they were seeking. They were impressed by his assertion that spirituality was noncoercive. According to Berg, "He who follows these laws just because they are written—he is totally crazy." Berg explained further,

> In Kabbalah we have a very firm principle: there is no coercion in anything spiritual. It is a fact that God does not compel us to be religious, and thus we do not compel anyone who comes to learn with us, and we hope that on their own people will come to the right conclusions.[58]

Young Israelis who were seeking spirituality but rejecting the Orthodox Israeli model would have found these words refreshing and attractive. In 1978 Berg boasted of having more than 400 students involved in the Research Centre of Kabbalah in Israel.[59]

In short, Berg had devised an ingenious method of reaching out to young Jews alienated from religion: remove the element of compulsion and obligation in order to attract followers. The presumption was that Jews—and in America, non-Jews as well—would be drawn to a form of spirituality that was rooted in the past and yet honored individual freedom. It was an effective and the least offensive mode of outreach. The strategy was to get their attention, draw them in, and not reproach them for their lack of commitment. Instead, neophytes were encouraged to choose the extent of their own practice. They were applauded when they accepted commitments. Neither guilt nor a sense of obligation was used as a means to get them to do more. It was acceptable if they never progressed beyond an elementary level. It was easy to join and belong.

Because of the acceptability of minimal performance of rituals and prayers, Berg's religious community has always contained participants whose various commitments to religious practice cover a wide range. At the outer margins of the movement are the people who accept kabbalistic ideas and engage in a minimum of ritual behaviors, such as meditations. Moving inward are people who are interested in kabbalistic ideas and engage in a few more rituals, such as meditations as well as mitzvot performed with kabbalistic consciousness. An inner core of followers fill their lives with meditations and mitzvot performed with kabbalistic consciousness in accordance with religious law, much like Orthodox Jews. In one sense, this range is similar to conventional American religious communities that make room for the most devout as well as people who barely practice at all; it is different because of the principle that it is worthless to do more than you truly feel drawn to do. Within the Israeli religious context, however, Berg's tolerance was exceptional.

The Orthodox characteristics of Israeli religious culture presented severe obstacles to the growth and even the existence of the Kabbalah Centre movement in Israel. Orthodox religious groups in Israel increased their power over the course of the 1970s and 1980s. The political divisiveness within Israel after the devastating 1973 Yom Kippur war meant that, in Israel's parliamentary system, the larger, secular parties had to make alliances with the minority parties—such as the religious parties—in order to form a government; the price the minority parties demanded for their alliance was greater influence in the government. Consequently, more public policies were determined by the Orthodox, and the religious, social, and economic needs of Orthodox Jews received greater attention and funding from the state. The features that made the Research Centre of Kabbalah attractive to nonreligious Israelis drew the hostility and opposition of the Israeli rabbinate and its agencies within the government. Its operation and efforts to expand were increasingly frustrated. In 1981 Philip and Karen Berg decided that the United States was a more conducive environment for the growth of the movement. They moved back to New York, taking with them some disciples and leaving others behind to lead the Israeli Centres under Berg's long-distance guidance. Berg returned several times a year for varying lengths of time.

The growing power of the Orthodox in Israel handicapped the movement internally as well and ultimately led to a major crisis within the Israeli Research Centre of Kabbalah. Unlike in the United States, Orthodox Jews in Israel were a highly visible part of the population. Secular Israelis who noticed

Berg's kabbalistic Judaism could hardly ignore its similarity to non-kabbalistic Israeli Orthodoxy. Some people rejected Kabbalah Centre teachings on this basis alone. In addition, the similarity also caused some internal tensions. Delving deeper into Kabbalah studies and the observance of mitzvot, Berg's followers often came into contact with non-kabbalistic Orthodox Israelis who would ridicule or otherwise undermine their unorthodox principles.

Such a development occurred with one of Berg's students, Michael Laitman.[60] Eager to learn more of the source of Berg's Kabbalah, Laitman contacted Rabbi Baruch Ashlag, the living son of Yehuda Ashlag, who resided near Tel Aviv amid a religious community in the town of Bnei Brak. Baruch Ashlag had been taught Kabbalah by his father and possessed most of his father's unpublished manuscripts. Laitman became Baruch Ashlag's personal assistant in 1979, all the while participating in the activities of the Kabbalah Centre in Tel Aviv. He grew more sympathetic to the strict, legalistic outlook of the Bnei Brak Orthodox Jews. When Berg left the country, Laitman began to criticize Berg's mode of teaching and the libertarian style of his community. A Kabbalah Centre teacher described how Laitman's approach differed from Berg's:

> The two of us were standing next to each other during the prayers. I was new and so I forgot to do the three jumps during the *kedusha* prayer. Laitman noticed I was not jumping and he elbowed me in the side so I would jump. That was not Rabbi Berg's way. He insisted that no one should be told to change their personal behavior as if there were a code. There should be no pushing. Laitman, because of the Bnei Brak influence, disagreed.[61]

Laitman's knowledge of Kabbalah and closeness to Baruch Ashlag increased his influence, however, and a growing number of people in the Tel Aviv Research Centre of Kabbalah community agreed that they should impose Orthodox religious law. They questioned Berg's claim to mastery of Kabbalah. According to the anecdotes shared by Kabbalah Centre teachers, Laitman made an official break after Berg took more teachers back to the United States with him in 1984. All but one of the Tel Aviv group's senior members abandoned Berg and joined Laitman in his own kabbalistic movement called Bnei Baruch. Yet Berg did not change his approach. He described his unique position to his disciples as a policy of outreach: "The gates were open, wide open, and because of those wide open gates, we got inside. We cannot close the gates to others." People who are deeply "inside the gates," having freely committed to a life of Kabbalah, practice in accordance with Jewish religious law. That regimen needs to be invisible to people on the outside, for it will discourage them and shut them out.[62]

The crisis within the Tel Aviv center hampered but did not end the Kabbalah Centre movement in Israel. It was, perhaps, the first sign of the diversification and multiplication of popular Kabbalah in Israel. During the 1990s (and continuing at full force at the present time), Israelis of all religious backgrounds began to show an avid interest in Kabbalah and in related phenomena: they visited tombs of rabbis, consulted and sought the blessings of reputed holy men, engaged in ceremonies and events that offered ecstatic religious expressions, and so on.[63] Berg was one of the first to teach Kabbalah to a nonreligious audience, and others adopted that mission and modified it according to their own tastes. After Laitman's departure from the Kabbalah Centre and the loss of so many followers, the sole senior teacher to remain loyal to Berg's principles was assigned to reconstruct the community in Tel Aviv and supervise the fledgling centers elsewhere in the country. The Bergs remained involved as supervisors from a distance and on their frequent trips to Israel, and the press of the Research Centre of Kabbalah continued to publish books and other materials in Hebrew. The Kabbalah Centre movement in North America remained very connected to Israel through holiday retreats and by absorbing Israeli-trained students.[64]

Perhaps it was the sobering experience in Israel, or perhaps it was the opposition of rabbis in North America when Berg returned there, that prompted the strengthening of the antiauthoritarian theme within Berg's teachings during the 1980s. This progression can be seen in Berg's *Kabbalah for the Layman*, the Kabbalah Centre's primary textbook in the 1980s and 1990s. In the book's first edition (1981), Berg mentions the alienation of the young with conventional Judaism, their disgust with the squabbling between different denominations, and their ignorance of the spiritual content of Jewish rituals. Berg insists that knowledge of Kabbalah is utterly essential to an accurate comprehension of the Torah, a spiritually fulfilling religious life, and social harmony among Jews.[65] Yet these Jews cannot learn Kabbalah, and Berg blames the rabbis:

> The ordinary Jew who wants to find out more about the nature and content of the study of Kabbalah will, therefore, find himself set about with difficulties: if he approaches "religious figures", he will inevitably be dissuaded—either through the widespread ignorance that exists even within Orthodox circles about Kabbalah, or by the stringency of the qualifications that will be demanded before he can undertake even preliminary investigation.[66]

By the 1987 printing of *Kabbalah for the Layman*, Berg's anger toward rabbis had increased noticeably. Appended to the body of the book was a new epilogue that contained, among other points, a harsh denunciation of men "who pose as religious leaders who, for their own selfish reasons, spread false prerequisites for the study of the *Zohar*." Berg conceded that there were parts of Kabbalah that should be kept secret, unpublished, and taught to just a few; but this only applied to a small part of the teachings. The leaders who refused to teach Kabbalah to laypeople Kabbalah were simply protecting their (false) reputations as learned men, Berg wrote; they were fearful lest they be embarrassed by the questions that would be asked by the people who now know Zohar. They are withholding benefits from others. He writes, "These *Kat* (cults) of Rabbis have been, and are still in some quarters, blemishes and disfigurements on the face of Rabbinic Judaism."[67] In this way, Berg associates rabbinic guardedness toward Kabbalah with power-hungry cult leaders. By implication, his desire to spread kabbalistic knowledge is democratic and genuinely Jewish.

THE GROWTH OF THE KABBALAH CENTRE MOVEMENT IN NORTH AMERICA: THE *HEVRE* AND *HARISHA*

In 1984 Philip and Karen Berg's main residence and headquarters was a large house in Queens, New York. Around them, in addition to their children, was a core group of between 5 and 10 Israeli disciples. These were young men and women—the women who were included were the wives of the men. From the base in Queens, they launched their campaign to spread knowledge of Kabbalah in North America. The term for the core group of disciples was *Hevre*, Hebrew for "group of friends." The term *hevre* is used in Israel for one's buddies or the member of one's army unit; it can also be used for a spiritual fellowship, and this is the understanding that the Hevre prefers. Like the circle of disciples (Aramaic: *Hevraia*) around the Kabbalist Shimon Bar Yohai, so too did this group rally around Philip and Karen Berg to study and spread Kabbalah.[68] The Hevre was a type of religious order. Philip Berg conferred ordination on the male students in the Hevre whom he deemed proficient (within Orthodox Judaism, it is accepted practice for rabbis to ordain their students), but the Hevre experience was not a path to ordination for most. Also, the membership of the group was not constant over the years: some who left the Hevre stayed involved but could no longer handle such a demanding life; some left the movement altogether; and currently, the Hevre is a much larger, less intimate group based in a number of different cities.

The interpersonal character of the first Hevre was fundamental. There were siblings and family connections among the members. Being in the Hevre was not a part-time activity; it was the result of a mutual decision between the Bergs and the individual to take on what would be a seven-day-a-week all-day activity. The members would study Kabbalah, live in accordance with Jewish religious law and kabbalistic principles as interpreted by Berg, and spread the teachings. They would not work at other jobs, and so the Research Centre of Kabbalah provided for their basic needs. The Bergs designed the Hevre experience to be an intense, life-changing process. Being part of the group was, in some aspects, reminiscent of training for military service or a religious order: one was being prepared, reshaped, given a new sense of awareness necessary for a crucial mission. They were taught to be prepared for any eventuality. Furthermore, each person's motives and behaviors were held up to frequent scrutiny so as to increase self-awareness. Here is a description of the Hevre training from the 1980s by someone close to the group:

> The training involves learning that everything that occurs has a spiritual cause—everything. Every bad thing or obstacle is there to teach you what you need to know. Karen would tell someone, "Prepare to move to such-and-such a place tonight." And then the person would pack and prepare, and then— nothing. It was a way to "break ego." It was deliberate. There was the constant criticism—24/7. From the other Hevre and from Karen and the Rav [Rabbi Berg], you would always be hearing "Why are you doing this? Why did you say it that way?" You learned that this constant scrutiny was for your benefit. They were trying to make a change in your life, and that's how it will happen. When you are Hevre, they are making that change at an accelerated rate.[69]

The necessity to change the individual and "break ego" is connected to Ashlag's description of human psychology. According to Ashlag, God constructed every living organism with an inborn will to satisfy its needs called the Desire to Receive. In human beings, the Desire to Receive expresses itself as self-centeredness; at its basest level, it is a Desire to Receive for the Self Alone. A maturing person learns to curb this impulse, to share with others, and to be concerned for their benefit. With effort, the impulse is transformed from a Desire to Receive for the Self Alone to a Desire to Receive for the Sake of Sharing. As one becomes more sharing, one ascends to higher levels of spirituality. Kabbalistic knowledge and practices facilitate this ascension. The Kabbalah Centre describes this process of personal transformation as one in which one's ego is broken. The ego is that part of the individual personality that manifests most strongly the Desire to Receive, and improvement involves breaking the ego's need for gratification. The quickest way to break one's ego and transform oneself is to serve others. Spreading kabbalistic teachings will multiply the number of people who understand and follow the ideal, and the end result is a perfected world.[70]

The principle means of spreading kabbalistic teachings during the 1980s was called *harisha*, Hebrew for "plowing," referring to the door-to-door missionary work engaged in by the disciples. This was primarily the work of the males within the Hevre. Laden with Berg's English-language books, they would knock on doors of residences or businesses asking to speak to Jewish people about Kabbalah. They sometimes narrowed their approach in a city by asking the location of Jewish neighborhoods or the location of the homes of Jewish people. The Hevre would go to businesses as well. Karen reports, "We used to have Eitan walk into offices asking, 'Are there any Jews here?'"[71] The harisha workers tended to take a global approach, however, because they found Jewish people living in unexpected places, or they found interest in

Kabbalah from people who were not Jewish (there was no objection to teaching Kabbalah to non-Jews, but the principle focus in this period was on Jews). In places distant from Queens, groups of two or three Hevre would drive or fly to a city and canvas the area from about 8:30 A.M. to about 9 P.M. They had very little money to cover their expenses, and where possible, they would be housed by a friend of Rabbi Berg. If Berg did not have a contact in the city and there were no other options, the harisha workers would go back to the car and sleep there, or they would accept people's offers of donations, food, or a place to sleep in their homes. "We must have contacted every American Jew," said a Kabbalah Centre teacher in reference to his harisha work of the late 1980s. "We went to every state, to Canada, Mexico, and Guatemala. We would go to little towns, places where you could not imagine that any Jews lived, but we would find them there."[72]

Of course, this type of missionary work had many precedents. Jehovah's Witnesses, Mormons, and all kinds of Christian groups send their members door-to-door in order to spread the word. Among American Jews, this door-to-door contact was frowned on. American Jews did not like being subjected to proselytizing, private or public, and they tended to congratulate themselves on not engaging in what they felt was an intolerant and offensive practice. Door-to-door solicitation of money for charitable causes was also sharply discouraged. In the 1920s, most sizable U.S. Jewish communities organized a local Jewish Federation to manage the fund-raising for a number of Jewish agencies and organizations, and door-to-door solicitations were not allowed. Only Orthodox and Hasidic Jews continued to engage in door-to-door solicitation of funds and missionary work, but the efforts of the latter were strictly addressed to Jews only. For them, it was an effort to bring nonreligious Jews back to Judaism; they called this effort *kiruv*, the Hebrew term for "bringing closer." As mentioned previously, during the 1960s, the Habad Hasidic organization engaged in outreach on college campuses and in cities and suburbs where Jews were concentrated. From the late 1930s until his death in the mid-1960s, Levi Krakovsky would go door-to-door with his books, seeking customers and students. Any of these may have been the inspiration for Kabbalah Centre harisha.

Harisha served at least three purposes. First, the books and tapes were sold in order to generate funds for the movement, enabling further publishing and the payment of expenses connected to other teaching. Second, it was regarded as the means of building a community. The disciples made personal contact with people and arranged one-on-one teaching. They kept track of those who were interested and those with whom they had left materials, and at later times, they checked back with them to see whether their interest had been piqued by the books and tapes. They tried to set up an ongoing class with a number of interested individuals in one area. Even after the harisha workers moved on to other regions, the students in the classes were guided to meet together and study from the books and tapes. In this way, a nucleus of a kabbalistic community was established.

The third purpose of harisha was to turn the disciples into effective teachers and Kabbalists. The initial Hevre was composed of Israelis with limited English skills, and those who were involved with harisha had to communicate with people of very different backgrounds. They were instructed to teach gently, without pushiness or guilt-inducing messages. Yet for the harisha participants, the work was brutal. It was bruising to one's ego to face repeated rejection and pick oneself up and continue forward. There were many personal discomforts. Harisha workers were taught that a Kabbalist should be able to overcome these challenges; if not, it was a sign that one's ego—one's Desire to Receive—was too strong. Engaging in harisha work (as well as other types of service to others) was considered the quickest way to transform and refine one's soul. The result would be a person who was a model for others as well as a capable educator who could build the movement and spread kabbalistic knowledge. One current Kabbalah Centre teacher who engaged in harisha believes that the experience was not helpful in attracting followers and may have done damage to the reputation of the group. Yet he credits it with enabling people to gain control of their ego and teaching them how to become sharing individuals and channels for God.[73]

It is in the institution of the Hevre that the Kabbalah Centre movement resembles most the stereotypic image of a "cult." Philip and Karen Berg were surrogate parents to the Hevre, instructing them and providing them with a way to interpret the world around them. The members of the Hevre were financially dependent on the Bergs. Their work was intense and demanding, and there was an effort to mold their personalities in accordance with religious principles. This is no different from other intense religious orders, such as the Catholic priesthood, and missionaries serving a church away from home. Such groups often appear insidious to unsympathetic outsiders, as well as to ex-members who leave in dissatisfaction. Those who could not abide the system and left the Kabbalah Centre have written bitterly about it.[74] The experience of the insiders is quite different. In the case of the Kabbalah Centre, members of the first Hevre who are still involved describe the early years as a time of hard work as well as joy, warmth, joy, excitement, tremendous personal growth, and satisfaction. Successful harisha work could be personally rewarding. The Hevre was a small, intimate group that debated, discussed, and made decisions together with the Bergs. They were part of the Bergs' extended family, and they watched the Berg children grow and watched each other find spouses. Each week, they together celebrated a Sabbath filled with food, rest, and fellowship, and Jewish holidays were also a time of great intensity. The Hevre did not consider Karen and Philip to be perfect or infallible, but wise, loving, insightful, open to suggestions, and utterly committed to their mission.

KABBALAH CENTRES AND THE EXPANSION
OF THE OUTREACH EFFORT

In the late 1980s, the Kabbalah Centre movement took on a new shape. Harisha was successful in Toronto, and by 1987, one of the senior teachers, Eitan Yardeni, was flying there once a week to teach. Among the students were some very dedicated and accomplished individuals. They advised the Bergs to adopt some of the organization and language used by religious communities in North America. Generally, devotees of a religion establish a nonprofit corporation for the religious group, headed by a board of directors and governed according to the bylaws agreed upon by the board. Among the advantages of adopting this model is that the corporation can more easily purchase and manage property, such as a building, that serves as a center for the group. The Bergs agreed to this structure. In 1988 the Canadian government granted the Toronto group's request for status as a charitable religious organization. The Toronto followers raised funds and rented a building and, with the Bergs, designed a center for the community. It was called the Kabbalah Centre or the Kabbalah Learning Centre, designations that differentiated the place from a synagogue and highlighted its educational and social functions.[75] The Toronto Kabbalah Centre was a model for Centres subsequently established in other cities. Classes, prayer services, and communal Sabbath and holiday meals were held there. It was felt that Kabbalah Centres should be headed by a team of rabbi and wife. They would be helped by a locally based Hevre, which would include teachers, and the board and volunteers would handle other aspects of the operation. Karen and Philip Berg were board members and provided oversight: Rabbi Berg was the chief rabbi, designated for life, and the one with the sole power of ordination. By the beginning of the 1990s, about 50–100 people would gather every Friday evening at the Toronto Kabbalah Centre for prayer services, and approximately 30 would stay for dinner. They were predominantly but not entirely Jewish, from all walks of life and all ages. By 1993, the Toronto Centre claimed between 1500–2000 active members—that is, people who enrolled in classes, attended special lectures, and sent their children to its Sunday school. Kabbalah Centre leaders in that year estimated that 5,000 people had passed through the Centre since its inception.[76]

The Toronto community was also instrumental in assisting Philip Berg to adapt his teaching for North Americans. The primary target audience for Kabbalah Centre outreach at the time was the vast majority of North American Jews who were assimilated to the extent that they had abandoned serious engagement with Judaism. Those who fit in this category were Jews who were not following *halacha* (Jewish religious law) and did not feel a spiritual connection with or understanding of Judaism. Reports one man, who was active in the Centre at the time, "Our stated, explicit goal was to reach 95 percent of the Jewish world in North America. That 95 percent are assimilated Jews, and they have to be approached with sensitivity."[77] Among the devotees of the Centre in Toronto were business professionals skilled in advertising, marketing, design, and public relations. They were eager to channel their talents in the service of spreading Kabbalah, and the Bergs invited their assistance. Berg and the teachers were taught the cultural associations and knowledge base of the audience they were trying to attract. Berg's explanations were highly dependent on the use of Hebrew and Aramaic, and his senior disciples were, for the most part, Israelis. Everybody was trained to adjust their teaching to the needs and tastes of North American students. The curriculum was simplified and revised. Less knowledge of Jewish culture was assumed, and named references to this or that rabbi or book were removed; at the same time, the professionals urged Berg to use his rabbinic title. Newly written books were more accessible, and older books had their covers redesigned, their pages reformatted, and their content revised. The scientific and space-age themes that filled the 1980s books were replaced by topics that were of greater appeal to the public in the 1990s. Brochures and advertisements were professionally designed to attract a wide audience of spiritual seekers.[78] This approach is still followed.

One of the consequences of this skillful marketing is that there is some discrepancy between the advertising and the actual teachings of the group. The ads promise happiness, prosperity, and love—without great effort or sacrifice. One has to search for a reference to "breaking ego," although this is a central concept of Kabbalah Centre teachings. In addition, the terms "Judaism" and "Jew" began to be heard far less frequently and appear less frequently in the books. The logic behind this is that assimilated Jews ("that 95%") had already demonstrated their rejection of and disinterest in Judaism and the Jewish community's tight social bonds. This change in strategy is evident in the revisions of *Kabbalah for the Layman*. In the 1981 edition of *Kabbalah for the Layman*, Berg writes:

> Kabbalah lies at the very heart of the system of holy actions and deeds known as *mitzvot;* without these actions, the life of a Jew is considered incomplete and lacking. However, inner devotion is also an important element of Jewish teaching, and this aspect, too, is emphasised by the teaching of Kabbalah.... We feel that many Jews who may read this book, and who have grown up without knowing the taste of mitzvot, will benefit from a contemplation to help link the teachings of Kabbalah with their application in the world of action.[79]

It is clear here that Berg is writing for a Jewish audience that identifies positively with Judaism and the mitzvot, and his concern is for the religious lives of Jews. As noted earlier, the same book evinces a harsh disdain for contemporary Jewish authorities, describing them as cult leaders. Yet by 1991, when Berg issued a significantly revised edition of *Kabbalah for the Layman*, he omitted mention of rabbis. He expressed his disdain for the distorted form of Judaism they had created. Furthermore, these comments about Judaism were just a passing reference in the book's larger message that Kabbalah is meant for all humanity. For example, the book opens with a description of the Zohar as a quintessentially universal book:

> As we enter the years ahead, the Zohar will continue to be a people's book, striking a sympathetic chord in the hearts and minds of those who long for peace, truth and relief from suffering. In the face of crises and catastrophe it has the ability to resolve agonizing human afflictions by restoring each individual's relationship with the Force.[80]

This type of message was designed to bring in a large audience, Jews as well as non-Jews. The revised edition of *Kabbalah for the Layman* signals the directors' reconsideration of their mission to spread Kabbalah. The universalism that was, perhaps, implicit in Ashlag's teachings was now going to be an explicit and important goal of the Kabbalah Centre. They had likely been moving in this direction for quite some time.[81]

Furthermore, although the first editions of *Kabbalah for the Layman* included many pages devoted to the unique role of the Jewish people in world history and in the future redemption, this concept was omitted in the 1991 revised edition. There, non-Jews are by no means marginal to the possibility of connecting to divinity. Nor were the mitzvot relegated to Jews. For example, the Jewish practice of designating a 13-year-old boy and a 12-year-old girl as Bar or Bat Mitzvah—typically understood as the change in status as the child becomes responsible and culpable for his or her obedience of religious laws—is described as the time when "the individual is incarnated with a *Yetzer haTov*, a good inclination, which is a potential metaphysical form of energy similar to the Creator's Desire to Impart." From that day onward, each individual then has the capacity to share, to love others, and to transform into a being who can emulate God and ultimately dissolve into God at the end of time. Berg explains, "Man is the channel through which the Creator's beneficence and grace flow from the upper heavenly spheres to the corporeal world." In the earlier edition of the book, as well as in the other books published in the 1980s, Berg teaches that Jewish souls have greater capacity than all others. In the 1990s, the distinction between Jews and others is not mentioned, although Berg admits that there are variations in people's capacities to channel.[82]

It is important to point out that the omissions and stylistic changes described here do not constitute a rejection of previous doctrine. They are simply more diplomatic and less explicit about hierarchical distinctions. Berg was no longer in Israel, where it was safe to assume the Jewishness of his audience and where his listeners were comfortable with the belief that Jews alone were pivotal and central to a cosmic drama. Outside of Israel, he was writing for and teaching a diverse group of people. There it might be insulting to address oneself only to the Jews. To Berg, Kabbalah included teachings that were of great importance to non-Jews as well as Jews. For example, all humanity could—and should, he believed—be taught that the purpose of human existence as well as the key to happiness was the individual's transformation of his or her soul into a sharing, less egocentric entity. Berg found a basis for this in Ashlag's writings and in Brandwein's. Although neither man taught Kabbalah to non-Jews, and Brandwein was loathe to have them financially support the propagation of Kabbalah, both believed that all humanity could benefit from kabbalistic knowledge. Berg took this universalism seriously. He put it into effect; indeed, he made it a priority.

Within a few years, the Kabbalah Centre movement began to increase its impact and its reach. Over the course of the 1990s, Kabbalah Learning Centres were established in New York, Los Angeles, Chicago, and other American cities where a base had been created through harisha. Karen and Philip Berg enlisted people to assist them in acquiring a building and designing and running the operations. Centres were also set up in London, Paris, Mexico City, and elsewhere. Door-to-door harisha diminished significantly and was eventually abandoned. Each Centre had teachers, a small Hevre, and a head teacher or a rabbi ordained by Berg. The senior personnel was drawn from the original Hevre that had been based in Queens in the 1980s as well as leaders who were groomed later, and they were rotated from Centre to Centre as the Bergs saw fit. Karen and Philip Berg spent many weeks of the year traveling from Centre to Centre, residing in each as they saw the need for their presence. (In the mid-1990s they moved their main residence and Kabbalah Centre headquarters to Los Angeles.) Wherever they were, they maintained frequent phone contact with the people working in the different Centres and the prominent members. Philip Berg continued to teach the Hevre and other participants. The Hevre and teaching staff was expanded and included people of non-Israeli and non-Jewish background. An increasing number of Jews and non-Jews were attracted to the Centre.[83]

Once the Kabbalah Centre movement became visible, it attracted the attention of Jewish communal leaders, educators, and rabbis. They uniformly denounced Berg and the Kabbalah Centres. Not surprisingly, Toronto was the site of the first skirmishes. In 1990 the Orthodox rabbis of Toronto published a statement disapproving of the Centre.[84] In 1993 the first major journalistic treatment of the Kabbalah Centre, focusing on the activities of the Toronto Centre, appeared in the *Canadian Jewish News*.[85] Although the article presented positive and negative views of the group, the effect of publicizing the unconventional practices as well as the complaints of ex-participants was to alert the Canadian Jewish community into combating what appeared to be a new and dangerous sect. Within months, a Toronto rabbi, while speaking to a Jewish audience in South Africa, publicly cast ridicule and aspersion on Philip and Karen Berg and the Kabbalah Centre. His lecture was taped and circulated to Jewish communities throughout the world. In response, Philip Berg sued him for libel and slander, requesting several million dollars in damages.[86] Consequently, the hostility between the Jewish community and the Kabbalah Centre became broadcasted throughout the Jewish world. Invariably, the Jewish media and Jewish communal leaders criticized the Bergs and all their doings, labeling the Kabbalah Centre a cult.[87] The vehemently negative reaction from the Jewish community affirmed the decision of the Kabbalah Centre leadership to regard their target audience as larger than the Jewish community, and the criticism strengthened the leadership's alienation from the organized Jewish community.

Another factor in the expansion of the target audience was the growth in the number of non-Jews at the Centre. They bought books, attended courses, participated in the communal celebrations and prayer services, and volunteered their labor at the Centres. Among the new participants were popular entertainment celebrities. Their involvement was broadcast in the popular media, creating free publicity for the Kabbalah Centre and great interest in the teachings. The most prominent celebrity, and the most seriously committed to the work of the Centre, was Madonna Louise Veronica Ciccone. Madonna is one of the most internationally known popular music artists of the last 20 years. Religion has always appeared as a theme in her music and videos, and her rebellion against Roman Catholic doctrines and norms has received much attention. Her approval of this new religious group was a powerful statement, and she did not hesitate to describe the Kabbalah Centre as a worthy spiritual alternative to organized religion.[88] By all accounts, the media attention given to celebrities' participation in Kabbalah Centre events contributed substantially to the increased attendance by people of all backgrounds to the Centre, and it still does.

One of the unique features of the Kabbalah Centres was (and is) its casual attitude toward membership. Most American synagogues maintain an official membership roster, and one becomes a member by paying annual dues. These dues theoretically pay for the many benefits that come with membership: adult education classes, schooling for children, pastoral counseling, and so on. Typically, all prayer services are free and open to the public except for the "High Holiday" prayer services on Rosh Hashanah and Yom Kippur, which are accessible only to members. The Kabbalah Centre did not adopt this model. Prayer services are generally free and open to all, but there is no official membership roster or annual dues. Individuals who attend meals, classes, or special events pay for that separate activity. Requests for personal or spiritual counseling are handled in a variety of ways—one common response is to encourage the person to consult his or her teacher—but not on a fee-for-service basis. Funds for the operating expenses of the Kabbalah Centre and funds for expansion are raised through donations, and the sale of books, educational material, and paraphernalia such as posters, jewelry, and clothing branded with the Centre's logo or other designs.

The rejection of the conventional Jewish system of membership is consistent with the "organizational phobia" of New Age religious movements and appeals to an audience resistant to organized religion and the appearance of conformity. It is an expression of the Centre's policy of outreach. Technically speaking, no one is a "member," and anyone may enter. This is one reason that accurate appraisals of the size of the community, locally or nationwide, are impossible to obtain. This system enhances the sense among the attendees that their participation is entirely in their own hands. People who are used to the usual mode of funding synagogues and churches frequently criticize the Kabbalah Centre for commodifying religion and turning it into a business. Of course, all religious organizations that offer benefits and services to others must depend on financial donations, donations of labor and in-kind donations, and actual payments. In the Kabbalah Centre, the system of financial support for the benefits and services is plainly visible. Instead of apologizing for it, Kabbalah Centre teachers point out that the transparency is consistent

Rabbis Michael Berg, Philip Berg, and Yehuda Berg, singing during Rosh Hashanah prayers, 2005. Copyright © The Kabbalah Centre International/Kabbalah University Archives/ university@kabbalah.com/www.kabbalah.com.

with an important kabbalistic principle called "Bread of Shame": one must earn the right to receive, whether one is receiving divine bounty or material wealth; unearned benefits will turn sour and destructive and will ultimately vanish. Furthermore, Kabbalah Centre directors are convinced that their spiritual paraphernalia have genuine spiritual power, and producing and selling it to the public helps and inspires others.[89]

The establishment of Centres in the major cities of the West, as well as the international reach of the Centre's Spirituality for Kids project, led the directors in 1999 to incorporate the movement as Kabbalah Centre International and to standardize the curriculum and operations.[90] The organization had clearly achieved a firm financial basis. By that time, its mission was explicitly about spreading Kabbalah to the world, rather than to just a Jewish audience. Philip and Karen Berg's son Michael explained it to me as follows: "In the past, we worked at encouraging 3 percent of the world to follow 97 percent of the Kabbalah. Now our realistic goal is to get 97% to follow 3% of the Kabbalah."[91] This strategic change had been in the works for years, and it did not falter when the Bergs' sons Yehuda and Michael began in the mid-1990s to take more important roles within the movement. They had studied Kabbalah with their father, and they attended schools of advanced rabbinic learning

Karen Berg, 2003. Copyright © The Kabbalah Centre International/ Kabbalah University Archives/university@kabbalah.com/www. kabbalah.com.

in Israel and the United States, receiving ordination from Knesset Yehezkel rabbinical seminary in Jerusalem. Yehuda and his father worked on producing a prayer book suitable for the Kabbalah Centres. Michael took charge of translating Ashlag's Hebrew version of the Zohar and his commentary into English. Highly educated in classic Talmudic and kabbalistic texts, the sons nevertheless have been adept at moving the Kabbalah Centre toward its universalist goal. "The Kabbalah Centre's goal is not to make better Jews," Michael explains, "but to make better people."[92]

CHAPTER 3

———— ✳ ————

Main Teachings

Kabbalah Centre teachers have cultivated a large group of followers of all religions and backgrounds who adopt a few doctrines and a relatively simple spiritual practice. They have also produced a smaller cohort of intense and highly educated practitioners who live according to a highly demanding and specialized behavioral code and complex doctrines. The latter are predominantly Jewish, with a high proportion of Israelis among them. The group as a whole is taught that the distinctions between them in terms of religious background and extent of ritual performance are not important; they are bound together in a community devoted to "revealing Light," that is, celebrating God's love, receiving spiritual energy from it, and behaving lovingly and generously toward others.

There are two recognizable periods in Berg's popularization of Kabbalah. The first is from 1969 until the early 1990s. During these years, Berg taught and wrote for a largely Jewish audience, one that was familiar with the concepts and assumptions of Orthodox Judaism. Nevertheless, he was popularizing Kabbalah, in that he was explaining it in the vernacular in layman's terms. The second phase of popularization begins in the early 1990s. At that point, Philip and Karen Berg accepted the guidance of marketing specialists in adopting language that would be comprehensible and more attractive to a wider, more diverse, and less Judaism-educated audience. From that point and continuing today, there has been a deliberate effort to make Kabbalah truly popular. None of the Kabbalah Centre directors denies this or apologizes for it. They believe that spreading kabbalistic knowledge to all of humanity is a fulfillment of the teachings of Rabbi Yehuda Ashlag. The two modes of presenting Kabbalah are different but not mutually exclusive, and the first mode is still available in the Centre for those who want it. The distinctions between these modes highlights the internal distinctions within the Kabbalah Centre community. This chapter presents Kabbalah Centre doctrines and beliefs in both forms and differentiates between them.

Everybody at the Kabbalah Centre is taught some basic principles from the kabbalistic system of Yehuda Ashlag: a view of God and the creation of the human race, a description of the human ego with its needs and drives, and the goal of elevating one's soul from base, selfish desires toward love for others and attachment to God. Since the major revision of the curriculum in the 1990s, kabbalistic ideas and their implications have been described as "12 Rules of the Game of Life." They provide people with a simple method of recognizing their impulses and channeling their desires in a direction that will elevate, improve, and refine their soul. People who remain associated with the Centre eventually filter out into concentric circles. The larger, outer peripheral group of supporters and spiritual seekers accept the kabbalistic principles as an answer to questions about the origins of the cosmos and the purpose of life; and they use these kabbalistic principles as a guide to moral and spiritual living, among other principles that they have gathered from other sources. Their engagement in ritual and meditation is minimal.

Moving inward are people who have added to the kabbalistic principles some "spiritual tools": these are rituals and meditations, the mitzvot—the commandments of the Torah—such as the Sabbath and holidays, and the wearing of special items such as the red string. The innermost circles include those who, in addition to the behaviors just described, commit themselves to the regular study of Kabbalah and the regular performance of mitzvot as they are interpreted by Jewish religious law. Their behavioral commitment is very similar to Orthodox Judaism, except that the mitzvot are explained quite differently; they are the tools God provided for enabling metaphysical energy to flow into the earthly realm. Their beliefs and behavior are best understood in the terms clarified by Berg in the first phase of his popularization of Kabbalah. The boundaries between these circles is not sharp; it is a matter of degrees.

The Kabbalah Centre movement is, consequently, a unique mix of people of different religious and ethnic backgrounds that make up a new religious movement. One could, at the same time, describe it—especially the inner circle—as a sect of Judaism.

GOD—THE LIGHT

God is at the center of Kabbalah Centre teaching. Some religions teach about God with a series of attributes—for example, God is one, good, moral, compassionate, and so on. Kabbalah teaches about God through a narrative about the creation and evolution of the universe; this is what religious studies scholars call a cosmogonic myth. Chapter 1 of this book includes an outline of the cosmogonic myth in the Zohar, in the writings of Isaac Luria, and according to Yehuda Ashlag. This chapter presents Ashlag's version in greater detail, for it is the foundation of all Kabbalah Centre beliefs. Philip Berg learned it from Ashlag's students and from his own study of Ashlag's books. Drawn almost entirely from literature that most Jewish religious authorities would describe as esoteric and fit only for an elite, it is a creation narrative quite unlike any other. It sounds nothing like the biblical account of God and creation with which most people attending the Kabbalah Centre have familiarity, but they learn that the Bible is written in code and the kabbalistic narrative is the revealed meaning of the biblical text. The narrative is quite complex, and although many members of the Kabbalah Centre cannot recite it with much clarity, they understand its implications and importance when they hear it repeated throughout lectures, prayers, and ceremonies. They know that the creation narrative provides the reasons for why the world is the way it is, and they believe that it shows the way for bringing our broken world back to wholeness.

Those who learn about the creation story today are introduced to it in an unusual manner. Beginning students are told that they should not believe the story because they have been told it; instead, they should decide for themselves after putting the principles of the story into practice. Kabbalah Centre teachers call this Rule Number One of Kabbalah's 12 Rules of the Game of Life.[1]

The story begins before there was anything material whatsoever, before there was anything created. In the beginning, there was simply God: endless, infinite divinity, entirely self-sufficient, and lacking nothing. God is a sharing, good power. God is like light, a beneficent light, incapable of burning or blinding, and God is often called simply "the Light." The Light is warm, life-giving, loving, and completely and utterly devoted to fulfilling all the needs of the recipients of its glow. God is spiritual Light inexhaustibly and effortlessly filling infinite space with its positive energy. God desires only to share and never to withhold Light. God is the manifestation of a drive that pulses through the cosmos called Desire to Share.

This picture of God is, for many people, quite unlike the conventional one, and they welcome it. People who turn to Kabbalah want something other than what is offered by established religions. They do not imagine God as a king on a throne, and they do not want to believe that God acts like a judge who rewards and punishes. "The word 'God' has so much garbage put on it by all the religions," my teacher explained. "If you want to call it God," he said, "go ahead, but give it the attributes that we have learned about the Light. Light cannot get angry, or command, or get upset." As for the biblical story that God gets angry, the teacher explains, "According to Kabbalah, the Bible is in code. People put the wrong meaning into the words."[2] Those who are uncomfortable with *any* personal, anthropomorphic image and who find it impossible to believe that behind all of existence is a single, ruling personality explain that they can accept this image of God as the Light. They do not believe that there is nothing out there because they feel something flowing in and through everything. People of all outlooks may be attracted to this image of God as energizing, loving, nonjudgmental, and unifying, but it is an image that is especially prevalent within New Age religious circles.[3]

The next few elements of the cosmogonic narrative are quite complex, and they are explained in the introductory Kabbalah classes with far less detail than appears here. People who read beyond what is presented in class and people who attend the worship services will learn these details and understand how they are connected with meditations and rituals.

At this initial phase in the emergence of the cosmos, God, or the Light, or pure Desire to Share, is all that exists. However, God wants to share, and he cannot share unless there is another to receive what he gives. This leads to the first of many paradoxes in the narrative: the Light creates a vessel to receive, but that vessel, which is one as well as an infinite number of vessels, is indistinguishable from the Light. The vessels are emanated into existence, but being divine, they are not differentiated from God, who is pure Desire to Share. Being filled with the light of sharing, they too wish to share. Consequently, the vessels empty themselves out so they can be the recipients of the others' sharing. Thus, the Desire to Receive is created. These two impulses, the Desire to Share and the Desire to Receive, constitute the basis of all existence.[4]

Only one of these vessels, Malchut, is truly a vessel—that is, a container with nothing of its own to give. The 10 major vessels, or sefirot, should be understood as different stages of divinity. They are different degrees in the process of creating the lowest vessel, or sefirah, called Malchut, kingdom. From the point of view of God, Malchut is the completion of the process of creation. The other nine sefirot contain Light of their own, and so they are giving as well as receiving. Malchut is a vessel that, entirely empty of divine Light of its own, is entirely the Desire to Receive. Divine Light flows into it. This stage of creation, and this "place" of Malchut, is called the Endless, or Ein sof, in the sense that Malchut endlessly receives Light and is totally filled and fulfilled. Within the Endless is Adam, containing all souls. This is still not the material world; at this point, materiality—the "lower world"—has not been created. The world of the Endless is one of utmost perfection. The souls have endless love, endless receiving, and endless fulfillment. When the souls lose this by entering the material world and immerse themselves in physical life, the deepest part of them will remember the Endless and seek to return to it.

BREAD OF SHAME AND THE RULES OF THE GAME OF LIFE

The next step seems to be an inadvertent one. It occurs when the vessels within Malchut, receiving Light continuously, filled with Desire to Share, want to share as well. They want to be like the Creator and give, but they cannot offer anything of their own; and there is no other to whom they can give because the Creator lacks any Desire to Receive. They feel shame. Kabbalah Centre teachers liken this to the human reaction to an undeserved gift: "In the beginning you will be happy, but after a while you feel patronized and diminished and shamed; you may even resent the giver."[5] The name for the vessels' feeling of embarrassment is "Bread of Shame."[6] The shame causes the vessels to voluntarily shut off the light as if to say, "No more handouts!" It is a drive for independence, an effort to take charge; actually, it is a desire to be like the Creator. When the vessels shut out the light, there is a deflation, a restriction, called *tsimtsum*. The lack of light and sudden emptiness that result shatter the vessels of Malchut. The breakage results in the creation of the finite, physical world.[7] The divine Adam is dislocated, and on earth there is a "fall" of Adam. (All this occurs simultaneously because time does not yet exist.) Twenty-two energy forces—the letters of the Hebrew alphabet— emanate into the empty space as the "building blocks" of the world as we know it, and this emanation is hinted at in the biblical account of creation, in which God constructs the finite world through Hebrew words.

The finite "lower world" is an imperfect one. The Light continues to shine endlessly, but in the lower world, we stop perceiving it. We create an illusory world of deprivation in which the divine light is blocked, as with veils, so that we are more aware of the darkness than the light. The veils are like the broken shards of the vessels, called kelippot, and they are spread throughout the lower world as negative forces creating chaos and disharmony. In the Kabbalah Centre community, the physical world that we know through our five senses is called "the world of the 1 percent," denoting its insignificance and illusory nature in comparison with the metaphysical realm, "the 99 percent world." This distinction between the two realms is summarized as Rule Number Two.[8]

Human souls, like all other entities in the physical world, are imprinted with unfulfilled Desires to Receive. Desire to Receive is important because it pushes animals and humans to seek food, rest, shelter, knowledge, sexual pleasure, power, wealth, and so on; but when it is unrestrained, it is exceedingly selfish and is called Desire to Receive for the Self Alone. Human souls feel incomplete, and this is because when they left Malchut and descended to earth, they split into separate male and female halves; people spend their lives seeking their soul mates, rarely finding them. Human beings, marked by unfulfilled longing, take what is not theirs and hurt others. The evil that tempts a person to act selfishly and impulsively is personified as *Satan*, a lurking and constant presence.

In reality, though, the Light is always there, giving energy and warmth. Divine light is abundant in this world: it is evident in love, creativity, beauty, health, generosity, and in all other such plenitude. Rule Three is

"Everything that a human being truly desires from life is spiritual Light." The introductory lecture of the Kabbalah Centre—this is a one-hour free class designed to entice people to sign up for the basic Kabbalah course— does not include all the preceding details of the cosmogonic narrative, but it does emphasize a fundamental point: Kabbalah is the Hebrew word for receiving, and kabbalistic wisdom teaches people how to receive lasting fulfillment by connecting to spiritual Light. Several participants I interviewed told me that by the time they heard this point, they realized that they had found what they were searching for. They knew that the Kabbalah Centre would be their "spiritual home."[9]

The first hard truth that students learn is that they are not simply entitled to have an easy life. One might think that life would be easier with such a benevolent God. But shortages of sustenance and satisfaction occur because of the Bread of Shame. Bread of Shame, that basic truth that one should not receive without earning merit, prevents human beings from receiving God's beneficence in any lasting manner unless they merit it. That is, God is not responsible for human deprivation and unhappiness; humans' own behavior is the cause. Human beings do not know this. Their souls, having originated in the Endless and endowed with the energy of Desire to Share, once possessed this knowledge. Upon entering the world, the souls forget the lesson of Bread of Shame and are weighed down by the body's powerful energy of Desire to Receive for the Self Alone. At this base, most natural level, humans are selfish and egocentric. They react impulsively to their base impulses. Being "reactive," they have difficulty learning how to be a better person. They transform their souls slowly or not at all. They endure much suffering because of their ignorance, because bad behavior produces a negative consequence—if not during this life, then during later lives (reincarnation is fundamental to Kabbalah Centre teachings). The best and quickest way to fulfillment is to follow the guidelines for self-transformation given by the Creator in the form of revelation—Kabbalah. Those guidelines help people be "proactive," that is, take positive steps toward elevating their souls. Rule Number Four summarizes this as "The purpose of life is spiritual transformation from a reactive being to a proactive being."

Through Kabbalah, a person learns not to eliminate his or her Desire to Receive, but to transform it. The Desire to Receive for the Self Alone can be elevated and transformed into a Desire to Receive for the Sake of Sharing. Sharing with others connects a person to the Light. This is summarized as Rule Five: "In the moment of our transformation, we make contact with the 99 percent realm." Sharing involves "restriction." It is the ego, or the Desire to Receive for the Self Alone, that is being restricted. For example, a person restricts his or her greed and shares food with others; a person restricts his or her desire for instant gratification and follows a sensible plan for earning a livelihood; a person restricts his or her ego and takes responsibility for what has occurred instead of acting like a victim. This last point is summarized as Rule Number Six: "Never lay blame on other people or external events." When a person "restricts," the Bread of Shame is removed. Hence, Rule Seven is "Resisting our reactive impulses creates lasting Light."

Berg likes to use the language of electrical currents and "columns of energy" to describe the process of transformation. Conceptualizing the dynamic of the 10 sefirot as a "three-column system" is a very old tradition. The left column contains the sefirot that are conceptualized as female, the right column contains the male sefirot, and the middle column contains the sefirot that join and harmonize the two polarized side columns. Berg's innovation, however, is to describe these in terms of positive, negative, and neutral harmonizing energy. He likes to equate Kabbalah to the highest wisdom and technology—to science—and so he compares the dynamic of the sefirot (and actually, all reality) to the atom, with its positively charged protons, negatively charged electrons, and neutral neutrons; or to electrical circuitry. He calls the left column of sefirot negative energy, and the left-hand sefirot are identified with Desire to Receive. He calls the right column of sefirot positive energy, and the right-hand sefirot correspond with Desire to Share. The two energies are opposites, and when they are unassisted or unmodified, their combination will be unproductive or destructive. They may be productively joined and utilized only with the presence of a third type of energy (or, "central-column energy") that restricts and harmonizes them. Productive activity in the lower world shares the same dynamic as that in the upper world, and the two realms affect each other.

CAUSE AND EFFECT

The lesson that is derived from the cosmogonic narrative, and also from the axiom that God only spreads good and positive sustenance to all, is that the events of the physical world are connected to the metaphysical realm and to consciousness. Consciousness is the cause; physical reality is the effect. There are no accidents or random events. Everything that occurs was put into place by the metaphysical forces available: God gives Light to all unless the emanation has been blocked by the kelippot, the evil forces activated by Desire to Receive in a person's life (or past lives). A person who does good receives the benefits of divine Light. The benefits may not arrive immediately (they may even be postponed until one's next lifetime), and they may not be the benefits that one expects. A person who acts selfishly receives negative consequences—again, maybe not immediately, or in this lifetime, or the negative consequences that one expects. Kabbalah Centre teachers avoid terms like "good" and "bad" in describing human behavior, however. Instead, they use the term "reactive" to refer to actions emanating from one's ego and driven by one's Desire to Receive for the Self Alone; "pro-active" refers to behaviors designed to bring Light into the world. Rule Eight teaches that "Reactive behavior creates intense sparks of Light, but eventually leaves darkness in its wake." For example, a person who is dishonest in business may become wealthy, but the wealth will not last, or unhappiness will come in its wake, or, the negative effect will appear in the person's next life.

In short, everything that happens to a person is a consequence of his or her behavior in the past. There are no victims, and there is no such thing as luck. This concept is called "Cause and Effect." Some Kabbalah Centre teachers liken it to karma. It is not to be regarded as a system of punishment and reward from God. Events are an automatic, neutral effect of the system put into effect by the original restriction of the souls in the Endless world. Berg and Kabbalah Centre teachers take great pains to emphasize that God cannot be blamed for negative events: "God didn't create evil—the Bread of Shame (or, the human souls in the Endless) created evil!"[10] In order to turn the focus away from blame, Rule Nine teaches that bad things or obstacles that occur should be regarded as opportunities to resist "reactive" behavior and connect to the Light. Rules Ten and Eleven are reassurances: the greater the obstacle, the greater the potential Light; and when the challenges seem overwhelming, be assured that the Light is always there. Rule Twelve teaches that all negative traits perceived in others are merely a reflection of one's own negative traits; changing oneself is the only way to change others.[11]

This approach to life's difficulties provides many people with the certainty they crave. "There were no explanations for why bad things happened in the religion I was raised in," says a Kabbalah Centre devotee whose childhood friend died at an early age from cancer. "People would say it is God's will, or we don't know why, or, we cannot know why but we need to accept it." He felt that at the Kabbalah Centre he was given convincing answers to these difficult questions.[12] I asked my teacher why a congenital disease that appeared in a young boy might not simply be a matter of random mutation in the genes. "There is no such thing as random," he insisted. Perhaps it was God's test, I suggested. "Impossible. The Light does not do that. It gives indiscriminately, and so the illness is the result of a blockage, a simple cause and effect." I persisted, "What could a child do to deserve torture?" He said, "If something befalls a child under the age of 13, it is because of a past life. It has to be."

The lesson of Cause and Effect can be applied to the most mundane as well as the most serious events. Students are taught that Satan is always present and providing obstacles that activate their weaknesses. Satan is most evident when people are in the process of receiving, or trying to receive, and there is a glitch. Kabbalah Centre teachers suggest a basic "transformation formula" that should be followed. When I began my studies at the Kabbalah Centre in 1999, the formula was summarized neatly on a card that could be carried around or posted in the home and workspace. Ideally, the formula becomes internalized and a more automatic response to difficulty:

1. An obstacle occurs.
2. Realize that your reaction is the real enemy.
3. Shut down your reactive system and let the Light in.
4. Express your Proactive Nature.

Here is how a young woman named Alissa illustrates this in her daily life:

> I'm late for an appointment but stuck in traffic behind a slow-moving truck. Normally, I'd be frantic and honking the horn. When I'm conscious of the kabbalistic principles, I realize that the Light has sent this truck: the Light is telling me that I've been too hyper. I calm down and turn into a mellow person.

Alissa has learned that the negative things that occur to her are opportunities for personal improvement.[13]

Others emphasize that the kabbalistic principles infuse their lives with an awareness of God's presence. "I stopped being so stressed," Simone explains. "It is because I connected to this metaphysical energy, and I felt fulfilled." These feelings have to be nurtured in order to present throughout her day. If Simone abandons her discipline of meditation, her stress returns. She seeks simple ways of connecting to the Light throughout the day. It happened that a coworker told her, in passing, that his days improved when he started the morning with positive thinking. Simone told me, "I realized that he was my messenger. The Light sent him to me." So she asked her Kabbalah Centre teacher for a kabbalistic prayer to say in the morning upon wakening to express her gratitude, and she now recites it daily. Simone has learned that spending Shabbat at the Centre is particularly helpful for strengthening her awareness of the Light. "The Kabbalah Centre teaches that on Shabbat you can connect to the metaphysical force without having to overcome Satan; you receive Light without having to earn it!" she tells me. Her husband Alex believes that the effect of Shabbat is enhanced by joining together with others to celebrate the day. "You know," he says, "it has been scientifically proven that when more people are involved, the connection to the metaphysical is stronger."[14]

The kabbalistic principles are also understood to teach the intrinsic value of each and every human being; each human soul had its origin in the Endless, and here on earth, each and every human being has the capacity to be connected to spiritual Light. People are putting this value into action through the community projects of the Centre, in which people work to improve life for others by "revealing Light" in various ways. In the project called Spirituality for Kids (SFK), the "Rules of the Game" are taught in abbreviated form to elementary school–age children who are guided to use them on a daily basis. The SFK classes—which are designed to be fun and engaging—teach social skills, self-empowerment, and nonviolent conflict resolution. Alex, an adult volunteer for Spirituality for Kids, describes his participation as mentor for a disadvantaged cohort of SFK children who were guided to help serve a Thanksgiving meal at a homeless shelter on Thanksgiving. The children were taught that even though they were poor themselves, they could still give to others. These particular children, because of the kabbalistic principles they had absorbed, had a profound effect on one of the homeless men at the shelter. Alex reports, "The man was crying, and I asked him if he was okay. The man said, 'Lots of people come in here and feed us and talk to us. This is the first time I feel like people really *mean* it.'" Alex felt that the children had absorbed the lesson that everybody has the same soul connection to the Light. Their sincere respect and love for the residents of the shelter was obvious. "You can convey an unconditional love," he said, "when you feel that you are part of the Light and so is every other human being."[15]

What happens when individuals lack knowledge of Kabbalah and its rules, or if they learn the rules and do not apply them? Because of Bread of Shame, they will not have lasting fulfillment. They will not behave well, and they will have difficult lives. When they die, they will not merit the afterlife known as *Gan Eden,* or Paradise. Instead, their souls will have to return to earth and be reborn. Their merit and misbehavior from their previous life—if not already given its due consequence in the previous life—will follow them into the new incarnation. Each lifetime presents the opportunity to transform the Desire to Receive, as well as to cleanse oneself of sins from previous lives. When individuals do connect to spiritual Light in their lifetime, they receive the metaphysical energy that is otherwise obscured in this 1 percent world. Their lives will be filled with calm, contentment, and satisfaction. Or, if their lives remain difficult, they can be assured that they must be paying off sins from a previous lifetime, and the next one will be better. When this individual process of transformation and cleansing, called tikkun, is completed, they enter Paradise upon death. The dynamic is slightly different for males and females, in that women are not forced to reincarnate, but often return to earth voluntarily.

"Connecting to the Light" occurs on a global level as well. The repair of the world is a gradual process, spanning many centuries. Prior to the final correction is a long era called *yemot ha-mashiah,* the Messianic Days—this is the Jewish term, but Philip Berg prefers to use the astrological term Age of Aquarius. During this penultimate stage, the world is populated by souls with excessive Desire to Receive. Life becomes more and more difficult and full of tremendous suffering as well as tremendous creativity and groundbreaking discoveries. The chaos and disharmony, however, lead people to a spiritual awakening. Berg began publishing kabbalistic books in English in 1970 to facilitate the spiritual awakening of the Age of Aquarius that he believed was apparent all around him. In the Age of Aquarius, people realize that they must transform themselves and their way of life, and consequently, they become interested in Kabbalah. This interest indicates that souls are awakening to the truths they possessed prior to their descent to earth, and they are thirsty to learn from Kabbalah how to return to their roots in the Endless. As more and more individuals learn to connect to spiritual Light, life on earth improves. People learn how to harness metaphysical energy for the sake of healing individuals and repairing the damage to the earth, for knowledge that will lessen the impact of hurricanes and earthquakes, and so on. According to Berg, by 2000, the accumulated Light began to have a noticeable effect on scientific achievement. That year marks the beginning of a new phase in which extraordinary advances in all fields of knowledge and technology occur. Berg began to teach that physical immortality actually becomes a possibility.[16]

"Connecting to the Light" occurs on a cosmic level as well. If enough people learn Kabbalah and live it, transforming themselves into sharing and loving creatures, a qualitative change in reality will occur. Physical reality will be purified of evil and will be drawn back to its roots. The fracture that was created by the restriction of the souls responding to the Bread of Shame will be repaired. All will be divinity—the Age of Messiah. The souls will again be united in the perfect world of the Endless, receiving divine light endlessly, and perfectly fulfilled.

Although there is much similarity between Kabbalah Centre rules and the techniques suggested in contemporary self-actualization psychology, there are important differences. The Rules of the Game of Life are integrated with a specific religious cosmology. People are taught a method of relating to others that is very spiritual, in that they are taught to understand their personal behavior as a means to connect to cosmic forces and as a function of that connection. As will be explained as the chapter continues, the "transformation formula" itself, or one's own desire to change, is not enough; one is urged to engage in Hebrew meditations, wear amulets, and participate in communal rituals that are thought to link one directly to divine energy, thereby maximizing one's own efforts to transform. Yet the Kabbalah Centre is also presenting a pragmatic, result-oriented system that avoids the language of morality and service to God. The nonpersonal, mechanistic character of the system renders it, to many people, attractive and plausible in a way that the religions of their upbringing were not. Kabbalah Centre attendees who were raised in conventionally religious families and who attended religious schools told me that they did not recall learning clear-cut guides to personal behavior such as they learned at the Centre. In regard to the teachers in his Catholic school, Alex says, "They just said, 'Be good and go pray,' but they never taught *why* to be good or to take communion." This type of education did not inspire him to get involved in community service, whereas the

Kabbalah Centre presented Spirituality for Kids as a logical outgrowth of its principles. "Of course we were taught 'The Church says so' and 'Jesus wants you to do it,' but that was *just faith*. It wasn't an *explanation*," he insists.[17] The Kabbalah Centre's rules of life, apparently, are not "just faith." They appear to be simple, logical, necessary laws of nature. Kabbalah lacks the associations to organized religion. Kabbalah as it is presented in the Kabbalah Centre lacks the elitism of an esoteric system; it is anti-esoteric.

NEW AGE AND BERG'S KABBALAH

It is no accident that the kabbalistic ideas that have been described already, and others that will be described as this discussion continues, are compatible with New Age beliefs. Philip Berg understood the importance of explaining Kabbalah in an idiom that would be attractive to his listeners and readers, and he found no shame in employing the metaphors and concerns that moved them. Consequently, the fundamental principles of his kabbalistic philosophy, which were first recorded for posterity in his 1980s publications, reappeared over the years in different forms, reflecting the changing cultural tastes of the audience. New Age concepts were popular among young Israelis as well as young Americans during the first two decades of the Kabbalah Centre movement. In trying to win over people for whom New Age was deeply appealing, Berg magnified those elements of Kabbalah that were in harmony with New Age ideas. There were common elements in New Age and contemporary Kabbalah because, to a great extent, New Age ideas are a revival of earlier Western esoteric beliefs, and Kabbalah had been part of the Western esoteric tradition. For example, belief in reincarnation was present in both. The New Age themes have continued to find appeal into the twenty-first century and remain prominent in the Kabbalah Centre.

However, the New Age character of Berg's kabbalistic teachings is not merely a consequence of Berg's attempt to find followers. Berg's Kabbalah and New Age are products of the mid- to late twentieth century. They incorporate the cultural assumptions of the era, and their emergence was influenced by the same political and economic realities. For example, one of the features of this period is that minorities and marginalized cultures have been granted greater legitimacy; their histories, values, and symbols (or, what is imagined to be theirs) are held up for admiration and compared favorably to those of the dominant social groups and cultures. Consequently, in the mid- to late twentieth century, new religious movements gained followers by positioning themselves against conventional religious orthodoxies. They offer a vision of a new era and "new people who will transcend the limitations of narrowly chauvinistic cultures, religions, and political systems, and will surpass the outmoded thought forms of 'old age' theologies and beliefs."[18]

What exactly are New Age ideas?[19] It is important to keep in mind that there has never been a "constitution" associated with New Age. Indeed, one can only speak of a New Age movement in a strict sense during the early 1950s until the late 1970s, when separate groups formed to study the writings of Alice Bailey (1880–1949) and Rudolf Steiner (1861–1925). They emphasized the importance of altruistic love and community values, and they believed that present civilization would soon be destroyed, followed by an era of universal brotherhood called the New Age of Aquarius. By the 1980s, however, New Age was best understood not as a movement, but as a diffuse cluster of spiritual seekers who subscribed to a number of alternative beliefs and practices drawn from Western esoteric philosophies, Eastern religions, and ideas of evolution and psychology. These spiritual seekers are less inclined toward community. Instead, they tend to focus on the development of the individual, advocating that he or she choose religious elements from the diverse resources available without feeling the need to make a commitment to one particular community or tradition. Many believe that their individual and collective efforts will improve the world and make it more spiritual, but the belief in an imminent new age is no longer a shared, central conviction. Therefore, the following ideas are commonly described as New Age beliefs, but they may be accepted by those who do not identify themselves as New Agers and rejected by those who do.

I have isolated five that correspond closely with Kabbalah Centre principles already explained. The table shows how closely Kabbalah Centre teachings match five fundamental New Age beliefs:

Table 3.1

New Age	Kabbalah Centre
God is best understood as a nonpersonal sacred force immanent within all of nature and embodied within the material world. This force is described as a universal spiritual "energy," and it may express itself in human consciousness. There is no sharp distinction between spirit and matter.	God is best understood as cosmic, metaphysical energy—The Light. Consciousness is primary, creating physical reality and influencing it. There is no sharp distinction between spirit and matter.
Humanity is about to enter or has already entered a new era of human consciousness and cosmic transformation known as the Age of Aquarius. (For some, astrology is a reliable source of knowledge about the individual and the potential development of the era.)	We are entering the Age of Aquarius, otherwise known as the Messianic Age. (Kabbalistic astrology reveals truths about human souls and opportunities to connect to divinity.)

(Continued)

Table 3.1 (*Continued*)

New Age	Kabbalah Centre
Humanity progresses in self-understanding and in spiritual development. Reincarnation occurs, enabling the individual to progress through different lifetimes. (Some believe that unworthy people can be reincarnated at a lower level.)	Reincarnation is necessary for all but the most angelic men; female souls reincarnate voluntarily. The purpose is to progress spiritually, although regression occurs when people are unworthy.
There is a cosmic principle of balance and justice. This is "the law of karma." Everything good that happens to an individual is a reward for a previous good deed, and everything bad that happens is a punishment.	The principle of Bread of Shame has created a world in which "Cause and Effect" prevail for the sake of the individual's tikkun (repair).
Allegiance to the planet and to humanity supersedes loyalties to clan, nation, race, or region. Some call for a single "universal religion."	Kabbalah is universal wisdom. Its lessons are applicable to all human beings.

KABBALAH AND OTHER RELIGIONS

Berg could account for the similarity between New Age and Kabbalah Centre concepts by his fundamental conviction that Kabbalah is the source of *all* wisdom and religions. Kabbalah Centre teachers present their students with a simple history of world religions that makes sense of the confusing multitude of religious beliefs and affirms their wisdom in choosing Kabbalah. This historical narrative has been altered slightly over the years. The first version—both are presented here—was constructed when Berg addressed himself almost entirely to Jews, whereas the second version is the one used currently.

The First Historical Narrative

This history starts with the Creator who, being all sharing and loving, created human souls in order to share, and it is not his intention to abandon them in the difficult, physical world of the 1 percent with no guidelines. Kabbalah is the gift of wisdom provided by God to humans, instructing them how to receive Light. To the first human, Adam, and to select individuals such as the patriarchs, God imparted a measure of the wisdom necessary for fulfillment. Abraham the patriarch was particularly important in spreading divine wisdom; he traveled from Mesopotamia to Egypt, and he sent the teachings to the Far East. This accounts for the similarity between Kabbalah and the Eastern religions of Hinduism and Buddhism. However, human beings, trapped by their own Desire to Receive for the Self Alone, did not follow these prophets. Moses received the full measure of wisdom, recording only the surface level of the wisdom in the written words of the Torah. This wisdom would have perfected the Israelites' personal behavior and given them the spiritual tools to connect to the Light. By virtue of their actions, all of humanity would connect to the Light. Many of the Israelites strayed from the core principles of the Torah, and eventually, the true wisdom became unknown to all but a few special individuals in each generation.[20]

The full measure of wisdom was revealed by the prophet Elijah to the sage Shimon Bar Yohai, who lived in the second century C.E. and whose soul was the reincarnation of Moses. Shimon Bar Yohai wrote down the wisdom in the books that make up the Zohar. The leading sages and spiritual figures associated with Judaism possessed this knowledge and recorded it—in a veiled way—in Jewish books such as the Talmud, but over the centuries, knowledge of the Zohar diminished until Isaac Luria appeared in sixteenth-century Palestine. His soul ascended every night to the heavenly realm where it was instructed in the esoteric wisdom. His students recorded Luria's teachings, and important kabbalistic masters proclaimed that the Zohar and all the works of Kabbalah should be revealed to humanity. However, people were not capable of understanding Kabbalah. Finally, Yehuda Ashlag (a reincarnation of Luria) published a clear, concise explication of the Zohar. From this time onward, the Jews would be able to follow the Torah correctly; that is, they would understand that they needed to behave lovingly and generously to others, and they would perform the ritual commandments with the proper consciousness. The other nations of the world would have a better understanding of the universe and behave better as well. With this knowledge, humanity would be able to complete its long path of self-correction, bringing the era of universal peace known as redemption, the Messiah, or the Age of the Messiah.[21]

The Second Narrative

The second history is virtually the same as the first version, but it includes the formation of organized religions. It begins with the Creator giving the gift of wisdom—Kabbalah—to all humanity, although the locus of God's revelation was in the Land of Israel. The use of the word "karma" illustrates this point. Hebrew or Aramaic kabbalistic texts never used the term, which originated in Hinduism, but Kabbalah Centre teachers may use the term to explain Cause and Effect. The similarity between Cause and Effect and karma is a result of the latter's derivation from the former.

Most human beings could not accept Kabbalah because they were addicted to their Desires to Receive for the Self Alone. Had the Israelites followed Moses's guidance, they could have completely connected to the Light and ended the alienation between the entire physical and divine realm (this complete connection is called redemption, or the Messiah, or the Age of the Messiah). Resistance to Kabbalah resulted in it "going underground." Despite the general ignorance and evil, there were always great spiritual figures who understood kabbalistic principles. These Kabbalists, who moved from the Middle East to other parts of the world, spread the Light of the Creator to many. Unfortunately, their real messages were distorted and quickly turned into dogmatic belief systems—organized religions—focused on trivialities and divorced from the ideals of love for the Creator and all humanity. These Kabbalists' actual teachings and deeds were forgotten, and they were erroneously credited with establishing the world's organized religions. Nevertheless, within these religions, individuals did appear from time to time—usually the great mystics—who retrieved the pure elements from within the religion and presented them to their neighbors. There were others who searched for this divine wisdom—the search for the Holy Grail was an example of this—and some actually found it. Yet oftentimes, these individuals were feared and persecuted as heretics, or their words were misinterpreted so as to remove the true, pristine meanings, or their words were understood only on the shallowest of levels. Thus, kabbalistic teachings *can* be found in all religions. That is why people raised in other religions feel a vague sense of familiarity with the Kabbalah when they learn it. They realize that Kabbalah is an older, purer form of spirituality; it is not "religion," but it is also not always contradictory to certain elements in organized religions.

Judaism, like the other organized religions, originated far later than Kabbalah. Kabbalah preceded Judaism because Kabbalah was given by the Creator at the beginning of time. Judaism, like other organized religions, represents a narrower and corrupted form of Kabbalah. Yet of all religions, it has been the closest to Kabbalah because it includes the Torah and everything that flows from it: the mitzvot, prayers, and Hebrew language and the sacred literature. One can say that the structure of Judaism "housed" and "protected" Kabbalah and Kabbalists over the centuries when the world was so resistant to that wisdom. That is why kabbalistic teachings can be found in the books and traditions and behaviors valued by non-kabbalistic Jews. The latter are fiercely opposed to the Kabbalah Centre because they do not know the true history of Kabbalah and the real meaning of Torah. Kabbalah is a spiritual wisdom meant to teach all humanity to connect to the Light. When a critical mass of people connect to the Light, there will be no more boundaries between the physical world and the Creator; this is the Age of the Messiah.

These historical narratives are rarely presented in such a compact, summarized fashion. Kabbalah Centre lessons contain very little history. Most religions do not present themselves historically, probably because the subject seems extraneous to the issues at hand, and most people are bored and confused by a recitation of historical events. Whereas the earliest editions of *Kabbalah for the Layman* began with 20 pages describing the origins and history of Kabbalah, the major revision that appeared in 1991 considerably shortened this section and placed it at the end of the book. At the Los Angeles Centre there have been occasional special film-lectures illustrating the history of Kabbalah in accordance with the second version, but these have not yet been published or widely distributed.[22] People in the Kabbalah Centre are most likely to learn the history by asking a teacher in the course of classes or privately. They have, however, grasped the principle that Kabbalah is a universal spiritual wisdom that preceded all religions and are compatible with them.

Thus, although Berg teaches Kabbalah through New Age referents, he argues that the most accurate, complete, and original versions of the concepts are found in Kabbalah. The secrecy in which Kabbalah was veiled prevented the world from realizing this. Berg believes he does the world a service by revealing that which had been—wrongly, he claims—hidden away. This is a central theme of Berg's teachings, and it appears quite prominently in his discussions of reincarnation. *Wheels of a Soul*, Berg's book on reincarnation published in 1983, opens with a preface declaring the universal importance of knowledge of the Jewish view of reincarnation:

> Much has been written in recent years about reincarnation but little of it has been valid simply because the authors have not had access to Kabbalah, the ancient body of Jewish mystic wisdom in which an understanding of reincarnation—be it Eastern or Western in concept—is rooted.[23]

Through Berg's *Wheels of a Soul*, specifically Jewish teachings on reincarnation were added to the diverse mixture of religious traditions drawn on by New Agers and modern spiritual seekers. There is no evidence that the larger cohort of New Age and spiritual seekers accepted Berg's claim that the kabbalistic view of reincarnation is the most accurate and complete one, but people within the Kabbalah Centre community could feel that they were embracing the best available version of the belief. This is the Age of Aquarius, Berg writes, and it will also be an Age of Enlightenment when people learn about reincarnation: "What is needed today is a master key to unlock the apparent chaos and find order within it. Reincarnation stripped of superstition and half-truth, can be that key."[24]

REINCARNATION

Both Philip and Karen Berg have taken great interest in the subject of reincarnation and other topics that flow from it: marriage, divorce, and gender roles. These were all subjects that were—and still are—of great interest to their audience. Reincarnation is a particularly useful way to justify God in the face of the existence of evil, and in the Kabbalah Centre, it is linked with sexual relations, marriage, divorce, and gender roles. New religious move-ments tend to target their outreach efforts to people in the 20- to 45-year-old age range, for whom these issues are the most salient, and it is clear that this is the target audience of the Kabbalah Centre as well.

Yet teaching about reincarnation through kabbalistic sources presents dif-ficulties. *Gilgul*, reincarnation—sometimes translated as transmigration in ref-erence to its connection to the Hebrew word for wheel—does not appear in the Bible, and the Talmud does not endorse it. Reincarnation appeared in Jewish writings only sporadically before the sixteenth century, and so it is not widely mentioned in the Zohar, the chief book of Kabbalah that is the focus of so much Kabbalah Centre attention. However, soul transmigrations played a major role in the teachings of Isaac Luria. Berg's main source for knowledge of reincarnation is a book attributed to Luria and recorded by his students called *Sha'ar Ha-Gilgulim* (The Gates of Transmigrations). When Lurianic Kabbalah spread throughout Jewish settlements, belief in reincarnation spread as well. Whether its source was Kabbalah or another factor, reincarnation entered into Jewish popular belief and folklore in the early modern period.[25] Yet belief in reincarnation does not seem to have become deeply rooted among Jews in the West. It was abandoned or went underground, especially in European lands, as rationalism spread. Many Western Jews dismissed the idea as en-tirely foreign to Judaism. Even some modern Kabbalists such as Ashlag paid little attention to the subject, although Ashlag did claim that Luria's soul had entered his own and served as his guide. Berg, however, must have found no good reason to ignore a subject that seemed so essential to Kabbalah and that was of such intense interest to contemporary spiritual seekers.

The general purpose for reincarnation in Lurianic Kabbalah is that it oc-curs when a person has violated God's commandments; rather than descend to Gehinnom (Hell) for punishment, the soul is punished by being required to live again. In his writings, Berg focuses on reincarnation as a consequence of bad personal behavior outside of the realm of ritual such as murder, exces-sive anger, embezzlement, and bank robbery.[26] He also connects reincarna-tion to the three-column energy dynamic and the cosmogonic narrative:

> Each and every one of us is a communications system whose purpose is to draw metaphysical energy from the Creator, thereby fulfilling His desire to share. Like any system known to science and technology, we must complete our en-ergy circuit by means of a positive, negative and central column. It is that system that was lost to us in the endless world. The need to regain that system within our individual souls is what keeps us coming back to this earth plane again and again.[27]

One basic principle is that the number of chances granted to an individual soul is not specified, but a soul who is forced to return to earth three times without making progress undergoes "reversion to the abyss."[28] A soul that is particularly evil and has not exhausted its chances may be transmigrated into a beast, plant, or stone. The usual type of rebirth, however, is as another person. Reincarnation occurs differently for men and women. As a group, women completed their tikkun when, at Mount Sinai, Israelite women refused to engage in the idolatrous worship of the Golden Calf. This act of piety repaired the misdeed of Eve (and all female souls) at the time of the fall. Since their tikkun during the incident of the Golden Calf, women have returned to earth voluntarily. They may return in order to help their male soul mates complete their tikkun and thereby hasten their soulmate reunification on earth and after death in Paradise, or they may return for other reasons.[29]

Berg admits that an important function of reincarnation in Kabbalah is to account for the inequality of human beings in terms of their health, happiness, and success. From Kabbalah, the concept developed into the doctrine of karma found in Eastern religions. Berg cannot imagine how anyone can believe in the existence of a caring, loving God without the concept of reincarnation.[30] The truth is, Berg writes, God is not responsible for evil:

> The degree of evil and injustice abounding on this earth has nothing whatsoever to do with God. War, murder, violence, deceit and oppression are not the result of His will. Rather they are the result of millions of souls struggling to balance their karmic debt and failing.[31]

Birth defects, the death of a child, and the appearance of mental illness in a person may all be accounted for as the consequence of the behavior in its previous life:

> In all the universe there is no such thing as an accident. All misfortunes or "accidents" encountered in the present are but the logical outgrowth of some action in a past life or in the present one. Misfortune and illness are merely the effects of causative factors operating under the laws of *tikkun*.[32]

Positive events can also be explained as a result of reincarnation. One may benefit in this lifetime from a previous lifetime's good behavior that did not then receive its positive consequence. Or a person may benefit for the sake of tikkun, such as when a skilled surgeon is given his skills as an opportunity to redeem his past life behavior when he was a homicidal bank robber. The surgeon can really only advance his tikkun if he realizes that his skill is only a tool to benefit others and not a tool to enhance his ego and fame.[33]

Reincarnation can also explain a whole host of phenomena. Berg and Kabbalah Centre teachers have many anecdotes "proving" that the reincarnation of a particular soul can account for amazing coincidences, mind-boggling events, unexpected discoveries, and strange affinities. "Reincarnation is not a question of faith or doctrine, but of logic and reason," Berg writes. Reincarnation is simply the most reasonable explanation for many observed phenomena, including haunted houses and the feeling people have that a forest is "malevolent." Someday, Berg predicts, scientists will realize this.[34]

Although reincarnation is influential in shaping the present, Berg insists that it does not determine the future. A particular soul is put in place at birth, and the soul's proclivities and tikkun agenda will be part of the newborn. Yet free will is granted to human beings in order that they may shape their lives, and they may shape their future positively by applying the Rules of the Game of Life. Kabbalah Centre literature and classes since the mid-1990s have used the metaphor of a film script to describe this dynamic: each person is born with a life script, and Kabbalah enables a person to rewrite the script from this point forward. This outlook gives people much hope and a feeling of control over their lives. Knowledge of a person's past lives is very beneficial to this process. It gives a person information about what he or she may voluntarily do in a proactive manner in order to avoid a harsher tikkun for past behavior. In his writings, Berg describes how he discovers peoples' past lives through "logic and reason." Another method is "kabbalistic meditation," although he does not explain how this method of discovery works. Eventually, the Kabbalah Centre offered the service of a kabbalistic astrologer—trained by Berg—who could access some past life information for people to use for their tikkun.

REINCARNATION AND THE ETHIC OF MARRIAGE

Reincarnation is closely linked to marriage. Most marriages are difficult and unhappy, the rabbi observes, and ignorance of reincarnation is at the source of this sad situation. There is a basic problem of a bad "fit" of the male and female souls because of the reality that people rarely marry their soul mates. It could hardly be otherwise because marriages between soul mates occur only when the male soul has been transformed to a very high level (the last one prior to completion of a soul's tikkun), and that does not happen very often. Without knowledge of Kabbalah, such ascension is well-nigh impossible. A couple who is certain they are soul mates (this is the case for Philip and Karen Berg) can be quite pleased with themselves. In a rather transparent reference to himself and Karen, Berg explains that it is quite acceptable for a man to marry a divorcee or to find his soul mate only after his own troubled first marriage. The tikkun of a painful marriage helps the soul become elevated and merit its soul mate.[35] A teacher in the Centre informed me that, according to Berg, even when the female and male souls are not soul mates, if the wedding ceremony is performed properly with a supportive and joyous community in attendance, the couple can be "seamlessly" joined under the wedding canopy as if they are soul mates.[36]

Yet Kabbalah Centre teachers tell people not to hastily undergo divorce. They take a pragmatic attitude: "What's the point?" they say. "You're bound to marry the same type of person again and have the same problems"—unless, that is, you learn your tikkun lesson and really change first.[37] One teacher told me that people are too focused on finding their soul mates. She explained that it is difficult to know whether one has met one's soul mate; really, only a skilled Kabbalist like Philip Berg can know for sure. But it does not matter, she insists. People can have a happy, fulfilling relationship if they behave in accordance with kabbalistic principles.[38] Marriage difficulties are to be treated the same way as other life difficulties: a person must accept that these are the consequences of his or her past misdeeds. One is never the victim of one's spouse, but the opposite: the "victim" is the cause of the marital strife. The marital difficulty should be regarded as an opportunity sent by the Light to aid in transformation. For example, a man with a problem controlling his anger will be drawn toward a woman who provokes his weakness, thereby giving him ample opportunity to control himself and elevate his soul. "A successful marriage must rest upon an understanding of the reincarnation process," Berg writes, for in order for a marriage to succeed, a man has to understand "why he happens to be with the woman in his life." That is, the kabbalistic law of Cause and Effect teaches that he was attracted to her because she would help him repair aspects of his character and rectify problems remaining from his past lives. Knowing this will help him tolerate her criticisms, accept her guidance, and appreciate her.[39] If the situation simply cannot be tolerated any longer, it may be part of one's tikkun to press for divorce.

Working from first impressions, a person might deduce that the Kabbalah Centre wants men and women to treat each other equally. After all, the Kabbalah Centre is a place where women learn Kabbalah as well as men, Karen Berg is codirector, and Kabbalah is presented as universal wisdom that is free of the dogma and parochialism of organized religion. Indeed, a person who attends Kabbalah Centre classes and listens to the public lectures could easily conclude that men and women connect to spiritual light in an identical manner. For example, the "Twelve Steps to Everlasting Love" that I learned in the advanced Kabbalah class I attended did not differentiate between male and female obligations.[40] However, Kabbalah Centre prayer services, in which women and men are segregated and only men take leadership roles in the worship, indicate that the reality is more complex. Advanced and specialized women-only courses and literature—such as Karen Berg's lectures and her book *God Wears Lipstick: Kabbalah for Women*—teach that men and women have different and complementary roles. Egalitarian feminism, one soon learns, is considered misguided and a bit ridiculous.[41]

The Kabbalah Centre presents a fairly conservative view of gender roles in general and within marital relationships in particular. In the general teachings of the cosmogonic narrative, all human beings are essentially Desire to Receive, and the Light is Desire to Share. However, in the context of male–female relationships, the situation is more complex. People learn that men and women are essentially different, and their differences to some extent fit traditional stereotypes. The goal of life, which is to transform one's Desire to Receive for the Self Alone into a Desire to Receive for the Sake of Sharing, is ideally or best achieved by a man and woman united in marriage. Men are described as givers, as generators and sharers of Light, and as the embodiment of Desire to Share. Women are described as receivers, as vessels, and as the embodiment of Desire to Receive. It seems that men are like God, and women are quintessential humans. The couple, if they operate harmoniously, are compared to the three-column energy system: men are right-column energy, women are left-column energy, and they apply central-column energy of restriction in order to complete a circuit. If they are soul mates, it will be a perfect circuitry.[42]

Both men and women "restrict" their egos within the marital relationship, but in different ways. Both are taught to give to or serve their spouses without the expectation of receiving in return; if one gives with the expectation of receiving in return, this is not really sharing, and consequently, one will not find fulfillment. In the women-only classes, women are taught that a man's primary responsibility is to provide financially for the family, and women's primary task to create a home for a man and keep it clean, through either her own labor or hired help. The energy that is expended by the wife in keeping a clean home must be positive and loving because this energy passes through the home into their relationship. Another way a woman receives Light is by "manifesting" her male partner's energy; that is, she helps him reach his potential by recognizing his abilities and guiding him to reach that potential without his awareness of her designs.[43] It is in this latter role that Karen describes women as both receivers and givers:

> The Vessel, the female, is a creation that is a bit unbalanced. The woman has not just one aspect, receiving, but also sharing—two divergent aspects in the same person. If we want to understand why we may not feel equal to men, this is the reason. We are imbued with dual energy, and that is twice as much to handle....A man can say, "I go to work every day. That's what I know." But a woman must adapt to a multifaceted lifestyle. We have to juggle because we must create some kind of balance between sharing and receiving.[44]

Women are, indeed, superior to men. This status dates from the ancient period when Israelite women refused to participate in the idolatry of the Golden Calf and consequently no longer were required to undergo tikkun. This is how Karen states it:

> Women are born with tremendous spiritual power, whereas men must earn theirs. Indeed, *The Zohar* teaches us that the least spiritual woman on earth still has the potential to be the greatest psychic, which means she has the ability to see beyond the limitations of her senses. God, indeed, does wear lipstick.[45]

In contrast to the complicated composition of women, men are rather simple. According to Kabbalah Centre teachings, men want to master the world and exercise power. Their self-esteem depends on their sense of themselves as powerful and capable of doing manly tasks such as governing, leading, protecting, building, performing tasks that require physical strength and agility, and so on. Yet they are incapable of fulfilling their ideals unless they are guided by women. Indeed, every female soul takes upon herself some of the tikkun of her male soul mate; it becomes her obligation to help him complete his tikkun. Men do not have a reciprocal responsibility toward their female soul mates.[46]

Karen and Philip Berg refer to this model when they describe their joint work in the Kabbalah Centre. Philip reveals Light through his study of Kabbalah, and Karen "manifests" it. According to Kabbalah Centre history, when Karen and the rabbi were first married, he spent all day shut up in a room with a group of men studying Kabbalah together. When she asked him what Kabbalah was about, and he told her, "It is about sharing," she informed him that his method of teaching was not the way to share. She advised him to teach Kabbalah to all men, women, and children. According to Philip's retelling of the story, he refused to believe her until Rabbi Brandwein appeared to him in a dream: "'Listen to Karen,' he said to me. 'Listen to Karen, for she is a reincarnation of——.'"[47] Because Philip accepted her advice then and thereafter, the Kabbalah Centre opened its doors to all and took the steps that have led to its phenomenal growth.

This productive male–female dynamic requires much subtlety, however. In the women-only settings, women are told not to flaunt their innate sense of how to produce good results. They are most effective at directing men's behavior when they appear to be deferring to them. Women are advised to pretend incompetence, to refuse to be self-sufficient, and to avoid careers or other activities that put them in a competitive or superior role in relation to men. Although a woman may work outside the family, she must be careful to do this in a way that does not threaten her husband's self-esteem and role as family provider, and her primary responsibility is taking care of him and their children. Paradoxically, this ethic promises that women will achieve spiritual liberation by being economically and socially dependent on men. If this bothers them, they can console themselves by realizing that they are superior and that these methods will achieve their goals. One woman at the Centre admitted to me that when she was younger, she felt she would not be honest if she acted that way toward her husband. But now, "I am older and have more experience. Now I feel you have to speak to someone on their level. You wouldn't speak to a child in the same way that you'd speak to an adult, right?"[48]

This outlook allows women and men to reject egalitarian feminism without overtly insulting women's capabilities and diminishing their value. It frees women who so desire from the obligation of achieving the feminist ideal of superwoman, and it honors the choices of men and women who are drawn to the "traditional" familial roles. The Kabbalah Centre is by no means unique in advocating such an ideology; it is found in other groups that have retained traditional gender roles but absorbed certain lessons of feminism. Since the 1980s, for example, this has been the predominant mode of explaining gender differences in Modern Orthodox Judaism and Habad Hasidism, and it is likely that Karen derived it from there.[49] The Kabbalah Centre's approach differs from these other Jewish approaches by applying it to all—not only Jewish—couples and including in it principles of reincarnation.

Reincarnation is also a factor in the couple's sex life. According to Philip Berg's understanding of Kabbalah, the process of reproduction and birth is designed to furnish a soul with a body that "will conform to the behavior of that soul as it existed in a prior lifetime." The consciousness of the father and mother at the time of conception—that is, while they are in the midst of the sex act that leads to conception—determines which soul is reborn into the child that they are creating. When conception occurs in anger, it attracts an angry soul; when it occurs in a lustful passion, it attracts a soul who has left a lust-filled life; and so on. The reason for this is because a soul needs to spend the lifetime "correcting" for the "uncorrected" life that it left behind. "Those who know nothing of Kabbalah or who dismiss reincarnation gamble with their very lives in the act of procreation," Berg writes.[50] He illustrates this point with an example of a couple whose baby was born with a defect in the right side of his neck. When the father asked Berg to discover the cause of the defect, Berg learned that the couple had given their baby a name similar to the father's sister. The sister had been murdered by a bullet wound on the right side of her neck. Clearly, the man had been thinking of his sister's murder at the time of conception. This all could have been prevented if the couple "had been able to understand and apply the principles of reincarnation when the child was conceived."[51] Not everybody who understands these principles can actually apply them during the sex act, Berg acknowledges. Soul mates, however, "are so happy in each other's company that no thought less than the most benign could intrude upon the act of making love."[52]

HOMOSEXUALITY

Given the Kabbalah Centre's conservative approach and dependence on seventeenth-century writings for its teachings on gender and marriage, the organization's tolerance toward homosexuality is quite striking. Jewish tradition, Kabbalah included, frowns on sexual relations between males. Luria's *Sha'ar Ha-Gilgulim* teaches that for this sin, the male will be reborn in his next lifetime into a female body. Such a mixed-up female will not be matched with a soul mate and will be infertile; only through great piety may she (he) merit the assistance of another woman's soul "impregnating" her (his) soul and thereby enabling her (him) to give birth—but only female babies are possible. This is just one example of the many teachings that warn against succumbing to homosexual impulses; there are many others that counsel men who have engaged in homosexual sex to enact rites of penitence lest they suffer severe punishment in their current lives and after death.[53] Whereas Berg paraphrased this text in *Wheels of a Soul* in 1984, by the late 1990s, it was removed from the curriculum.

Kabbalah Centre teachers respond very carefully to questions about homosexuality. The following question was posed to Michael Berg on his Web site: "How does Kabbalah look at homosexuality? Do they draw a distinction between homosexual desire and homosexual actions? Can one be a queer Kabbalist without contradicting themselves?" Michael's answer is a model of diplomacy:

> While Kabbalah and its cardinal text, the *Zohar*, has little to say about homosexuality, it is a main focus of The Kabbalah Centre and Kabbalah in general to stay away from judging others for any reason, external or internal, physical or metaphysical. Kabbalah also explains that the most sharing act we can achieve on this planet is childbirth, which is unattainable between two members of the same sex alone. However, that is not to say that two same-gendered people cannot have the same or more loving, rewarding, and lasting relationships as heterosexual couples. Kabbalah is all-inclusive rather than exclusive, and I hope you feel comfortable continuing your study.[54]

"We have to deal with the subject of homosexuality very subtly," I was told by a Kabbalah Centre teacher. Yes, he admitted, the Kabbalah teaches that homosexual behavior is a sin, but, he continued,

> Why be cruel to people? Why insult them? It is not politically correct. This is 2006. Should we tell people who are 40 or 50, who've never married and do not have children, that they should have acted differently? Of course not! Not everybody does everything according to all the rules, so should we drive them out? There are people in the Centre who take drugs, who gamble, who steal, who cheat on their spouses—why would we want to drive them out? They are here and we want them to learn what we have to teach. Who knows? After learning from us, after experiencing the Light, they may change.[55]

And indeed, the teacher personally knew two gay men who, after a few years at the Kabbalah Centre, became heterosexual. They found wives and had children. Still, he knows that does not always happen. The Kabbalah Centre's mission of outreach is of paramount importance, superseding its commitment to teach unvarnished Kabbalah.

Consequently, there are gay people and couples who have found their spiritual home in the Kabbalah Centre community. One of the participants that I interviewed, who happened to be gay, described his experience in the Los Angeles Centre.[56] Jonathan told me that he is not interested in theoretical issues such as whether a gay man has a female soul. He has learned, however, that gayness is not an indelible part of a person's soul; the soul can be born into a heterosexual in one lifetime and reincarnate as gay because of the tikkun that it needs to make. (Jonathan has had an astrological reading and has learned about his own past lives when he was not gay.) Although he serves as a mentor for beginning Kabbalah students, he is unaware of the kabbalistic teachings that regard homosexual behavior as a sin. His knowledge of Kabbalah is based only on what he has been taught at the Centre, and he has found that it affirms his individuality and worth. Jonathan illustrated this with an experience that occurred when he first began to study at the Centre. A woman made advances to him, and he let her know that he was gay and not interested in her. She responded, "You can change yourself! Kabbalah is about transformation, and you should make that change." Jonathan asked two teachers, separately, if this is what Kabbalah demanded. Both were emphatic in dismissing the woman's opinion as a reaction to her own ego needs and Desire to Receive. They told Jonathan that he must accept who he is and not try to change in that way. He has since learned that this is how all the teachers talk about the subject, and so he attributes the few unpleasant comments he has received to the people who have made them, not to Kabbalah. He believes the tolerant atmosphere is also fostered by the kabbalistic teaching that those who are judgmental will have the judgment come back to them (this is Rule Number Twelve). He attests that gay and lesbian couples feel safe at the Los Angeles Kabbalah Centre in Los Angeles, and probably in other Centres.

Since that initial incident, Jonathan has learned that Kabbalah Centre teachers do understand that being gay is a tikkun. To him this means that it is a challenge put before you in this life that you need to cope with, like having a physical handicap; that is, it is less than ideal, but it cannot be changed. This assessment does not offend him. Anyone who is gay recognizes that being gay is a challenge, Jonathan told me, because it is hard to find lasting and good relationships. "Will you find your soul mate?" I asked him. Jonathan has heard conflicting answers to this. He has learned that because of his gayness, he will not be with his soul mate in this lifetime—unless, as Karen Berg has taught, the soul of one of the males in a gay couple is actually female. Still, gay and lesbian relationships can be loving and satisfying, especially when the couple lives in accordance with kabbalistic principles. Being involved with Kabbalah will increase the likelihood that you will find a good match, he thinks. Kabbalah helps a person transform into a giving person, and such people are attractive and draw others toward them.

ASTROLOGY AND KABBALAH

Consciousness shapes reality, according to Kabbalah Centre teachings, but so do the celestial bodies. Astrology is very important in Berg's Kabbalah, and astrological symbols and influences are given prominence in all Kabbalah Centre events. To many, this immediately identifies the Kabbalah Centre as a New Age movement.

The first expressions of New Age spirituality affirmed the astrological belief that the world was passing from one astrological age to a new one. An astrological age is defined by the constellation in which the sun appears at the vernal equinox. For the last 2,000 years, the sun has been passing through the zodiac of Pisces, and the next constellation is Aquarius. There is little agreement about when the Age of Aquarius begins; the dates have ranged from 1781 to 3000. New Agers explained that the character of the Age of Pisces was indicated by its symbol, the fish: people were dominated by Christianity, and like fish, they were mute and dull, and they passively followed their leaders. The Age of Aquarius, they promised, would be liberating and harmonious. People would become independent, strong, and intelligent. Aside from this use of astrology, New Agers modified Western astrology by making it less determinative for the individual. A key principle of New Age was the belief that humans have unlimited potential, and so astrology was regarded not as an instrument for ascertaining one's future, but as an indicator of one's inborn traits. An astrological reading was a guide to the individual's psychological makeup, a starting point for one's life (or multiple lives) journey. When the New Age movement in a strict sense evolved into a large network of diverse spiritual seekers by the 1980s, astrology became one element that was not held in common, and some dismissed it outright as a baseless superstition.[57]

Belief in astrology can be found in the Jewish tradition. Talmudic sages believed in the power of the stars and planets over human affairs, and in the medieval era, philosophers and exegetes expanded Jewish astrological teachings. Some authorities emphatically regarded astrology as nonsense and idol worship, but they seem to have been a minority. The kabbalistic book *Sefer Ha-Yetzirah* and the Zohar take the truth of astrology for granted, as do later Kabbalistic works. The 12 houses of the zodiac are identified with the 12 tribes of Israel, the 12 lunar months of the Jewish religious calendar, and 12 permutations of the Divine Name; the 7 celestial bodies (sun, moon, Mercury, Venus, Mars, Saturn, and Jupiter are the only ones with influence) are linked to the 7 days of the week, and there were other connections as well. Yet a persistently recurring opinion was that the impact of celestial bodies on Jews was different than on the other nations of the world. One version of this opinion is that God limited the power of stars and planets over the Jews because of their observance of the Torah laws. Another understanding is that God alters the conventional astrological laws for the Jews, or God specially constructed them for their sake. Kabbalistic writings endorse the conviction that the study of Kabbalah and performance of the mitzvot mitigate the power of the planets and stars. Nevertheless, Kabbalists generally regarded the celestial bodies as force to be reckoned with and to be taken into consideration when engaging in certain activities.[58]

Despite astrology's appearance in Jewish tradition, Berg was undeniably influenced by New Age astrology. Neither Ashlag nor Brandwein had paid much attention to astrology, and Berg had to independently find kabbalistic sources for it. It is likely that this search brought him to the New Age and Theosophical publications whose ideas and phrases are evident in his writings.[59] Putting Kabbalah in astrological terms had the effect of moving it beyond its narrow confines in the Jewish community and making it more universal. Through astrology Berg developed his fervent conviction that Kabbalah contains within it the most advanced scientific knowledge and is the authoritative guide to the mysteries of the universe. Kabbalistic astrology explains seemingly random events as the result of age-old universal laws, and it also teaches how one's consciousness can lessen the power of these laws. This, to Berg, has the rigor and authority of science. It has succeeded where conventional science fails: Kabbalah—and this includes kabbalistic astrology—gives certain knowledge of the past and effective means of improving the future. Kabbalah is the *best* science, the most advanced technology. It is a most distinctive feature of New Age to conflate science and religion and to insist that one's faith is not faith at all, but pure science.

Similar to New Age, Berg uses astrology to indicate the potential of an era or shorter units in a calendar. The late twentieth-century interest in Kabbalah and the revelation of its esoteric doctrines is connected to the astrological era. Berg explained the origin of all the Jewish holidays as being the dates when, because of the astrological forces dominant at that time, certain metaphysical energies could be accessed the best, or certain human traits could be adjusted.[60] He did this even for holidays connected to historical events. For example, in the Jewish calendar, there is a three-week period of semi-mourning in which one limits intake of certain foods, avoids the beginning of new projects, and does not schedule celebrations. Virtually all sources, including kabbalistic ones, connect this somber interval to the three weeks leading up to the destruction of the Jerusalem Temple on the ninth of Av; tragic biblical events such as the idolatry of the Golden Calf and the betrayal of the Israelite spies are also said to have occurred then. The Kabbalah Centre, however, explains the three weeks as a period of danger because the position of the planets during Cancer and Leo make human affairs highly vulnerable to disruption. The previously mentioned events in the history of the Jewish people are merely exemplary effects of a universal problem that affects all people throughout the world during these weeks. Every human being can avoid difficulty by reciting the prescribed meditations and by following the prescribed restrictions of these three weeks.[61] For those who want astrological guidance throughout the year, a kabbalistic calendar is available that specifies the capacity of every month, week, and day for the harnessing of spiritual energy and the advisability of restrictive and proactive behavior.[62]

Astrology is also a tool enabling the individual to better accomplish tikkun. A kabbalistic astrology reading of the position of the planets and stars at one's birth will generate an accurate assessment of a person's character, weaknesses, strengths, and life path. The thoughts of the parents at the time of conception produce an embryo into which a certain type of soul will be born, and the position of the stars and planets are an additional shaping force. Similar to New Age astrology, the astrology of the Kabbalah Centre is not fully determinative; a person can freely decide to change his or her behavior, and every change will affect other aspects of the person's life.[63] The astrologer can read how far one has progressed from the birth forces, and indeed, it is advisable to get a reading every year in order to learn how to best utilize the celestial forces to advance one's life purpose. Unique to kabbalistic astrology is the evidence found in the natal chart for past lives.

For my session with the kabbalistic astrologer, I submitted in advance the place, date, time, and hour of my birth and my parents' birth dates. She correlated the information to the Jewish lunar calendar date and identified the latitude and longitude. The astrologer generated a natal chart—with the aid of a special computer software program—containing a great deal of information, and kabbalistic astrological writings guided the astrologer in interpreting the data. Luria's *Sha'ar Ha-Gilgulim* was laid open on the table next to the charts—not to be consulted by the astrologer, but "just to aid the process." She told me about my inherited traits and present behavior with regard to love, career, spending patterns, friends, health, interaction with the larger world, and so on. I was advised which of my inborn traits need to be curbed and which need to be activated more fully. I learned about three of my past lives. In one I lived in South America and was, in all likelihood, a poet who explored spiritual matters. I was told that my soul is the type that rebels against unjust authority, and in two of my past lives, I took a public role in assisting people who were vulnerable to such abuse. Although this behavior led to my death at a young age in one life and to my being born into a male body in another life, it is for these virtuous and important deeds that my soul has been sent to earth repeatedly. The astrologist informed me that according to her reading of my current chart, I am not fulfilling my soul's purpose; I am too studious and retiring. She advised me to find opportunities for greater leadership in my career or community. I know from my studies of the kabbalistic principles of the Centre—the astrologer was too gentle to tell me this—that according to Kabbalah, if I do not voluntarily channel my energies in this direction, I will endure suffering that provokes me to leadership, or I will simply suffer. In addition, she told me that in my household there is currently a "leakage" of money, and she warned me to check into this and make sure money is no longer wasted. "Why does the Light care?" I asked. She reminded me that the Light is the source of the money we earn, and if it is being squandered, the Light will no longer give.[64] The session ended with the instruction that I should listen to the audio recording of my session, take notes on it, incorporate the suggestions into my life, and utilize the spiritual tools taught at the Centre to assist me in improving my life.

FAITH AND SCIENCE

Why should anyone believe that something called Kabbalah contains all this terrific information or that these objects or behaviors will lead to the fulfillment and success that they promise? On one level, it is a simple matter of faith. People who bother to walk in the doors of a Kabbalah Centre, pay for a series of classes, and attend them to the end, or people who pay for and complete the online classes, at some point choose to believe in the divine source of the Kabbalah and the version of it that is taught by Kabbalah Centre teachers.

Yet at the Kabbalah Centre, "faith," like "belief," is not an ideal. The first rule in the 12 Rules of Life is to *not* accept Kabbalah on faith. "Don't believe me—decide for yourself" and "Try it out and see for yourself if it works" are frequent refrains in the courses. The Kabbalah Centre leadership trains teachers and mentors not to be aggressive or pressuring. The most cutting response I received to my skeptical queries was "I guess this is not for you. You're happy in the 1 percent world." Of course, to people who are emotionally vulnerable, the strong, absolute certainty of Kabbalah Centre long-timers can be quite pressuring. There are many people who walk around testifying to the amazing results they have gotten from kabbalistic principles and practices, or who readily talk about the miracles that occurred to others. A board member admitted that he thinks this may become distorted and turn into a kind of "idolatry":

> We tell people, "Find out for yourselves. Don't trust our words." We have our stories, our miracles that we tell people, but no one has to believe them. And if you come in because of the miracle stories, *that's* a problem—you should not be trusting someone else's words for it. You have to know yourself.[65]

In short, the rituals and meditations will not be effective unless there is certainty, and you should not be doing them unless you have certainty. Being certain means that you are practicing not out of a Desire to Receive, but out of a certain conviction and a pure motive that the practices are connecting you to the Creator. Those who do not believe and do not want to be persuaded leave the Centre. To my knowledge and in my experience, there is no "retention policy" of pursuing, threatening, or denouncing people who stop attending the Centre.

Certainty is a concept that is very important in the Kabbalah Centre. At first, when the newcomer tries scanning the Zohar (gazing at its letters, a ritual discussed in the next chapter) in order to receive an infusion of Light, there is a leap of faith. Simone described how, initially, she would look at the Zohar and say, "What am I doing?? This is a book!" But then she would say, "That's the point—it looks like a book, it *is* a book, but it is a tool to connect." She became convinced that the scanning made a difference. Alex admitted that at the beginning it was difficult. "But you say, 'Well, let me try this.' And every time I did it, I had a much better day. I felt better!"[66] For the teachers and students at the Kabbalah Centre, the most convincing proof is personal experience. They are not seeking carefully controlled and thoughtfully interpreted experiments whose conclusions meet the critical scrutiny of the scientific community.

Yet Philip Berg has always been deeply convinced that what he has discovered is scientifically valid, and he has passed this conviction on to his sons, teachers, and followers. From his earliest writings, he explained that the Zohar and other kabbalistic writings constitute the most complete scientific textbook in existence, containing the information necessary for understanding the root causes for the functioning of the physical world. The claim that Kabbalah is perfected science is not new. Medieval Kabbalists were convinced that Kabbalah anticipated and surpassed science in its apprehension of reality, and the modern Kabbalists from whom Berg drew his knowledge of Kabbalah— Yehuda Ashlag, Yehuda Brandwein, Levi Krakovsky—said the same.[67] Berg was following an old kabbalistic tradition when he claimed that Kabbalah was equivalent to science, but he seems to be outstanding among twentieth- and twenty-first-century Jewish religious leaders in developing this theme.

Berg's books are filled with scientific references, but the most obvious one is the use of atomic theory to explain the basic dynamic of the spiritual realm. He points out that the basic unit of all physical reality is an atom consisting of positively charged protons, negatively charged electrons, and neutral neutrons. At the quantum level, mass is interchangeable with energy. Berg makes a leap of faith in declaring that all of physical reality is energy that is imbued with divine intelligence, and all physical things are the surface manifestations of the hidden realm of the divine sefirot. The positive, negative, and neutral components of the atom are a physical manifestation of the three-column energy system of the sefirot. The differentiation in appearance, strength, and other features of physical reality are merely variations in the amount and intensity of divine energy received. Divine energy can be activated by the meditations, rituals, and restrictions recommended in the Torah.

Although the scientific theme in Berg's writings owes much to kabbalistic teachings, his use of scientific language in his writings and in Kabbalah Centre curriculum fits the pattern followed by contemporary religious leaders. Religions in the twentieth and twenty-first century are under considerable pressure to seek some rapprochement with science. They would rather not take an explicit stance against science because that would throw them into the so-called "fundamentalist" camp and alienate them from the modern people they want to attract.[68] The influence of New Age "scientific" teachings are especially obvious in the Kabbalah Centre. Berg included them in his writings in the 1980s, and the teachers present them in their classes and lectures. Modern scientific developments are interpreted to affirm a religious worldview, but they are also presented so as to discredit the existing scientific consensus and lead to a turn to kabbalistic concepts for authority.[69]

The way this conclusion is reached follows a well-established New Age discursive pattern. It begins with a description of the now-discarded assumptions of Newtonian physics that the universe is an enormous mechanical system that runs according to exact laws in which time and space are absolute and distinct. It then moves on to the revolutionary advances of early twentieth-century physicists: Albert Einstein, Max Planck, Neils Bohr, Werner Heisenberg, and others. The teachers explain that Einstein's theory of relativity destroyed Newton's worldview because he found that time and space are not absolute and distinct, and neither are matter and energy. They then turn to quantum mechanics, in which physicists showed that subatomic elements act unpredictably and that the subatomic realm cannot be measured and charted exactly. The very act of observing prevents an accurate measurement of the object observed and interjects an element of subjectivity into the results. At this point, Kabbalah Centre teachers point out that the best scientists learned that they cannot trust their senses in assessing reality, and neither should we. For example, to a person who argues against reincarnation because he cannot see a soul being transferred from one person into another, Kabbalah Centre teachers respond, "Science has shown that you cannot trust the five senses." To someone who maintains that there is such a thing as objective reality, they respond that objectivity is a man-made construct, and we discern with our senses only the 1 percent world.[70]

Like many New Age spiritual teachers, Berg knows that it is more convincing to use scientific-like reasoning to arrive at these beliefs. New Age writers like to quote physicists who have reflected on twentieth-century research to posit a new approach to the physical world. The physicist David Bohm is often cited because he suggested that we need to view the universe as an undivided whole that is kept intact in a flowing, dynamic movement. And what keeps this holistic universe together? New Agers conclude that it is a sacred force immanent within all the cosmos. They also conclude from the new physics that ultimate reality is mind or consciousness, and this contains the divinity that flows through the cosmos. Berg arrives at the same conclusions. He claims that the leading scientists have arrived at a *kabbalistic view* of the universe in that it is sustained and guided by an underlying consciousness. He explains that quantum theory "provided impressive scientific evidence…that consciousness plays an essential, if not deciding role in the nature of physical reality."[71] Or,

> The new age of physics tells us that particles or mass as such does not exist. Rather everything in the universe is energy. Things that we observe are really only mental structures and have form only so long as they are observed as such…. We discover that the closer we examine energy, the more easily it disappears into consciousness.[72]

In short, twentieth-century discoveries brought science in line with Kabbalah. Human beings, on their own, arrived finally to the truths that were present in kabbalistic writings thousands of years ago. It is *because* of the scientific advances that Kabbalah can be taught to the intellectuals at this time; they had been resistant before because they felt that Kabbalah went beyond the scope of science. The nonscientists have been brought to the Kabbalah because they have been affected by the spiritual awakening of this Age of Aquarius. They too benefit from this scientific age, in that it enables them to understand far more Kabbalah than people in the past: "Only when knowledge of electricity, basic physics and even the general principles of quantum mechanics were in possession of the average person could Kabbalah be taught in any span of time shorter than a lifetime," Berg wrote.[73] They can easily understand kabbalistic principles such as the three-column energy system, the effect of consciousness (i.e., Desire to Receive or Desire to Share) on the physical world, and so on. "Science Catches Up with Kabbalah" is the title of one of the chapters in Yehuda Berg's *The Power of Kabbalah*, his 2004 summary of his father's teachings. There one hears repeatedly statements such as "Two thousand years after the ancient Kabbalists revealed that…, physicists arrive at the same conclusions."[74]

Yet clearly not all scientists agree with Kabbalah Centre judgments; only those whom Berg considers at "the leading edge" really understand. This recognition produces an expression of frustration that there is still strong resistance on the part of scientists. Berg laments the loss this represents to the advancement of knowledge:

> Were the scientific communities amenable to accepting the hypothesis that terrestrial activity is subject to celestial cosmic influence, as so clearly stated in the Zohar, much of scientific data, now shrouded in mystery, might just open up endless new frontiers in nature never before imagined.[75]

The references to science were significantly reduced in the books from the 1990s and later, but the scientific basis of Kabbalah is still a major theme in the Centre's teaching. Philip Berg is still the source within the Kabbalah Centre of this intense belief in the power of Kabbalah to achieve wonders. His book *Immortality* seeks to prove that a new era of human history began in 2000 in which aging could be reversed and physical immortality could be within reach with the application of the right kind of consciousness.[76] During Kabbalah Centre Connections, during the shouted Kaddish prayer, cries of "Immortality!" (*Lichiyot la-netzach*) resounded throughout the synagogue. When Philip suffered a stroke prior to Rosh Hashanah 2004, and it was not clear how well he would recover, many were taken aback, and some left the Centre altogether. By spring of 2006, it was being said that his recovery was phenomenal and miraculous, and filmed testimony of a neurologist that affirmed this was broadcast in the Centre community. The next generation in the Berg family, however, is assuming leadership. The sons are not as focused on Kabbalah as a vehicle for science. "Immortality!" has given way to shouts of "Unconditional love!" (*Ahavat chinam*).

CHAPTER 4

———— ❄ ————

The Spiritual Tools and Who
Gets to Use Them

The principles and concepts described thus far provide an outlook on life and death, a method for interacting with others, and a guide to the calendar that indicates the type of consciousness and behavior that will be the most successful on a given day. There are people who make use of the Kabbalah Centre to provide this type of enlightenment. They may occasionally attend Centre events, but unless they attend frequently enough to learn how to participate and make friends, they remain at the margins of the community, and the Kabbalah Centre doctrines are at the margins of their religious lives.

People who are strongly attracted to the doctrines, practices, and people at the Centre, however, quickly accept the advice that *real* transformation of their souls and *significant* success in connecting to spiritual light require the assistance of spiritual tools. This is the term for the rituals, prayers, ceremonies, and other practices that have the extraordinary power of bringing the energy of the Light into their very bodies and souls. They are taught that these tools, in the short run, accelerate the process of transformation and bring calm and joy and contentment; in the long run, they make the contented, joyous feelings a permanent part of life, and they help the individual achieve tikkun.

The tremendous variety of spiritual tools advocated by the Kabbalah Centre can be explained by the organization's evolution and complexity: the Kabbalah Centre began as a sect of Judaism that tolerated a wide range of commitment within it, and years later, Kabbalah Centre directors fostered alongside, and in support of, the core community a much broader, universal religious movement. When Berg began to teach and attract disciples, he was constructing a kabbalistic Judaism for Jews. The rituals, prayers, ceremonies, and other prescribed spiritual activities were much the same as those in non-kabbalistic Judaism; added to these were practices that were taken directly or derived from kabbalistic teachings. At that time and today as well, these behaviors would have been and still are regarded by other Orthodox Jews as having a long and legitimate history within Judaism—they are the mitzvot, the commandments of the Torah. When the Kabbalah Centre directors altered their mission in the 1990s with the goal to reach and persuade the multitudes—non-Jews—to join them, the intricate and demanding religious practices posed a daunting challenge. In the previous chapter, I showed how Berg's fundamental principle of noncoercive spirituality attracted people who wanted the freedom to choose the intensity and extent of ritual performance. Removing the element of compulsion and obligation made the Kabbalah Centre's spiritual practice more attractive, but that flexibility was not sufficient for building a mass movement. It was unreasonable to expect everyone to accept a spiritual discipline that included the dietary limitations of *kashrut*, a dress code, work prohibitions on Sabbath and on the many holidays, and restrictions on marital sexual relations, among other prohibitions. Consequently, when Kabbalah Centre directors expanded their outreach effort in the 1990s, they created new spiritual tools that were easier, less time-consuming, and less restrictive and that did not require specialized knowledge (these tools were not entirely unprecedented in Jewish tradition). The most important of these was scanning—that is, gazing at the Hebrew letters of the Zohar and divine names. The practice of wearing a red string tied around the wrist began to be widely advocated, as well as drinking special "Kabbalah water." Another spiritual tool—this had deeper roots in the Jewish tradition—is the recitation of the prayer *Ana Bekoach*. These four spiritual tools are common to virtually all participants in the Centre. A much smaller cohort practices the mitzvot as well.

Although the Kabbalah Centre rejects an ethnic understanding of Jewishness in favor of universalism, it does not mean the end of Jewishness, nor does it end categories of difference within the community or within humanity. This is because a kabbalistic Judaism was the starting point and remains important at the center of the Kabbalah Centre movement, and the texts affirmed as authoritative and sacred by the Kabbalah Centre affirm—certainly in their literal meaning and in the interpretive tradition—distinctions between Jews and the rest of humanity. Reading these texts and applying them to people's lives has not meant denying differentness, but reinterpreting it or applying it in a different way.

This chapter's explanation of the spiritual tools, then, is linked together with the themes of ethnicity, religious background, and conversion.

JEWS AND THE MITZVOT

When Berg first explained the way to receive divine Light, he showed that the repair of the entire world was in the hands of Jews when they lived in accordance with the Torah. (Torah, for Berg, means the Torah in accordance with a kabbalistic understanding.) According to Jewish teachings, humanity is divided into two groups: the Jewish nation and all the other nations—70, according to the Jewish tradition. Most Jewish religious authorities date the beginning of the distinction with the biblical figure of Abraham, who was chosen by God to be the father of a great nation. Kabbalistic writings uniformly regard distinctions within humanity as beginning prior to the creation of the physical world. Berg, following Ashlag, taught that the fundamental characteristics of each nation were already present before they descended into physical bodies. Jewish souls are distinctive because they are endowed with larger Desires to Receive, "the most powerful of any nation."[1] The strength of their Desires to Receive explains what to Berg is the notable Jewish record for creativity, ambition, power, scientific achievement, and so on. Berg learned this from his teacher Brandwein, who he recalled telling him,

> The claim of Jew-haters—that Jews want to rule the world—is actually true, in that Jews' spiritual vessel and light has great capacity to influence others and to give abundance, order, and certainty to the rest of humanity.[2]

The size of the Jewish nation's Desire to Receive also explains their notable record of suffering and persecution:

> Through his limitless Desire to Receive he can create potent forces of negative energy, causing the Creator to turn his face away from the Jewish people as a father chastises his favourite son. If these negative energies created by the imbalance of the Desire to Receive are allowed to build up, the Angel of Death is given access to the Jews, and his power reigns over them until they eliminate the negativity by balancing the Desire to Receive with one of Imparting.[3]

In other words, Jewish persecution occurs when the Jews are receiving without giving. Giving, for the Jews, consists of connecting to God through the precepts of the Torah. The Jewish souls prior to their birth know this, but once they are born, they are enmeshed in the force of the evil inclination and the kelippot and forget. The imbalance in the divine realm produced Bread of Shame, causing the vessels to turn off the light; likewise, in the lower realm, an imbalance causes a restriction. The Light ceases to reach the Jews, and so they are subject to discrimination, violence, hatred, and expulsions. Ultimately, they are responsible for the troubles they experience. This applies to the Holocaust as well.[4]

Although Jewish religious literature teaches that God sends hardship upon the Jewish people when they neglect the mitzvot, Berg's explanation is extraordinarily harsh, and it may seem to absolve the persecutors of their crimes. His explanation for anti-Semitism, which is echoed by Kabbalah

Centre teachers, is out of step with contemporary, rational views of history and finds little support in the Jewish community. Yet it is consistent with the doctrine of Cause and Effect, and Jewish participants at the Centre do not take offense from it. They understand that the perpetrators of evil are not blameless, and they are subject to the laws of Cause and Effect as well; they will face the negative consequences of their deeds in their present life or in later ones. Most contemporary American Jews do not take responsibility for what happens to them, complained a Jewish man who attends the Kabbalah Centre. "In the synagogue I used to attend," he told me, "peoples' explanations were invariably about how Jews had been victims and scapegoats. Again, no understanding of cause and effect, no taking responsibility." But at the Kabbalah Centre, he continued, the story of the Israelites' slavery in Egypt is

> not taken literally, and that's a good thing, because I really don't believe that there was a sea that split and the Jews walked through on dry land. The story of slavery is not about being victims, because people are not victims; the slavery is explained as a time when there were choices.[5]

If the stories are regarded as real events with the Jews as victims, there is no incentive to change. Consequently, anti-Semitism remains. The lesson is that Jews need to learn that God has a special relationship to them in terms of his beneficence, in that they will receive more; but they have a special relationship to him in terms of giving, and they must give abundantly.

The Jews' lot is to follow the mitzvot, the commandments of the Torah. According to Jewish tradition, there are 613 commandments. Following the teachings of Yehuda Ashlag, the Kabbalah Centre teaches that the most important of the commandments is "Love thy neighbor as thyself," and indeed, the other 612 commandments were given in order to make it possible for the Jews to fulfill this one. Because of a person's ego and strong Desire to Receive (and especially for Jews, whose Desires to Receive are so large), it is very difficult to truly act at the level of "Love thy neighbor as thyself." Performing the 612 commandments makes it easier to "restrict" sufficiently to fulfill "Love thy neighbor as thyself." The myriad commandments are those that have always been part of Judaism, including the many different acts of worship; specific restrictions on diet, dress, sexual relations, and labor on certain days; and ceremonies for different moments in the life span and for different times of the year. Berg, expressing these ideas in kabbalistic terms adapted from Ashlag, describes the Jewish commandments as tools given to the Jewish nation to rectify the prevailing forces of chaos on earth. Because Jews are so central to the energy of the entire world, their neglect of Torah causes hardship and distress for themselves as well as for other nations. Therefore, Jews have been given the mitzvot for their own protection as well as for the good of the entire world. However, to be effective, the mitzvot must be per-formed out of the desire to connect to the Creator. When this occurs with a sufficient number of people, the Jews are then actually repairing the devasta-tion that was wrought by the restriction.

Ilana, a devout member of the Kabbalah Centre community, explains this dynamic to me using the language of "vessels," a term commonly used by the teachers in reference to one's capacity to receive and give Light. Jews are people with greater Desires to Receive, with larger vessels than others. The size of the vessel influences how much Light one receives as well as how much Light one may give to others; or, if one is not restricting one's ego, how much pain one receives and gives. The ritual mitzvot help you so that restricting will not be so hard, Ilana explained. "Why else would you do Shabbat?" With Jews' bigger vessel, they can get more light, and they can do a lot more for the world.[6]

Berg introduced the language of electrical currents and "columns of en-ergy" to describe how the Jews' performance of the mitzvot originated in the divine world. According to Berg, when the vessels were being formed during the creation process, they were endowed with either right-, left-, or central-column energy. The divine vessel known as the sefirah *Chesed*, grace, is the right-column positive energy of Desire to Share. Chesed corresponds to the patriarch Abraham, renowned in Jewish tradition for his kindness and generosity. The sefirah *Gevurah*, power, is the left-column negative energy of Desire to Receive, and it corresponds to the patriarch Isaac. When God commands Abraham to bind Isaac for slaughter, but not—in the end—to kill him, God is teaching that Desire to Receive must be reigned in by Desire to Share, but that it cannot be destroyed.[7] Isaac gave birth to Jacob, who is the earthly counterpart to the heavenly sefirah *Tiferet*, beauty. Both represent central-column harmonizing energy. Jacob produced the 12 tribes of Israel, all of whom possess central-column as well as the left- and right-column energy.

Only Jews were given knowledge of these energy forces and the three-column system, according to Berg. Other religions had knowledge of opposite energy forces, but they lacked knowledge of central-column harmonizing energy.[8] The Jews were given the entire system, but they were to use it for the whole universe:

> On Mount Sinai, where the souls of all Jews were present, we were shown how to live within the framework of these three columns—how to organise our lives so as to connect with these three forces. In this way the energy represented by the Torah was established and connected for all time to this universe by the presence of the Jewish people and their exodus from Egypt. Our heritage, therefore, is to channel these energies constructively, avoiding and eliminating clashes and disruptions in the world, in order to bring about the reign of peace and harmony for all people.[9]

This explains the Bible's term for the Jews, *am segulah*. Usually translated "a treasured nation" or "a chosen nation," the term should be connected to the Hebrew word *segol*, the vowel sign consisting of three dots. Jews are the nation that knows how to operate the three-column system.[10]

The kosher food laws can be used to show how this three-column energy system operates through the commandments of the Torah. The Torah prohibits the eating of milk (and products derived from milk or containing milk ingredients) and meat together, the cooking of milk and meat together, and deriving any benefit from their mixture. The explanation for this, according to Berg's reading of kabbalistic texts, is because the white milk is the energy of Desire to Share and the red meat is the energy of Desire to Receive. There is no way to join their energies harmoniously. Another example from the food laws is the Bible's permission to eat the meat of mammals that chew their cud and have split hooves, while prohibiting meat from mammals that do not have both features. This makes sense only in reference to the energy system explained in kabbalistic texts, Berg teaches. The animal with split hooves contains the two opposite energies, and the cud-chewing feature provides the central-column energy that restricts and harmonizes. Thus, the meat of a cow, an animal with both features, may be eaten, but not that of a pig, which has split hooves but does not chew its cud.[11] In short, when the Jews on earth implement the three-column system—that is, when they perform the mitzvot—they are creating harmony in the lower world. Furthermore, their acts actually draw down the metaphysical energy of the divine world to the earth, uniting the upper and lower realms. To regard these mitzvot as signs of obedience is to miss the point, Berg writes. Such an outlook will turn Judaism "into a rigid moral code, repellent to all but a small minority of the faithful."[12]

What Berg is doing, then, is presenting Judaism as it should be. He is promoting the performance of mitzvot, but with explanations and rationales that differ from the conventional ones. In the Bible the stated purpose of the food laws is to make the Israelites holy. What exactly does this mean? Jewish religious authorities who were not Kabbalists and who suggested *ta'amei ha-mitzvot* (the reasons for the commandments) offered a number of possible explanations—for example, that they were given for health reasons, or to prevent social intercourse between Jews and non-Jews, or to encourage self-discipline. According to Berg, however, performing the mitzvot for anything other than the desire to connect to the Light, or doing them without the metaphysical understanding (the exact connection to the energy forces in the divine world), is worthless. This harsh judgment is found in the Zohar, and Berg agrees.[13] Kabbalistic knowledge is vital for present-day Jews, Berg believes, especially those who are plagued by questions of meaning.[14] Berg was convinced that the standard approaches are erroneous and damaging. From his perspective, he was not supplanting Judaism, but purifying it and restoring its power.

MITZVOT AT THE KABBALAH CENTRE

The Kabbalah Centre calendar of events revolves around the celebration of Shabbat (Sabbath), Rosh Hodesh (beginning of the lunar month),
and the holidays. These special days are identical to those of Judaism, and
the practices fit the range available in the Orthodox Jewish community.
The innermost circle of Kabbalah Centre participants will perform rituals
and meditations unique to these days whether or not they are near a Kabbalah Centre community. Because it is best to engage in prayers—these are
called "Connections"—communally rather than singly, local Centres organize and publicize the times of the Connections in advance. Everybody is
invited to these. They are free and open to all, except for the Rosh Hodesh
events, which require advance registration and a fee.[15] The Sabbath and
holiday are high points in the calendar. People are dressed nicely, and the
males in the congregation wear white. The Kabbalah Centre explains this
as follows:

> The *Zohar* states that on Shabbat men should dress in white, since white is the
> color of giving. The white dress enables the prayers to connect with the energy
> of giving the energy available during Shabbat. Women are not obliged to wear
> white dress on Shabbat since they are naturally on a higher spiritual level than
> men. For women, giving, showing kindness and concern for others are easier
> and come more naturally.[16]

The Connections are very lively, filled with singing or chanting the Hebrew and Aramaic prayers in unison. During gaps in the prayers, the leader
calls out the names of the sefirot or Hebrew letters upon which the congregants should focus their attention. He also calls out the function of the
upcoming prayer—for example, "this prayer is for healing the body, soul, and
the world," or "this carries us to the next higher level of consciousness," or
"these divine names drive out chaos." The liturgy is based on the prayer book
of Isaac Luria, with additional meditations of other Jewish mystics, and the
melodies and style of the service are taken from those used in Jewish communities native to North Africa and the Middle East. The service always includes a sermon in which a teacher explains a kabbalistic concept and spells
out how it can be applied in one's life; invariably, the lesson explains how
one can become a better person and live with greater fulfillment. People pay
very close attention to the sermon. Every Sabbath and holiday includes a
designated Torah reading, every word of which is considered to be very beneficial in giving metaphysical energy for the present and future. The women
and children who have not been sitting in the synagogue during the prayers
(women do not "need" the prayers, and the children have been playing elsewhere) come into the synagogue for the Torah reading and gaze at or read
the Hebrew words as they are being chanted by a prayer leader. Designated

volunteers roam the aisles on the lookout for people who look confused or need help. In between prayers, readings, and sermons, the congregants greet and embrace each other, and during some prayers, they link arms and sway to the music. Although people may not first walk through the doors of the Kabbalah Centre because they are seeking a community, they will find that the place is quite social.

Shabbat is the mitzvah that gets the most attention in the Centre. Shabbat is a time of celebration and special attention because, it is taught, spiritual energy is available on that day without anyone having to work for it. One day out of seven, and only on that day, Light is given freely. Shabbat starts just prior to sundown on Friday and continues until an hour after sundown on Saturday, and at the Los Angeles Kabbalah Centre, there are two communal meals and three Connections. Connections are free of charge, and the meals, which are kosher and bountiful and filled with singing, require advance registration and payment. The Connections and meals provide many opportunities to replenish one's store of metaphysical energy for the coming week and for the purpose of healing.

The other holidays of the year are set by the Jewish lunar calendar. The beginning of each lunar month, Rosh Hodesh, is celebrated at the Centre by special Connections, lectures, and meditations. Each month is identified

The men's side during the Rosh Hashanah prayers at the international Rosh Hashanah retreat, Anaheim, California, 1999. Copyright © The Kabbalah Centre International/Kabbalah University Archives/university@kabbalah.com/www.kabbalah.com.

by its zodiac name and has a distinct character supplied by the astrological tradition. The Connections and meditations, it is explained, allow the participants to draw power from the month's positive aspects, defend themselves from its negative ones, and influence the month ahead as it begins. This is called "shaping the month at the seed level."

The holidays—Rosh Hashanah, Yom Kippur, Sukkot, Hanukkah, Tu-Bishvat, Purim, Pesach (Passover) Shavuot, and Tisha Be-Av—total about 20 days per year. They are considered opportunities supplied by the Light in which one may draw down special energy, cleanse, put oneself in order, rid the world of chaos, guarantee the future, and so on. They are compared to "cosmic windows," each one supplying access to a different form of cosmic energy. The holidays are acknowledged with special Connections, communal meals, and special meditations. In addition to the regular events at the local Centres, an international retreat is held each year on Rosh Hashanah and Pesach at a large hotel, bringing thousands of people together from around the world to celebrate and engage in the Connections together.

Outside of Shabbat and the seasonal holidays, people who are looking for ways to connect to the Light may learn about and follow the life cycle rituals, sexual codes of behavior, dietary laws, and daily prayers said in one's own daily routine at home, work, or outside. These are the same as the mitzvot that are performed by religiously observant Jews, although Kabbalah Centre members explain them in accordance with the Centre's teachings. For example, the recitation of the *Shma* at bedtime, which Jews have traditionally understood as a fulfillment of the duty to declare allegiance to God and Torah, is explained as a means to enable the soul to return to the body after vacating it during the night and elevating to the Upper Worlds of divinity.[17]

PEOPLE WHO ARE NOT JEWISH

Although Berg accepted the notion of Jewish uniqueness in his writings, even then he would not adopt past teachings on this subject unconditionally. Kabbalistic and other Jewish sources transmit a number of quite unflattering accounts explaining why the nations refused to accept the Torah (as well as some unflattering accounts of the Jews' decision to accept it). For example, according to Ashlag, all souls are born on earth at the level of nature in that they are egocentric and capable of acting toward others only from the motive of self-love. The souls of non-Jews are enmeshed in nature, and "they cannot be raised even the smallest amount above the natural levels" to the point at which they can follow, selflessly, the dictum to "Love thy neighbor as thyself." Thus, when they were offered the Torah, they rejected it. In contrast, the Jews were already at a higher level, raised up by the preparatory work of their forefathers, and they accepted God's rules.[18] Of course, Berg is familiar with Ashlag's disparagement of non-Jews, for in 1984 he had the Research Centre of Kabbalah publish Ashlag's essay containing these remarks. For Berg, however, it is Ashlag's conclusions that are more important: the nation of the Jews has a role toward the other nations similar to what the patriarchs did for the Jews. Here is Ashlag's explanation:

> That is, the merit of our holy forefathers enabled us to develop and purify our-selves until we were worthy of accepting the Torah.... Similarly, the Israelite nation must keep the Torah and *mitzvot* for their own sake to enable themselves and all mankind to develop and eventually accept upon themselves this exalted duty of loving one another. This as we have said is the ladder to the purpose of creation which is cleaving unto Him.[19]

The process of repairing the lower world will not be complete until *all* of hu-manity is elevated, Ashlag taught, and Jews should be well aware of their role in achieving that goal. He believed he was living near the end of time, in the Messianic Age, an era when—because the understanding of the Zohar was now complete (Ashlag himself took credit for this)—the world can be filled with the knowledge of God.

It was the universal message within Ashlag that Berg embraced. In the 1980s, when Berg elaborated his ideas about the distinction between Jews and non-Jews, he consistently adopted a dispassionate tone. He interpreted the negative assessments of non-Jews found in religious texts as referring to the distant past, when the other nations were ruled over by evil angels. Under the influence of these malevolent forces, they perceived the Torah as extremely demanding, and so they rejected the Torah when it was offered to them. Berg refused to use the language of moral superiority or inferiority in referring to Jews and other nations, instead describing the Jewish willingness to receive the Torah as a matter of their "unique metaphysical structure":

> This unique cosmic energy force provides the Jew with a different metaphysical structure from that of the non-Jew. When a Jew decides to make use of this third column force, he can determine the basic unity of the cosmos, the way it manifests, and thereby influence the world. When Jews overwhelmingly decide to make use of this force, a basic connection between the two polar forces of negative and positive will emerge and create an indivisible all-embracing unity based on the third, or central, cosmic energy force.... essential to the survival of our entire civilization.[20]

Berg insists that Jews were made distinctive in order to improve the entire world.

Berg developed Ashlag's universalism to an extent that Ashlag could probably not imagine. While living in Israel during the 1970s, Berg did not attempt to teach Kabbalah to Muslims and Christians, but he did welcome women and non-religious Jews into classes to learn Kabbalah. It was out-side of Israel that the universalistic approach was implemented. Philip's son

Michael explained to me that there was no real discrepancy between Ashlag's approach and the Kabbalah Centre's. Michael pointed out that Ashlag was writing in a land in which there were only Jews, so when Ashlag meant "everyone," it made sense to refer to them as Jews. This is how Yehuda Brandwein conveyed it to Philip Berg, and it took some time for the latter to change his "voice" to include truly everybody—and it was everybody who was meant all along.[21] Eventually, the Centre's publications and oral presentations adopted the universal voice. This is evident in the new prayer book that was issued in the late-1990s, a project undertaken by Yehuda Berg under his father's supervision. The morning blessing, "Blessed are You, Lord, our God, King of the universe, Who did not make me a Gentile," is explained as follows:

> On the surface level, this blessing appears to be discriminatory. The word Gentile in this context does not mean a person who is not Jewish. It refers to a person who does not have a powerful and severe desire to receive, be it a spiritual or a physical desire. How many millions of people awake each day and live a life of routine and habit? They live 70 years of their lives as if they were the same day. They experience no inner change or spiritual transformation. They have not accomplished anything worthwhile that they can leave behind in this world. This blessing ignites our appreciation for the power of the Torah and its ability to help us transform our large desire for the self alone into one of sharing and spirituality. We learn to live one day as if it were 70 years, filling our lives with spiritual growth, inner change, and positive transformation. By changing ourselves, we effect change in the world around us.[22]

This explanation erases the common understanding of "Gentile" and "Jew" as ethnic or religious terms, and it reinterprets the terms as different levels of spirituality. A Gentile is someone with an underdeveloped Desire to Receive, and who therefore does not have the capacity to share or transform much. This interpretation is actually consistent with Ashlag's teaching that Jews have larger Desires to Receive than all other nations. The impression given is that there are no barriers to throwing off one's Gentile status; indeed, by virtue of saying this blessing, one affirms that one is not a Gentile. Other writings from the Kabbalah Centre make this point more directly by replacing the term "Jew" with *Yisrael*, Israel. The Centre rejects the Bible's explanation that the name Yisrael was given to Jacob after he wrestled with God's angel and was not defeated, and rejects any genealogical or national associations. It is a spiritual designation only. It refers to people who struggle with Satan and try to connect to the Light. In short, everyone at the Kabbalah Centre is Yisrael. The new terminology gives the congregation a common identity and unites it in its elevated goals.

In public discourse, non-Jewish people who attend the Kabbalah Centre lessons and ceremonial events do not hear statements differentiating them from Jews. The term "Jew" is not used. A few distinctions are made, however.

Philip Berg was ordained an Orthodox rabbi, and although he has departed from Orthodox Judaism in his inclusive stance toward teaching Kabbalah, in many matters of Jewish law he is quite strict. When Jewish law requires Jewish status for a particular ritual, he honors that. This inequality, however, is treated like the other inequalities that arise through the obedience to Jewish law, such as when Jewish law requires performance by someone of priestly genealogy or when Jewish law frowns upon women's leadership in communal prayer. These are explained as a function of the different and necessary energy levels of the variety of human souls; for example, men and women have different energies, so they connect to the Light with different spiritual tools. Yet these distinctions do not matter much, I am told. "People who are not Jews cannot have *aliyot* [public blessings over the Torah scrolls], but everybody gets the Light from them." After making the blessing, the person—men only are assigned this role—hugs and greets each man in the congregation, "spreading the Light" that he generated by the ritual. Another person explains, "When someone goes up and says the blessing, *everybody* actually does it: just meditate and *you have it*."[23] All participants are important, but not equal. All are assured that they can derive benefits at the level that fits their souls.

Some people in the Centre are scornful of Jews who want to guard the distinctions between Jews and non-Jews. The term "Jew" is a misnomer, a modern invention, and certainly not rooted in the Bible, I am told. Those people outside the Centre who commonly represent themselves as the *best* Jews—Jewish community leaders—are actually the worst. They are *erev rav*, the mixed group of outsiders who accompanied the Israelites out of Egypt (Exodus 12:38). According to one strain of Jewish tradition, the mixed multitude was a motley crew of opportunists who instigated all the rebellions against Moses. Contemporary opponents of the Kabbalah Centre, I was informed by an influential member of the community, are simply today's version of *erev rav*. Throughout history, these are the types who have conspired to suppress the study of Kabbalah and persecute Kabbalists. "In every generation there is a group, the *erev rav*, that wants to keep the chaos going. . . . The worst ones were the Ashkenazic [Germanic, European] Jews, who persecuted Kabbalists and invented this modern 'Judaism' that hates Kabbalah."[24] This adversarial outlook is not universally endorsed among the Kabbalah Centre leadership. "I call it Taliban Kabbalah," one senior teacher muttered to me in disgust when I asked about it.[25] It is not unusual to hear an "us versus them" refrain from the senior leaders of the Kabbalah Centre community, who have received the brunt of the sharp criticism from the organized Jewish community, but pains are taken to keep these comments to themselves. Being judgmental is an expression of the egocentric Desire to Receive impulse. Such talk is counterproductive to the universal mission of the movement and the generation of positive energy in the community. In general, discussions of issues of Jewish and non-Jewish status are discouraged on the grounds that they cause disunity and destructive divisions between people and interfere with connecting to the Light.

CONVERSION TO KABBALAH? OR, WHY MADONNA DOES NOT NEED TO CONVERT

It is not surprising, then, that one does not hear within the Kabbalah Centre any calls for conversion to Judaism. When a neophyte raises the question, he or she receives the simple response, "There is no need." When I question people in the Centre what they think about conversion, they are invariably dumbfounded, "Why would people want to convert?" People who ask their teachers if they should convert to Judaism are told that it is neither necessary nor desirable. A senior teacher tells me that only when a person sincerely and repeatedly—on three separate occasions—insists that he or she deeply desires to convert will assistance be offered. This is consistent with Jewish tradition.[26] Conversion makes sense only in the context of religion, and the Kabbalah Centre leadership does not claim to be supplying religion to its non-Jewish participants. Actually, since the mid-1990s, the leadership has insisted publically that it is not giving religion to *any* participants. As the Kabbalah Centre leaders have concentrated their outreach efforts on people outside of the Jewish community, and as more and more people of non-Jewish background have become involved in the Centre, the declaration "Kabbalah is not religion, but universal wisdom" has been heard more clearly and more frequently in the advertising, classes, Web pages, and books.

What is a religion, if Kabbalah is not it? Within the Kabbalah Centre community, "religion" is a pejorative term. It refers to established organized religions at their worst. These are necessarily exclusive, separatist, and dogmatic. Religions are groups that demand unquestioning obedience, promote hostility, foster guilt in their followers, and insist that anyone not of their religion is condemned to hell or is inferior. This is a trope adopted from New Age spiritual leaders.[27]

The most influential expositor of the "not religion, but universal wisdom" message is Madonna. In 1997, Madonna's participation in Kabbalah Centre classes was publicized, and her persistent involvement has had the effect of turning her into a public defender of the movement. In a radio interview in 2004, Madonna presented the main points of the "not religion" theme:

Terry Gross [interviewer]:   Is studying Kabbalah a sign that you're going to become Jewish, or is it just Kabbalah?

Madonna (in an exasperated, angry voice):   Oh, no, please, don't make me sick! I'm never going to be Jewish, and I hate that phrase. And I've not converted to Judaism, and I'm not a member of any religion. It just makes me sick when people say that all the time, because nobody ever bothers to do the research to find out what it actually is. It's not religion. It's a belief system, a philosophy, a body of wisdom that's been around for thousands of years and it predates religion.... Religion fragments people, and Kabbalah unifies people.

Terry Gross: You didn't mean that Judaism makes you sick.

Madonna: I don't want to convert to any religion. I don't want to *be* a member.... The reason it makes me sick is because I hear a lot of people, like rabbis and religious Jews say, "Oh, she shouldn't be dabbling in the Kabbalah," or they think I'm converting to Judaism. They couldn't be further away from the truth. I was raised Catholic and I've had enough of religion. I don't want to judge other people for their religious beliefs. If it works for you, that's great—if it's working for you. Once you join a group because you say, "I'm going to join because this group is superior, and other groups are inferior"—I don't want any part of that. Unfortunately, most people who are part of a religion think that. People say, "If you're not my religion, you're going to hell," or "If you're not Jewish, and you're not part of the 'chosen people,' tough luck for you." Kabbalists—and I include myself in that group of people—don't look at the world that way, in that fragmented way. I do think it's rather impossible to say, "I'm religious and I want to help unite the world." It's a major paradox.[28]

The resistance to oppressive authority and exclusivity expressed here is widely shared by Kabbalah Centre participants. Indeed, Madonna's association with the Kabbalah Centre has done much to bring in people who are seeking spirituality and want to avoid what they regard as the trappings of oppressive religions. One person tells me how as an adult she became dissatisfied with the Presbyterianism in which she was raised and educated. She found it boring and filled with duty and required behaviors that held no meaning for her. She tried out other denominations, but nothing felt right. While attending one of Madonna's concerts, she saw the Kabbalah Centre books on display. She thought, "If Madonna likes it, and you know *her* attitude toward religion, there might be something there." She bought a book, read it, loved the ideas, and began attending the Kabbalah Centre regularly.[29] Madonna's approval of the Kabbalah Centre testifies that this group lacks the narrow and oppressive features of established religions.

The use of the term religion as a pejorative is a strategy of outreach to people dissatisfied by or alienated from established religions. "Religion" is that rigid, empty, and dead habit, whereas "spirituality" and "wisdom" are nurturing, alive, and useful. The leaders realize that they are presenting a stereotype and that the Kabbalah Centre does indeed offer people a religion. "You know how people react to the term religion—so we say we're not a religion," says the head of the organization's legal department. She had asked me to write a letter on behalf of the Kabbalah Centre to a government agency testifying that the Kabbalah Centre deserves status as a religious organization.[30] I clarified the matter with Karen Berg, codirector of the Kabbalah Centre. Karen and I quickly agreed that the Kabbalah Centre presents what religious studies scholars define as religion, although she pointed out that some people engage in it as religion whereas others utilize it for other purposes. I asked Karen how she thought the followers would respond were they to be aware of the legal request and of Karen's belief that the Kabbalah Centre is a religion. Karen replied, "They wouldn't like it. Most of them do not like religion at all." I asked her how she thought Madonna would respond. Karen replied:

> Madonna wouldn't like it! She doesn't want religion. But look at her: she keeps a kosher home, she observes Shabbat, she circumcised her son and had her husband circumcised. But she doesn't want to convert; she was born Christian and wants to keep it that way.

I asked Karen how something could be a religion and not a religion at the same time. Karen explained it as similar to people who practice yoga for the exercise and the calming benefits, without accepting Hindu religious principles. They are adopting only the elements that are universal, and they are not detracting from Hinduism.[31]

The approach to "religion" is consistent with the outreach strategy that characterized the Centre from its beginnings. It has enabled the Kabbalah Centre to disparage organized religions for those who want to hear the disparagement and to respect organized religions for those who want to hear that. The belief that Kabbalah ideas are compatible with all other religions has

Distributing the Zohar in Israel. Copyright © The Kabbalah Centre International/Kabbalah University Archives/university@kabbalah.com/www.kabbalah.com.

led the directors to augment the Zohar Project—the widespread and free distribution of sets of the Zohar to people in troubled parts of the world—with meetings with leaders of other religions. These meetings consist of interfaith dialogue and lessons to the religious leaders on kabbalistic principles.[32]

JEWISH SOULS, GENTILE SOULS

Few people are aware of the leadership's and the inner core's loyalty to traditional conceptions of Jew and non-Jew. In private discussions with Kabbalah Centre teachers and directors about the appropriateness of guiding non-Jews in the performance of the Jewish commandments, no one challenged the belief that a distinction between Jews and non-Jews exists within human souls. They referred to Ashlag's axiom that Jewish souls have greater Desire to Receive for the Self Alone. That is, more than non-Jews, they have a greater hunger for physical, emotional, intellectual, and creative attainments and power; this greater capacity to receive means that they also have greater capacity to share and give and to connect themselves to the Creator. Their particular function as human beings is to combine the negative energy of receiving and the positive energy of restriction so as to reveal the energizing, loving, nonjudgmental, and unifying Light that flows in and through everything. They are designed to connect to the Light through 613 commandments, or channels, whereas non-Jews ("the nations of the world") need to fulfill the seven Noahide commandments. These seven are the obligation to establish and obey a judicial system and the prohibitions against murder, idolatry, blasphemy, theft, sexual immorality, and cruelty to animals.[33]

Affirming their belief in this distinction, Kabbalah Centre leaders have explained the participation of non-Jews in the performance of the 613 mitzvot in a number of ways. One pointed out that non-Jews who participate in the mitzvot designated for Jews are, in the process, performing the seven Noahide commandments.[34] Another leader, acknowledging the difference between the effect of a Jew's performance of a mitzvah such as Shabbat and a non-Jew's, feels that the non-Jew's participation is nonetheless beneficial: "If that person wants to join in, if that person feels the light that Israel is generating, why should I stop him? It's not my business! And it's a good thing, it makes them feel connected."[35] As for the Jewish tradition that the mitzvah of Shabbat should only be fully and completely performed by Jews, I was told that it is quite difficult to fully and completely perform the mitzvah of Shabbat, and non-Jews were certainly not performing it to that exact standard. "They are not exactly following the Torah, but they are getting a portion of it which is helpful to them," the teacher told me, and there is no good reason to deny them that. The non-Jews who do the mitzvot, another person told me, "are very special people."[36] Throughout all these discussions, the attitude was a feeling of delight that kabbalistic principles were being well received by people of different backgrounds. Their participation was regarded as an enhancement to the community and a step toward perfecting the world. Jewish people who want a more insular, ethnic spiritual community of only or mostly Jews leave the Kabbalah Centre.[37]

According to Kabbalah Centre teachings, however, no one really knows the status of one's soul. Over the generations, Jews mixed with others biologically and took on the religions of others through assimilation and as a result of the difficulties during the exiles, migrations, and persecutions. "Being Jewish is simply presumptive," one teacher explained, "and you can find this in the Talmud. Elijah will come in the future and verify people's status."[38] In other words, to exclude non-Jews may actually be excluding people with Jewish souls. I was told, "There are many Jewish souls out there who need to be brought back, like the 10 Lost Tribes, those who were converted forcefully, and those who converted voluntarily. Making this distinction explicit will scare off these potential souls."[39] Karen Berg testified to the success of the Kabbalah Centre's approach in returning Jews to Judaism. "The people who come in who are Jewish," she said, "90–99 percent are from backgrounds where they have nothing, they never learned anything Jewish, they were so turned off....Now they marry Jewish, observe Shabbat, the whole works."[40] Several senior teachers repeated to me that they had heard Rabbi Berg say that anyone who completes the Kabbalah I course probably has a Jewish soul. They believe that when an ostensibly non-Jewish person is so passionately determined to reveal Light, it is an indication that his or her soul is Jewish. Yet only when that person repeatedly insists that he or she wants to be Jewish is discussion of conversion warranted. "At that point," a teacher said, "it's a mitzvah! But it has to come from them. That's part of Jewish tradition—you don't push people. They have to keep insisting to you. And once they do, you help them along. You go to a *bet din* [rabbinic court], the whole works."[41]

Wouldn't such a tolerant environment foster intermarriage? I wondered aloud to a teacher. He responded, "I see very little of it here. They want to marry one of their own. After all, they want to find a soul mate, and that comes with finding someone similar." Ilana explains it to me using the language of vessels. "It doesn't work [for a Jew to marry a non-Jew], because you need to marry someone whose vessel is like yours. A big vessel with a little vessel—they don't fit together right."[42]

Nevertheless, in private as well as public, Kabbalah Centre leaders express distaste for Jewish exclusivity and separateness in regard to Torah and Kabbalah. They are well informed about the Kabbalists who believed that Kabbalah should be propagated to all of humanity. Some are familiar with the passages in rabbinic literature that describe the Jewish sages engaged in discussions with non-Jews about Judaism. "The traditions that demonize non-Jews and keep them far away from mitzvot come from a *shtetl* mentality," I am told by one teacher with a historical bent. *Shtetl* is the Yiddish term for the medieval Eastern European Jewish community, isolated from non-Jews because of anti-Semitism and Jewish desire for separateness. The Kabbalah Centre inner core has disdain for the Ashkenazic heritage and prides itself on being allied to the mystics of Spain, the Sefardic Jews. They have accepted Philip Berg's explanation that *Sefard* is the Hebrew anagram for a person who puts the *sod*, secret teachings, first.[43] Nevertheless, one of my teachers connected the Kabbalah-loving person with actual Sefardic Jews. Sefardic Jews did not abandon Kabbalah in the modern period like the Ashkenazic Jews did, he taught, and that is why they were spared during the Holocaust (in fact, thousands were killed). I was also taught that the Sefardic Jews, most of whom settled in North Africa and the Middle East, erected fewer barriers between themselves and non-Jews. Their point is that the fearful, exclusive policies prohibiting non-Jews from worshiping and studying with Jews are a legacy from some of the harsh regimes of the Middle Ages and should not be continued.[44] Finally, aside from the "proofs" originating in historic Jewish literature are the distinctly modern arguments for open, mixed communities. Exposing non-Jews to Kabbalah and Judaism, people have told me, fosters their appreciation of Jewish culture and decreases anti-Semitism.[45] Many Jewish participants tell me that they feel good about being part of a movement that is so tolerant and international. They want a spiritual community with a diverse membership. They have the benefit of some familiarity with the Jewish elements in the rituals, but without the tribalism, guilt, and victim mentality of the conventional Judaism they disdain.[46]

THE SPIRITUAL TOOLS THAT ARE NOT MITZVOT

When Kabbalah Centre directors began to make a deliberate effort to teach Kabbalah to non-Jewish people in the 1990s, they did not have to radically alter either their outreach strategies or their practices. They already had spiritual tools in place for Jews whose knowledge of Jewish tradition was very minimal. As explained in chapter 2, from the start of his independent career in Kabbalah, Berg addressed his teachings to young Jews who were alienated from Judaism in particular and organized religion in general. Whereas in Israel he could count on these types to have fluency in Hebrew and basic familiarity with Jewish history and religion, this was not the case in the United States and Canada. With the establishment of the locally based school-synagogue centers called Kabbalah Learning Centres, other challenges appeared. Worship services and communal Sabbath and holiday meals were held in addition to classes, and the rituals and ceremonies required knowledge of Hebrew and Aramaic. Unless they were of Israeli background, many of the participants would not be able to participate. There are precedents in Jewish culture for accommodating those Jews who cannot read Hebrew or who can read but not understand it. The deep belief in the sanctity and power of the Hebrew language meant that it was considered preferable to utter the prayers by rote, use transliterations, or read the Hebrew without understanding rather than resort to translations. There was also the hope that the ignorant congregant who vocalized the Hebrew would eventually gain greater understanding. In Berg's first writings, he expressed tremendous disdain for the practice of reciting Hebrew prayers through rote memorization and without understanding, insisting that such prayers were empty gestures with no spiritual content. Yet constrained by the low level (or nonexistence) of Hebrew language proficiency as the Centres began to attract non-Israeli Jews as well as non-Jews, Berg developed a variation of it for the Kabbalah Centres. After all, a new religion that seeks to become widely followed must be inclusive, accommodating people at all levels of spirituality and knowledge.

Scanning

Consequently, the Kabbalah Centre introduced to its students the practice of scanning the pages of the Zohar, primarily, as well as scanning the text of the Torah and *Siddur* (prayer book). Scanning is the Centre's term used for the practice of passing one's eyes over the lines of text as if one were reading, without understanding the words. It is explained that this will confer spiritual and physical benefits on the individual, and when many people scan at the same time, it can have an effect on a much larger number of people, on the environment, or on a region. Scanning was introduced to the Kabbalah Centre gradually. According to senior teacher Shaul Youdkevitch, Berg first mentioned scanning casually in 1983, again raised the subject in a lecture to advanced students in 1986, and recommended it on a broader scale at some point after that.[47] A longtime participant in the Los Angeles Centre insists that widespread encouragement of the practice began in 1987–88 when the Kabbalah Centre's edition of the Zohar was published.[48]

There actually is a precedent for scanning in Jewish tradition, although very few modern Jews (including rabbis) are aware of it. Beginning in the eighteenth century, Kabbalists began to recommend that the individual male would derive spiritual benefit from reading or reciting pages of the Zohar even without understanding it. Such recitation became part of the daily and holiday liturgy as well as customary on certain special occasions. Scanning pages of the Zohar by people who could not read the text, however, was not practiced. Some Kabbalists taught that the mere placement of the Zohar volumes in a place was believed to confer spiritual benefits there. Belief in the intrinsic holiness of the Zohar grew more widespread after the eighteenth century, and this belief remained firm in non-European lands through the twentieth century.[49]

Rather than explain scanning with reference to the kabbalistic precedent, however, Berg found a metaphor that associated the practice with a modern invention: the bar-code scanner used in retail stores. When the bar code is passed in front of the scanner, the scanner decodes it and processes a great deal of information in an instant. Berg took his logical leap from here: "If an inanimate object such as a bar-code scanner can produce such activity, imagine what the human mind can do," Berg writes. Yet, it is really not a matter of the mind at work, Berg continues: "As we scan, our eyes, more than our rational consciousness, make the absolute connection and therefore permit us to tap into the awesome, flawless universe of Tree of Life [the divine realm of the sefirot]."[50] He does concede that people—especially "the layman without any prior Hebraic background"—might have a hard time believing this. Such a person would resist the idea that the words of the *Siddur* and Zohar would have such a uniquely powerful effect. Nonetheless, it is the truth, Berg writes. "Once we have come to the realization that we have no other choice in our efforts to rid this universe of chaos," we will accept it. Then there are the tangible rewards that follow: "When an individual begins to tap this awesome Lightforce of God, he or she instantaneously experiences the sensation of being surrounded by the warmth of the Lightforce."[51] That is, experience will prove what logic cannot.

The Kabbalah Centre's 2006 Web site expresses the benefit a bit more extravagantly:

> Kabbalah teaches that each letter [of the Hebrew alphabet] is a channel to a unique form of energy—and this is true whether or not we know how the letter sounds, or how it fits into a given word. As you begin your spiritual work

Kabbalah Centre volunteers prepare to distribute mini-Zohar gift packages to children in hospital. Copyright © The Kabbalah Centre International/Kabbalah University Archives/university@kabbalah.com/www.kabbalah.com.

with the *Zohar*, simply scanning the pages—allowing your eyes to pass over the words and letters—opens a direct connection to the divine spark hidden within each of us. The more you bring the *Zohar* into your life, your connection to the Light becomes stronger. The Kabbalists tell us that by just being in the presence of the volumes creates an impenetrable shield of spiritual protection against the forces of chaos and negativity in the world.[52]

Students are advised to scan the Zohar on a daily basis, and the Kabbalah Centre informs the community which chapters are best to use on which days. Scanning the prayer book and the text of the Torah as they are read in the synagogue on Shabbat is considered important spiritual practice. People are advised that they should do it with the correct consciousness, that is, with an understanding of what the text is supposed to be accomplishing. Scanning requires the possession of a set of the Zohar. This is not an insubstantial expense; the 24-volume set can be purchased through the Kabbalah Centre for approximately $350.[53] Active participants of the Kabbalah Centre own a Zohar set; certainly by 2002, and probably earlier, it was regarded as basic equipment. The teacher of the "Healing and Consciousness" course that I took was pleased to learn that virtually all the students owned Zohar sets. He told us, "When I started here [in the late 1980s], it was *so hard* to convince people to buy and scan the Zohar!"[54]

For people who cannot afford to buy a complete Zohar set, there is a cheaper option in a pocket-size edition of the section of the Zohar commenting on the section of the Torah portion called "Pinchas." Because of the intrinsic holiness of the Zohar, simply carrying part of it around is thought to guard against danger; the Pinchas portion, which deals with matters of disease and healing, is thought to provide protection from physical illness. "This miniature volume is ideal for travel bags, your car, children's backpacks, and even in your purse. Don't leave home without it!" advertises the Kabbalah Centre Web site, and many people take this to heart.[55]

Scanning also occurs in the worship services that include Torah reading. The morning Connection of every Shabbat, new moon, and holiday includes a trained reader melodically chanting a designated portion of the Torah. Everybody listens attentively and follows every word in *The Kabbalistic Bible* books that are supplied, pointing their finger under the Hebrew text so that every Hebrew word passes in front of their eyes. Recently, the synagogue at the Los Angeles Centre was outfitted with a huge screen in front, and a camera projects on the screen an image of the reader's hand pointing at each word of the Torah scroll as he reads it. This is especially helpful for those people who cannot actually read Hebrew and would have difficulty scanning each word by themselves. The literal translation of the portion is so unimportant that it can be found only at the end of *The Kabbalistic Bible*. After all, the Bible is considered to be a code. What is most important, the congregants are told, is to absorb the metaphysical energy of the Hebrew letters while scanning and meditating on the deeper kabbalistic lesson, which is available in summaries on the bottom of the pages and in the explanations of the prayer leader. This approach to the literal meaning has some grounding in Kabbalah. The Zohar teaches that the words of the Torah are merely its outer garments, and the true meaning is found in the secret teachings that are found within. Nevertheless, the Kabbalah Centre takes this perspective to lengths probably never imagined by previous Kabbalists.

The directors of the Kabbalah Centre clearly and unequivocally teach that the actual volumes of the Zohar have power whether or not people believe in them. Belief in the absolute power of the Zohar volumes is the basis for the Zohar Project. Copies of the Zohar are distributed to areas of the world suffering from poverty, violence, and disease—simply to be there in boxes, sit on shelves, or be scanned. Yet when one listens more attentively to Kabbalah Centre teachers and to members of the core community, it becomes apparent that they believe that the Zohar's power manifests itself in degrees of intensity, increasing as one's knowledge and application of its principles increase. People who can read Hebrew gain more light than those who can only scan, and those who understand the words gain even more, as long as they are understanding the real, kabbalistic meaning (as opposed to the literal meaning) of the text and they act on it at the level of "Love thy neighbor as thyself." During the Shabbat connection at the time of military hostilities between Israel and Hezbollah in July 2006, this was voiced to the congregation in terms of a passive and active power: "We hope that the Zohars that we have distributed to the countries in the Middle East become activated at this time, and bring peace to the region." The teacher explained afterward that the Zohar is a force in and of itself, but it will have more power—its latent powers will become "activated"—if people focus on it with consciousness and change their ways.[56]

It is obvious that scanning was introduced to the Kabbalah Centre as a strategy of outreach. It has provoked outrage and derision from Jews across the denominational spectrum who are, in principle, opposed to the popularization of Kabbalah and unaware of the precedents in the tradition for reading without understanding or using the Zohar as a protective measure. They regard the Kabbalah Centre's scanning as a cynical ploy to expand the market for Kabbalah Centre publications and to legitimize meaningless rituals and promote belief in "magic." Kabbalah Centre leaders, however, are unapologetic about their mission. At a public conference in 2006 on popular Kabbalah, Michael Berg cited passages from respected Kabbalists from the past who recommended similar practices. In response to skepticism that such a practice is spiritually efficacious, he and other teachers have explained that when people with no knowledge of Hebrew want to feel a part of the community and pray with the others, guiding them to scan with proper consciousness and the right intention is an act of compassion. In his experience, continuous participation in the Connections leads eventually to learning the alphabet and reading.[57] There is a hint of this in the Kabbalah Centre *Siddur* in Yehuda Berg's explanation of scanning:

> There is just one other prerequisite for those not versed in the Hebrew language: You must meditate to be one unified soul with your fellow congregates [*sic*]. A thin, weak string might not have the strength to lift up a heavy chest filled with wonderful treasures. Combine and weave many delicate strings together, however, and eventually you form a rope strong enough to accomplish the task.[58]

In short, scanning increases in benefit when the scanners are in a community with others. Kabbalah Centre members also believe that new students receive Light with less effort than experienced practitioners. One person explained it as follows: "Initially there is a 'gift,' so that when you start to learn Kabbalah, the Light gives you fulfillment whether or not you believe in it. After a while, your 'gift' is used up, and it will no longer work unless you have the consciousness."[59] Another person described it as a function of one's vessel size. When people begin at the Kabbalah Centre, she explained, they get Light right away and feel great. The reason is because their vessel is not very developed, and a little Light fills it all up. When their vessels have grown and stretched with all the restricting, scanning, and meditations, they need more Light in order to fill their vessel and find satisfaction.[60] It sounds as if scanning were developed expressly for neophytes who need immediate results. As they mature, they will find other spiritual tools.

Meditating on the Divine Names

Another spiritual tool used in the Centre that is not a mitzvah is meditating on the divine names. This, like scanning, can be enacted by someone with little background or knowledge, although unlike scanning, it is rooted in the highest levels of kabbalistic tradition. The meditation practices that were adopted and adapted for use in the Centres were those that involved silently reading or gazing upon Hebrew letter combinations that had no meaning as such. They were to be contemplated, not recited, and they were incorporated into the established prayer service, varying according to the time of day, week, month, and year. Called *kavvanot*, meaning intentions, these originated with the emergence of Kabbalah in medieval Spain, and their function is described in a multitude of ways. Some believed they enabled the worshiper to contribute to the harmony of the different dimensions and processes within God, whereas others described them as the means to adhere to God without any separation, and some regarded their kavvanot as sustaining and protecting the Jewish people.[61]

Since the late eighteenth century, the recitation of kavvanot has been based on the system developed by an eighteenth-century Yemenite kabbalist named Shalom Shar'abi (also known as RaSHaSH).[62] Shar'abi claimed that his particular formulas were the product of revelations received through the soul of Isaac Luria implanted within him, and Kabbalists throughout the world accepted his kavvanot as the most authoritative. Under Shar'abi's leadership, an elite class of Kabbalists in the Jerusalem community called Beit El were assigned to worship with the kavvanot in shifts around the clock, thereby ensuring the peace and protection of the community. Shar'abi's kavvanot spread to Kabbalists in many communities. When Yehuda Ashlag moved to Palestine in 1921, he came into contact with the Beit El kabbalistic circles that still recited the kavvanot in the prescribed manner. He was not impressed with their practices or their knowledge of the teachings of Luria.[63] Yet these Hebrew meditations were still in use at the end of the twentieth century by kabbalistic rabbis in Israel who were highly regarded by Jews of Middle Eastern origin. They were quite pleased when, in 1995, Yehuda Berg produced a Hebrew prayer book for the Kabbalah Centre that included the kavvanot in the liturgical framework established by Isaac Luria.[64] Four years later, a Hebrew version with English translations and explanations was published, and this constitutes the basic liturgy for Kabbalah Centre "Connections" and summarizes many of the movement's doctrines.

The integration of the kavvanot into the worship service of the Kabbalah Centre exemplifies how kabbalistic practice is popularized. The customary way of utilizing the kavvanot involves hours of silent meditation. In contrast, the kavvanot in Kabbalah Centre Connections are interspersed through the prayers, and participants devote short intervals of less than a minute to gazing at them; alternatively, the prayer leader calls out a sequence of Hebrew letters in between the phrases sung by the cantor, and at other times, the congregation sings phrases made up of words whose initials spell out a divine name. The synagogue and auditorium walls are decorated with short Hebrew formulas rendered in the calligraphy of classical Torah scribes, and when they are the subject of meditation, someone will point to them and explain. Important meditations are projected on the screen in front of the room in order to facilitate the in-unison gazing at or singing of the words. One important quieter meditation called *Tikkun Ha-Nefesh* (repair of the soul) includes meditating on different formulations of the Tetragrammaton (the four letter divine name consisting of the Hebrew letters *yod, hey, vav,* and *hey*) while waving one's hand over different areas of the body, so as to send healing power there.

Quiet meditation, however, is not the general form of the worship service. There is unison singing, chanting, and some jumping, and the Connection is punctuated regularly by the *Kaddish* prayer. The Kaddish is an ancient Aramaic prayer that is chanted by the prayer leader between different segments of the service, denoting a new theme in the liturgy, and at the end of a service, it is recited several times (at least once by mourners). In traditional synagogues, it is chanted at times at breakneck speed, or slowly as a dramatic closing or opening of the next section of the service, or solemnly by the mourners; the congregation intones specific phrases in response throughout the prayer. In the Kabbalah Centre Connections, the Kaddish is recited by the prayer leader (except when the mourners lead their designated Kaddish), and the congregation shouts, gesticulates, waves, and focuses on meditations.[65] The intense Kaddish is a result of its appearance in the liminal, in-between space between prayers; the fervent congregational response functions to prevent Satan from entering in and the specific Aramaic words are said to trigger cosmic forces of immortality and healing. During my first years at the Centre, people regularly shouted out the names of places in the world in need of healing—Chernobyl, for example. These were replaced with phrases in different languages calling out "Immortality now!" and currently the phrases revolve around unconditional love and unity. In short, the worship service is designed to be stimulating, exciting, and not taxing for those with short attention spans. The atmosphere is one of joyous communal enthusiasm, rather than somber and serious devotion.

The literal meaning of the text is irrelevant not only in scanning the kavvanot; most of the prayers, according to Kabbalah Centre teaching, have no value in their plain meaning. The fact that words of the prayer are words of praise, thanksgiving, request, and penitence is irrelevant. Yehuda Berg laments, "The idea that a prayer book is meant to praise and thank is merely the handiwork of Satan. He stimulates our reactive intelligence and diverts our attention from the true power of prayer."[66] This false notion of prayer explains why prayers have never accomplished anything, Philip Berg writes. He teaches that the true function of prayer can be learned from the original form of worship, the sacrifice, or *korban*. *Korban* originates from the word *k'rav*, warfare. The sacrificial offerings were the forms God provided to fight all the negativity that people produced, according to Philip, and prayers have the same function. This is why the Hebrew term is not *sefer tefila*, "book of prayer," but *siddur*, order; the purpose was "to restore order in one's life, to remove oneself from imminent danger or chaos." To be efficacious, however, the prayers must be recited with an understanding of the connection between the words and the divine energy force to which the words connect.[67]

The Red String and Kabbalah Water

There are two items developed by the Kabbalah Centre that serve as spiritual tools. Rabbi Berg introduced Kabbalah water in the late 1990s. The main function of this water is healing, and so it is be dealt with at greater length in the next chapter. Aside from healing, however, Kabbalah water confers one of the important benefits attributed to the presence of the Zohar and the scanning of it: it facilitates connection to the Light; it helps diminish the ego and elevate the soul from the state of Desire to Receive for Oneself Alone to Desire to Share. Like the other spiritual tools, using Kabbalah water is considered the *most* effective when it is accompanied by the person's directed consciousness.

Wearing a red piece of cloth or thread or jewelry to ward off "the evil eye" is a very ancient and culturally widespread practice, according to anthropologists. The notion is that a person deliberately or unwillingly causes disease or evil to a person by looking at him or her with envy, hatred, or other negative feelings. Wearing a red item—red may be preferred because it is the color of blood, signifying death and life—is thought to form a protective shield or to nullify the threat. As early as 1992, Kabbalah Centre teachers instructed people to wear a red string around their wrists, and they explained the practice with kabbalistic concepts. However, there is actually no precedent in kabbalistic literature for this practice. Wearing a red string was, however, a practice endorsed by some Jewish people over the ages, despite the declarations of rabbis that it had no efficacy and had its origins in "foreign" teachings.[68] Consequently, it is fair to say that it is part of Jewish tradition, and it is not difficult to attach to it kabbalistic symbolism.

Yehuda Berg explained his understanding of this spiritual tool in his 2004 book *The Red String Book: The Power of Protection, Technology for the Soul.* Similar to his father's equation of bar-code scanning and the human body's absorption of divine energy of the Hebrew letters, Yehuda equates television technology and the red string:

> The question is, can the power of spiritual protection actually be transmitted through a simple strand of wool, colored red, worn on one's left wrist 24 hours a day, seven days a week? Then again, you might also ask, can movies and television shows actually be transmitted through a simple strand of copper wire, connected to the back of a television set, 24 hours [a] day, seven days a week? The answer to both questions is a resounding yes! Spiritual and physical technologies both work the same way.[69]

This "spiritual technology" is based on an extrapolation of passages in the Zohar that use red as a metaphor for sin or harsh judgments and describe the world as "spinning" with judgment and mercy.[70] Injecting red into a wool thread is "a diluted strain of negative energy," serving as a vaccination against the evil eye. The spun wool is a manifestation of the powers of mercy and judgment spun together, and in such a combination, mercy dominates. Winding the string around the tomb of the matriarch Rachel (situated in the occupied territory near Bethlehem), Yehuda explains, imbues it with the force of Rachel's love and protection of her children.[71]

Like the other spiritual tools, consciousness plays a role. In order for the red string to protect against others' jealousy and ill intent, the wearer should make every effort to overcome his or her own jealousy and ill intent toward others. "In addition to wearing the string, you should also wear the garment of humility," Yehuda advises, because people who speak about their successes will become the focus of others' hostility. Following this are other suggestions for behavior and attitudes, and it becomes clear that the red string is another entry point for a person to make the kabbalistic "12 Rules of the Game" a guide for one's life.[72]

CHAPTER 5

———— ✠ ————

Religious Healing

Healing is currently a central concern of the Kabbalah Centre community. Kabbalah is presented as a means of eliminating "chaos," the catch-all term for personal, social, economic, and political distress. Communal worship and the application of the Centre's "spiritual tools" are believed to improve health, lessen political strife, prevent natural disasters, and diminish environmental pollution. Community service projects organized by the Kabbalah Centre are frequently described as acts that heal the world. Many of the teachings and the explanations for the healing rituals focus on the individual rather than on national or international distress or natural calamities, and so much of this chapter focuses on individual healing, but the distinction between individual and global chaos is somewhat artificial; they all share the same cause, and the solutions are similar too.

Kabbalah Centre healing has roots in Jewish and kabbalistic sources as well as in New Age and alternative healing. Although most of the elements of the healing philosophy were present from the beginning of Philip Berg's popularization efforts in the 1970s, healing as a theme and function of the teachings expanded greatly in the 1990s. This reflects a larger trend in America at the turn of the twenty-first century, when spiritual and religious healing increased in popularity and legitimacy.[1] Among the most popular of the spiritual alternative healing philosophies and therapies are the Western Hindu-derived Aryuvedic teachings. These explain that the divine spirit enters human beings through the astral body (the aura), and from there it is diffused into the body's seven interior centers (*chakras*). Sins or uncompleted tasks from past lives may clog the chakras like so much karmic debris, producing pessimism, sluggishness, destructive behavior, and illness. Traditional Chinese medicine is often referenced to describe the disrupted flow of energy through the body. Prior to the 1980s, kabbalistic ideas were just barely present amid the alternative healing philosophies, and much of that emanated from Theosophical

Society writings that used kabbalistic diagrams of the sefirot as the model of the individual human body and the pathways along which energy flows and may be blocked.[2] Berg's early writings include very little on the flow of the life force through the sefirot and much more emphasis on the enormous role that astrology plays in disease. When the theme of healing entered Berg's writings in the 1990s, he presented his kabbalistic perspective as the most advanced system of them all and as the earliest and the starting point for all other points of view.

Fundamental to Berg's outlook is the principle that individual health is an effect of astrological forces *and* a person's moral behavior in this life or in past lives. Good health is earned when a person seeks to be close to God by sharing with others. This behavior enables divine energy to flow into the body and sustain it at its optimal level. Bad behavior produces blockages in the flow of divine energy, leading to bad health. Environmental pollution, natural disasters, and regional conflicts are also caused, in part, by bad behavior that blocks divine Light. Healing requires the adoption of good behavior, but there is a particular understanding of what good behavior entails. Additionally, there are many kabbalistic rituals and meditations, as well as astrological factors, that are considered essential in enabling the individual to reform. Then there is the matter of intent, or consciousness. Rituals and meditations are often described as having intrinsic power to remove chaos. That is, the community believes that rituals and meditations can solve the health problems of others and fend off or mitigate natural calamities and violence. Often, however, there is the insistence that healing occurs only when the people who are directly stricken by chaos elevate their own consciousness and activate or reveal the divine Light within.

Berg has never been content to establish the legitimacy of the healing powers of kabbalistic spiritual tools on religious faith alone; instead, he has insisted that they represent the most advanced science and technology, and it is merely a matter of time before all leading scientists and doctors affirm their effectiveness. Yet Berg and Kabbalah Centre teachers see no need to establish the authority of their healing therapies in the normative manner—through carefully controlled and thoughtfully interpreted experiments and through the critical scrutiny of scientists not personally invested in the success or failure of the research—and they often deny the relevance of scientific verification. The result is a complex relationship to science: the Kabbalah Centre adopts scientific language and cachet while rejecting scientific standards. This approach to science is characteristic of New Age healing and some types of alternative medicine. The one exception to this is the healing project called Spirituality for Kids. Even though Spirituality for Kids has emerged naturally out of the kabbalistic principles and uses some spiritual vocabulary, it is a secular educational program that has been tested, revised, and continually modified in response to measured assessments.

In previous chapters, I have emphasized the hierarchical structure of the Kabbalah Centre community—that is, the core community's resemblance to a sect of Judaism with intense and strict performance of mitzvot, and those surrounding them practicing with less regularity and strictness. This distinction pertains as well to healing. The core community perceives itself as unequalled among all of humanity in its knowledge of the astrological forces and personal weaknesses that cause individual disease, and they also feel the best equipped to fend off these harms, as well as environmental disasters and wars. Those on the periphery, whose lives are less restricted by the discipline of Jewish law and whose kabbalistic practice is less intense, have less capacity to ward off problems. However, all members of the community feel themselves at a tremendous advantage to outsiders; they believe that people ignorant of Kabbalah lack the defenses to prevent physical and mental infirmities and to protect the world from disaster.

THE MEANING AND SOURCE OF DISEASE AND DISASTERS

In the Kabbalah Centre, disease is explained by reference to the fundamental religious beliefs and the cosmogonic narrative described in chapter 3. Briefly, God, or "the Light," is understood as an energy force that continuously pulses throughout the universe, infusing life into all creation. The Light is entirely benevolent and sharing. Prior to the creation of the physical world, when the human souls in the divine realm received divine Light without meriting it, they felt embarrassed about their sustenance; this is called eating the Bread of Shame. The souls shut off the flow of divine Light. "Restriction" resulted, producing the lower realm in which we live, where deprivation, suffering, evil, and ill health occur. The action of the souls established thereafter the basic principle that one must earn Light by one's good deeds. The purpose of life is to fulfill the commandment "Love thy neighbor as thyself." When people live according to that principle, their souls will receive Light. They become more and more elevated until they finally adhere to God (*devekut*), achieve affinity with the Light, and all is Light. Like all other types of evil and suffering, disease occurs when people in their present or their past lives violate the principle "Love thy neighbor as thyself." Instead of love, people act "reactive"—this is the Kabbalah Centre term for self-centeredness and behavior that disrespects others' human dignity. The reactive behavior and negative consciousness accumulate and create obstructions that block Light from parts of the body.

Berg and Kabbalah Centre teachers call the internal blockages of Light negative energy or Satan. At times, the descriptions of these blockages are quite colorful and dramatic. Here is an example of Philip Berg's use of medieval mythical symbols:

> The invasion by the Dark Lord has breached our natural, birth-given defenses and immunity systems, and has thus given rise to the Dark Lord's negative energy forces.
>
> Once negative energy forces have established a beachhead within our system, these forces begin to spread at highly increased rates of attack. They continue to fan out throughout the natural immune system establishing pockets of resistance to any attack by the immune system.[3]

Although this language sounds as though the enemy is an external force, the enemy is actually within. People create Satan and negative energy inside them, and the body loses its capacity to function at peak level; it becomes imbalanced and cannot heal itself or guard against the intrusion of foreign or destructive elements. All physical ailments are the consequence of accumulated bad behavior and consciousness; this is the principle of Cause and Effect. Eventually, the person is overtaken by suffering, disease, and death. The problem does not end there. No one is born entirely pure (except new souls and saintly souls brought back to help others). The soul will be reincarnated in another human being or life form, to enable it to pay off its "debts" accrued from its previous life. That is, it will possess the same array of emotional tendencies that hindered its fulfillment of "Love thy neighbor as thyself" in its previous life, so that in its new incarnation, it will have the opportunity to improve. Unless it can overcome its emotional weaknesses, the same sorry events will recur.

All evil and suffering are consequences of Cause and Effect. Whether it is personal disease or disasters of a natural kind, the disruption is caused by egoistic human behavior that has accumulated to such a degree that chaos results. Writing about earthquakes, hurricanes, floods, and tornados, Berg comments, "Natural disasters are our own doing. We have the power to prevent and stop these unnatural [sic] phenomena from taking place."[4] Wittingly or inadvertently, human behavior is responsible. There is no such thing as luck or random occurrences in the realms of health, climate, or politics or in any aspect of life. Only one factor is an exception to this equation: the position of the celestial bodies. Astrological conditions enhance people's susceptibility to innate weaknesses, and sometimes they give an added boost to people's ability to overcome them. Yet the stars and planets are influential but not determinative. People have free will, and by choosing to be emotionally mature and elevate their souls, they can surmount the power of the stars and planets, overcome the debts from their past, live healthy long lives, and prevent larger disasters from occurring.

These principles even apply to children. Disease that afflicts children up to the age of 12 (for girls) and 13 (for boys) is explained as an effect of their past lives. The teacher of my "Healing and Consciousness" course told us that it is only an illusion that children are young; they are just extensions of their previous incarnation, like adults in children's bodies. Nevertheless, adults have to do the healing work for them until they reach the age of majority. However, children's birth defects or congenital problems may be caused by their parents' thoughts during conception. (This is explained in chapter 3.) In these cases, the children are extensions of their parents and their parents' faults. Animals, who have no free will according to kabbalistic teachings, are the only creatures whose diseases are solely the result of natural laws alone. Human beings are enjoined to heal them.[5]

Kabbalah Centre teachers explain that disease exists in order to make humans strive for perfection. The typical first response to ill health is fear and anxiety, and this produces a "reactive" response—impulsive and self-centered. The correct response is to apply the "transformation formula": realize that your reaction is the real enemy, shut down your reactive system and let the Light in, and express your proactive nature. Say, for example, you stumble and break your arm. Rather than panic and become angry, you should realize that the pain and suffering have been sent as an opportunity to solve a problem that you yourself created. The accident is actually an opportunity to achieve tikkun. Perhaps you have not been compassionate—either in this life or in previous ones—to handicapped people, or perhaps there are other emotional shortcomings the produced the breakage; there is no such thing as purely physical clumsiness.[6] Whatever the exact reason, you should realize that the accident was a warning that you need to change your behavior. You should be grateful and use the opportunity to transform. You need to act more calmly and thoughtfully, take responsibility, and be more compassionate toward others. In addition, you need to remember that your broken arm is just a small thing. It is part of the 1 percent world of the five senses, but ultimate reality is the 99 percent world of divine light. The 99 percent world affects everything else, and you can gain access to it by applying the right consciousness. Had you maintained the proper consciousness, you would not have broken your arm in the first place.[7]

There is definitely much overlap between these ideas and those found in the broader Jewish religious tradition, but also significant disagreement. The notion that ill health is to be regarded as a God-given opportunity to reform has its roots in biblical stories and was affirmed by post-biblical sages.[8] However, Jewish tradition also teaches that disease is decreed by God as punishment for sins. Berg has always insisted that God does not punish because God should not be regarded as a personified deity but rather as an eternally giving, sharing energy. Negative occurrences, Berg and his followers insist, are not from God but are an automatic consequence of peoples' negative deeds. Any biblical text that indicates otherwise must be understood metaphorically. Additionally, Kabbalah Centre teachers do not accept other beliefs found in the Jewish tradition teaching that God may impose ill health on the righteous in order to receive their prayers or to achieve a larger national goal. Finally, whereas there have certainly been Jewish sages who attributed health problems to astrological conditions and as the result of previous lives, these beliefs were not axiomatic in the Jewish tradition.

The cause of specific diseases is not generally taught in the Kabbalah Centre, but it is available for those who are interested. Because it is specialized and detailed, it is reserved for advanced students and may also be found in Philip Berg's writings. The latter contain many details and quotations from kabbalistic texts that were not included in the Kabbalah Centre publications composed in the late 1990s and after. The more recent literature, much of which is authored by Yehuda and Michael Berg, is designed to appeal to a very broad audience, and consequently, there are no footnotes and few mentions of historic Jewish figures or book titles.[9] A positive tone dominates, and insofar as health is mentioned, it is in the context of healing rather than the factors that contribute to disease.

In the "Healing and Consciousness" course I attended in 2002, the teacher focused on a number of different diseases explained in the Zohar commentary on the Torah portion called "Pinchas." In the initial class sessions, we focused on diseases of the brain as an example of the diagnostic system and its connection to kabbalistic concepts. We learned that because the brain relays instructions to the rest of the body, it plays a crucial role in responding to the demands of the ego: it activates, suppresses, or channels the Desire to Receive for the Self Alone. If I think something negative and self-serving—for example, "I will insult that man who was rude to me"—I have a choice about whether to convert it into action, and the decision occurs in my brain. If I choose not to insult him, I am "restricting," that is, limiting my ego's Desire to Receive impulse. That is good, and I will not face a consequence for having negative thoughts. It is best not to have them at all; if I have too many negative thoughts, they will accumulate in my brain and block the Light and cause damage. When a person is rude to me, I should immediately realize that he is under the control of Satan—that is, he is acting out of the Desire to Receive for the Self Alone, and so he feels the need to oppose me in order to feel like a winner. Aware of this, I will "let in Light" and respond politely and respectfully. No negative energy will enter my brain. If I only *intend* to respond positively, but I remain silent and do not follow through with my intention, the positive energy that accompanies my good intentions will turn negative. Satan has in this way entered my brain. The same dynamic occurs with promises: making promises and not fulfilling them creates negative energy. The long-term consequence of accumulating negative energy in the brain is brain cancer.

It is important to understand an overarching kabbalistic principle that is relevant to both the cause and the curing of disease. The human body is considered a microcosm of the divine world, which comprises the 10 sefirot, the 10 different stages of emanated divinity.[10]

The highest three sefirot—*Keter, Chochmah,* and *Binah*—correspond to the skull, right brain, and left brain, respectively. The right arm connects to *Chesed,* the left arm to *Gevurah,* and the body to *Tiferet,* and so on. That is, the human body in the earthly, lower world is a mirror of the 10 sefirot. The sefirot of the body receive Light from their parallel sefirot in the divine realm, as well as from the other sefirot. A blockage of Light in a particular part of the body means that the body is not receiving the Light from the sefirah that corresponds to it.

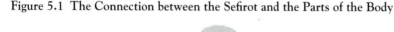

Figure 5.1 The Connection between the Sefirot and the Parts of the Body

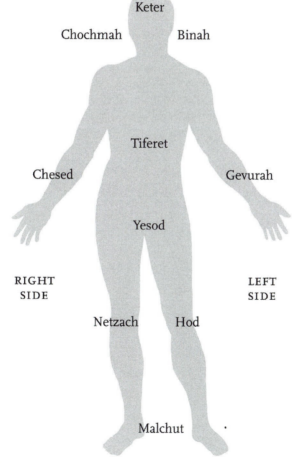

Diagram: Kathryn de Boer.

The connection between the sefirot and the parts of the body is evident in brain diseases that include memory loss. Memory is connected to channeling Light, the "Healing and Consciousness" teacher told us. The Hebrew word "remember" (*zachor*) is connected to the word "male" (*zachar*), and *zachar* is the term for the group of six male sefirot called *Zeir Anpin* that channels Light to the female sefirah called Malchut. Thus, remembering is channeling Light, and forgetting is blocking Light. People who are in the habit of willfully or inadvertently forgetting things are blocking the flow of Light between Zeir Anpin and Malchut.

The blockage positions itself in the repository of memory, the brain. The result is a disease such as Alzheimer's. Upon hearing this, a woman in my class gasped in horror and then said scornfully, "That is simplistic!" The teacher responded, "It *is* simple. That is why it is so important for us to learn how *not* to block Light and how to transform accumulated negative thoughts into positive Light."[11]

Figure 5.2 In a Condition of Health and Harmony, Divine Light Will Flow from the Male Sefirot to the Female Sefira Malchut

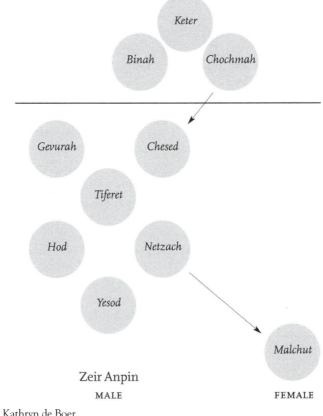

Zeir Anpin

MALE   FEMALE

Diagram: Kathryn de Boer.

The position of the stars and planets can have a deleterious effect on health, too. In the Kabbalah Centre, certain times are known as "cosmic danger zones." In his book *Astrology: The Star Connection*, Philip Berg quotes long passages from the Zohar teaching that the adverse position of the moon relative to the sun and the earth at the time of a child's birth will produce lifelong harm. This is the case even for a truly righteous person. Specifically, souls born when the moon is waning are sentenced to lives of great difficulty and suffering, whereas souls born when the moon is waxing will be blessed with all good things and bodily health.[12] Another example offered is the effect of the twilight hours. Berg is convinced that a person is likelier to be the victim of violent robbery as sunset approaches, because in those hours criminals are "driven by a cosmic energy force that compels people so inclined to exercise the violence of their greed."[13] Then there is the effect of the planetary conjunction of Jupiter and Saturn: to Berg, this explains the untimely death of American presidents in office between the years 1840 and 1960.[14] To Berg, this is a metaphysical, not a physical, phenomenon, and scientists have yet to grasp that the metaphysical origin of all sorts of physical suffering.[15]

Some "cosmic danger zones" need to be understood in reference to holidays and seasonal observances. In the Kabbalah Centre, the dates of the Jewish holidays are understood as "cosmic windows" that, because of the astrological forces dominant at that time, allow people to more easily acquire certain metaphysical energies or adjust their traits. In Berg's early writings, he admitted that the Jewish nation's Desire to Receive is so great that Jews need to "share" or "restrict" a tremendous amount in order to achieve balance. This is why they were given so many mitzvot, or precepts of the Torah. The mitzvot of the holidays, he explained, were designed to balance the Jewish nation's energies so that it could avoid harm to itself and others. In other words, one is courting danger if one does not do the prescribed "restriction" at the time of the holiday. Occasionally—disease is not mentioned much in Berg's early writings—he points out that the harm may manifest itself as disease. For example, on the day before Pesach, the firstborn male is enjoined to fast. This is because the firstborn has an exceptionally high level of negative energy, so much that he *radiates* negative energy. This problem is solved for the firstborn by the commandment to fast:

> The subtle influence of the body is gradually transformed through their discipline of fasting and concentration, permitting us to be nourished by more positive forms of energy and to leave the radiation stemming from our bodies behind.... If we can maintain the balance of body with spirit, we can avoid *dis-ease* since it is the result of blockage within the body of the free-flowing energy of light....Dis-ease—and the word should be hyphenated for the sake of its true definition—is nothing more than the result of conflict between opposite forces radiating in a magnetic field of disunity.[16]

The belief that ill health may be the result of behaviors enacted or not enacted on certain days of the year has remained a principle of Kabbalah Centre life. It is no longer described as a condition peculiar to Jewish people, but to humanity in general.[17]

Even an ostensibly positive cosmic era, if not responded to appropriately, may cause problems. This occurs when there is a mismatch between the Light that is revealed to humanity and humanity's response to it. Signaling the greater prominence of the healing theme in Kabbalah Centre teachings, in 1991 Berg devoted a chapter in a book to emotional stress. He believed that the problem had become widespread at the end of the twentieth century, and its root cause of stress is metaphysical: in this Age of Aquarius, there is an increasing amount of energy from the Light, providing us with greater opportunities to remove Bread of Shame and negative energy. Because the Light is revealing more energy than usual, the vessel of humanity has to expand to receive more Light, and then it must give more in response. Humanity is under great pressure to act in a sharing manner. The failure to expand one's giving capacity causes stress. However, accepting the responsibility to increase one's giving capacity also causes stress; it is like a growing pain in one's vessel as it expands. The solution to stress is not to do less, take tranquilizers, or meditate to achieve quietness of mind, Berg wrote. The solution is for human beings to expand their capacity to accept more of the creative "Light Force." The study of Kabbalah and kabbalistic meditations will definitely help, he explains:

> The study of Kabbalah enables us to gain a deep state of rest which repairs the damage incurred by previous excess stress because the action of the Light Force vaporizes body obstructions. Those black spots that appear on X-rays are merely indications of the impasse created by the body consciousness in hampering the steady flow of the Light Force.[18]

POWER AND POWERLESSNESS IN DISEASE AND HEALING

There seems to be some tension between the seemingly indiscriminating power of the celestial bodies and the other, highly moralistic components of Berg's theory of disease. This can be partly attributed to the historical gap between his two sources: Berg's astrology is drawn primarily from the medieval books *Sefer Ha-Yetzirah* and the Zohar, whereas his highly moralistic theory of disease is based on the twentieth-century writings of Yehuda Ashlag. Ashlag wrote very little on astrology, and so Berg himself had to reconcile Ashlag's teachings with the astrological principles found in the earlier kabbalistic writings. He did this by arguing that those people who are hurt during the "cosmic danger zones" are deserving of the harm inflicted upon them; for example, the souls who require a difficult tikkun are put into babies born during the cosmic danger zones or are put into the path of violent criminals who are stimulated by the astrological conditions.[19] At times, however, Berg applies no real blame to the victims. He repeats throughout his books that people suffer needlessly because of their ignorance of the intricate and highly complex doctrines of Kabbalah. For example:

> [One] cause of the breakdown or damage to the immune system is exposure to various negative cosmic danger zones. The responsibility to avoid these time frames rests with all of us. Ignorance of these devastating cosmic events will not prevent their invasion of a healthy body. Zoharic teachings reveal that cosmic predisposition can play a role in infinite illnesses. Kabbalists zero in on these cosmic markers, with sufficient information to map the location and time frames.[20]

Berg had to harmonize this seemingly arbitrary evil with his belief in the Light's unstinting generosity—can it be that everyone who is ignorant of Kabbalah has earned the consequent suffering? Does the Light have any compassion for those who, through no fault of their own, had no access to Kabbalah? He found the solution to this quandary in the kabbalistic community: people who study Kabbalah have a responsibility to solve the problems of unsuspecting humanity. This is a central theme in Kabbalah Centre worship services. Many prayers are introduced with explanations such as "This meditation is for bringing healing to all who are sick" or "Focus on these words to end violence and repair environmental pollution." One notable example of this was the prayer leader's warning to the congregation prior to the public reading of Deuteronomy 27–28, which contains the curses that befall people who do not observe the Torah's commandments:

> These are real curses, and reading these could unleash tremendous chaos and destruction in the world—*if* you don't do it right. Kabbalah gives us the antidote, and we are going to use it today. Kabbalah teaches us about three words that must be pronounced differently than you would expect, and when you meditate on them and pronounce them correctly, you have used the antidote.... Very few—*very* few—people know this. And if you do it wrong, you unleash these curses upon humanity! There are only a few congregations where they know Kabbalah who will do it correctly like us. So you have a huge responsibility to pay attention and meditate, and say it right. That will protect you, and it will remove the harm caused by all those other congregations.[21]

Comments such as these were received with somber attention.

The Kabbalah Centre teaches that it is particularly powerful when a large group of people scan the same sections at the same time, whether they are together or not. After the massive destruction of Hurricane Katrina in the summer of 2005, the Kabbalah Centre responded by donating funds to the victims, and there was also a special meditation effort at Kabbalah

Centres around the country. With the approach of Hurricane Rita, people were instructed to scan and read a section of the Zohar, the commentary on the Torah portion called "Balak," which reputedly has the power to minimize storms and water damage. One member explained, "I don't discount global warming and other meteorological causes for these hurricanes and the tsunami [in Indonesia, 2005], but there's no doubt that all the negativity in the world is having an effect." She was convinced that the Kabbalah Centre's scanning was influential in diminishing Hurricane Rita's intensity from a level 5 to a level 3. During the Rosh Hashanah Connection, she told me, people were congratulating themselves for their accomplishment and encouraging each other to do more in the future.[22] Benjamin, an enthusiastic member of the Kabbalah Centre told me about Rabbi Berg's exhortations to the congregation,

> the Rav would tell us that the burden and responsibility of the world's problems fell on the Centre. He would tell us, "We have so much work to do: to take care of AIDS, and wars and tragedies! We are hardly pulling the wagon, and Satan works double-time! He will use any trick in the book to prevail!"

This message makes Benjamin feel that he is contributing to the betterment of humanity. He said, "When you learn Kabbalah, you know why you are in this world."[23]

Communal responsibility for health is taught in another way. Kabbalah Centre teachers emphasize that the most effective path to healing oneself is by praying *for others*. During the introductory lecture at the "Shabbat of Healing" (this is the Kabbalah Centre name for the day when the Torah portion called Pinchas is read), the speaker explained the day's power as follows:

> Many of you probably came here in order to heal yourself: physical health, mental health, relationships, or business. But it will not work that way. You cannot use this Shabbat of Healing by focusing on healing yourself. You cannot heal yourself by focusing on your own pains. You do not get Light that way. You get Light by giving to others. So you need to have other people—other specific, individual people—and their problems in mind and concentrate on them. When you scan the Zohar and do the meditations and experience the Shabbat here, you will serve as a channel for those people. The healing will go through you to them, but it affects you, too. You are like a water pipe connected to a faucet. The water flows out to other people, but it is there in you on its way to them, so you will be healed.[24]

The logic behind this lesson is based on the Ashlagian principle that a person receives Light only by sharing. To pray for one's own health is an example of acting on one's Desire to Receive for the Self Alone; one needs to pray for others in order to earn any benefit. Yehuda Berg reflected on this in one of his Weekly Meditation e-mail messages:

> Believe me, it's an uphill battle. I have to work at it all the time, constantly reminding myself to get out of "me" consciousness. That's literally what I do. I tell myself, "focus on this person, focus on this person, focus on this person." And guess what? It works. Sure, 30 seconds later I have to repeat it again, but I do it. I do it because I know the joy, health, and safety I want for my family, friends, students—for the world—depends on my connection to the Light force of the Creator.[25]

Acknowledging—perhaps even by commencing with—a person's selfish desires, Kabbalah Centre teachings propel that person toward consideration of others.

Furthermore, in the Kabbalah Centre community, there is utmost concern to pray for the health of others and show compassion toward those members who are suffering from disease. There are "Rules of the Game of Life" that warn against reactive behavior and judgment of others. People speak in respectful, hushed tones about the one-on-one involvement of the directors and teachers in aiding members of the community who are seriously ill. Specific prayers for healing are included in all worship services (these are described later). This may seem at odds with the prevailing belief that sickness is earned and not accidental. As I have mentioned before, the principle of Cause and Effect leads people to blame themselves for their own troubles. Yet, people are encouraged to reject a punitive explanation for their health troubles. Here is how a young woman who suffered from a life-threatening disease explains her illness:

> At first I thought all my negative actions in the past caused this. I've cheated, I've lied, I had an abortion. But then I thought, "How could that be?" So I don't think of my illness as a punishment as much as it is a situation that happened for the best: it helped me connect to my family, to learn how to be dependent, to teach me other things. I've looked back at the actions I did with dismay, but now I realize that I was doing the best I could at the time, and I must have done those things because they would get me to be where I am now.[26]

I asked a mother whose little boy spent months in and out of hospitals in treatment for leukemia and accompanying problems whether Rabbi Berg and Karen told her the spiritual source of her son's illness. "Oh no, they wouldn't do that! Besides, how would one know? I mean, it must be past life, and we rarely know why, so why talk to people about that?" She felt the deepest gratitude to the Bergs for their emotional support. Once, when she confessed that she must be doing something to cause her son's sickness, Karen said to her, sharply, "Who told you that?! There's no reason to think that way!"

The important lesson she learned from this rebuke was not to be so rough on herself. "We have to be compassionate with ourselves as well as toward others," she told me.[27] Although Kabbalah Centre teachers criticize conventional religion for not providing definite answers, its own answers are not that precise either.

Members of the Kabbalah Centre tell me that they find the movement's teachings on illness to be empowering. They do not seem anxious about the apparent ease of blundering and getting sick. They are pleased that Kabbalah supplies answers to why bad things occur, and they are pleased to not live in doubt and in "limbo" over these ultimate questions. The doctrine of Cause and Effect teaches that there is nothing random, accidental, or meaningless about life. Everything that happens, happens for a purpose. The individual really matters: all the details of one's life are connected to the larger cosmos. Most important, you can shape your own future. There are kabbalistic tools to prevent trouble in the first place, and when trouble occurs, there are tools to resolve it. All participants have these tools. When Ilana's father became sick, she ran to Rabbi Berg for help, and he reminded her that he had taught her what to do to effect healing. She felt sheepish because he had always stressed that they were not to depend on him or on another outside force, but on their own ability to make a connection. "Of course I knew what to do," she said. "I was just panicking and not thinking."[28]

KABBALISTIC VIEWS IN COMPARISON WITH
CONVENTIONAL VIEWS OF DISEASE AND HEALING

The Kabbalah Centre's explanations of disease are strikingly different than the ones suggested by modern Western physicians. In the latter, the body is regarded as a very complex organism that is best studied following established, scientific methods. Scientific research has shown that there are factors contributing to health that go beyond the physical, such as a person's temperament, will to live, lifestyle, membership in a loving community, religious commitment, and so on. However, the notion that health and illness are a reflection of one's moral condition is, from the viewpoint of Western medicine, simply a subjective belief that has not been verified scientifically. Nor is there any support for the conviction that the position of the stars and planets produces health problems.[29] Furthermore, conventional Western medicine tends to be far more tentative about its conclusions than alternative medicine. It is common to hear conscientious doctors admit that their knowledge is limited and that healing therapies are not foolproof or have pros and cons. In contrast, diagnosticians and therapists whose procedures are based on religious conviction typically brim with the certainty that comes with faith. Their optimism is not simply a matter of faith, but is fundamental to the healing process. This is because according to the spiritual teachings described earlier in this chapter, the sick person's positive attitude is absolutely critical for the success of the healing modality.

In ascertaining the position of Philip Berg toward conventional Western medicine, my research shows a contradiction between the written and the ethnographic evidence. The former shows great disdain toward Western medicine, whereas the latter shows much more respect. When Berg increasingly addressed the subject of healing in his books during the 1990s and beyond, he had little but derision for conventional medicine. The following is from his 1991 volume *To the Power of One*:

> The extension of the biomedical approach in physical medicine to the treatment of mental illness has been very unsuccessful. A tremendous amount of time and effort has been wasted in trying to arrive at a basic diagnostic system of mental disorders, without the realization that the search for this kind of physically based diagnosis will ultimately prove futile for most mental disorders.[30]

Berg thinks that one of the problems with standard psychiatry and psychotherapy is that they merely suppress the symptoms of a deeply rooted disease and give the false notion that the problem has disappeared. Instead, Berg advises that "true therapy should consist in facilitating the body's natural healing process by providing an emotional, metaphysical supportive atmosphere for the patient."[31] This consists of learning Kabbalah, engaging in kabbalistic meditation, and practicing "restriction." These will enable people to harness the power of the Light and activate the body's healing forces.[32] In *Immortality: The Inevitability of Eternal Life*, written in 2000, Berg's faith in the power of Kabbalah to advance healing and life expectancy seems as strong as ever, as does his scorn for the limited and shortsighted methods of scientists. Were they only to accept the methods and assumptions of Kabbalah, he states repeatedly, they would be able to accomplish far more and understand the real cause of the world's problems.[33]

There is no official policy or "rule of Kabbalah" pertaining to the use of conventional Western medicine.[34] In the course of my interviews with a range of Kabbalah Centre participants, I have heard much evidence that Philip and Karen Berg recommend that people accept the counsel of medical experts—without abandoning one's common sense, value for human dignity, and caution toward the occasionally overblown promises and questionable procedures of some doctors. Kabbalistic healing therapies (Kabbalah water, meditations, and others described later) are *always* encouraged and utilized in support of conventional treatments, or in place of them; belief in kabbalistic healing therapies is as fundamental in the Centre as belief in the Light.[35] Yet the senior teachers at the Los Angeles Kabbalah Centre boasted to me about the excellent, free (or reduced-cost) medical care they and the Hevre receive from doctors who are Centre supporters or participants.[36] The senior teachers and longtime Los Angeles members repeat anecdotes about Philip and Karen's wisdom in supporting their efforts to find good physicians, help in seeking second opinions from medical specialists, and encouragement in taking prescribed drugs and surgery. Everybody was informed that the Rav was treated by the top doctors after his stroke in 2004. People in the Kabbalah Centre community have told me about medical advice that they have rejected, but this stance has not been unusual in the West since the late 1960s, and I find no evidence that there is a greater rate of rejection within the Kabbalah Centre community than outside of it. What is certain is that within the Kabbalah Centre community, there is deep conviction that the most effective healing occurs through the power of the Light. One person told me her concern that some parents in the Kabbalah Centre were not sufficiently utilizing the benefits of the 1 percent world. "They count on Kabbalah to get them out of trouble and don't use the vehicles that are there," she said. Through her involvement in the Kabbalah Centre elementary school, she knows that some do not allow their children to receive vaccinations. She explained, "They do not believe that immunizations will cause harm. They just figure their kids don't need it, because of Kabbalah."[37] Other parents in the school, when they heard of this, were dismayed; they are vigilant about preventative medical care for their children. One older man, involved in the Centre since the 1980s, told me that people in the Centre simply do not get sick. He invited me to check around and to ask anyone who had been there for many years and was intensively engaged in the practices. "Kabbalah protects," he explained.[38] "I'm not certain that we have less sickness than other communities," said another longtime member, "but I am sure that we handle it better."[39]

In recent years, there has been a greater effort to reach out to the medical community through lectures on kabbalistic healing beliefs and practices. The lectures of senior teacher Shaul Youdkevitch to health care professionals contain a more compassionate and conciliatory approach toward conventional medicine than is evident in Berg's writings. Perhaps Berg's stroke and the aging of the core community have contributed to this. Youdkevitch employs a hierarchical model in describing the Kabbalah Centre's approach to healing. A disease is like an iceberg, he explained. The uppermost, visible part of the iceberg above sea level is in fact just a tiny portion of the tremendous part that extends far below, and similarly, the physical disease is just a tiny manifestation in the 1 percent world of a problem that exists in the 99 percent world. The disease manifests itself in stages. The root source is in an emotional issue that is part of a person's tikkun. If the source is not addressed in an appropriate way, it will eventually give rise to an "energy imbalance" that manifests itself in subtle mental or physical disturbances. The energy imbalance will eventually produce a physical disease that is evidenced by symptoms.

Figure 5.3 The Source of Physical Disease and the Ways of Curing Its Symptoms and "Root Cause"

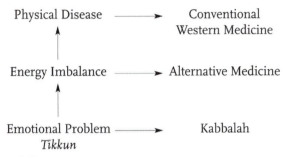

Diagram: Kathryn de Boer.

True healing must be cognizant of these stages. Conventional doctors only treat the symptoms, Youdkevitch said, because they think only in terms of the 1 percent world of the five senses and do not believe the disease extends deeper. Their medications, surgery, radiation, and so on may eliminate the symptoms but do not eliminate the root cause. Tackling the problem closer to the root level are alternative and New Age healers. Youdkevitch affirmed that alternative healing therapies such as acupuncture, physical touch, homeopathy, herbs, naturopathy, and so on can solve the problem of a person's energy imbalance and eliminate physical symptoms. Nevertheless, the root cause still remains. When disease is attacked with conventional and alternative medicine, it will not disappear. Problems will eventually return, sometimes in worse form. A real cure can be found only through kabbalistic healing, which involves various forms of behaviors, rituals, and meditations. These connect the individual to the Light and dissolve blockages, and the free flow of light allows the body to heal itself.[40] Healing is understood to be nothing short of a scientifically measurable cure of physical illness.

Youdkevitch teaches that according to Kabbalah, it is acceptable to use conventional medical treatments and alternative healing therapies, but one should be aware of the limitations involved. Sophisticated medical knowledge similar to that known by modern doctors is evident in kabbalistic literature that dates back millennia, he says. However, the Kabbalists hid this knowledge because had people used the medical treatments, they would have had no incentive to make the deeper changes necessary to fully repair themselves. Without the deeper changes, they would have felt well enough—although they would have probably remained miserable, discontent, and unkind to others. The problems would have reappeared in future lives. The Kabbalists wanted people to understand that true healing comes from God.[41]

This hierarchy of values and recommended treatment of disease, I have found, is not relevant in serious or emergency cases or at times of great pain and distress. In those situations, the Bergs and the teachers consider it sensible, desirable, and compassionate to seek and accept conventional medical treatment. This would be augmented by kabbalistic healing therapies. For example, when a teacher was found to have a problem in his heart valve that required surgery "in the next month or so," Karen advised him to seek surgery immediately. In addition, there was no question but that the child who had leukemia would be treated with chemotherapy in accordance with the oncologist's prescriptions. Meditations, prayers, and Kabbalah water were also used, but no one counseled these people to "solve the problem kabbalistically" at that time.[42] The conventional and kabbalistic treatments were used in tandem with one another.

VARIETIES OF PERSONAL KABBALISTIC HEALING

The goal of all Kabbalah Centre healing methods is to allow divine energy to flow freely into and within the body and sustain it at its optimal level. Theoretically, a person who lives entirely in accordance with the commandment "Love thy neighbor as thyself" will have a soul so elevated that it has achieved an affinity with the Light and will enjoy perfect health, indefinitely. Because only the rarest of saints can ascend to this level through the force of their free will alone, the Creator supplied spiritual tools to assist them (these are the spiritual tools described in chapter 4). The same spiritual tools that make calmness, joy, and contentment a permanent part of one's life, and that help an individual achieve tikkun, also bring perfect health. Some people will need to do more than others; for example, people who are already sick need to perform more in order to cure themselves. Jewish people, who by definition have larger Desires to Share than non-Jews, will have to do more. "Doing more" means performing the prescribed spiritual tools more often, thus enabling greater control over one's ego so as to live in accordance with "Love thy neighbor as thyself." There are healing therapies that are supposed to remove accrued obstructions to Light in the body and rejuvenate parts of the body that have become diseased or malfunctioning. These are of special interest to sick people, but everybody at the Kabbalah Centre is urged to perform them as preventive measures and for spiritual advancement.

Changing One's Name

One of the first healing therapies mentioned in Berg's writings is changing the name of the sick person. This is a very old practice based on the biblical precedent of the name change as a mark of a changed destiny or status—for example, from Abram to Abraham, from Jacob to Israel, and so on. The custom developed of giving an additional name to a person who was dangerously ill or terribly troubled in the belief that the Angel of Death would no longer recognize the victim. The additional name would be one like Hayyim or Hai or Hayyah (life) or Raphael or Raphaela (may God heal), and it would be conferred formally in a ceremony and always used thereafter.[43] Berg offers a slightly different reason for this practice. The person may be ill *because* of bearing a wrong name, he notes. If a person was named after someone who had vices, the live person bearing that name could be suffering because of the tikkun—in this case, the negative consequence—that the dead person was working out at his death. In short, the sick person possesses the flawed soul of the deceased. Changing the name has the effect of changing the soul and, of course, the future. Berg believes that biblical names are best names to choose because the Hebrew letters can be matched to a positive biblical verse for every letter, and meditating on the verses can generate positive energy. According to Berg, he "who meditates on his own verse will find himself at the threshold of the time tunnel that leads back to memory of previous incarnations when his body and his circumstances were different, but his name, essentially, was the same." Looking back at one's previous lives, Berg suggests, can help eliminate fear of illness and death, and it can provide comfort by enabling the person to retreat back to a happier time.[44] Berg admits that a name change, like every other kabbalistic healing method, is not foolproof. Furthermore, although people learn about the effect of changing names and are often eager to change theirs, it is not the practice of the Centre to hastily change peoples' names. One teacher told me, "I tell them that they can wait. I had to wait ten years before the Rav changed my name!"[45]

Lifestyle Changes

Teachers inform new participants to the Kabbalah Centre that "lifestyle change" is the easiest and most basic path to healing. There are three recommended lifestyle changes, and they are similar to those suggested by a wide range of health experts. First, the teachers recommend that people find a supportive community in which to live and participate in the lives of others. Second, volunteering to help people and engaging in community service will help. The logic is that healing occurs when an individual is connected to the Light, whose essence is Desire to Share, and so sharing one's time, labor, and skills with others is an easy way to connect to the Light and activate the body's healing powers. The third lifestyle change recommended is for people to cultivate a habit of study. Although this sounds intellectually challenging, it may actually amount to a daily period in which one thinks positively and makes an effort to feel gratitude, optimism, and compassion toward others. Actual study of kabbalistic texts is ideal, for it will foster the correct kind of positive thinking. These three lifestyle changes are labeled "kabbalistic" because they can be found in a book like the Zohar. The teachers are aware that other religious and medical authorities have made the same recommendations; indeed, they are eager to tell you that medical research has shown the salutary health benefits of community membership, service to others, and optimism. To them, the similarity demonstrates two Kabbalah Centre convictions: Kabbalah is universal wisdom at the source of all wisdom, and Kabbalah's scientific basis will eventually be recognized by leading scientists throughout the world.

All three lifestyle changes can be easily accomplished by joining in the activities of a local Kabbalah Centre. People who are impressed by the free introductory lectures are encouraged to enroll in the three-semester Kabbalah course. The first course in the series introduces them to the "12 Rules to the Game of Life," and within a few weeks of beginning, students are shown how to scan the Zohar and perform basic Hebrew meditations. Ideally, each class of students is assigned several mentors, who are more advanced students volunteering to answer simple questions and to encourage deeper involvement; typically, the mentor will suggest a way that the student can volunteer at the Centre or in one of the community service projects. The teacher of the course becomes the student's "official" teacher, someone with whom a student may meet regularly for counseling and guidance. The mentor or teacher may arrange for the class to attend Shabbat or Rosh Hodesh "Connections" and meals as a group, thereby helping them become friends and together learn how to participate. In this way a person develops a community, engages in volunteer work, and gains a regular study habit. People who live at a distance from a local Centre are at a disadvantage. They (as well as people who live near a Centre) can sign up to receive the free daily, weekly, or monthly e-mail inspirational messages from Yehuda or Michael Berg. They may enroll in distance learning of Kabbalah (online or through videos or CDs) and are assigned a mentor, and this will facilitate the right thinking. If there are enough students in their area, they may be able to get a teacher to come and teach a class face-to-face or through a webcam. They can elect to be active members of a community and volunteer their labor somewhere, but if they want a kabbalistic community, they will need to travel to a Kabbalah Centre–sponsored event outside their local community.

Community participation, volunteering, and positive thinking are described as ways to connect to the Light, to find contentment, to achieve success, and to eliminate chaos. Virtually all of the activities of the Centre, whether they are spiritual tools or communal meals, are described as having the power to eliminate chaos. The word "healing" describes the resolution of any of these problems, as well as the actual cure of disease.

Mitzvot

Likewise, the performance of the prohibitions and positive precepts of the Torah can influence healing. Virtually any mitzvah can be explained as beneficial to health because mitzvot are understood not as "laws" or "commandments," but as tools for connecting to spiritual energy. One mitzvah that is considered especially effective for healing is donating money for charity. *Tzedaka* is the Hebrew term for charity, and its literal meaning is "righteousness."

In the Jewish tradition, tzedaka is understood not as an extraordinary act of generosity, but as an expected behavior of a righteous person, no matter how poor. Nevertheless, it is considered a behavior that has great benefits, and this is captured in the Talmudic maxim "Tzedaka saves a person from death."[46] Jewish literature over the ages has contained many stories of people whose acts of charity toward the poor or generosity in feeding or caring for others delayed the divine decree of their death. A pledge of charity was—and still is, among many Jews—considered essential to a prayer for healing. The Kabbalah Centre regards this teaching as a central tenet of Kabbalah. The lesson of the Bread of Shame is that one can receive only after earning merit. To receive spiritual Light, one must first give, and giving money to charity is an important mode of giving. Students are told generally, and they are counseled one-on-one, that it is to their benefit to tithe.[47]

One student recounted a discussion between students and an instructor during a class about whether it was sufficient to donate to an organization other than the Kabbalah Centre, such as the American Cancer Society. The instructor, Jamie Greene, responded that it is best to give to an organization that promotes Light, and this means limiting your donations to the Kabbalah Centre. Within the Kabbalah Centre there are several different projects and causes to which one may designate a donation. Members of the class were not pleased with this answer, and they asked for the opinion of the senior teacher, Eitan Yardeni. Yardeni pointed out that simply donating money is not sufficient if it does not actually go toward good causes. It does happen, he said, that charities mismanage funds or channel them toward a purpose that is not that worthy, and then the donor is not getting a benefit; he, personally, could testify to the good effects of the money given to Kabbalah Centre projects. But either way, "you must give—or the universe will take it from you!"[48]

The Kabbalah Centre has been sharply criticized for its practice of asking for donations from people who are desperate for a cure for themselves or for their loved ones. Although one teacher admitted to me that there are times when it may not be appropriate—for example, when the sick person truly does not have the funds to donate, or when someone is not of sound mind—the Centre does not deny that it asks for donations as a means of alleviating serious illness or death.[49] Their belief in the power of tzedaka is fundamental. It is considered a very powerful way of becoming a "being of sharing" and thus meriting Light in response. "It will *always* do good," Billy told me.

But remember, when you share enough, you will then merit to receive *what you need*, not necessarily *what you want*. Kabbalah teaches you that *tzedaka* saves from death—everyone [in the Jewish tradition] tells you that. This is nothing extraordinary. And if you give, and you die anyway, it's because first, you did not do it 100 percent. The consciousness was not there. Second, perhaps death is what you need. Death could be your cleansing process.[50]

And, he explained further, the charitable donation might do you good in alleviating your condition in your next life. It is like a store of merit that acts on your behalf in the face of something worse. Billy believes that when the Kabbalah Centre gets attacked for this practice, it is the ego talking. Satan takes root in people, convincing them that they are entitled to their money and their comforts without giving anything in response.[51]

The Kabbalah Centre does not promote the performance of all the mitzvot equally. People are urged to celebrate Shabbat and the holidays at the Centre, but the teachers do not routinely encourage people to say blessings before and after eating, to observe the dietary laws, or to commit to the Sabbath work prohibitions. They are more concerned about promoting the right consciousness than they are with the observance of the mitzvot. Men and women who insist that they want to take these obligations upon themselves will be guided to do so, and some mitzvot have specific healing benefits. One example of this is the mitzvah known as *tefillin*. Deuteronomy 4:8 instructs the Israelite, "Bind them for a sign upon your arms and for frontlets between your eyes," and this is manifested in ritual leather straps (one circling the head, one wound around the arm), each of which is threaded through a small leather box that contains a tiny Hebrew-inscribed scroll. Tefillin is a weekday morning ritual that in both the Kabbalah Centre and the Orthodox Jewish community has been considered appropriate only for men. Because of Berg's principle of noncoercive spirituality, no male is rushed into the observance of this precept, even those Jewish males who attend the Centre's weekday morning prayers.[52]

According to my "Healing and Consciousness" teacher, tefillin is especially effective for brain health. The instructor explained that the four compartments in the box on the head straps correspond to the different parts of the brain. Reciting the blessing and meditations on this part of the tefillin, while sustaining the consciousness of how it connects the wearer to the sefirot, actually draws spiritual Light into the brain, clearing the pathways and removing the negativity there.[53] Yehuda Berg's commentary in the Kabbalah Centre prayer book explains the effect of the tefillin headpiece as follows:

> An evil inclination usually targets our mind when it is trying to take control over our lives. It bombards us with negative thoughts, which in turn lead us to negative actions. By placing the *tefillin* on our forehead, we are overriding the Satan's signal. This action helps to prevent negative thoughts, fears, and insecurities from manifesting in our consciousness. We feel a great sense of positivity and a higher state of mind throughout our day.

Yehuda explains that the head and arm tefillin function like an antenna, drawing spiritual energy from the upper world to the lower world: "Each part of the body tunes and receives a different frequency of spiritual energy. The left hand [around which the arm tefillin is bound] is the main antenna for drawing all the signals to the body."[54]

This explanation for tefillin is discordant with the blessing formula connected with the ritual, which reads "Blessed are You, Lord our God, the King of the universe, who has sanctified us with His commandments and has required us to put on [or, with the commandment of] tefillin." In the Kabbalah Centre community, this literal translation of the blessing—which is found in the Kabbalah Centre prayer book—is regarded as a code, and in accordance with Berg's principle of noncoercive spirituality, "required" does not really mean "required," and "commandment" does not really mean "commandment." Yehuda Berg has, however, constructed an explanation for tefillin that establishes an immediate and long-term benefit to the one who wears them. Alex, a Kabbalah Centre participant who is not Jewish, attends the communal weekday morning prayers twice a week, where many of the participants wear tefillin. He told me that when he first saw them wear tefillin, he thought it was "really weird." Now he's attracted to the idea. He has not been asked to wear tefillin, and he has not requested to do so. He thinks that tefillin are a very powerful spiritual tool, and he imagines that those who wear them must feel they have been injected by divine energy at the start of the day. He was impressed to learn that the place on the head where the knot and the box touch are, in some Eastern religions, considered important pressure points.[55] For people who are aware that negative thoughts accumulated in the brain may cause brain disease, tefillin must be even more compelling and gratifying.

Kabbalistic Nanotechnology Healing

Nanotechnology is a word for the branch of engineering that deals with things smaller than 100 nanometers (a nanometer is one billionth of a meter). In 1961 physicist Robert Feynman envisioned a type of molecular manufacturing in which scientists build things from the level of the atom upward. In 1986, with the publication of K. Eric Drexler's *Engines of Creation*, nanotechnology received popular attention. Drexler anticipated that scientists could manufacture mini-machines or even living organisms to repair human organs and reprogram human genes. Nanotechnology experiments began a few years later, along with more speculative writing. It is clear that Philip Berg was excited by this new field. Because of his deep-seated conviction that Kabbalah is divine wisdom and the source of all human achievement, he "found" nanotechnology healing in Kabbalah.

I have already mentioned in chapter 3 how Berg articulated his kabbalistic theory to conform to atomic theory with its positive, negative, and neutral subatomic components. For Berg, the 10 sefirot, each one corresponding to a less intense and more veiled level of divine Light than the one above it, represents positive energies, negative energies, and neutral harmonizing energies.

The 22 letters of the Hebrew alphabet, the actual instruments of creation, represented different pulses of energy or Light. He believes that the power of the sefirot and Hebrew letters may be harnessed, through kabbalistic meditation, to receive an infusion of divine energy and to recreate the world.

The next generation of leaders unreservedly accepts this viewpoint. Here is one typical explanation of the Hebrew letters and their connection to the universe and the human body, written by Yehuda Berg:

> Just as a human being is built from a four-letter genetic alphabet (A, T, C, and G) found in his DNA, the universe, according to Kabbalah, is built from the 22-letter genetic alphabet of the Hebrew letters. In a human being, each letter represents a different chemical. The letters combine to create a set of instructions to build a human being. The Kabbalists teach that each of the 22 Hebrew letters represents a particular energy force. The Hebrew letters combined in various sequences to create the forces that built our universe. We tap into the power of the 22 Hebrew letters via the prayers and blessings in this [prayer] book.[56]

In nanotechnology healing, a person uses prayers and meditations on the Hebrew letters to refresh the body's cells or the basic material of the physical universe. The power of healing is already there inside each individual. Through prayers and meditations, the person makes the connection to the power inside. "We have to connect to the God inside of us," Ilana told me. "We can do anything, but we don't believe that."[57]

Listening to the prayer leaders at the Centre, reading the advertisements, or attending to the words of the outreach workers, one gets the impression that kabbalistic nanotechnology produces instantaneous, unconditional success. Upon greater scrutiny and questioning, the path to success is more difficult. First, the meditations must be accompanied by the right consciousness: love for the Creator; the desire to connect to the Light; a pure desire to share with other human beings, recognizing them and oneself as part of the totality that is the Light; the recognition that one is responsible for one's life; and certainty in these beliefs and in the power of one's meditations. Second, a successful outcome may be subverted by one's past emotional behavior, which may require the balance of the present suffering. One teacher told me,

> Between us, the letters are simply the tools; they do not achieve anything without the consciousness, which is essential. The letters are like the wheels on a plane: they get it to the speed where he can take off, but that's it. Each person has to do the work to get the plane off the ground and fly.[58]

This, of course, is quite a challenge.

For people in the Kabbalah Centre who see the relationship between the divine and physical realm as one of precise, minute correspondence, a real

Kabbalist is someone whose meditations have the power to transform an object or body part. The Kabbalist focuses his or her consciousness on Hebrew letters in such a way so as to draw divine Light into the body and transform the tissue. "The Rav could walk in this room and regenerate someone's amputated finger," Chaim Solomon, the instructor of the "Healing and Consciousness" course, informed the class. (But the Rav would not do it, Chaim told us, because what would be the point? It would simply activate our Desire to Receive.)[59] Without any surgery or the usual chemicals, the cells would revert back to their state at the point of creation. This process is described as "returning cells to their DNA level" or "returning cells to their embryonic, or stem cell, level."[60] Berg and Kabbalah Centre teachers sometimes call this power by the general term "mind over matter." Every human being potentially has this power, but it is greater among those who have transformed themselves to a level at which they may receive more Light in order to give it back and make change in the world.

Although prayers are used in these healing rituals, their literal meaning is often ignored. As I have already explained, at the Kabbalah Centre, the regular liturgy is regarded not as a means of personally or communally addressing God, but as a way of waging war against the negativity within the soul. Then it becomes possible to receive enough Light so that people can save, heal, and protect themselves. Kabbalah Centre teachers reinforce this idea by calling the room used for Kabbalah Centre communal Connections "the war room," rather than "the synagogue." Using less militant metaphors that conform to the notion of Kabbalah as "spiritual technology," instructor Jamie Greene explains the Centre's outlook on prayer:

> Prayer is a code word in Kabbalah. We don't actually pray to God, because remember the infinite Light of the Creator, or God, is endlessly, infinitely sharing, and therefore, there is no energy of receiving. So in effect, literally, God cannot receive our prayers. Not in that way. Just like we're trying to get online to the Internet, so that we can draw down, or download, whatever energy we need, we're making a connection. We're dialing God in that way, we're connecting to those realms of energy. Therefore we can download whatever we need. The whole notion, the whole code about dialing God, is how I can connect into this realm with my consciousness.[61]

This language makes prayer sound easy and immediately satisfying. It gives the impression that one merely has to "dial" correctly, and one is connected to God, who will, it appears, automatically fulfill human desires. As I have shown, Kabbalah Centre teachings for the more advanced students reveal that results are not so simple or instantaneous.

Although the Kabbalah Centre's explanations for the Hebrew meditations are expressed in its distinctive style and very much in accord with other New Age spiritual approaches, the Centre's Hebrew letter meditations are adapted from older kabbalistic traditions. For the most part, these are the divine names in linguistic formulas known as kavvanot, described in chapter 4.[62] Many of these Hebrew letter meditations are thought to activate the connections between the sefirot. When the sefirot are in the proper relation to each other, divine Light flows freely from one to another and finally into our world. This dynamic is relevant to healing because our good health is dependent on receiving divine Light from above. The problem is solved not by addressing it in the physical realm of the five senses, but by controlling it at its root level in the upper realm of the sefirot. It is a fundamental kabbalistic rule that when changes are made in the realm of the sefirot, there will be parallel effects in the realm of physical reality.

According to Berg's explanation, the top sefirah, Keter, is the most like the Creator in its constant emanation of divine Light—it is almost purely Desire to Share. Below Keter, each sefirah represents a greater veiling of divine Light and is therefore less intense until the tenth sefirah, Malchut, which has no divine Light of its own but simply receives divine Light from above and as such is purely Desire to Receive. Our physical universe is a manifestation of the sefirah Malchut in that "we have no metaphysical energy of our own, and we cannot exist without energy forces drawn from outside ourselves."[63] The sefirot are often likened to the sun and the moon and to members of an extended family. Like the moon, dependent on the light of the sun, humanity is Malchut, dependent on the "sun" of the six sefirot above Malchut called Zeir Anpin. Zeir Anpin and Malchut also relate to each other as a couple; Zeir Anpin, the male, couples with Malchut, the female, and fills her (an empty vessel with no Light of her own) with his nourishing Light (see Figure 5.2, p. 144). Zeir Anpin, however, cannot do this unless he is nourished by the sefirah above him called Binah. He is like a son, a product of the unification of his "parents," Chochmah (male) and Binah (female). Binah is the very beginning of creation; she is the storehouse of energy, and all the Light that may be revealed in our world flows from her. Malchut will only benefit from the nourishing Light of Binah when she unites with Zeir Anpin. The Zohar describes this dynamic using the metaphor of a family feast. Malchut is not automatically invited to the feast, as is Zeir Anpin; she has to attract and sustain a connection with the son before the parents-in-law invite her to join the festivities.[64]

Our chaotic, imperfect world reflects the severance of Malchut from Zeir Anpin. Disease, poverty, hostility, and war are a manifestation of the blockage that obstructs the flow of Light from Zeir Anpin to Malchut and keeps Malchut from receiving nourishing Light. Malchut, our world, is dominated by the Desire to Receive for the Self Alone; this is because we do not share, and so we do not receive sufficient Light and are constantly in need. We/ Malchut need to attract the Light of Zeir Anpin, and the way to do this is to establish an affinity with him. This occurs through sharing and by restricting our impulses, as is accomplished by performing the mitzvot of the Torah and meditating. These actions on earth (when performed with the correct consciousness) "mate" Malchut with Zeir Anpin, and the nourishing Light of Binah is brought down to Malchut. Another way to describe our accomplishment is to say that "we ascend to the level of Binah." At the level of Binah, obstructions of Light are entirely dissolved. Intense injections of Light from Binah lead to healing. Different meditations, restrictions, and mitzvot produce different amounts and intensities of Light from Binah.[65] Kabbalah Centre teachers will recommend these meditations to people who want to pray for others who are sick, or for the sick people themselves. Simply by fully performing the prescribed behaviors with the correct consciousness during the 10-day period from Rosh Hashanah through Yom Kippur, a person receives such intense exposure to Binah that one can reshape one's very cells and—in Berg's language—"perform surgery on our DNA."[66] In short, when a person engages in the rituals of these holidays while maintaining the proper consciousness, he or she may be cured of disease.

Virtually all of the healing meditations include meditations on specific combinations of Hebrew letters, or a single letter, that are thought to enable a connection to God. There is a meditation called *Tikkun Ha-Nefesh* that includes meditation on the sefirot as well as different formulations of the four-letter divine name made up of the Hebrew letters *yod hey vav hey* (also known as the Tetragrammaton). This meditation is predicated on the belief that the sefirot correspond to different parts of the human body. Starting with the highest sefirah and the top of the head, the meditator simultaneously meditates on the sefirah associated with it, on the body part (while gently waving his or her hand over that body part), and on a different formulation of the four-letter divine name. Moving down the parts of the body while meditating on the sefirot associated with them, the meditator draws healing energy to each part in turn. The Kabbalah Centre has made this multitasked meditation easier by printing a numbered chart of the meditation. The chart begins with box number one which contains the words "skull," "Keter," a Hebrew formula and an English transliteration of it to be contemplated silently; the last box contains the word "feet," "Malchut," a Hebrew formula and an English transliteration of it to be contemplated silently. Each communal worship service will include at least one interval designated for the members of the congregation to perform Tikkun Ha-Nefesh. Individuals can do the meditation by themselves outside of the synagogue, as needed. When Ilana does Tikkun Ha-Nefesh, she feels warmth rising in those parts of her body where she is concentrating her attention. She is not painstaking about how her hands circle over the different parts of her body. She explains, "As long as you're looking at the different combinations of letters, you're doing it okay." She does Tikkun Ha-Nefesh about three times a day.[67] People may also choose to focus on a particular part of the body. Those who are concerned about preventing or curing brain disease, for example, may perform

Tikun Hanefesh

the top three Tikkun Ha-Nefesh meditations—for the skull, right brain, and left brain—many times each day. In the Kabbalah Centre community, among the most important of the letter combinations are those known as the 72 names of God. These are 72 clusters of three letters each that were derived from Exodus 14:19–21. Historians maintain that they have been part of kabbalistic practice since the late twelfth century, but Kabbalists insist that they were given to Moses encoded in the Torah, and they were first used by the Israelites to split the Red Sea.[68] The following explanation of the names, which appears on the Kabbalah Centre Web site, ties the names' power to their universal scope and the kabbalistic energy system:

> The shapes, sounds, sequences, and vibrations of the 72 names radiate a wide range of energy forces. The Light they emit purifies our hearts. Their spiritual influence cleanses destructive impulses from our natures. Their sacred energy removes rash and intolerant emotions, fear, and anxiety from our beings. The Hebrew letters are instruments of power. In fact, the Hebrew word for "letter" actually means pulse or vibration, indicating a flow of energy. The Hebrew alphabet transcends religion, race, geography, and the very concept of language. The three letters signify three spiritual forces—a positive charge, a negative charge, and a ground wire—to create a circuit of energy.[69]

כהת	אכא	ללה	מהש	עלם	סיט	ילי	והו
הקם	הרי	מבה	יזל	ההע	לאו	אלד	הזי
וזהו	מלה	ייי	נלך	פהל	לוו	כלי	לאו
ושר	לכב	אום	ריי	שאה	ירת	האא	נתה
ייז	רהע	וזעם	אני	מנד	כוק	להחו	יוו
מיה	עשל	ערי	סאל	ילה	וול	מיך	ההה
פוי	מבה	נית	ננא	עמם	הוזש	דני	והו
מוזי	עזו	יהה	ומב	מצר	הרוז	ייל	נמם
מום	היי	יבמ	ראה	וזבו	איע	מנק	דמב

Chart of the 72 names of God, reading from right to left. Copyright © The Kabbalah Centre International/Kabbalah University Archives/university@kabbalah.com/www.kabbalah.com.

Yehuda Berg, expanding on earlier kabbalistic texts in his book *The 72 Names of God: Technology for the Soul*, articulates a different function for each of the 72 names of God.[70] Theoretically, meditating on any of the names will diminish one's Desire to Receive for the Self Alone, thereby enabling the individual to have greater access to the Light and improve his or her health. However, at least four of the 72 names—*mem hey shin, yod yod yod, yod lamed yod*, and *mem vav mem*—are given prominent mention for their salutary effect on personal health.

The divine name *mem hey shin* is used the most often for healing. The Kabbalah Centre prayer book teaches that these three letters

> release the force of healing. We should close our eyes and visualize these three letters emitting rays of light bathing our entire body in a flood of white light. We should also send this energy to others in need of healing. We can meditate upon their Hebrew name or visualize the *mem, hey, shin* radiating light over their body.[71]

The *mem hey shin* divine name, like most of the other divine names, does not spell out a word and does not have a single explanation. Some prayer leaders have pointed out that the letters are the same as in the Hebrew name of Moses, Moshe (spelled *mem shin hey*), implying that the meditation calls on his help. Yehuda Berg's commentary on *mem hey shin* makes two points. First is the general principle that the healing power of the name is activated for ourselves when we pray on behalf of others. The second point is a reference to Cause and Effect, in that healing begins when we accept responsibility for creating our own diseases:

> We must lose the victim mindset. We must realize that it was something we did—in this life or a past life—that brought about illness. Immediate causes such as the foods we eat, or even our genetic makeup, are simply the weapons that inflict illness upon us. They are not the causes, they are the effects.[72]

Other teachers have pointed out that the numerical value of *mem hey shin* (each Hebrew letter has a fixed numerical value) is equivalent to the numerical value of the Hebrew word *ratzon* (desire). The lesson here is that a person who desires to be healed must reject the belief that he or she is the passive victim of illness. Armed with the proper consciousness, the person will fight the Satan within and begin to heal.[73]

This divine name is the centerpiece of the Kabbalah Centre's recitation of the communal healing prayer called *Misheberach La-Holim*. This old Jewish prayer used to be recited very infrequently in synagogues because it was reserved only for people who were gravely ill. In the last few decades, however, it has become a fixture of the Sabbath service in many congregations, and new modes of recital have been developed to accommodate the large number of people who include in it the names of their friends and relatives who are suffering from all types of illnesses.[74] It is no different at the Kabbalah Centre, where the prayer draws quite a bit of attention from the congregation. *Misheberach La-Holim* is recited during the Torah reading, which, as the high point of the Shabbat Connection, commands the presence of the entire congregation. Prior to the prayer's recital, volunteers distribute handouts (prepared before the Sabbath), upon which are the many names of men and women who require healing prayers (one may call the Kabbalah Centre during the week to add names to the list). The Jewish custom is to mention the Hebrew first name of the ill person and mother, such as David *ben* (son of) Rachel, or Sima *bat* (daughter of) Rachel. In the mixed Kabbalah Centre setting, one will see names such as Jorge *ben* Consuela or Jennifer *bat* Lisa. If a mother's name is not known, the person is always called the daughter of Sarah (the matriarch). At the front of the synagogue is an easel—or, if a projector is used, a huge screen—displaying the Hebrew letters *mem hey shin*.

The prayer announcer declares, "The first recitation is for males who are sick," and he directs everyone to concentrate on one or more names of the sick and the letters *mem hey shin*. The prayer reciter chants in Hebrew,

> He who blessed our pure and holy forefathers will bless all the sick of Israel and among them may he bless (the sick male's name) the son of (the mother's name) and may He send complete healing to his 248 organs and his 365 sinews. Please, God, heal him, please. Please God, heal him, please.

Without missing a beat, the congregation takes over, singing the next phrase in unison, three Hebrew words that start with the letters in reverse order: *shabbat hi miliz'ok, shabbat hi miliz'ok, shabbat hi miliz'ok.* This phrase means "for Shabbat prohibits crying out," and it refers to the belief that because the Sabbath is a day of blessings and plenty, it is not seemly to request more from God—although this is exactly what the worshiper is doing. ("You see," the teachers explain, "the literal meaning does not make sense. It is a code.") The prayer reciter completes the prayer with "and healing will come soon. May it so be pleasing and we shall say, Amen!"[75] Then the ritual is repeated, this time for sick women. It is a dramatic, unifying experience for the congregation. Whereas the literal meaning of the prayer calls on an omnipotent God to cure the sick, the prayer's meaning for this congregation is a request for assistance in curing themselves.

There is also a wide gap between the literal and the "kabbalistic meaning" of another prayer considered to be a powerful healing tool. This is the prayer known as the *Shma*, which is a declaration of belief consisting of Deuteronomy 6:4–9; 11:13–21; and Numbers 15:37–41. It has been a central element of Jewish liturgy for over two thousand years. In addition to proclaiming God's oneness, it asserts the principle that one should teach the Torah to one's children, and it mentions three ritualized reminders of the mitzvot: the tefillin (described earlier), the *mezuzah* (affixing words of Torah to one's door-post, usually in the form of a small box containing a tiny scroll of writing), and wearing the special fringes on one's garments called *tzitzit* (these have been traditionally worn by men on an undergarment and on a prayer shawl). The *Shma* also contains a stark statement of the principle of God's earthly reward and punishment for performing or neglecting the mitzvot. In the Kabbalah Centre, the prayer retains its place of prominence in the communal prayers. The prayer book contains a literal translation of the *Shma*, so all can read the ideas that conflict with the Centre's teachings (e.g., a punitive God, the duty to perform mitzvot), but during the Connections and in the Kabbalah Centre prayer book, the *Shma* is described as important for healing because of its numeric attributes:

> Before we actually start the *Shma*, we must think about the concept of loving our neighbors as we love ourselves. Even more powerful is to meditate upon someone else who needs healing. The first verse of the *Shma* channels the energy of *Zeir Anpin*, the upper world. The second verse expresses our world, the *Malchut*. There are a total of 248 words in this prayer that transmit healing energy to the 248 parts of the human body. The first section of the Shma is built of 42 words signifying the 42-letter name of God in the Ana Bekoach [another prayer]. The next section is composed of 72 words that connect to the 72 names of God. The following section contains 50 words, which link us to the 50 gates of Light that are contained in the sfirot known as Binah. This link helps us rise above the 50 gates of negativity.[76]

Thus, like Tikkun Ha-Nefesh, there is a correspondence between the body parts, the divine names, and the manifestation of God's presence in the sefirot.

Another divine name, *mem vav mem*, plays a role in the practice of using bundled sage leaves to spiritually cleanse a space. At the Kabbalah Centre Internet store, this practice is described as follows:

> You'd be amazed if you could see the entities that may be lingering around your home or clinging to your physical body! Negative actions leave behind a residue that can clutter up your emotional and physical life. Mem Vav Mem has the power to cleanse your body and your environment. Used in combination with Sage, this potent duo absorbs negativity and enhances the flow of life. It will drive away any negative forces and tensions that can give rise to misfortune.[77]

This ritual combines kabbalistic nanotechnology with the folk remedy that figures prominently in Native American and Chinese healing.

Another prayer with healing powers is *Ana Bekoach*. Historians date this liturgical Hebrew prayer to the medieval era, but the Kabbalah Centre accepts the Jewish tradition that it was written by a rabbi in Roman

Palestine named Nachunia ben ha-Kana. At the Kabbalah Centre, its literal meaning—which is a poetic beseeching of God to purify, protect, and hear the prayers of his devout worshipers—is ignored; instead, following a kabbalistic tradition, the structural elements of the poem represent the sefirot and God's name. The six verses symbolize the six sefirot of Zeir Anpin, and the seventh verse is Malchut. Each verse contains six words, and the initial letters of all 42 words are considered to spell out a 42-letter divine name. People are taught that *Ana Bekoach* is the oldest and most powerful daily spiritual tool, designed to draw the light of Zeir Anpin into Malchut and thereby eliminate chaos in our world. In the communal recitation of *Ana Bekoach* at the Kabbalah Centre, the congregation intones the first verse while meditating on the six initial letters within it, and the prayer leader calls out the function of the sefirah and the two 3-letter divine names in that verse.

According to Kabbalah Centre teachings, the third verse, which is connected to the sefirah Tiferet, has special healing power. The first three initial letters in the verse (*nun, gimel,* and *dalet*) refer to the power of sustenance and abundance. The prayer leader explains that when we focus on these letters, we gain an affinity with the Creator's generosity and are then empowered to act generously. This earns us true prosperity. When we contemplate the next three letters (*yod, kaf,* and *shin*), we are focusing on a sequence that gives us access to healing power. He explains,

> *Yod kaf shin* is the consciousness within each of the cells of the body, creating that perfect state of balance, harmony, unity, and taking every cell back to its original, undifferentiated state of oneness. The power of love, and total balance and harmony. So we're created balance and harmony within our own immune system to have perfect health.[78]

Included in *Ana Bekoach* is a meditation on the angels of the day and month. Angels are the divine powers that are said to be assigned to each and every element of creation, protecting and encouraging its potential development. The angels meditation involves scanning other Hebrew letters. *Ana Bekoach* also includes a recitation of Tikkun Ha-Nefesh. The entire meditation ends with the silent meditation on the seventh verse, Malchut. The silence is regarded as an exercise in "restriction," and it is considered to help people limit their ego more easily. Kabbalah Centre teachers recommend that people start the day with a five-minute meditation consisting of *Ana Bekoach*, Tikkun Ha-Nefesh, and the angels-of-the-day meditation. This meditation "plants a seed for the day," shaping it in accordance with the values articulated and the powers that were "activated." It is good to end the day with *Ana Bekoach* as well, so that "at night you're ensuring that when you sleep there's rejuvenation and reception of whatever messages you may need to receive in your dreams. You'll be really connecting to the right levels."[79]

I have been told several stories about people who have had success with the kabbalistic meditations after receiving a terminal medical diagnosis. Typically, such people come to the Centre after their doctors have given them no hope, and they are desperate for a cure. Shaul Youdkevitch told me his experience with a young woman who came to the Kabbalah Centre after her doctor told her that her cancer was terminal and she did not have much time. She had two little kids. "We prayed and prayed for her," he told me. "Her name was in the *Misheberach,* they said her name before the *Shma* and before and after other prayers." He recited her Hebrew name to me, "Leah bat Malka. Leah bat Malka. We said it over and over again in the prayers." The woman's husband was not happy with her involvement in the Centre, he told me, "but she was a wonderful woman, and everybody loved her. And she lived for 6 more years! Her children reached their teens." In the end, he told me,

> the Angel of Death was stronger. But also, she gave up near the end. I can't talk about why, because it has to do with really private matters about her own life that she didn't resolve, that she didn't want to face, that were troublesome to her.[80]

I asked him whether it wasn't better to help people accept the ending of their life. "She wanted to live! When people want to live, you help them," he responded. He told me about an 89-year-old man who had studied at the Kabbalah Centre for a while and was sent to the hospital with a serious ailment:

> I visited him in the hospital and he was very depressed, and he told me what had happened. The doctor checked him and left the room, and then the man heard the doctor say to the nurse, "Make him comfortable." He knew that meant that they were giving up on him and he was going to die. I said to him, "Do you want to die? Are you ready?" The man said no. So I said, "Say *Ana Bekoach*—shout it!" And together we shouted *Ana Bekoach. Very* loud—the hospital staff didn't know what to do with us, but they left us alone. We worked with him, we said prayers at the Centre, and a few days later he was out of the hospital. The doctor was amazed. The man lived two more years. Then he got sick again, and he was 91, and he told us, "It's time." So we helped him go peacefully.[81]

Kabbalah Water

Kabbalah water is the one of the simplest modes of healing that is offered by the Centre, and like the carrying of the pocket-sized volume containing the Zohar commentary on Pinchas, people believe that it is effective even when the user exercises no kabbalistic consciousness. It is sold at the Kabbalah Centre in plastic bottles and serves as drinking water. Less typically, people cook with it, apply it to their body, splash it on objects, or bathe in it.

Many cultures around the world accept the notion that water may acquire or may naturally possess healing or sacred qualities. Kabbalah water acquires its special qualities because of the meditations enacted upon it. Kabbalah Centre teachers occasionally refer to the water as "liquid Zohar," as if by drinking it one absorbs the power and sanctity of the holy book.

Water rituals have always been part of Judaism and the kabbalistic tradition. Water immersion, which was a fundamental biblical purification ritual, became institutionalized in the Jewish community as the *mikveh*, a ritual bath built according to exacting specifications and filled with rain or spring water. In the absence of a mikveh, prescribed purification must take place in natural bodies of water. The water immersion is thought to remove impurities and change the status of the immersed object or person, or, as some argue, it confirms that an essential change has already occurred. For example, the process of conversion to Judaism involves immersion, some Jewish traditions require dishes and cookware to be immersed before they are considered kosher or fit to be used, and women who have menstruated or given birth must immerse themselves after a prescribed amount of time before they can resume physical contact with their husbands. Women's immersion is a private, not public, ritual, although it may be supervised by a female supervisor; men's immersions—which, unlike women's monthly immersions, are no longer mandated by Jewish law—may be private or occur with other men present. Among Kabbalists, immersion for men was considered essential to establish the high level of purity required before engaging in prayer, study, rituals, or other sacred activities. From its beginning, the core Kabbalah Centre community that follows Jewish law has honored all of these immersion practices. At the international Rosh Hashanah and Pesach retreats, the Centre makes provisions for men's immersions, and all men are informed of the option. In addition, both men and women engage in immersion as a spiritual cleansing to enhance health and for various spiritual benefits. In the New York and Los Angeles Kabbalah Centre communities, and likely elsewhere, there are men who immerse on a daily basis. When the Los Angeles Kabbalah Centre established its permanent site on Robertson Boulevard, the directors included within it a beautiful room containing two *mikvaot* (plural) for its members.[82]

Nevertheless, the Kabbalah Centre does not explain Kabbalah water by associating it with the tradition of mikveh. The theoretical foundation of Kabbalah water is in the cosmogonic narrative, in which God created the world in order to share Light. The primordial waters mentioned in the biblical account of creation were a physical manifestation of the Creator's Desire to Share. According to Berg, the original water was pure positive energy imbued with the essence of sharing. The world was filled with abundance and vitality, and the human life span extended hundreds of years. However, water's purity was sullied by the increasing evil of human society. By the time of Noah, water had acquired a dual nature, negative and positive, and has been that way ever since: it is crucial for all life and refreshes and purifies, but it also can be terribly destructive.[83]

Figuring out how to produce such water was not a simple matter, I was told; it took Berg many years of experimenting with ways to restore water's original purity by following the guidelines contained in kabbalistic writings. By the end of the 1990s, he was satisfied enough with his results to provide some of his special water to sick people that he knew personally; some time later, the Centre produced enough to sell in the Kabbalah Centre stores. In 2003 and 2004, visitors to the Los Angeles Kabbalah Centre synagogue could see cases of bottled water piled high along the walls and back of the room, and people told me that its power was strengthened by the Light produced during Connections. In addition to the regular Kabbalah water, there is a version that has enhanced healing power called Pinchas water. Pinchas water is not produced in large quantities and is more expensive; it is reserved for people who can show they are under a doctor's care for a serious illness. All the Kabbalah water sold by the Centre is the product of Philip Berg's meditations. His son Michael told me that this is a pragmatic matter of ensuring that the water is of consistently high quality. Everybody has the power to improve the quality of water through their own exertions, just as we all have the power to bless someone in such a way that it makes a difference. This power is not just reserved for a few, although someone whose soul is at a very high level can do it better than someone whose soul is lower.[84]

Like many of the other spiritual tools provided by the Centre, Kabbalah water has both elitist and populist elements. The meditations for producing it are not taught in any classes. Like the kavvanot, the process that generated this spiritual tool remains shrouded in mystery; it is found in teachings that are mediated by the Kabbalists whose spiritual level is thought to be beyond that of most humans. Yet Berg and the Kabbalah Centre, in their mission to spread Kabbalah to all humanity, have made it available to everyone. In addition, it is taught that any water can be made into Kabbalah water. Berg, however, has insisted on special mountain springs that meet the specific geological and climactic conditions he derived from kabbalistic literature. In Kabbalah Centre teachings, holiness is associated with physical and emotional pleasure, and it is crucial that the experience of drinking the Kabbalah water is a positive one. The Kabbalah Centre's water provider stopped supplying the Centre in 2005, and despite the demand, Berg refused to produce more until he found a spring that met his standards. One of his students told me, "For weeks I saw all the maps, all spread out on the table, because the Rav was looking for just the right source." She tried other bottled waters during the interim, but she did not think that they tasted as good.[85]

It is characteristic of the Kabbalah Centre to bolster its religious beliefs with scientific language and claims, and this applies to Kabbalah water too. Teachers who are more comfortable talking about chemistry will describe the structure of a water molecule, making reference to a hydrogen bond that connects the elements together and helps enable multiple water molecules to form "clusters." The body's DNA, they may mention, forms a double helix structure that is held together by a hydrogen bond. All the teachers can recite water's importance in transmitting oxygen, nutrients, and information to all parts of the body and the huge percentage of water that makes up the brain and the body as a whole. Listeners are impressed by this information and can easily agree that consuming a sufficient amount of high-quality water will enhance their health. At this point the explanation glides smoothly to points that cannot be verified scientifically. Kabbalah Centre doctrines hold that there is no real distinction between the physical and the spiritual world. In this context, it makes sense to explain that water may harbor anger, pessimism, joyousness, and optimism. Water that is infused with positive feelings will be good for the body, and good feelings directed at the body will positively affect its water stores. This positive energy is essential for the optimal functioning of the body from the DNA level upward.[86]

Those who are interested in scientific proof of this belief are directed to the research of Dr. Masuro Emoto, available on the Web or in books. Emoto recounts his experiments in which people utter words directed at samples of water, or they tape messages onto bottles of water. Before and after, photographs are taken of the water in its crystallized frozen state. Invariably, the water subjected to positive messages (such as "thank you" or "I love you") crystalizes into lovely, delicate forms, whereas the water subjected to negative messages ("you fool" or "Adolf Hitler") forms structures that are chaotic or that are incapable of crystallization.[87] Similar work has been produced by Professor David Schweitzer, who has lectured widely on what he calls "thought form photography," that is, photographic evidence of the transformative powers of thought. His photography of water trapped in a meteor, never exposed to human beings, shows a marked difference from water exposed for an extended time to human society. He has been credited with taking a photograph of water exposed to kabbalistic meditation, showing that the sefirot in their Tree of Life formation are evident in the crystallized form.[88]

The claims of Emoto, Schweitzer, and other proponents of structure-altered water have never been subjected to standard scientific measurements or evaluated in peer-reviewed scientific literature. Most chemists, biochemists, and physiologists would dismiss these authors as quacks and hucksters promoting "New Age pseudo-science" to ignorant and uncritical people. Nor would they regard Emoto or Schweitzer as authorities in the field; Emoto's doctorate is from a university of alternative healing, and Schweitzer's academic credentials are not established. Emoto uses scientific terms inappropriately, and his discussion of water's properties is inconsistent with long-established research. Scientists explain the photos by pointing out that water crystallizes in many different ways, and the end result is dependent on the conditions, rates of freezing, and whether there are other substances in the water.[89] One retired professor of chemistry has constructed a sophisticated Web site that chronicles and exhaustively details the multitude of waters on the market claiming to be enhanced or structure-altered. The advertisements of many different brands of structure-altered water, he has found, make unsupportable claims. One common one is virtually identical to that of Kabbalah water: that the water has been altered so that it is now a pure form of water that was once common on earth before the spread of evil and pollution.[90] The closest that Kabbalah water has come to being scientifically reviewed occurred when a Kabbalah Centre director in Florida succeeded in getting the state's Department of Agriculture to consider it as a curative to the disease then harming the orange crop. The state's chief of entomology, nematology, and plant pathology declared that the "product is a hoax and not based on any credible known science."[91]

Kabbalah Centre directors have made no effort to subject their water to the rigors of scientific testing, and their members who drink the water make no such demand. For years, Kabbalah Centre teachers described the salutary effect of Kabbalah water on the radiation-contaminated water in Lake Chernobyl. "A small amount of Kabbalah water was added to the lake," my teacher told the class, "and the radiation level went down significantly." Unfortunately, we learned, the Ukrainian government did not allow the Centre to continue with its ministrations or to conduct experiments so as to verify these results.[92] I asked Leilani, a drinker of Kabbalah water, a licensed pharmacist, and a holistic healer, why she felt the water to be so beneficial for healing.

Question: Do you think there is a different structure to the water?

Answer: Yes there is, once they do the blessings and meditations.

Question: Have you examined it yourself, like through a microscope?

Answer: No, I haven't. But you can see it explained online. There's this Japanese doctor. The same photographs were taken of Kabbalah water, and it had the Tree of Life in it.... I can tell you for a fact that the pH changes after the blessings.

Question: Have you checked that yourself?

Answer: No, I haven't.

Clearly, people who desire scientific proof are not going to buy Kabbalah water or remain at the Centre for long. The issue of scientific verification was not important to Leilani, nor is it for most members of the community. Kabbalah Centre doctrines describe the realm of physical reality that we perceive with our five senses and that is known and measured by scientists as "the world of the 1 percent," a somewhat illusory sliver of existence. True reality is the 99 percent world, the realm of spirituality. In short, there are lots of things that are true that cannot be proven, and people who insist on scientific proofs are limited by their 1 percent thinking. Their own experience, and their knowledge of the experience of others, is more persuasive. The pharmacist *knows* that Kabbalah water is effective. Also, she pointed out, "just on the 1 percent level, it's good for you because it tastes good and you'll drink it," and everybody knows the benefits of staying hydrated.[93]

Furthermore, there are convincing ways of explaining when the water works and when it does not. In the pharmacy where Leilani works, one of the other workers kept stretching his arms and wrists at different times during the day, and he told her he was having pains in his wrists. She persuaded him to drink a glass of Kabbalah water and let her rub some on his wrists. He felt better immediately and has not had any further pain. The man had never attended the Kabbalah Centre and had teased her for her association with it, but he now affirms that the water cured him. The pharmacist, who drinks Kabbalah water all day long and still has minor aches and pains, asked one of the teachers to explain why it worked for him and not for her. Yael Yardeni told her, "He's got a smaller vessel than you, so a little bit of Light fills it." Leilani knows that her vessel has grown and stretched as a result of her scanning, meditations, and restrictions, and so she will need far more Light than he does to produce a cure. Besides, she added, her aches and pains may be part of her tikkun.[94]

Placebo Effect?

Belief in the effectiveness of a medication or treatment will not cure all ills, but it is a factor. There are scientific studies showing that for certain chronic ailments, placebos are successful for approximately 40 percent of people who use them. Consequently, even doctors who regard Kabbalah water as mere water will concede that almost half of the people who believe in the efficacy of Kabbalah water and who use it for minor problems are likely to be cured. Relieved of their problems, they broadcast their experiences around the community, building faith in the water's power. The expense of the water and the effort involved in acquiring it from the Centre are also likely to increase peoples' desires to have their commitment confirmed. Those who are not cured will, like Leilani, find other explanations.

One member of the Kabbalah Centre community who was well aware of the lack of scientific basis for Kabbalah water and kabbalistic nanotechnology referred to the research on placebos to explain to me why he supported the Centre's healing therapies. "Most people come to the Kabbalah Centre for the placebo effect," he said, and because they think the water and the meditations have a proven basis, "about half of them will get positive results." He did not think that was such a bad thing. What frustrated him was that few of them really believe in the principle of mind over matter, which holds that one's consciousness can actually cure the body's ills. Were they to accept this, he told me, the rate of success would be far higher.[95]

Spirituality for Kids and World Peace

Karen Berg is credited with the idea of developing a curriculum for teaching young children the guidelines for personal behavior contained in the "12 Rules of the Game of Life." She knew that children raised in the Kabbalah Centre community and educated in the Kabbalah Centre elementary school would be learning these lessons from their parents and teachers, but she believed that it was the Centre's obligation to carry the teachings outside the community; it is an important aspect of the mission to spread Kabbalah to the world. Healing the world and bringing world peace, Karen explains, starts with each individual. The best way to produce people who will live in accordance with sharing values is to shape them while they are young. Naomi Ricardo and Sarah Yardeni, two educators within the Hevre, designed interactive, fun lessons for children aged 6–12 in after-school and summer-camp settings. Spirituality for Kids (SFK) began in Toronto and Los Angeles for children (and those parents who could join in) who could enroll in the classes as enrichment activities and for children (and those parents who could join in) living in high-crime and poverty-stricken areas, who would be given the opportunity free of charge. By 2004 the program was also available in New York, Florida, and Israel.

Michael Berg, Moica Berg (seventh and eighth from the left), Centre teachers, and teachers from Malawi at the Los Angeles Kabbalah Centre in 2006, training to be Spirituality for Kids facilitators. Copyright © The Kabbalah Centre International/Kabbalah University Archives/ university@kabbalah.com/www.kabbalah.com.

Spirituality for Kids is a different type of healing than all those previously mentioned. First, although Spirituality for Kids was started as a project of the Kabbalah Centre, it has been an independent legal entity since 2001 and does not aim to bring the people it serves into the Centre. SFK has offered its program through contracts with public school–sponsored after-school programs, secular agencies (such as the Boys and Girls Club), and religious organizations that would not be comfortable being associated with Kabbalah (such as the YMCA); for organizations such as these, it is important for SFK to be distinct from the Kabbalah Centre.

The Spirituality for Kids curriculum is essentially secular. "If you want to teach children Kabbalah," I was told, "you send them to the Kabbalah Children's Academy. SFK is not Kabbalah."[96] Children are taught that within them are two conflicting impulses, the "Good Guy" who leads them toward sharing and treating others with human dignity, and the "Opponent" who pulls them toward self-centered, mean-spirited behavior and immediate (but only short-term) self-gratification. The lessons—which are fun and lively— are reinforced and then practiced through group games, drama, dance, crafts, recitation, and writing. The teachers do not put the lessons within the framework of theology. Instead, they direct the children "to see that they have the power inside them to overcome challenges and improve the quality of their lives and the world around them."[97] Insofar as there is mention of "the Light," it is connected to those feelings to which all people aspire: happiness, comfort, contentment, love, and so on. If they wish, children and their parents may identify the Light and the Good Guy with Jesus, God, or Mother Nature. In the SFK class I observed, a teacher respond enthusiastically, "Yes, that's one way to look at it!" when a child identified the Light with Jesus. When a child said, "The Opponent is the bad guy in us, like the devil," the teacher responded gently, "We don't see it that way. The Opponent is in us, and *we're not bad*; the Opponent is our inner voice that says 'me me me.'"[98] There is no appeal to an all-powerful force that solves problems; the emphasis is on the dynamic within each child. The teachers acknowledge that life is hard and the world is unfair, but the lessons teach that although the children cannot necessarily change everything around them, they do have the power to control their reactions.

The Kabbalah Centre, with its emphasis on meditation, Zohar scanning, and "restriction" as vehicles for world peace, seems at first glance to teach that political activism is irrelevant or unnecessary. Yet it is in projects such as Spirituality for Kids that one sees an alignment with progressive social-welfare and peace movements. "We think it's most productive to change the world from the ground up," explained one of the organizers. The main target for SFK expansion is in the "outreach" work in impoverished and violence-torn areas. Since 2004, Spirituality for Kids has also expanded to London, Mexico, and Malawi, and plans are in development for Panama and India.

The practice is to work with faith-based or community-based organizations who can supply the staff and local constituents to lead the classes themselves. In Malawi, where the basic human needs of the huge population of orphans are so huge, the launching of SFK classes was held off until other services were first provided. To this end, the Kabbalah Centre assisted in the establishment of the Raising Malawi Foundation (also independent from the Kabbalah Centre, although cofounded by Michael Berg). Raising Malawi channels funds and technical expertise to the community- and faith-based organizations in Malawi who are running the orphanages, schools, and health clinics. After some time, a small group of Malawians was brought to Los Angeles to train as SFK teachers, and after more training in Malawi, SFK classes for about 400 children were started in fall 2006.[99]

The "leftist" sympathies of the Kabbalah Centre outlook are most apparent in its Middle East activities. Israelis who have experienced military duty in Israel dominate the leadership of the Centre, many of the Hevre are Israeli, and the sacred primacy of the land of Israel is fundamental to Kabbalah Centre teachings. Yet in the communications from Kabbalah Centre directors and teachers, Israeli nationalism is clearly secondary to the universalist principles. In Israel and in the occupied territories of Palestine, Spirituality for Kids has organized classes and summer camp programs that bring together Jewish children with Israeli Arab and Palestinian children. The staff is made up of Jews and Arabs of different religious backgrounds who have been active in coexistence efforts and peace movements.[100] During the outbreak of war between Israel and Hezbollah in the summer of 2006, while members of the community kept in frequent contact with their families and friends in Israel, and Kabbalah Centres in Israel stepped up the distribution of Zohars to soldiers and to people under attack, the message of the prayer leaders at the Los Angeles Centre was consistently universalistic. Of course, privately, people expressed less tolerant opinions, and public opinion in the United States indicated that a majority of U.S. citizens were supportive of the Israeli military efforts. In response to this, Yehuda Berg sent the following e-mail weekly meditation:

> Kabbalists are not pro-Israel, pro-Zionist, pro-Arab. Kabbalists are pro-humanity, pro-human soul, pro-God's children. This includes Christians, Muslims, Jews, Buddhists, Hindus, Atheists and all people who populate this planet.... The teachings and tools of Kabbalah help us eradicate and destroy the self-centered aspect of our being that only allows us to cry for ourselves, both individually and as a particular people of specific faith. When we remove that destructive selfish part, we will have the ability to cry over the pain of our individual neighbors and other nations. With everyone concerned for one another, the hatred and conflict will cease.... But no one gets it. The result? Wars and bloodshed for 2000 years. Sometimes we win battles. Sometimes we lose battles. In both cases, the blood keeps flowing and the tears keep shedding.

The idea is to win the war. And the only war is the war on one's own ego and self-interest. Please pass this around instead of anything that only serves the interest of one people.[101]

The message continued with a reference to the effort to distribute Zohars in Lebanon and Syria and a request to recipients of the emails to aid in this effort.

Another way that Spirituality for Kids distinguishes itself from other aspects of Kabbalah Centre healing is that its directors are eager to have it tested by independent social scientists. To this end, SFK hired an accomplished scholar to design and implement internal assessment mechanisms for the program. These measures were in place in the SFK class I attended: the staff practiced and critiqued each other immediately prior to the class, they held a group session afterward in which they evaluated the session orally and in writing, and they scheduled an additional training session prior to the next SFK class. Each of the teachers and aides had a teacher's guide that spelled out student learning outcomes and step-by-step growth in understanding over the course of the lessons. SFK is now being evaluated externally. "We want SFK to be data-driven," I was told by Heath Grant, "and in order for people to be assured that our claims are credible, we went to the top research agencies, the Rand Corporation and Nova." The studies are funded, respectively, by private donors and the Children's Trust, a foundation in South Florida.[102]

CHAPTER 6

———— ✻ ————

Profiles of Participants in the Kabbalah Centre Community

All new religious movements are under pressure to build a sufficient following. Numbers establish legitimacy, a sense of community, and the financial footing and labor pool for a sound infrastructure. During the first two decades of Kabbalah Centre history, when the movement struggled to establish itself in Israel and then to attract followers in North America, the charismatic leadership of Philip and Karen Berg and a small circle of disciples were critical in establishing a stable and lasting community. By the turn of the twenty-first century, the Kabbalah Centre was on a firm footing, and like other new religious movements that become established, charismatic leadership is less of a factor in the commitment of individuals to the group; leadership is more diffused, and to a greater extent, members sustain each other in their commitment.

New religious movements are made up primarily of new converts, and this remains the case for the Kabbalah Centre. Outreach efforts are ongoing. This is not motivated by fear that the community is shrinking or experiencing a low retention rate. Outreach is important because the leaders of the movement have defined their mission as spreading knowledge of Kabbalah to as many people as possible. Retention and community building are not major concerns, and in this the Kabbalah Centre differs from many other new religious movements.[1] Nevertheless, there are many people who have stayed involved at their local Centres for years, or who are part of a community that reassembles itself at the retreats, and who therefore give the gatherings a sense of continuity and fellowship. In this chapter I show why and how people enter the community. In their own voices, they explain why they find the teachings compelling, what practices they follow, and what difference Kabbalah makes in their lives.

The individuals described here were chosen out of the many people that I became acquainted with and interviewed. (Their names have been changed, and in some cases, identifying details have been altered.) They were chosen for a number of reasons. First, I wanted to present the diversity of people that participate in the Centre in terms of the intensity of their commitment—from those who have committed themselves to the observance of Jewish law and who engage in many rituals to those who are less inclined toward ritual and are content with a spiritual outlook. Second, the profiles present individuals who find Kabbalah Centre teachings important to their physical and emotional healing and recovery from personal crises. Third, I wanted to depict people whose involvement in the Kabbalah Centre has caused conflict with or has been harmonious with their involvement in conventional, organized religions. These people, I expected, would enable me to demonstrate the extent to which the Kabbalah Centre is what it purports to be: a universal, spiritual wisdom and not a religion. Finally, I chose people whose experiences I found particularly interesting. With regard to all whom I interviewed, I feel enormously privileged to have been given the opportunity to listen and then to edit their stories according to my own vision.

LIVING WITH SPIRITUAL CONSCIOUSNESS

Catherine's father was the force behind the family's commitment to Catholicism; her mother was less knowledgeable and less enthusiastic. Catherine was sent to Catholic school from kindergarten through high school. The Catholic teachings did not make much of an emotional impact on her or, according to her, on the other children. They would read Bible stories, memorize the creed, hear about the Eucharist, and learn how to pray, but "it was not *spiritual*," she says. Her father died when she was nearing the end of high school, and with his loss, the family's Catholic routines fell away. Over the next decade, Catherine did not find a religious community for herself, although in other ways she established herself successfully; she trained for a career and held responsible positions, worked for several years in Europe, married and divorced, and had around her a comfortable circle of friends and family.

A few years ago, Catherine decided that it was time she contributed to the community through volunteer work and donating money. While looking at and listening to the various causes available, she heard about the project Spirituality for Kids (SFK). She was impressed by the SFK Web site and a note at the bottom of the page said that SFK was a project of the Kabbalah Centre. She gave a donation online to SFK and ordered a couple of books authored by the Bergs that were listed there. Catherine had read other spiritual books over the years and felt they were "nice, but not compelling." But Yehuda Berg's *The Power of Kabbalah* was quite different: she had an immediate, positive reaction upon reading it. She understood that it just scratched the surface of Kabbalah and that there was a lot more to learn if she took classes. She signed up for the Kabbalah I class.

Catherine was exposed to a spiritual system that felt to her remarkably unlike anything in her past. The thing that was so startling to her was that the teachers kept saying, "Don't believe this because we're telling you—try it and see if it works." Growing up, she believes, she was told not to think for herself, and the prevailing instruction was "Believe this because the Church *knows!*" Catherine feels that another difference was that the kabbalistic spiritual teachings were directly tied to a person's life and provided a daily guide for relating to people. They explained one's place in history and within humanity. The Kabbalah teacher encouraged the students to volunteer, and Catherine began working as a teacher's aide in a Spirituality for Kids class for economically deprived children and parents in Los Angeles. She began to scan the Zohar and recite *Ana Bekoach* daily; and she regularly attended the Los Angeles Centre for the Friday night Connection and meals and the Saturday morning Torah reading.

"I saw such a huge difference in my life because of the principles," Catherine told me. She used to be anxious all the time. She would worry. She would be restless at night. She was ambitious, "but only in 1 percent ways. I'd say, 'I've got to get a better job, to make more money, to have more friends.' And when I did that, it was not satisfying. There was always a 'heaviness' inside." The classes give you the intellectual information, Catherine told me, but you have to *live* the lessons. "The teachers would keep saying, 'Do this only if you believe it,' but there's also the necessity to leap in and be open to it working, so at first you're doing it and you're not sure what you think. Eventually I saw that it made a big difference in how I felt. I stopped being so stressed." Catherine attributes part of that to the actual lessons: overcoming ego; not being a victim; the more you share, the more you get; you create Satan so that you will have something to overcome; Cause and Effect; you are getting messages all the time and may not be noticing them; it is hard to do the work; and you have to be held accountable for what happens.

In addition, Catherine became convinced that part of the change in her life was a result of the meditations. She explains, "I connected to this metaphysical energy, and I felt fulfilled." Like others who tell me why they are drawn to the Kabbalah Centre, Catherine tells me about the "energy" that suffuses the place: "It's in the air, because everybody is making that effort and the energy has been drawn down into the place. Everything is so powerful! Do you know that when people are preparing the Shabbat food, they are reciting *Ana Bekoach* over it? So of course the food has a special effect." When Catherine stays away too long, or if she neglects to do the scanning or prayers, some of her old negative behaviors come back. She finds herself getting stressed.

When that occurs, she just goes to the Centre and volunteers at anything—it does not matter what—and her calm returns.

For Catherine and for others at the Centre, there is a direct relationship between suppression of one's ego and awareness of the Light. An inflated ego blocks out the Light; all you see is yourself. If people would really think about it, she told me, they would realize how much of their time is spent satisfying their ego, even when they think they are helping other people. When Catherine first discovered Kabbalah, she was so excited: "You feel like you've discovered the key to the universe, and you want to tell everybody about it." Only after she began to pay attention to people's reactions—they were uncomfortable and not eager to listen—did she realize that her desire to share was prompted by her ego. "You have to learn that if they are not ready to hear you, then what's driving you to tell them is ego. If you really want to share, you have to talk to them at the level that they are at. Otherwise, it's just about you." Now she is much more aware of this dynamic, and she realizes how much work she has to do to improve herself. Plus, she is more conscious of other peoples' ego drives. She is quieter, and she does not enjoy hanging around gossiping people or people who are like her former self, people who "coast through life," unconscious.

Catherine's spiritual awareness played a major role in her wedding to Edward, another member of the Kabbalah Centre community. Both of them had been married before, and their weddings had been fancy church affairs. "Our families did not need another fancy wedding, and I wanted a wedding that was about 'connecting to consciousness,' not about ego," Catherine said. A regular wedding is very much about ego, she explained, with all the fuss over the bride and groom, the effort to make them feel so special, and all the pageantry. Catherine wanted this wedding to be a ceremony that planted a "seed" for their marriage—that is, to create the potential for what developed later, which was to be their joint connection to the Creator and their collaboration in bringing Light to the world. With this in mind, they decided that the wedding should be held at the Centre with only their teachers and their friends from the Centre who understood these concepts. Yehuda Berg told her that because they were not Jewish, he would conduct only a simple spiritual ceremony that contained some but not all of the elements of the regular Jewish ceremony, and they would have to go afterward to a Justice of the Peace to be legally married. They set a date and time—not an easy thing to do, working around the teachers' obligations and adjusting the scheduled time of the basketball game played by the Kabbalah Centre team, of which Edward was a member.

The day of the wedding began according to plan. The bride and groom fasted, stayed apart, went separately to the mikveh (ritual bath), and prepared for the ceremony. But when Catherine was at the beauty salon, Edward called her and told her that the basketball team had decided to follow its original schedule. The teammates would come to the wedding, but they would be quite late. Catherine told me about her reaction: "I went a little crazy for about 10 minutes, exclaiming 'How can they do this! This is terrible! No one will be there!'" Then, she said, she suddenly "got it" and started laughing. She had been given her chance to have a wedding that was not about ego, but consciousness!

At the wedding there were lots of women (because they preferred a wedding over a basketball game) and two men other than the rabbi and the groom. Yehuda explained the rituals, and Edward signed a document saying that he would protect and take care of Catherine. He gave her a ring and recited to her a Hebrew phrase dictated to him by Yehuda, Catherine circled Edward in the traditional fashion, Hebrew blessings were recited, and they drank wine. The members of the team drifted in late, and Catherine and Edward's teacher never managed to arrive. It was a beautiful, spiritual wedding, Catherine told me, all about consciousness.

HEALING AND LEARNING AT A DISTANCE FROM A CENTRE

Learning the principles and practices of the Kabbalah Centre is a big challenge when one lives far away from the cities with Centres, but it has been happening more frequently with the development of Web technology, the Kabbalah Centre's Student Support system, and the regional and international retreats. Creating a religious or spiritual community is not easy because it is not local, and it requires significant planning, expense, and travel to sit with others and share meals and worship. Without experts close at hand, there is more extemporaneous teaching, and it is harder to feel competent and confident. One's spiritual home is away from home. Consequently, coming together with other Kabbalah Centre followers at the regional and international gatherings is very powerful and exhilarating. It is an experience that can tide a person over for months.

Molly is a single woman of 30 who lives in a town of 2,000 in central Illinois, where her family has lived for several generations. She describes her family as "not that warm—they are not the type of people who hug or say 'I love you' to each other," she told me a bit wistfully. Molly is a bit shy, but she is friendly when people approach her. She looks fit and healthy, but when she was 25, she became seriously ill with a terrible disease and was hospitalized for three months. "I was dying," Molly told me. "They did not think I would make it." Some of her internal organs were impaired, and she was plagued with serious staph infections. Her mother would not visit Molly in the hospital, finding it too depressing, and Molly was terribly distressed and felt abandoned. When she was finally released from the hospital, it took her months to walk again and find the strength to stay awake. She is still not entirely healthy, for her kidneys sustained permanent damage. During the months of recovery, Molly thought people were acting very insensitively and unsympathetically toward her, and she became depressed, went to therapy, and took antidepressant medication.

While Molly was in the hospital and throughout her convalescence, she kept asking people, "Why me?" She told me, "I knew there was some reason why I had this and other conditions." People told her not to ask why, or that one could not know, but that she should just accept her situation. Molly was not satisfied with the Catholic, Protestant, or secular responses. She researched on the Web to see how different religions looked at disease. After hearing about Kabbalah on television, she went to the Web site www. kabbalah.com and signed up for the Weekly Consciousness e-mails. The teachings she was exposed to made sense to her. Molly summarized the les-sons she first learned from the e-mails:

> Kabbalah Centre teachers were saying that it's okay to ask questions. They said that when people act mean and insensitive, it's because they are looking at the world through a hazy window. When you see clearly, you see that human beings and everything are all connected, and you will act better. Here I was getting mad at them, and I realized that they weren't seeing clearly. I had to let that go.

When Molly told her therapist about the teachings and how much better they made her feel, her therapist encouraged her to continue. Molly bought the book *The Power of Kabbalah* from the Centre. She tried sharing her new ideas with her friends. "I thought that all of my friends would feel this way, too," she said. "I sent them the e-mails, but they weren't interested or even reading them."

Molly found a community in which to explore these new ideas. She learned that there would be a Rosh Hodesh evening program at a hotel in a larger town 40 miles away. Typically, the Centre will organize such an event and notify people in the region who have been in touch with the Centre through the Web or through the free Student Support phone line. They then send a teacher from one of the Centres to lead the Connection. Molly drove there and got a taste of kabbalistic meditation and community. The teacher gave a short talk about the month's consciousness (that is, the particular energy for the month and the challenges and opportunities that this entails) and the symbols for the month that should be the focus for meditation. The group watched a video of Karen Berg lecturing about the new month. Molly went to three different New Moon events at the hotel. The faces of the people became familiar, but most important to Molly were the concepts: "I had this conviction that if I could keep this consciousness every day, I'd feel better: I'd have a better focus on my health and jobs and friends, and a better outlook, instead of focusing on the negative." She joined a core group of about 20 people who signed up and paid for a Kabbalah I class taught by a teacher flown in from Los Angeles, held at the home of a man in the group. After the completion of the course, they continued to meet once every few weeks in the man's home. "I guess they are my spiritual community," Molly says. They are predominantly Protestant, with a few Catholics and one man of Jewish heritage. Some are single, some are married couples, and a number are gay and lesbian couples. One married couple has impressed Molly as "deeply spiritual." "They live in tune with the Kabbalah and in tune with the earth," she told me, "and they'll keep referring back to the Zohar and the lessons they've all learned when things come up. They learned from the Centre that the best time for meditation is between midnight and 4 A.M., so they wake up every day at 4 A.M. to scan and meditate."

It is difficult for people living in the Midwest to advance in learning beyond the basic level. Molly would like to take the second and third part of the Kabbalah series, but enrollment has not been sufficient for those courses to be scheduled. One option is to find a couple dozen people to sign up for a seven-week distance-learning course. In this type of course, the teacher is in a studio far away, and the local group connects to him through a password-controlled Web site and projects the teacher's image to a large screen. They also have to set up a phone line through the computer (such as through a Skype system) so that the students can ask questions. A few members of Molly's group chose a slightly different option in which a number of people in small groups located in distant cities connect to the teacher simultaneously via the Web. The teacher talks, and then each group calls in questions. The teacher can then respond to the people and have people in each group speak to him in a way that all can hear. In between the sessions, the participants can call or e-mail the instructor up to a specified maximum of minutes per week. The class does not bond together in the same way, but one does get the sense of community. Molly enjoyed the novelty of it, telling me with some excitement, "There were people from different cities in Ohio, and one as far as Michigan."

Early on, Molly discovered the services provided by the Student Support phone line. If something is happening in your life and, for example, you need a healing prayer, the phone support workers will put your name on the list for the healing meditation at Shabbat prayers at the Centres. The Kabbalah Centre teacher who led the New Moon Connection urged Molly to call Student Support to find a teacher of her own, a person who would serve consistently as her guide. She did so, and their plan was that the teacher would call her once a week, or she would call in and ask for him, so they could develop a teacher–student relationship. Molly admitted that they have not spoken on such a regular basis because there are times she cannot speak, or the different time zones mean that their schedules do not mesh, but she did like him and appreciated the service. When her teacher was moved to the London Kabbalah Centre for several months, she did not take up his suggestion to switch to a new teacher for the interim.

For someone like Molly, the regional and international retreats are very important. She saved during the year to afford the cost of travel and the approximately $2,000 registration fee for the big Pesach and then the Rosh Hashanah retreats. The fee covers hotel, food, and preparatory classes that can be accessed online as videos before and even months after the retreat. Thousands of people attend from all over the world, their names and home cities displayed on their name tags, and the event is programmed in such a way so that people meet and talk to each other. "For me, the biggest thing was to see my teacher in the flesh, and to see the Rav and Karen," Molly told me. She was also thrilled with the prayer services, where people learn how to use the prayer book, follow a Torah reading, sing together, and "become one" in connecting to the Light. She experienced Shabbat and the holiday firsthand and came into contact with people who were performing rituals she had barely known existed. Inspired by the experience on Rosh Hashanah, the following week, Molly drove to a regional Yom Kippur retreat in Chicago. The regional holiday retreats are more intimate, and this one brought together 100 people. She told me, "At the time it was all new to me, but with every moment came more Light. It was a wonderful learning experience. The Chicago group has very nice people, and they were so welcoming and warm to us."

A few months ago, Molly called and let her teacher know that she was feeling very negative and needed to talk. She is waiting for a kidney transplant, trying to get on the list for donors, and her sister is a good match—but her sister is not sure she wants to donate her kidney. Molly was angry, sad, and confused about how she should feel about it. "My teacher really helped me," Molly said. "He helped me think differently about it." He pointed out that if her sister did not want to help, it may be for the best. He suggested that she spend a minimum of 30 minutes a day scanning Zohar and meditate on the principle that she has control over her life. " 'You're used to expecting the worst,' he told me. 'What do *you* want? Make that your outlook!' " Following his advice has brought Molly some peace, and she told me that this is how she has come to think about her sister and her situation:

> Knowing my sister, I know how anxious she gets regarding medical stuff. Could she emotionally handle it? I wouldn't be there for her while her kidney is being removed and help her during all the recuperation. My family is not the type to be really supportive. It's her body and it's part of herself. It would be *wonderful* if she would give up that part of her body, but she has to choose it. The old me— I'd sit at home and be depressed about my situation. Not now. I say to myself: you only have a certain amount of time here, and don't sit and be depressed

about it. And I'm not! I'm not on antidepressants. I'm thinking positively. My mom says, "This is really hard." She's always had a really negative take on the world. She only sees the bad stuff. But I think, "This is *not* really hard compared to what many people go through! I can work, I can walk, I can do lots of things. Many people out there are sicker than I am."

Molly's daily involvement in Kabbalah is rather simple. As soon as she awakens, she ritually washes her hands with the Hebrew blessing. She scans her pocket-sized Zohar, says *Ana Bekoach,* and meditates on several of the names of God from her 72 Names of God card deck. "It gives me more of a positive consciousness," Molly explains about the names meditations. "It gives me something to look forward to. When I look at the names, I try to visualize the symbols in my head, I think about the message, and I think about anyone in particular who needs help at the time." Depending on her schedule, this routine may take 5–30 minutes a day. The monthly New Moon events also contribute to her sense of control. "I think one of the concepts that make me think so positively now is the idea that astrologically you connect differently every month. Some months will be harder than others."

FINDING YOUR SOUL THROUGH KABBALAH

During the first year Jessica began attending Kabbalah Centre classes and events, more than a decade ago, she knew that she had found her real spiritual home. Although many people who participate are oblivious to the teachings differentiating between Jews and others, Jessica not only knew these, but also knew she was meant to participate on the level of a Jew. It is likely that her upbringing as a Mormon had something to do with this. Jessica's family of origin is quite devout and has a long history of leadership in the Church of the Latter Day Saints. She was educated to take seriously the difference between the sacred duties and special fate of the select "Israel," or the Mormons, and the other nations of the earth who are called Gentiles, or non-Mormons. As in Judaism, correct genealogy is a factor in religious status, and it is understood that souls have an essential religious identity. Yet her origins also made the decision to convert to Judaism all the more weighty, for her conversion would—and eventually did—result in her community excising her from her family of birth on earth and in the future afterlife. Jessica's determination to convert to Judaism, despite these serious consequences, demonstrated to her Jewish guides that she had a Jewish soul that was longing to return to its rightful identity.

Conversion to Judaism is currently a matter fraught with difficulties because it is enmeshed in the competition between denominations of Judaism. It is easiest to convert through the guidance of rabbis from the Reform or the Conservative movements; they require a course of study, a commitment to follow Judaism according to their standards, and—for a Conservative conversion—immersing in the mikveh and, for men, circumcision. But Jessica did not consider these options. "Why do that?" she said to me. "Reform and Conservative just do whatever they want, they allow women to do things they really are not allowed to do, they eliminate and change everything just because they feel like it. It's not really Judaism." To her the only authentic option was through Orthodox Judaism, which she believes is the only denomination that upholds Jewish law. She could have asked Philip Berg, an Orthodox rabbi, to convert her. However, she wanted her conversion to be accepted everywhere in the world, without question. People with this desire follow the standard set in Israel; there, the only valid conversion process is through the rabbinical courts recognized by the Israeli rabbinate. In order to convert in America, Jessica needed to find a rabbi to convert her who was associated with the Israeli-approved Rabbinical Council of America. The Bergs warned her that she would have to repeatedly ask for conversion before any of those rabbis would agree to sponsor her. Furthermore, because of the hostility with which the Kabbalah Centre was regarded, they suggested that it would be better if Jessica did not mention her involvement in the Kabbalah Centre; it might jeopardize the entire process.

Jessica regarded the task in front of her in the terms she had learned in the Centre. "I don't know why, but that's what my soul had to go through," she said. She explained that there is no absolute finite number of Jewish souls, such as the figure of 600,000 Jewish souls with Moses at Sinai. She said, "The 600,000 Jewish souls at Sinai fragmented, and that's why there are more Jews than that." Just how many there are is unclear. But also, "there is an idea that some non-Jewish people have Jewish souls that were put into them, and it will eventually be obvious." Jessica felt she was born into a non-Jewish family for a reason, but a reason that she cannot know: "It was my tikkun. For some reason I needed to go through that process."

Consequently, Jessica faced the difficulties of conversion with the belief that every trouble she faced was allowing her to repair previous damage and refine her soul. The rabbi whom she approached for conversion was rather rude to her. "But that's what he had to do," she told me. She kept returning to him with the same request, and eventually, he had no choice but to agree. He insisted on a two-year preparatory stage that included a very demanding course of study and her intense association with an Orthodox family in his synagogue's neighborhood. This would ensure that she was learning how to live in accordance with Jewish law and was actually committed to it. Jessica imposed a further restriction on herself: she stayed away from the Kabbalah Centre entirely. She spoke to her Kabbalah Centre friends, the teachers, and the Bergs, but she did not associate publicly with them or enter the building. She did not want to risk jeopardizing the conversion process, and she also believed that her situation was something that she had earned in a previous life. This is the principle of Cause and Effect. She was not bitter. "I did what I needed to do," Jessica told me.

At the end of two years, the rabbi decided that Jessica was ready to convert, and he scheduled her immersion in the mikveh and meeting with the *bet din* (rabbinic court). Jessica scheduled a separate conversion ritual with Rabbi Berg for the week before that. Jewish law demands that for the sake of conversion, a person's immersion must be observed by two male witnesses, but there are various ways to do this to preserve a woman's modesty. For example, another woman may be with her and serve as an agent reporting to the witnesses who stand behind a screen that the woman converting has immersed properly; or, the woman immersing may be covered by a sheet-like garment that floats above her when she immerses. In Jessica's case, in the conversion with Rabbi Berg, Karen Berg stood with her in the mikveh and reported to the witnesses. Jessica pronounced the blessings and dipped the prescribed number of times. "And then I passed out," she told me. "I felt my soul leave me. Karen had to grab me and pull me out of the water. Only then I revived." Rabbi Berg's explanation, Jessica told me, was that for a moment she was soulless: "You cannot have two souls residing in you at the same time. My old soul left, and my new soul came in." The experience in the mikveh was clearly transformative. Later, I spoke to a Michael Moskowitz, a senior Kabbalah Centre teacher, about the mikveh conversion process. He explained, "The experience is quite personal, and people feel it differently. For some, the mikveh is merely a sign for the 1 percent world that the person has changed, a change that preceded the mikveh. For Jessica, the change occurred during the mikveh." He told me further, "The thing about Kabbalah is that it's not 'this' or 'that.' It's 'this' *and* 'that.'" The next week, Jessica attended the Orthodox *bet din* and had an uneventful mikveh experience.

The meaningfulness of her own ordeal and experience motivated Jessica to ease the way of others in the Centre who wanted to convert. "Of course I could not train them or teach them," she told me, "but I could serve as a type of mentor." With the Bergs' encouragement, for a while Jessica counseled a few people in a group setting. "It fell apart," she explained. "It was quite demanding, not only for the students, but also for me." The conversion process *is* demanding, Jessica believes, and it is supposed to be that way, but doing it through the Orthodox *bet din* is extraordinarily difficult. Years ago, Jessica told me, the Kabbalah Centre used to have a conversion program, and some people were converted by the Rav. Perhaps it was too easy a process, Jessica speculated. "Some of them left the Kabbalah Centre entirely and Judaism, too," she told me. "I don't know why, but clearly it was their tikkun to go through that whole process. The people who are really serious go to the Orthodox *bet din*."

Subsequently, Berg decided not to conduct any more conversions, and Jessica thinks this is wise. Her reasons are largely pragmatic: it is best to have universally respected conversion (and this cannot occur with a Kabbalah Centre conversion), it is difficult to deal with vacillating potential converts, and the Centre would be obliged to provide a highly demanding course of study that is at odds with its primary mission. Jessica is just as happy that this matter of controversy can no longer be used to attack the Kabbalah Centre. "We don't need the trouble," she said. "It's not like before, when people used to spit on anyone wearing white, and there used to be posters denouncing us on the telephone poles along Pico Boulevard." Those were very difficult times, and Kabbalah Centre people were always on the defensive. She enjoys the relative tolerance and does not want it disrupted. "Times have changed," she observed. "Now all synagogues are teaching Kabbalah and astrology."

MONEY AND MARKETING

Danny was a young, highly successful Jewish businessman when, during the mid-1980s, in the time when the Kabbalah Centre sent its teachers door-to-door for outreach, a member of the Hevre came to his office asking if there was anyone within who wanted to learn about Kabbalah. Danny saw a young man wearing a yarmulke and invited him in the door, thinking, "Oh good, I'll have some fun stumping him!" Danny loved to read about quantum physics, the Big Bang, and other theories about the origin of the universe. "I understood maybe 5 percent of what I was reading," he admits to me, "but I could not imagine that any religious man could talk about these theories and find a place for God in them." Danny had also formulated his own personal "rules of success in life" that had helped him rise to the top in the field of marketing. So when the teacher discussed the role of God in the context of quantum physics and affirmed Danny's principles from a different frame of reference, Danny agreed to commence a one-on-one course of study with him.

Learning about Kabbalah Centre teachings over the next few years was very rewarding for Danny as well as for the Kabbalah Centre. He received private tutoring from the teachers, and he became close to the Berg family. He helped the Centre with its marketing. He donated many thousands of dollars to the Kabbalah Centre. "They treated me great in the Centre. I was like a king; they could not do enough for me!" Danny told me. Yet, despite his thorough knowledge of the 12 Rules to the Game of Life taught in the Centre, Danny was not following them. "I was all ego," he told me. "I was selfish and greedy; I swore all the time. I was obnoxious, and I could make life miserable for the people at the Centre and for my family." Danny recalls that the Rav used to warn him that he would face consequences for his poor behavior.

Danny explains that he was simply obstinate. He felt the teaching was excellent, and he describes one of the most important lessons as follows:

> Through my relationship with the Rav, I learned about awe. It wasn't awe that he had supernatural powers, because I could see that he was just human and far

from perfect. But I saw how he *shared*, I saw his unconditional love for me, how he didn't judge, no matter what we talked about. The Rav is very *concealed* like the Light is concealed. He's very humble, simple, and that really is who he is. But the more intensely you relate to him...over time, you realize how bright and revealed he is. That is how you learn to love the Light: first you love your teacher, and then you see that the teacher is just part of the Light. And then I saw that it was not that he alone contains divine Light; *everybody* does. There is divinity in all of us. We just don't always see it.

Danny illustrated this point with one of his favorite teachings about Moses and the burning bush. He asked, "What provoked Moses to approach the burning bush? It called out to him *in his own father's voice*. And once you are drawn in because of that, you realize it is God talking." He learned that the essence of Torah is "love thy neighbor." When you watch someone who is living that way, he explains, you are studying Torah. When you do it yourself, you are learning and living Torah. "The thing is," Danny admits, "I knew all that and I was doing some good things, but I thought they outweighed all the chaos I was creating."

Then the crash came. Danny's business went rock bottom, and he lost everything: the mansion, the fancy cars, the savings accounts. He was terribly dejected and frantic, and no matter how hard he tried, nothing would go right in business. Month after month, for two years, the family was just barely scraping by. Danny kept in touch with the Centre, attending the prayers every morning. He told me, "When I was going through my two years of hell, the Rav would say 'You brought this upon yourself—Cause and Effect. That's how the Light works, so that you can transform yourself.'" Danny did not understand. Why hadn't all his good deeds and charity protected him? He was humbled, and he became a bit nicer, but he was still desperately determined to raise himself up. He describes his moment of truth:

> There was a homeless man who used to stand outside the Centre in the morning and beg, and I would give him a bit every day. Then there came the day when I really had less than a dollar of loose change—not just in my pocket, but of my own. That was really it! I told the beggar and he clapped me on the shoulder and said, "Let me buy you some coffee!" It was the ultimate! I finally got it. Here I had nothing, but I was going to be okay. I finally began to let go of all the drive, the frantic need for success. I actually became content with what little I had.

Danny did not become instantly successful after that. It was difficult for quite some time, but it was better, he explained, because he was different and open to change.

Danny and his wife look back at that period in their lives as a time of Light, rather than one of darkness. I asked Danny whether his wife thought it was fair that she should suffer because of him. He laughed and said, "Let's call my wife and you can ask her!" She told me,

> It's Cause and Effect: no one is a victim. We bring everything upon ourselves. I knew that, even though Danny didn't at the time. It was my tikkun, whether from something I did in my life or in my past life. It gave me a good husband, finally. He had been a real jerk before that. It gave me a family. The kids didn't seem to have suffered at all during that period. It's like they were oblivious.

Danny explained to me that his crisis had been triggered by his donations of money. "All those donations led the Light to teach me, in this life, what I was refusing to learn in an easy manner. The only way I could learn was through the hard way. I got that chance." The donations helped in another way, he told me:

> Donating the money just gives you enough merit so that when you come back, your wife and kids haven't left you, and they still love you! Had I not donated the money, I would not have merited that, because I was really not a good person. And because of the money, I had the merit to learn the lessons so well when I finally did learn.

Slowly, "by baby steps," Danny tells me, he and his wife changed their family culture. During the day they began to say *Ana Bekoach* and meditate on the 72 names. They began to allocate times in the day and before bedtime to study the Zohar with their children. They eventually began to observe Shabbat and the holidays, keep a kosher home, and they enrolled their children in Orthodox schools. "We're not perfect, but we try to apply the principles. It's not easy, and we don't always succeed, but we try."

I asked Danny why the Kabbalah Centre does not tell the world about the disciplines of study, worship, and ritual performance that govern the lives of him and others in the core community. Danny laughed and replied, "Do you really think that would make it more attractive to people? It would scare them off!" He refused to concede that it might make the Kabbalah Centre look better to Jews: "Been there, done that, failed," he told me. Besides, he reminded me, the mission of the Centre is to reach 97 percent of the world. "If we told people 'It's going to be a workout, it's going to be hard,' they'd never come in the door! Marketing gets them in the door. *Then* they'll learn. Or they won't—we can't convince everybody."

CATHOLICALLY HEALING

Betsy lives in a town of 100,000 people containing a state university, two hospitals, a well-organized network of Catholic organizations, many Protestant churches, a synagogue, and no Kabbalah Centre. She was raised and educated in the Catholic tradition and still attends her parish church regularly. After receiving her RN degree, Betsy worked as a nurse in and out of hospitals and clinics, but for the past two decades, her professional focus has been on establishing and administering hospitals' home health programs, developing curriculum for preventive health (often called "wellness") and rehabilitation purposes, public speaking on topics connected to health, and her own private practice as a holistic health practitioner. She learned about Kabbalah from a friend in her meditation group who talked about the divine name she was "born under," information she had found in Yehuda Berg's book *The 72 Names of God* and from a Kabbalah Centre Web site. Betsy went to the Web site, bought a few books, and signed up for the regular e-mail messages and e-newsletters offered by the site. She was especially interested in the healing meditations. In her town there is a network of holistic and spiritual healers who have forged a collaborative relationship with one of the local hospitals. "We try anything that works," she said. "All the local nuns use Reiki." Reiki is a Japanese healing method involving "laying on hands" and is based on the belief that an invisible "life force energy" flows through and sustains the body. Through physical stimulation and focused meditation on Reiki symbols, a person can increase one's life force energy and activate the body's own healing capacity. Betsy decided to incorporate kabbalistic meditations into her array of healing techniques.

Betsy has taken a leading role in bringing Kabbalah Centre teachings to her town. She was assigned a teacher through student support, and the two of them used to converse once a week. "He's young in age but not in spirituality," she told me. "He must have come to this world wise." When he returned to his native Tel Aviv to work in the Kabbalah Centre there, Betsy found others to guide her. Explained Betsy, "The Kabbalah teachers are not masters, but people who push you along the way, like friends." They recommended that she attend a mentor workshop in Los Angeles in 2005. This was a three-day retreat for people in small cities who are considered potential leaders and organizers for the further dissemination of Kabbalah Centre teachings. Betsy agreed, and along with people from an array of cities across the United States, she paid her own transportation and a nominal fee for the program. She was housed at a local hotel and fed at the Kabbalah Centre. The group experienced the full schedule of Shabbat events at the Los Angeles Kabbalah Centre. They attended workshops with the senior teachers and directors where they learned about the Centre's mission, history, finances, and projects. Betsy explains,

> We heard quite a bit about the inner workings of the Centre, because they wanted us to know what we were getting into if we became mentors. They'd say, "Here are some of the things you'd need to do—do you want to do that? Are you comfortable with all of this?" The message was, "It's your decision."

They said, "We don't coerce people, and we don't want you to coerce people." They talked about cults and explained why they think they're not a cult. It was also very practical.

Betsy is very impressed with the teachers she met at the mentor workshop, on the phone, and at the international retreats. Like most participants in Kabbalah Centre events, she has had minimal or no contact with Philip Berg. About the rest of the Bergs and the teachers, she says, "They are awesome. They're not full of themselves. It is obvious that they work on their egos. They are *real* people." She decided to be a mentor.

When Betsy returned home, she utilized her network of healers to spread news of a free introductory lecture. The free introductory lecture is a general statement about the principles of Kabbalah and a "pitch" to encourage enrollment in the Centre's basic courses, and it is the chief mode of recruiting students to the courses. One of Betsy's friends was so excited about the prospect of learning Kabbalah that he sent news of the upcoming lecture to the Council of Churches in the area, a move that ruffled a few feathers. Then the local rabbi heard about it, and he sent a word of caution to his congregants to the effect that "some people look at this as a cult." The 80 people who attended included a diverse group of Christians and people who did not identify with a church, a minority of Catholics, and no Jews. Twenty-six of them signed up for a Kabbalah I class that was conducted via webcam and phone. Betsy has also arranged special lectures and streaming videos via webcam. She is excited about the international healing and retreat center that is being built by the Boca Raton Kabbalah Centre, and she would like to establish in her town a similar training center for healers and for those who wish to be healed; in hers, kabbalistic methods would be one technique of the many that would be offered.

Betsy sees great compatibility between Catholicism and Kabbalah. She has always been a deeply spiritual person, she says. "At age 8, I had terrible feelings of fear of sin and of God's judgment," she told me, "but at age 12, I had a type of epiphany with the help of a nun who said that God and religion were really only about love. I actually began 'counseling' my peers toward this point of view when they were going through spiritual distress." In response to the doctrine that salvation comes only through Jesus, Betsy responded,

> True, that is not compatible with Kabbalah. I guess that doctrine does pose a problem for some people, but not for me. I don't believe that only through him I can be saved. I love him, [but] he's not the only savior; we all have that capability.

She believes her point of view is expressed in John 14:11–13, explaining it to mean that Jesus is asking people to do the work with him. She elaborated,

Everyone has that potential. We *all* are linked to the Creator. We all need to work on bringing the vessel back together. It's not about coercing anyone, but seeing the Light. Whatever form that takes is good. You have to "*be* it."

She connects this to the prayer of Jabez from I Chronicles 4:9, which has become quite known through the book by Bruce Wilkinson, *The Prayer of Jabez: Breaking through the Blessed Life.* Betsy was delighted when Michael Berg mentioned the Jabez prayer in one of his New Moon meditations in the past year. "His point was that we are revealing Light at every moment. It's about '*being* it,' not looking for it elsewhere." To Betsy, Michael's reference to the Jabez prayer is more evidence that Kabbalah contains truths revealed later to others.

"I have heard them say at the Centre that Jesus is a Kabbalist," Betsy says, "but I'm not clear exactly how it works." Kabbalah Centre teachers do not know enough about the New Testament to answer her questions, Betsy told me, and she thinks it would be helpful if they had more knowledge about other religions. "I think that the world was ready for another energy level of love, and so he came. Every leader who comes has his own job to do." Yet, Betsy continued, the teachings of Jesus were turned into an organized religion, and that changed things:

> It's hard to soar above that. The way Christianity puts it, narrows the path: personal salvation through Jesus. In Kabbalah, there is no "wall" as in Catholicism with its dogma. We took x, y, z and made it into a religion. The Christian mystics, though, really *are* free and unfettered by the dogmas.

Betsy does not associate Kabbalah with commandments and prescribed rituals and dogmas. She believes that the Kabbalah Centre teachers "are pitching a particular school, but it's very universal." A lot of Catholics Betsy has met within the Kabbalah Centre community have left the Church in disillusionment and regard Kabbalah as a new direction. "They have not healed that schism in their lives," she says. "I'm different. I'm just adding to what I knew. Everything that I've studied is already in Kabbalah."

Betsy did not think that Catholics are drawn to the Kabbalah Centre more than Protestants, but she did find that her experience in Catholic worship made it easier for her to adjust to the Centre's practices. "I've sat through hours of Easter vigils," she said, "so I can handle the long Rosh Hashanah prayers." Kabbalah water was not hard to understand, either: "I drink it some. I splash it on my house and on people. It's like our holy water, which is blessed at a particular time in Holy Week, with a tiny amount of oil in it." She thinks that her Catholic background makes it easy for her to accept the kabbalistic tools. "In Catholicism you're used to the notion that you don't have to understand everything. Protestants don't usually think that way. To be Catholic, you have to be open to the mysticism, that is, to something that you don't

understand in a logical way." Consequently, Betsy is not hesitant to practice Tikkun Ha-Nefesh, meditate on the 72 divine names, and scan Hebrew
prayers in the *Dialing God: Daily Connections* book. "They are tools," she told
me. "They are gifts that have been handed down to bring in the Light. They
probably predate the Reiki symbols. That's my intuition. And because of that,
they might be more grounded and effective." Betsy's priest does not mind
that she is studying Kabbalah, she told me. And she believes it has strengthened and deepened her awareness of and commitment to God: "Kabbalah has
pushed me further than anything else."

RITUAL AND REFORM

Charles differs from most members of the Kabbalah Centre community in
that he did not join while seeking answers to ultimate questions or because he
was dissatisfied in any way with his church or his religious practice. He came
into contact with the Centre because his girlfriend, now his wife, was getting
deeply involved. Charles is a writer, highly educated and very well read. His
atheist parents raised him as an agnostic, but he became a devout Christian
in college and has never wavered since then. His faith is bolstered by his extensive knowledge of philosophy, theology, and history, and so he was skeptical about this new religion that seemed to appear out of nowhere. He read
through the Internet sites and magazine articles that make the case that the
Kabbalah Centre is a cult and that the Bergs are conducting a massive scam.
His girlfriend, Rafela, did not take these charges seriously. "Just come to one
Shabbat Connection and see for yourself," she told him. In the aftermath
of her sister's long battle with mental illness and subsequent suicide, Rafela
found the Kabbalah Centre teachings far more comforting and helpful than
the Christian faith of her parents. Charles believed that she was being pulled
into a group taking advantage of her vulnerable state.

Because he could not talk Rafela out of her admiration for the Kabbalah
Centre, he agreed to go to a Shabbat service and gather evidence to persuade
her to see reason. "I found it overwhelming and terrifying," he said. "All those
men wearing white, jumping and screaming," he said, "and they kept me away
from Rafela, and everything was so bizarre. I was convinced they were a cult.
I refused to go back after that." It took another six months for him to concede
that he should learn about the Kabbalah Centre in the recommended manner,
by enrolling in the basic courses. Besides, he was serious about Rafela, and he
had to see whether he could live according to the principles and practices that
meant so much to her. Rafela told me, "Some people come into the Centre as
tourists, and some as spies. Charles was a spy." A few weeks into the Kabbalah I
course, Charles admitted that his first impressions had been mistaken. He liked
what he was learning, and he felt it was compatible with his Christian beliefs.

Shortly after he began to add meditation and rituals to his daily routine,
Charles noticed the improvements in his behaviors. He explained,

I have always been an extraordinarily stressed person. I do a lot—writing, teaching, volunteer work with animal rescue projects and with the teens at my church—but I get very stressed. What I noticed was that just doing the meditations in the morning diminished my stress throughout the day.

Charles's morning practice became fixed: as soon as he awakens, he ritually washes his hands and then recites *Ana Bekoach* with the prescribed consciousness. If he has the time, he scans the Zohar, too. If he gets stressed during the day, he might recite *Ana Bekoach* "and a classical Christian prayer," he told me with a chuckle, "you know the one: 'Dear Jesus, I am really stressed out.'" Rafela, in contrast, added much more to her daily routine. She began to volunteer after work at the Centre several times a week, doing such things as helping at the store or setting up the tables for the Shabbat meals. When she awakens every morning and also at midnight (she sets an alarm clock), she ritually washes her hands with the blessing and then scans the Zohar and meditates. There are transliterations for people like Rafela who cannot read Hebrew, but she has memorized many prayers so that she can say them easily and independently of the written material. She knows all the blessings to be recited before eating (there are different ones for fruits, for vegetables, for bread, and for other categories of food) and after experiencing or seeing different things. On one night during the holiday Sukkot, she slept at the Kabbalah Centre in the *sukkah*, the booth erected outside in the courtyard roofed with palm fronds. "Perhaps next year we will build our own at home," she told me. There is enough flexibility in her job to allow her to be a regular helper in a Spirituality for Kids class, and recently she began training as a mentor for beginning students. Rafela and I met one morning at 8, after her 6–7:30 A.M. mentor training session. While sipping Kabbalah water, she told me, "I've found that once you do Kabbalah, you can get a lot more done every day. You just get so much energy!"

Charles believes that the greatest benefit he has received is in the power of "restriction." He has always had difficulty controlling his impulses and passions. "For years and years, I've been troubled by eating meat," he told me. "I never felt I had the strength to live out my principles. I always wanted to be a vegan. I've written checks to PETA and then wolfed down a burrito!" His sexual appetite was even more troubling. "I've always been a chronic womanizer. No control. I was married three times before Rafela, and they all ended in failure." With such a poor record of fidelity, he was sure that no minister would want to perform a fourth marriage for him. Charles met weekly with a teacher at the Centre for guidance, and Yehuda Berg agreed to perform the wedding. Charles describes his experience at the Centre:

The Centre is very unique, I think, in not judging people. Other churches say "no judgment," but I've only seen it with my own eyes at the Centre. People at the Centre would say to me, "You were married three times before? How interesting that that was in your script! What did you learn from it? I wonder what the women learned?" My teacher would say, "This is going to be different." He didn't see my past as an obstacle.

Charles was determined to make this marriage work. "I was determined before, too, but I couldn't do it."

What differed this time was Kabbalah. Charles explains, "The combination of scanning and sharing enables a person to resist the enormous drives of the Desire to Receive." Charles began to believe that by following Kabbalah Centre teachings, he could gain control of his passions. Prior to the wedding, he decided to undergo circumcision:

> There was no pressure about circumcision. It came organically to me. When I told my teacher I was thinking about doing it, he said he thought it was an excellent idea. They would have married me with a foreskin, too. Afterwards, people who had heard about it would walk up to me and congratulate me, like it was a normal good achievement!

Rafela explained it as follows, "It was something he had wanted to do before, but he did it then so it would make his marriage to me different than the others. Also, there's a lot of negative energy connected to the foreskin, so it's good to remove it." In the weeks leading up to their wedding, Charles and Rafela learned about the kabbalistic marriage tools. This information is not part of the regular curriculum. "It would scare people away," says Rafela, "so it's only taught in a one-on-one or couples settings, and only if people really ask for it." She is referring to the laws of *niddah* that govern sexual relations during marriage. These involve avoiding all physical contact during Rafela's menstrual period plus seven more days, after which time Rafela immerses in the mikveh, and they resume physical contact. Since their wedding two years ago, they have observed these laws.

Charles is very pleased with the results of all their efforts:

> Kabbalah didn't teach me anything I didn't want to be; it gave me the tools to match my ideals to my life. If I get an urge, I might say *Ana Bekoach*. I was unfaithful to my first three wives. A chronic womanizer! White knuckling it! Man, it's easy now! I learned how to keep healthy boundaries.

They also keep a kosher home; that is, they observe the Jewish dietary laws. They replaced all their kitchen items with new ones, there are separate meat and dairy plates and utensils, and the meat is kosher. Like many people in the core community, they store their meat and dairy in separate refrigerators. Rafela eats meat because, in accordance with Kabbalah Centre teaching, she believes she is elevating the animal soul to a higher level when she eats with the proper rituals and consciousness. Charles is proud that he has been able to become a vegetarian. "Here's my thinking: there are plenty of people elevating those animal souls. I feel very strongly that eating animal flesh is wrong. We are all one soul, and I let other people do that other work for me."

When I asked Rafela whether she had considered conversion, she was a bit disconcerted by my question. "No," she responded, "I don't know why I would." She is very comfortable where she is right now. She and Charles attend Kabbalah Centre Connections every Friday night and Saturday morning, and Saturday night and Sunday morning, they are at church. She thought a bit and then said, emphatically, "I really do not feel at all Jewish!" I asked Charles how he reconciles his Christian devotion with Kabbalah and with the performance of rituals that were rejected by Christianity:

> It's true, you don't need a circumcision of the body. You don't need circumcision for salvation. But there's no prohibition against it. Paul doesn't say "*Don't do it.*" Salvation is not contingent upon a measles vaccination, either, but the vaccination is a good practical tool.

Charles admits that he cannot as easily harmonize his belief in Jesus with Kabbalah:

> I do believe that Jesus is my savior. His death is profoundly efficacious. It remains the central fact of my spirituality. When I'm pushed too hard to explain how this works with Kabbalah, I can't do it. Yet, I am comfortable, even as an intellectual, holding two contradictory ideas simultaneously. It doesn't bother me.

More important for Charles are the similarities between the principles espoused by Jesus and those identified as kabbalistic by the Kabbalah Centre. "There is radical compatibility there," Charles tells me. He believes that Jesus, more so than Moses and Shimon Bar Yohai (the reputed author of the Zohar), had contact with the divine and was superior to them in embodying the kabbalistic teachings throughout his short life. Charles asserts, "There's something about Jesus that is without equal, in his person and his ministry. Jesus was the perfect Kabbalist."

IN THE HEVRE AND OUT TO CHANGE THE WORLD

At age 30, Lily has come full circle in her life, with a big difference. She is the youngest in a family that was always quite poor. The health problems of both parents precluded them from adequately supporting the family, and they lived in government-subsidized housing in a rough, high-crime neighborhood in Paris. Lily was familiar with drugs, gambling, and violence. She and her family were the only Jews in the neighborhood, and they were quite religious. Lily and her sister were scholarship students by day at an all-girls Orthodox Jewish school on the other side of town, and her brothers were sent to the parallel boys' school. The school was an escape from her neighborhood, but Lily recalls the feeling of being shortchanged there, too. The girls were restricted from learning certain subjects, some of the rabbis gave her the creeps, and she could not believe that what she was taught was the full picture, or even accurate. She remembers her feelings of extreme bewilderment and her frequent complaint in high school: "There has to be something more to this than what they're teaching us!" Whenever she expressed her own opinions, her teachers and family would say, "Shut up—you don't know anything!" Still, Lily was not an outright rebel. After high school, she moved to Israel, studied and worked successfully in the music business, and returned to a job in a better neighborhood near her family. Today she is a member of the Hevre, is living in Los Angeles, and is devoted to Spirituality for Kids (SFK) work in the impoverished, high-crime areas of Los Angeles. When she is not teaching children, she is helping people in other cities in North America, Central America, Europe, and Africa set up their own Spirituality for Kids classes, or she is studying Kabbalah.

Lily was drawn to the Kabbalah Centres in Israel and Paris because she felt she could finally learn that which had been kept from her in her religious education. Yet she did not become deeply moved by her experience there until she attended an international Pesach retreat in Miami. She explained, "In my family on Pesach at the Seder, they would tell the story of the slavery in Egypt and talk on and on, and people would go sit on the sofa and fall asleep, and then wake up and say, 'Where are we? Is it time to eat?'" A Kabbalah Centre Seder is quite different. Slavery in Egypt is a metaphor for enslavement to one's self-centeredness, and all the steps leading to the exodus are about "breaking ego." Lily recalls, "You would sit at the table talking about how you have wrecked things because of your ego, and people are crying and sharing and talking about how to improve. It was *very* intense." During one of the breaks between the prayers, a film about the community service project Spirituality for Kids was screened. Lily was enchanted by the sequences in which inner-city children told of their new abilities to resist the impulse to be mean, to slack off in school, and to steal and by the film clip of a mother in a jail who said, "Had I learned this then, I would have done better." Lily's reaction was, "*That's* what I'm looking for! I'm going to do *that*." Immediately upon returning home after the retreat, she requested a three-week leave from her job. She flew to Los Angeles and volunteered in Spirituality for Kids. After returning home, she spent her free time volunteering as an assistant in the Spirituality for Kids class. It was not long until she quit and moved to Los Angeles so that she could learn Spirituality for Kids from experienced teachers.

It took only a few more months for Lily to be asked to intensify her work with Spirituality for Kids as a member of the Hevre. In 2001 there were only about 30 Hevre members living in Los Angeles, but the expansion of operations in the Kabbalah Centre worldwide and in Los Angeles pushed its growth to 100—single people and married couples, not counting their children—based at the Los Angeles Centre in 2006. They live within walking distance in several apartment buildings, free of rent, and they receive their food, clothing, medical care, and children's schooling free of charge. The Hevre has the reputation of being on duty all day, seven days a week, but Lily tells me otherwise: "We're all so free! You have the capacity to concentrate on your work, to improve yourself. You're so guided, all the time! I'm not missing anything, and I get everything." In terms of work hours, Lily has Saturday nights and all day Sunday for herself—unless there are special assignments—and she recently returned from a two-week visit home with her family.

Lily described the Hevre's daily routine. When they awaken, they say their individual morning rituals and meditations. Only the males go to the Centre for mikveh and morning prayers. They eat breakfast together in the Centre dining room, and lunch is also together in the dining room with the paid employees. They can eat dinner there or—more often—pick up their food and take it back to eat at home or in their offices. During the day and sometimes extending into the evening, each member of the Hevre does his or her assigned job. Everyone follows Jewish law, but the non-Jews do the tasks not permitted to Jews; for example, a non-Jew operates the camera on Shabbat (to project the Torah scroll onto the screen for public viewing). About 60 of the Hevre work in Student Support, and the rest teach or work on the Centre's projects. The Hevre as a whole has a weekly class with Michael or Yehuda Berg and a class about four nights a week with one of the senior teachers. Individually, each person meets twice a week with an assigned mentor and once a week with his or her teacher. (Anyone who takes a course in the Centre has a designated teacher, and so Hevre members have teachers who have known them since they first began their studies.)

Lily is delighted to be in the Hevre. Her assignment is to facilitate the establishment of Spirituality for Kids in different parts of the world. She spends many hours of each day communicating by phone and online, in addition to the Spirituality for Kids training and work in the field. "In these past two years, since I joined the Hevre, I've achieved more than in all the rest of my life," she exclaims. "All my progress has sped up. Since I've been in the Hevre, everything has come to me where I've wanted to develop. There's always someone there to guide me." I asked Lily what she felt the mentors and teachers regarded as the most important thing to learn. "Teaching us to treat people with human dignity," she told me. "That's the mantra for everybody. The people here are not angels, but everyone believes in that, and everybody is trying."

When I asked Lily to tell me about her life, she responded emphatically, "SFK is my whole life!" She knows why she is so devoted: "It is healing my inner child. I did not have those skills at all—quite the opposite. The kids we deal with in the outreach areas are like me and the children around me when I grew up." She began to learn very basic lessons when she first studied Kabbalah:

> I had certain addictions. Kabbalah I teaches about addictions. You learn that you have choices. It's not the cigarette you want; you want the spiritual/non-physical feeling that you get from the cigarette—it's the Light in you that you want. When you understand that, you can make the decision "I want to be present, I want to feel healthy." You realize that taking the smoke is just getting a quick fix. You realize that you'll get the quick fix, but you'll feel bad, and you learn how to suppress that desire for the quick fix so you get the long-term benefit. This did not happen suddenly, but it seeped in.

The SFK curriculum, she saw, makes the kabbalistic principles more powerful. People are taught to recognize their two competing inner voices, the Good Guy and the Opponent, and they learn they have the power to listen to the Good Guy. Lily told me,

> I am more confident now, believing in myself, that I can reach a potential. I'm less shy. I realized that the voice inside me that's saying "Shut up—you're no good" is the Opponent's voice. I no longer think of myself as a victim. I'm not as reactive anymore. I am an impatient person, but it's more under control. I'm constantly learning about myself and how to live in the world. Constantly.

The real test of her application of the principles, Lily tells me, occurs when she goes home to visit her parents and siblings. "They act the same," she said, "but now I don't. And I don't try to 'fix' them. I tell myself, 'I'm not in control of them, I'm in control of me. I'm the one who has to act differently.'"

TEACHING KABBALAH

When Jason was 15 years old, he was earning hand-over-fist in the stock market. A cousin who was worried about Jason's neglect of schoolwork and his life priorities suggested that he attend a Kabbalah Centre introductory lecture. Jason grew up in Los Angeles in a nonreligious Iranian Jewish family, and his cousin was from a part of the extended family that was involved in the Centre. Other members of the family had had mixed experiences with the Kabbalah Centre or regarded it with hostility. Jason went to the class, was delighted with the teachings, and signed up for his first course. He admits that it took another year before he actually began applying the principles to his life. While he completed high school, received a BA, and worked in a family business, he volunteered at the Centre and took every class available.

The Kabbalah Centre encouraged Jason to take a leadership role. He is bright, attractive, energetic, and passionate about the Centre's teachings.

Jason became a mentor for students in the Introduction to Kabbalah series; this involves sitting through the classes and making himself available to a group of students for questions, for suggesting volunteer opportunities, and as an elementary-level guide. "I took Kabbalah I about 18 times!" Jason told me. He was deeply impressed with the teachers. "I thought they had a lot of power," he told me, "not power in the 1 percent sense of the word, but power in terms of truth—deep truth. I was such an avid learner, I would chase after them to ask questions." He found a senior teacher who agreed to instruct him privately once a week. When he was 19 years old, he was allowed to give introductory lectures, and by the age of 20, he was in the Hevre working in Student Support on the phones and as a teacher for short stints in the more isolated cities in the Midwest. Now only 22 years old, he also teaches Kabbalah I courses.

Jason's rapid rise in the Kabbalah Centre perhaps owes something to his ethnic and family background. Iranian Jews in Los Angeles have a reputation for being very ambitious in business and the professions. Jason explains it as follows:

> Iranians—and Israelis, too—have *huge* desire for success, or Desire to Receive for the Self Alone. That's why many come and go without staying. They come in because they think it will help them, and they leave because they're seeking a quick fix. It's not about that. It's the opposite. It's about transforming yourself. And you also have to realize that even if you've transformed, there are times when the Light is concealed and nothing will work.

Jason thinks it is important that people realize that Kabbalah does not disrespect monetary success. "Making money is good if it is used to create spiritual growth," he tells them. "Then you'll make more; otherwise, you'll lose it." He concedes that his family would be happier if he were a lawyer, or doctor, or something more conventional that is upscale and prestigious. "But they're 100 percent supportive, and they can see I'm happy and a better person."

Jason's training reflects the Kabbalah Centre's current mission to disseminate Kabbalah widely and broadly. Unlike the teachers trained in the 1980s, who were, for the most part, fluent in Hebrew and the recipients of Rabbi Berg's lectures on Ashlag's magnum opus *Talmud Eser Ha-Sefirot,* Jason and most of the non-Israeli instructors possess only reading knowledge of Hebrew. Before he joined the Hevre, Jason learned advanced material—the Zohar and the writings of Yehuda Ashlag—in translation from his teacher. The teacher's explanations would be laced with stories, lessons from Rabbi Berg, or commentaries. Now that Jason is in the Hevre, he joins the group in such a class given by the senior teachers. He also studies on his own, reading the English-language books and listening to the tapes of lectures from the Centre's huge archive of lessons delivered over the past 25 years. "If you do know Hebrew, you can bypass certain books and go right to some key texts," Jason says. "But that's not the most important thing. The Centre does not feel there is any advantage to Hebrew; there is no point to learn for the sake of amassing knowledge."

I spoke to Jason's supervisor, Yehuda Grundman, about the Centre's teacher-training goals. "First I will tell you what our goal is not: it is not to get people to perform rituals, or to master sacred texts. The Kabbalah Centre's objective is to refine people's consciousness." For both the teachers and the students they serve, the Kabbalah Centre's God-centered narrative is central. He summarized it succinctly:

> We're talking about the Light here. We are teaching about an evolution that started with the Endless Light, and the Endless evolved to the limited reality that we are in now. By looking inward, we will find that Endless in us. It is in everything that we do. If we realize that it is all there, we will transform our vessel nature back to the Light, to the Endless.

Yehuda's particular task is to elevate the quality of the conversation that takes place on the phone between the Student Support workers and the callers. He explains, "You have to make sure that they are guiding people, rather than telling them what to do. We don't want to tell people what to do. The act without consciousness has no point."

Consequently, Jason's description of his teaching focuses on the process rather than the content of the lessons. In order to be a successful teacher, he believes, you need to truly do the work of transforming your soul, beforehand. "When you teach, it is not about you. Just the opposite: the ego gets removed. You need to reach the students, not to focus on yourself." Jason is drawn to teaching because of the liberation from the ego. He exclaims, "I love teaching! Only while teaching have I been able to focus outside myself. When I teach, it opens doors. It's very fulfilling." Members of the Kabbalah Centre community understand the link between ego-suppression and self-fulfillment; it is central to Kabbalah Centre teaching. He concludes, "Anyone who says 'I want to be a giver all of the time' is in denial or is lying. We all know that here. We give because we get something out of it. I know that the only way I can receive is to give. Why else would anyone give? People give so they can receive."

JUST A LITTLE BIT MAKES A DIFFERENCE

Joel's Story

Joel is a man in his late forties who came to the Kabbalah Centre through the private classes held in the homes of wealthy, accomplished people. He is a successful divorce attorney. What that means, he tells me, is that he gets clients who can pay his very high fees, and they are pretty happy with what he has done for them. "In court," he says, "I'm awful. That's my job. I'm cutting, sarcastic, and I go for the jugular. You don't want to face me for cross-examining!" He thinks that in terms of his day-to-day behavior and over the course of his life, he has been a good person. He is divorced and has no children. "My girlfriend for the past 14 years—she'll tell you I'm impossible and sarcastic," he says with a chuckle. "But I'm always conscious of how I'm acting, and I'm trying to improve. I've always been that way."

Joel got involved with the Kabbalah Centre because he was invited by one of his clients, a man in the entertainment field, to attend a special class. It was to be held in the man's home every week, with Eitan Yardeni as the teacher. There were about 20 people. They were generally middle-aged American-born businessmen and women, mostly Jewish people, Joel said. "There were lots of people from the entertainment field, some *very* well known people—I don't want to divulge the names—but you'd be surprised at how high they are." Joel was part of the core group of people. "You'd call or you'd be called, and if you couldn't come one week, others would be called to take your place. It was definitely not a 'drop in' event." Joel was surprised when I asked if the teacher was paid. "I don't think anyone gave a dime. I was never asked for money, and giving money was never discussed," he said. Many of the people in the core group, however, were quite active in the Centre. He knew they attended programs or lectures at the Los Angeles Centre, and some would travel to New York or other cities for special events. They were on friendly terms with Eitan, and some had close relationships with him.

The topic of the classes was relating Kabbalah to life. Eitan would talk, but the class was participatory. People would ask questions and would apply the principles to their personal or professional experiences. Joel thought Eitan was a terrific teacher: he was very smart, showing a thorough grasp of his topic, and his interesting choice of words and melodic and soothing voice made it an easy listening experience. Joel was pleased that the talks were not proselytizing and were so relevant to daily life. "This canned Kabbalah for the masses—the books are very user-friendly—they are going to resonate at some level with each of us," Joel explains. He thinks they are insightful in showing "how we flub up." The teacher talks about the ways in which we are our own worst enemies, or how our petty ego-needs make life difficult for others and for ourselves. He talks about it with humor, with anecdotes that people can relate to, with sympathetic understanding. It is a cathartic experience. Joel continues, "So you sit there and realize that we all stub our toes, and you listen because how can you not want to be better at every chance you get?"

One of the important lessons that Joel learned—"an amazing lesson," he told me—is that just because you are nice does not mean that you are doing what you need to do in the world. In class, as well as in the books, the message is "you have to stretch yourself." This is Joel's way of describing the principle that one's natural Desire to Receive for the Self Alone must be transformed into a Desire to Receive for the Sake of Sharing with Others. "Unless you really stretch, or give until you hurt, you won't grow or change. The real growth is when there is some struggle, when you break your mold," he explained. Joel feels that the lessons have helped him look at "the big picture," at the world outside of himself. He thinks perhaps he is less self-centered and more open to trying new things.

One way that Joel has stretched himself is through meditation. He does not attend the Centre, and the holidays and Shabbat mean little to him. His meditation is individual: he tries to meditate every day on the 72 names of God and on the Zohar, and he keeps a book of meditations in his car. Joel is particularly concerned about the culture around him, which he thinks is amoral and full of distorted values. "Lawyers are getting worse, clients are impossible, and the stakes are higher—where will it end?" He also thinks "the world consciousness" has become quite sick. According to an article he read recently in foreign policy journal, "the U.N. cannot combat terrorism because they cannot define it," he told me with exasperation. "Isn't that indicative of the collapse of common sense? I can meditate on peace and hope there is a consciousness shift." Joel described his meditations as a vehicle with the potential power to change the world. "You do it for the hundredth monkey," he told me. This refers to the belief that a particular learned behavior spreads instantaneously from one group of monkeys, isolated on an island, to all other monkeys of that species elsewhere in the world, once a critical number of monkeys (in this case, 100) is reached. The "hundredth monkey effect" is the application of this phenomenon to human beings and human culture. No scientist has evidence of the hundredth monkey effect, on monkeys or on people, but the factual basis of the story is accepted by Joel, who learned it from Eitan; the story has circulated widely in New Age and alternative health and spiritual circles.[2] In other words, Joel's right type of consciousness, focused in the right type of way, may just be what is needed to add to others of like mind, and it may tip the balance in the world so as to transform others. "If 40 people act, it may have an effect," he tells me, "and besides, what harm could it do?"

Stella's Story

Stella is an independent person with a strong sense of self, and she is attuned to the social dynamics of Kabbalah Centre events. Observing another woman flitting from table to table where people are sitting and eating the Shabbat meal, Stella tells me, "She hasn't yet found a home here." Stella herself has had some difficulty finding her niche at the Centre. She is a striking beauty with a ready smile, so she has made friends easily. However, she has had problems finding a suitable teacher to guide her. When she first called Student Support and agreed to study Kabbalah by listening to the classes on CD, she was assigned Mira as her teacher. The assigned teacher is supposed to call weekly and answer your questions, or you can call her, and at Kabbalah

Centre events, you meet and talk in person. However, Mira was unreliable and full of excuses, and when she ignored Stella while sitting at the same table during a Shabbat meal, Stella decided that four months with Mira was enough. She called Student Support and asked to switch to a teacher named Peretz. There was considerable resistance to this plan, Peretz told her later: "She didn't want to give you up because—people don't know this, and don't quote me please—she's one of the workers here who gets a commission for each student." Stella found Peretz to be a fine teacher, but after several weeks, she received a phone message from Student Support informing her that he was no longer at the Centre. A woman named Tzippy phoned Stella and told her she would be her teacher. Tzippy was better than Mira had been, but Stella balked when Tzippy asked her to purchase items from her private business, and shortly thereafter, Tzippy left Student Support too.

Stella's next teacher was also inadequate. He is a senior teacher whose primary responsibility, Stella learned from a very wealthy friend at the Centre, is to mentor the members of the community who are affluent. These members—her friend is among them—meet with him individually every week or two weeks and attend dinners at his home, but Stella, who has a very modest income, was limited to a short meeting once a month. After a few months of this, she asked for more time, and when he encouraged her to find another teacher, she did. "Your main anchor is your teacher," Stella told me. "Otherwise you're just floating around." Yet despite Stella's exposure to this unattractive side of the Centre, she separates the principles from the institution. She explains it as follows:

> We all know at the Centre that everybody is equal, and some people are more equal than others. I understand that the celebrities are kept separate to protect their privacy. I feel sorry for them because their experience is so different than everybody else's. But they and the rich people are not being helped. If I give a million dollars a year, and you're trying to teach me that the idea is to transform my Desire to Receive for the Self Alone into Desire to Receive for the Sake of Sharing and reduce the ego, you're not helping when you suck up to me!

Stella feels that the most valuable lesson the Centre has to offer is to give people a different perspective. "Our society is so 'me' focused, and the Centre's idea is that you should always be open to the other person," she tells me. Even though she was raised in a family of average means, she admits that she has had a sense of entitlement that limited her. "There's Bread of Shame—you have to earn everything! When you give, you will receive. I can deal with the ups and downs so much better now."

Stella does not spend much time at the Los Angeles Kabbalah Centre. She has taken on-site courses, has attended special events and occasional Shabbat Connections, and has volunteered at the Centre. However, she lives about 30 miles away, and her work keeps her busy. She meditates and scans the

Zohar for about 10 minutes a day. Stella really enjoyed her astrological reading and plans on returning for an "update." Stella learned that her soul has
had the unusual experience of being the child of her same parents' souls in
the past. This, to her, explains the close family tie and her father's bond with
her mother, which has persisted beyond their divorce. She learned why she
occasionally gets jolts of panic about drowning. Stella is a physical therapist
who helps rehabilitate people's muscles in specially equipped swimming
pools, so she is quite capable in and familiar with water. "I learned that in a
previous life I was a pirate, and I died by drowning!" she told me, thrilled by
the thought. Perhaps her former evil deeds in water account for her current
career choice, she speculates: "It may be a tikkun for my past, even though
I enjoy my work." Stella would like to get more involved in the Centre's projects. "The minute they bring Tech for Soul [Spirituality for Kids adapted for
prisoners] to the prison system here, I'm signing up as a mentor," she asserts.
She wonders whether that interest, too, is connected to her criminal past.

Stella was raised Presbyterian, and "it never took," she says. She thinks
the Kabbalah Centre will always be her spiritual home. This is evident in her
reading. She has always enjoyed reading spiritual and self-help books, nonfic-
tion, and autobiographies. Her regular perusal of bookstores is what led to her
discovery of Yehuda and Michael Berg's writings and then the Los Angeles
Centre. A few months ago, she decided to take on the spiritual discipline of
reading one chapter of the Book of Proverbs every day. "It was up and down,"
she told me, "and not always that compelling." But the younger Bergs' books
do not disappoint. She loved the latest, titled *The Kabbalah Book of Sex*, and
the earlier ones too. "I picked up one I had read a couple years ago and read
it the second time around, and I'm surprised! Did I notice these good ideas
before? I'm going to read them *all* again!" She admits that this will limit the
variety of her reading material. "I don't know why, but reading *these* books
seems to take care of a lot of different things all at once."

AMERICAN-BORN RELIGIOUS JEWS PRACTICING
JUDAISM IN THE KABBALAH CENTRE

A small portion of the Kabbalah Centre community is made up of American Jews in whose lives Judaism and American Jewish communal institutions
have played a strong role. They participate in Kabbalah Centre life because
they accept its claim to represent the kabbalistic tradition of Judaism, and
they have chosen its teachings over those they were taught in their homes,
schools, and synagogues. They strengthen the community with their familiarity with the prayers, rituals, holidays, and knowledge of Hebrew, but this
does not propel them into leadership positions; the leadership is dominated
by those of Israeli or non-American backgrounds. Indeed, it is unusual for
North American Jews with religious upbringing to frequent the Kabbalah
Centre. It bears examining those who do, however, because their experience

in the Centre reveals the tug-of-war between American Jewish ethnicity and the universalistic outreach of the Kabbalah Centre, as well as the feelings of hostility and betrayal with which the Kabbalah Centre and American Jewish denominations regard each other.

Naomi's Story

Naomi describes her family as loving, stable, and rooted in the Jewish tradition. She attended afternoon religious school, Jewish summer camps, and a synagogue youth group and spent a summer in Israel as part of an organized tour with other teenagers. Consequently, when she became a parent, she joined a Conservative synagogue, and when her children reached school age, she enrolled them in a Jewish parochial school. She was attracted to the Kabbalah Centre because, as a fairly well-educated Jew, she wanted to learn about an exciting facet of Judaism that could not be explored elsewhere in her community. She did not want to simply read books about the subject or attend academic-style lectures on Kabbalah offered by synagogue rabbis (which began to be available only after the Kabbalah Centre made its presence felt in the city). She wanted a living, spiritual exploration of Kabbalah, and the Centre provided that.

Naomi had and still has no plan to abandon her American form of Judaism for Kabbalah, but rather wishes to integrate and synthesize the two. She and her children have managed over the years to have friends in both places and to frequent both communities. Yet they have learned that it is best not to broadcast their involvement about the one place when they are in the other. The teachings of the Kabbalah Centre, it seems, dominate Naomi's religious consciousness, and it is there that she spends most holidays and Shabbat. She told me, "It makes sense that the teachings of the Kabbalists are closer to the deep truths of the Torah than the nonmystical rabbis." Naomi appreciates how people at the Centre, especially those in the core group who follow Jewish law, regard the Jewish holidays as opportunities to perfect their souls and connect to the Light. "You know it's been so intense this month here," she told me with some self-satisfaction during the weeks before the New Year, "because we're doing so much self-examination in preparation for Rosh Hashanah. With the right consciousness," she told me, "you channel divine energy into cells." Naomi accepts the teaching that each person is born with a life path already determined by his or her previous life and the necessary tikkun (in Kabbalah Centre Hollywood jargon, this is a person's "life script"), but that Kabbalah enables a person to change the script from this point forward. Naomi believes this and thinks it creates a spiritual atmosphere more serious and engaging than the one at her synagogue. She prefers the botanical metaphors used by the teachers, and she tells me that each new moon connection "plants the seed" for the rest of the month, and Rosh Hashanah plants it for the upcoming year.

Yet Naomi likes many aspects of the Western liberal Jewish denominations: the way they encourage girls and women to engage in mitzvot traditionally reserved for men, their encouragement of broad learning, their support for Jewish communal social welfare organizations and cultural institutions, and the esteem they grant to the Jewish heritage. She complains about the stereotypes she hears at the Centre about American Judaism and especially the unwillingness of the Israelis to give it any respect. "I want my children to be proud that they are Jewish," Naomi said, "but they won't get it from here. I want them to value their family geneaology and Jewish history, but they won't get that here either." Naomi says to me frequently, in reference to the Kabbalah Centre and American Jewish synagogues, "They could learn a lot from each other."

Gabriella's Story

Gabriella was at the beginning stages of a career in education, and her accomplishments, enthusiasm, and attractiveness make her a great "catch" for any religious movement. She grew up with a strong Jewish identity but very little religious education. She attended college in New York, immersing herself in Jewish studies and engaging in jobs that prepared her for a career in Jewish education. After college, she tried out different synagogues, but she found most of them to be boring and unstimulating. When she sat through one of the free introductory lectures at the New York Kabbalah Centre, her immediate reaction was "I want to be here." She enrolled in the courses, drank up the teachings, became close to her teacher, and loved the Shabbat Connections. Having experienced them, she could not enjoy the prayer services in other synagogues, even those who catered to the young. "The service was so dead!" she exclaimed about a morning prayer service organized by young Jewish graduate students. She was disappointed by a Friday night service reputed to be lively and moving, telling me, "There was good singing, but the rabbi's sermon had nothing to do with spirituality. It was not uplifting, and it certainly didn't make me feel motivated to be Jewish." She stopped exploring synagogues and began regularly attending the Kabbalah Centre. During the time she spent in the Kabbalah Centre community, Gabriella says, she became "more Jewish" than she had ever been, in that Shabbat and the holidays really became a part of her life.

Nevertheless, she was deeply conflicted about the Centre. Although she had terrific teachers and made friends there, she felt that the intensity of her experience there pulled her away from the elements of her life outside of the Kabbalah Centre that she wanted to keep. Other American Jews, especially those who led the programs and synagogues in which she studied and worked, regard the Kabbalah Centre as a bizarre and dangerous cult. She found that the acrimony between the organized Jewish community and the Kabbalah

Centre also made its presence felt at the Centre. When she spoke about her professional commitment to Jewish education, her teachers and her friends in the Hevre made disparaging remarks and reacted with puzzlement, saying "Why would you want to do that??" They encouraged her to change her plans and dedicate her energies to outreach for the Kabbalah Centre, and she was eventually offered the honor of joining the Hevre. Flattered and sorely tempted, she refused.

"It was my family," Gabriella told me. They did not discourage her, but she knew that the round-the-clock activities of the Hevre would mean that she would never see her siblings or parents, with whom she is quite close. Even without being a member of the Hevre, Gabriella feels there is tension between the Kabbalah Centre and her family. "Traditional Judaism emphasizes family, but the retreat is a big expense, and the whole family can't and won't come. I could stay in town and do it at the Centre, but I want to have a Pesach Seder with my family." Another reason Gabriella decided not to join the Hevre was because it would mean abandoning her career in Jewish education. Shortly afterward, Gabriella stopped attending the Centre altogether. She wanted some distance to figure things out, to "find some balance," and to prepare for her teaching responsibilities in a Jewish school.

After months of feeling bereft without the spiritual stimulation of the Kabbalah Centre, she has begun to occasionally attend the Shabbat Connections on Saturday morning. "There's so much energy, and they're so inspiring," she tells me. She finds the sermons "amazing," and she feels "they go right to your heart." But this time, Gabriella wants to proceed more carefully and with more "balance." She has decided to remain silent at the Centre about her job. "I realize that they really don't like Judaism," she tells me. This saddens and confuses her. Why is it, she asked me, that they voice respect for all religions but Judaism?

Shalom's Story

For the first four decades of his life, Shalom was an active participant in American Jewish synagogues. His parents were born in the United States, but they spoke Yiddish at home, and Shalom's Eastern European–born grandmother lived with the family for years. He was enrolled in a supplemental religious school five days a week, almost three hours per day, and so he was relatively well-educated in Judaism and Jewish languages. He attended Orthodox synagogues with one side of his family and Reform synagogues with the other side. He had a powerful emotional response to Orthodoxy:

> When I was a kid, for the high holidays, I got enough Light for the year. I could get a hair-raising feeling that I was on the Western Wall, connecting to God. Every time I went back to that place—after my father died, going there was a connection to him, too—I was very filled with awe of God.

When Shalom reached adulthood and moved to a new area of town, he and his wife joined a Conservative synagogue, and Shalom quickly became one of the leaders. "They made me ritual chairman," he told me, which meant that he would assign the different parts of the prayer service and assist in them. He explained, "On Shabbat, the idea was to get people to sing out. The holidays became my show." It did not give him the same religious feelings as before, but it was the best option in their neighborhood, and it offered a supplementary religious school education for their children.

Shalom's involvement in the Kabbalah Centre was very gradual; his wife took the lead. She was resigned to their somewhat empty spiritual life, but being a "spiritual seeker" type, she read about alternative religious outlooks. When an Irish Catholic friend of theirs recommended Philip Berg's books on Kabbalah, she visited the local Kabbalah Centre and signed up for classes. Shalom thought it was a little crazy. He was still involved in his synagogue, but he attended the Kabbalah series because he found the classes interesting. His wife prevailed on him to spend a Shabbat at the Centre when Philip Berg came to town. "I didn't want proselytism, I didn't want a charismatic rabbi, and then I couldn't understand him anyway," Shalom reported. "It was way over my head—I liked Karen's talk, though—and I didn't like all the screaming and carrying on in the prayers." He continued to take classes and enjoy them, and eventually, he said, "I realized that I understood things from a different viewpoint and I understood the screaming." People urged him to attend a Rosh Hashanah retreat. He resisted, "I had family! My wife and I could go, but only us! Rosh Hashanah is about family!" The people at the Centre told him, "This is not a family thing. Do family for Thanksgiving. This is for something else: it's about making a connection for the whole year." Shalom relented, and he had a powerful experience at the retreat: "The awe and hair-raising experience from when I was a child came back." He decided that the Kabbalah Centre would be his spiritual home.

After several years in the Centre, Shalom looks at the family issues differently. To him, American Judaism has turned into "tradition" without understanding. "We were told '*Es iz geshribben*' [Yiddish: it is written]. Other reasons I've heard, like 'do it for historical ties, do it for a feeling of community, do it for family'—these are, excuse me, nonsense." He believes they will not be powerful enough reasons to perpetuate Judaism:

> Okay, so we can get a warm and fuzzy feeling about sitting around the table reading the Haggadah [Pesach story], but will my kids do it for those reasons? Intermarriage being what it is, where is it going? I have reasons now to do it, but not necessarily with my family. I invite whoever of my family who want to take part. I'm no longer part of their thing, and they respect that. It's hard to be a Jew—now I know what it means, it means restriction. It means the consciousness. I used to *davven* [recite prayers] pretty good, but when I came to the Centre, I learned that what I was doing was pretty ridiculous. Now I have to fight and keep the right consciousness during the prayers.

Shalom believes that when he works on refining his relationship with the Creator, his relationships with his family directly benefits. There is no longer a conflict there.

He looks at ethnic loyalties differently too. The presence of non-Jews was at first disconcerting. He realized that he had to be careful about the types of jokes he told so as not to alienate those who are not Jewish, and this annoyed him. "My first reaction was 'Screw this! This is who I am!'" The interaction with Israelis at the Centre was also somewhat difficult. Shalom felt that they focused too much attention on Israel, that they did not appreciate Yiddish culture, and that their personalities could be abrasive. He gradually modified his perspective:

> I realized that that was about *me*. Isn't the Centre trying to get us to change that?...Ethnicity is about separation. It's about "Mine is the best." It's a continuous battle to understand that that's not what it's about. I need to keep working on it. We learn to live and love each other in spite of our "stuff." It affected me much more than others, but I was able to overcome that. After all, none of it has anything to do with the teachings of Kabbalah.

Shalom is aware that the Kabbalah Centre has evolved since he joined, and he freely admits that at times he resents it, "because this is not why I joined." Yet he appreciates the distance he has traveled in his own evolution. "I've gotten a greater understanding that there's more to life than me in this world," he told me. "I'm continually trying to marry who I am to who I want to be. I'm working on my ego all the time. This is not an easy process, not an easy lifestyle for Jews."

FINDING A PERFECT SYSTEM

Abe grew up in a loving, stable, working-class Jewish family. When he was 13, his father died suddenly. Abe was devastated, and he spiraled downhill into depression. His family had been members of a Conservative Jewish synagogue, and he attended a religious school, but he found neither comfort nor intellectual satisfaction in religious teachings. He eventually dropped out of school and worked at a variety of jobs. By 18, he was totally disenchanted with Conservative Judaism. From that point forward, Abe investigated all sorts of religious systems, without committing to any one of them. He engaged in a number of different business ventures and found his niche in entertainment marketing and advertising. By his mid-thirties, he was earning millions of dollars a year.

It was not until he was in his forties that Abe discovered Kabbalah Centre teachings. The attraction was purely intellectual, he said. It was the science. Abe knew about quantum physics and the recent advances in research. "We and all matter in the universe are all connected," he told me. "It is an intricate and perfect system of cause and effect. How do some cells know to be a liver cell and not a blood vessel cell? They know. God is that energy of intelligence." Rabbi Berg in his books was the first to explain this, Abe believed, and the teacher at the local Kabbalah Centre was "the cat's whiskers" in his ability to convey Berg's ideas to a wider audience. Abe found a concept of God that he felt was far more plausible and satisfying than the one he had learned in his youth:

> Do you know the God of Conservative Judaism? He is Eichmann. He stood in front of the gates of Auschwitz and said, "You live, and you die." So my father dies of a heart attack. God kills my father! And some womanizer lives to be 80. No justice! "God works in mysterious ways," they said. I found it to be emotionally distasteful and intellectually dishonest. How could I pay homage to this type of God? The reason I embraced Kabbalah is that the Jewish God is not this thing. It's about the supernal energy. There is a manual and a plan about how the physical world works.

His new thinking was purely intellectual, not spiritual. It all made sense. He felt at home with it, even though it was quite different from the Judaism in which he was raised.

Yet Abe was still cautious about adopting the ritual and lifestyle changes that came with being a serious devotee of Kabbalah. He wanted to actually meet Philip Berg before deciding. "I'm very jaded and skeptical," he told me. "I'm in marketing. I think everybody is manipulative, lying, or an easy mark. And I didn't want to jeopardize my own reputation." He hired a private detective to investigate the stories about Berg, and upon meeting the rabbi, he put him to his own test to discover whether Berg lived the principles that he preached. Berg passed Abe's test, and Abe decided to allow him to be his guide. Abe's wife was not convinced, however. She found Kabbalah to be strange, and she watched her husband get very involved rather quickly. She thought that their marriage agreement was being breached. Abe explained how he dealt with her opposition: "I told her, 'If I don't become a better father, husband, and son to my mom, I'm quitting. If it doesn't change me as a human being, I'm leaving Kabbalah. You decide.'" According to Abe, it was the final test:

> I had been very self-interested, self-centered, mercurial. I stopped being that way. I really stopped. I started being more sharing. I was open to the idea that the world didn't revolve around me. She observed it. Then she decided it was good for her and good for me. She saw only abundance for us and for our family. She embraced it.

Abe told me that the switch, for him, was not easy: "Everything was hard for me, and it still is, but if you know how it works, it's insane *not* to do it. I don't give a damn about unity with God. What I want is for my friends and family: protection for everybody." Over the years, Abe has extended his concern to far wider circles. "I want the spiral of negativity gone," he told me, in reference to the human relations and politics. "Tit for tat isn't working. I don't throw out garbage any more! Recycling—I've got to do it! Otherwise, I'm going to get what I deserve."

Abe is convinced that the mainstream Jewish denominations are histori-cal aberrations. He thinks the French Revolution and the accompanying pressures on European Jews to assimilate prompted Jewish leaders to expunge mystical ideas from religious life. "They were *all* mystics before then," he told me. What about the Rosh Hashanah prayer written by a thirteenth-century rabbi that depicts God deciding who shall live and who shall die? I asked Abe. He informed me that all prayers are in code and cannot be taken literally:

> The Hebrew letters are like an energy channel. Think about the blessing over wine—it's absurd on its face.[3] God is "king"? Ridiculous. And why do *we* bless God? That's nonsense. You have to know that "*baruch*" [bless] is like *bereicha*, a pool of water. It's the source from which we draw down energy. There's a se-cret behind the words, and the concepts are so complex that they cannot be written.

I persisted, asking why the prayers could not consist of words whose literal meaning was closer to the kabbalistic meaning. He replied, "I never read the English anymore. It doesn't make sense. The prayer was written in the 1200s, so it was written to the capacity of the writer. And they were like children." Abe's concession to an evolutionary viewpoint was brief. "It's the value of the letters," he continued. "The letters have phonic and pictorial power, and it's the sequence of the letters that creates the power. Sequence trumps content—this is the most important principle in quantum mechanics, too. The latest scientists believe that." When all is said and done, Abe makes a confession: "Really, it's not about the intellect, the left brain. We're hung up on that, and it's the only way to get inside. Once you're inside, there is a right brain level, and that's where the magic is."

Conclusion

New religious movements form because they satisfy a need. A leader succeeds in building a community of people who agree with his or her convictions about ultimate reality and who find satisfaction in acting on those convictions together. Sociologists explain that new religions will form during a time of change when the older understandings of the world do not seem to apply anymore. The new viewpoint helps to interpret these changes and make sense of them, explaining the new reality as something recognizable and not entirely new. It connects these new interpretations to existing ones, so that people believe they are not really innovating, but continuing on the right path or rediscovering the purer form of an existing religion. The new religious viewpoint helps people adapt to the new reality by justifying changed behaviors that are now necessary.

New religious movements provide many immediate rewards to their members, probably more so than established religions. There are real satisfactions attendant upon being led by charismatic leaders who are kind and loving and who inspire and mentor directly. It is exciting to find a novel approach to life. The religious outlook is fresh and lacking a known record of disappointment and failure, and a person feels special at being present at the start of the group's promising emergence into history. The religious ideas, practices, and structure of the community are in flux as the group comes together and takes shape. Because new religious movements are made up of converts, there is no shortage of people who brim with the joy of their new discovery and the zeal born of firm conviction. Members of new religious movements typically behave in ways that outsiders find objectionable: they tend to proselytize too vigorously, they have difficulty showing respect for inherited or established religious traditions, and they often scorn moderation. As Eileen Barker and others have shown, however, new religious movements that endure and grow become more conventional. Leaders who want broader acceptance will rein in their members and instruct them to be more toler-ant and respectful toward outsiders. With a larger community, they are less desperate for survival, and they temper their zealous proselytism. Looking at long-term survival, the leaders develop strategies for perpetuating their teachings to the next generation and to a wider range of followers. This often means abandoning practices that are at extreme odds with the sur-rounding society. Furthermore, for a new religion to become established and followed by a large group, it needs to set clearly defined moral and doctrinal positions, and it must be inclusive—addressing people at all ages, levels of spirituality, and income levels.

The history of the Kabbalah Centre as sketched in this book follows this pattern, for the most part. Philip Berg presented an analysis of life's dilem-mas, as well as solutions to these dilemmas, that sounded plausible and fit the tastes of spiritual seekers in the late twentieth century, and these dilem-mas and solutions were refined and adapted to suit the needs of people over the years. During the time I examined the Centre's teachings, from 1999 to 2006, Kabbalah Centre directors and teachers were pointing to three trouble-some features of society. First, they critique the secular, scientific outlook that seems—for some people—to rob life of spiritual meaning and that has failed to prevent or cure diseases, predict natural disasters, and bring peace between people and nations. Second, they note the corruption, dogmatism, and insu-larity of many religious institutions and religiously identified people, as well as these religions' failure to provide a meaningful rationale for religious ob-servance for the spiritual seekers who are the Kabbalah Centre's audience. Third, they bring attention to the seemingly insatiable human appetite for power, goods, and status that wreaks havoc on society and breeds dissatisfac-tion in the lives of many individuals. The Kabbalah Centre provides a solution to each of these problems. Its version of Kabbalah appears to be a universal-istic, spiritual wisdom that improves on and transcends modern science and all organized religions. These teachings explain why human cravings are so strong, and they also provide a way to harness the cravings, achieve personal satisfaction, and bring the world to perfection. Many people are drawn into the Centre's rather exotic worship because of a very individualistic, pragmatic effort to improve their lives. If they become more engaged with the teachings through the courses and through one-on-one relationships with teachers and other students, they learn that improvement is possible only by reducing their self-centered focus and their egotistic desires. Their hard work is rewarded, if not by the actual results they had originally sought, then by the approval and fellowship of the group or through their revision of their personal goals toward others that are less materialistic.

The Kabbalah Centre, to some extent, has followed the pattern of other new religious movements in eliminating practices that outsiders have found offensive. The door-to-door canvassing of neighborhoods and businesses that characterized its initial efforts to create a following in North America was replaced by a less invasive form of marketing through carefully designed books, free public lectures, and the sophisticated use of Internet communication. Celebrities and wealthy followers attracted to the Centre (often brought in by their friends to private teaching sessions arranged for them) generated, by virtue of their own social prominence, free publicity in the popular media for the organization. Philip and Karen Berg's initial leadership of the group evolved into a leadership consisting of the Berg parents, the Berg sons, and the Hevre. Since Rabbi Berg's stroke in 2004, Yehuda and Michael have become more influential in the Kabbalah Centre community. There are also the members of the Kabbalah Centre boards, the professionals and the volunteers, including mentors. Many lurid tales have circulated, especially in the organization's early years, about the religious coercion that occurs in the Kabbalah Centre's recruitment of young people. I did not attempt firsthand research into those claims; my investigation of the Centre has convinced me that the people there are emotionally manipulated to an extent no greater than in many other established religions. The senior teachers did inform me that their methods of training have been undergoing reform, and I could see firsthand the professionalization of the training procedures. Over the past few years, I have seen minor changes in Kabbalah Centre practice: the phrases shouted during the Kaddish prayer were modified, and, most recently, the Hevre decided to eliminate all the shouting that accompanies the Kaddish prayer. Certainly, there were more changes made that escaped my notice.

In terms of modifying its doctrines, however, I could not find that any of those that had been ridiculed and found offensive by outsiders were abandoned. Berg's initial teachings have remained at the core of the Kabbalah Centre. His dense writing and arcane themes were eventually made more accessible and updated. In the last few years, the publications attributed to Karen, Yehuda, and Michael have been significantly less complicated and have presented themes that appeal to the contemporary audience: topics connected to personal fulfillment, acting compassionately toward others, physical and emotional healing, and improving the world at the grassroots level. The latest curriculum is a highly simplified version of the earliest. Greater depth and the teaching of mitzvot are reserved for people who have been in the Centre longer and who seek out greater commitment. These are stylistic changes, not substantive. The goal of spreading Kabbalah to the world, which may have been present in Berg's mind from the beginning, eventually won higher priority among the numerous objectives of the organization.

As I have shown in this study, the universal mission never supplanted entirely the desire to produce a kabbalistic form of Judaism. This has produced an interesting community structure. The Kabbalah Centre expanded its range of followers not by modifying its core teachings, but by producing a version of its teachings that is less demanding and more accessible to many,

Notes

PREFACE

1. Olav Hammer, "Esotericism in New Religious Movements," in *The Oxford Handbook of New Religious Movements*, ed. James R. Lewis (Oxford and New York: Oxford University Press, 2004), 446, 450–451. Hammer is unfamiliar with the Kabbalah Centre. For him, Theosophy is an example of an esoteric religion that has drifted toward democratization.

CHAPTER 1

1. See, for example, the broad treatments of mysticism in classic works such as Evelyn Underhill, *Mysticism* (London: Methuen & Co., 1911), and Walter T. Stace, *The Teachings of the Mystics* (New York: New American Library, 1960).

2. Gershom Scholem, a founder of the academic study of Kabbalah, insisted in *Major Trends in Jewish Mysticism* (New York: Schocken Books, 1946) that no such thing as mysticism in the abstract exists; each mystic can be understood only in the context of a particular religious tradition, such as Jewish, Buddhist, Christian, and so on. See also Steven T. Katz, "Language, Epistemology and Mysticism," in *Mysticism and Philosophical Analysis*, ed. Steven T. Katz (New York and London: Oxford University Press, 1978), 22–74; and Boaz Huss, "The Construction of Jewish Mysticism and the Politics of Teaching It" (presentation at the 14th Annual World Congress of Jewish Studies, Jerusalem, 2005).

3. Many books provide an introduction to the various forms of Judaism. See, for example, Steven T. Katz, *Jewish Ideas and Concepts* (New York: Schocken Books, 1977); Lavinia Cohn-Sherbok and Dan Sherbok, *A Short Introduction to Judaism* (London: Oneworld Publishing, Ltd., 1997); Marc Angel, *The Rhythms of Jewish Living: A Sephardic Exploration of the Basic Teachings of Judaism* (Northvale, NJ: Jason Aronson, 1997).

4. Gershom Scholem, *Kabbalah* (Jerusalem: Keter Publishing House, 1974); Moshe Idel, *Kabbalah: New Perspectives* (New Haven, CT: Yale University Press, 1988); Arthur Green, *Ehyeh: A Kabbalah for Tomorrow* (Woodstock, VT: Jewish Lights, 2003).

5. Moshe Idel, "On the History of the Interdiction against the Study of Kabbalah before the Age of Forty" [in Hebrew], *AJS Review* 5 (1980), 1–15; "Perceptions of Kabbalah in the Second Half of the 18th Century," *Journal of Jewish Thought & Philosophy* 1 (1991), 55–114.

6. Joseph Dan and Ronald Kiener, *The Early Kabbalah* (Ramsey, NJ: Paulist Press, 1986).

7. Yehudah Liebes, *Studies in the Zohar* (Albany: State University of New York Press, 1993).

8. Boaz Huss, "*Sefer ha-Zohar* as a Canonical, Sacred and Holy Text: Changing Perspectives of the Book of Splendor between the Thirteenth and Eighteenth Centuries," *Journal of Jewish Thought and Philosophy* 7 (1998), 257–307.

9. Arthur Green, *Ehyeh: A Kabbalah for Tomorrow*, 23.

10. Jochanan H. A. Wijnhoven, "The *Zohar* and the Proselyte," in *Texts and Responses: Studies Presented to N. Glatzer*, ed. Michael Fishbane (Leiden: Brill, 1975, 120–140). In contrast, non-kabbalistic Jewish literature generally affirms the equal status of proselytes.

11. Idel, *Kabbalah: New Perspectives*, 74–111, 156–200.

12. Idel, *Kabbalah: New Perspectives*, 2–7. Allison Coudert and Jeffrey S. Shoulson, eds., *Hebraica Veritas? Christian Hebraists, Jews, and the Study of Judaism in Early Modern Europe* (Philadelphia: University of Pennsylvania Press, 2004).

13. Gershom Scholem, *Sabbatai Sevi* (Princeton, NJ: Princeton University Press, 1976), 66–120; and Gershom Scholem, *Kabbalah* (Jerusalem: Keter Publishing House, 1974), 190. Against this assertion, see Moshe Idel, "'One from a Town, Two from a Clan'—The Diffusion of Lurianic Kabbala and Sabbateanism: A Re-Examination," *Jewish History* 7 (1993), 79–104.

14. Idel, "Perceptions of Kabbalah in the Second Half of the 18th Century," 61, 67–68.

15. On the spread of Hasidism, see Glenn Dynner, *Men of Silk: The Hasidic Conquest of Polish Society* (New York and London: Oxford University Press, 2006). Pinchas Giller, *Shalom Shar'abi and the Kabbalists of Beit El* (New York and London: Oxford University Press, in press).

16. Jonatan Meir, "Wrestling with the Esoteric: Hillel Zeitlin, Yehudah Ashlag, and Kabbalah in the Land of Israel" [in Hebrew], in *Be'er Rivkah: Festschrift in Honor of Professor Rivka Hurvitz*, ed. Efraim Meir and Haviva Padia (Beer Sheva, 2006), 595–602.

17. The main source for Ashlag's biography is written by his son's disciple, Avraham Mordecai Gottlieb, *Ha-Sulam: Biographies of Rabbi Yehuda Lev Ashlag and Rabbi Baruch Ashlag and their Pupils* [in Hebrew] (Or Baruch Shalom: Jerusalem, 1997). This is summarized in Mark Cohen and Yedidah Cohen, eds., *In the Shadow of the Ladder: Introductions to Kabbalah by Rabbi Yehudah Lev Ashlag* (Safed, Israel: Nehora Press, 2002), 20–26. A more discerning account of Ashlag's life is found in Meir, "Wrestling with the Esoteric." See also Micah Odenheimer, "Latter-day Luminary," in *Haaretz*, 16 December 2004, translated and on the Internet at www.haaretz.com/hasen/objects/pages/PrintArticleEn.jhtml?itemNo = 515439, (accessed December 18, 2004). The details of the difficult journey and family tragedies vary in the different accounts, but Gottlieb's sources regard Ashlag's decision to leave in such a manner as a positive testimony to his devotion to Kabbalah.

18. Lawrence Fine, *Physician of the Soul, Healer of the Cosmos: Isaac Luria and His Kabbalistic Fellowship* (Stanford: Stanford University Press, 2003).

19. Fine, *Physician of the Soul*, 304–314.

20. Ashlag's reference to Luria's soul within his own appeared in a letter written in 1926; a portion of the letter is quoted in Gottlieb, *Ha-Sulam*, p. 1, without further identification. Ashlag's discussion of his prophetic role in the transmission of Kabbalah is quoted in Gottlieb, pp. 1–3.

21. Ashlag's cosmogonic narrative departs from all previous ones in his description of the *tsimtsum* that occurs in Malchut and not prior to it. See David Hansel, "The Origin in the Thought of Rabbi Yehuda Halevy Ashlag: Şimşum of God or Şimşum of The World?" *Kabbalah: Journal for the Study of Jewish Mystical Texts* 7 (2002), 37–46.

22. For an English rendering of this final goal of creation, see the translation of Ashlag's *Hakdamah La-Zohar* [Introduction to the Zohar] in Cohen and Cohen, *In the Shadow of the Ladder*, 38–42. On Ashlag's distinctive ethical shift, see Boaz Huss, "All You Need is LAV: Madonna and Postmodern Kabbalah," *The Jewish Quarterly Review* 95, no. 4 (Fall 2005), 616.

23. Boaz Huss, "'Altruistic Communism': The Modernistic Kabbalah of Rabbi Ashlag" [in Hebrew], *Iyunim Bitkumat Israel* 16 (2006), 115–116. On Ashlag's relationship to other Hasidic

teachers, see Jonathan Garb, *"The Chosen Will Become Herds"*: *Studies in Twentieth Century Kabbalah* [in Hebrew] (Jerusalem: Shalom Hartman Institute), 100–102.

24. The institution (in Jerusalem) was called "Beit Ulpana deRabbana 'Itur Rabbanim' [House of Rabbinic Study 'Crown of Rabbis'] for the Teaching and Spread of Kabbalah in Jerusalem." Yet, according to Meir, "Wrestling with the Esoteric," 602–609, as well as Gottlieb, Ashlag kept himself aloof from the other Kabbalists in Jerusalem. For a list and description of Ashlag's known students, see Meir, "Wrestling with the Esoteric," 590–592.

25. Meir, "Wrestlings with the Esoteric," 594, 625–630.

26. For example, he managed to published one issue of a newspaper, *Ha-Ummah*, May 6, 1940. Most of Ashlag's essays are still in manuscript form. Some may be found in Hebrew and in translations on the Web site of Bnei Baruch (www.kabbalah.info).

27. Huss, "Altruistic Communism."

28. Huss, "Altruistic Communism," 129.

29. Meir, "Wrestling with the Esoteric," 44.

30. Herbert Weiner, *9 1/2 Mystics: The Kabbalah Today* (New York: Collier Books, 1969), 96–101, describes Weiner's recent visit to Baruch Ashlag's yeshiva and synagogue. See also Micah Odenheimer, in "Latter-day luminary," for firsthand accounts of Ashlag's poverty and social isolation.

31. Gottlieb, *Ha-Sulam*, 58–59, and Odenheimer, "Latter-day Luminary." These details are based on testimony from Ashlag's wife Rivka and acquaintances.

32. Interviews with Shlomo Krakovsky, February 25, 2004, and August 22, 2004. Meir's account in "Wrestling with the Esoteric" corresponds more closely to this version.

33. On the lawsuits, see Meir, "Wrestling with the Esoteric," 593, fn. 36.

34. Interview with Shlomo Krakovsky, February 25, 2004. In the United States, Levi Krakovsky studied at the Isaac Elhanan Theological Seminary, which later became part of Yeshiva University.

35. Interviews with Shlomo Krakovsky, February 25, 2004; August 22, 2004; November 22, 2005. The three boys were in Mossad Diskin, a religious boarding school for boys; the two girls were in Mossad Weingarten, an institution for girls.

36. Letter dated 15 Sivan 5697 (May 25, 1937). The letter is in Hebrew.

37. The reference to the Kabbalah Academy is in *The Omnipotent Light Revealed: The Luminous Tegument to Unite Mankind into One Loving Brotherhood* (Hollywood, CA: Kabbalah Culture Society of America, 1939), 43. Krakovsky described himself as the head of Yeshivat Chochmat Ha-Kabbalah in his edition of Ashlag's *Sefer Talmud Eser Ha-Sefirot Me-Haari Zal, im Shnei Biurim Maspikim Lemathilim, Hanikrain Or Penimit . . . Histaklut Penimit* (Brooklyn, NY: The Kabbalah Foundation, 1943).

38. Interview with Sidney Semel, January 3, 2006.

39. Interviews with Shlomo Krakovsky, February 25, 2004, and August 22, 2004.

40. Krakovsky complained of this in his writings, and this is confirmed by many other sources. See Jonathan D. Sarna, *American Judaism: A History* (New Haven, CT: Yale University Press, 2004), 289–291, 294–306.

41. In this volume, unlike that of his later book, Krakovsky writes for a universal audience, and he makes no mention of Jews. The address of the publisher of the volume was a private residence in the hills of Hollywood, California, which was at that time a center of avid interest in Theosophy, occult, and Eastern religions.

42. Levi Isaac Krakovsky, *Kabbalah: The Light of Redemption* (Brooklyn, NY: The Kabbalah Foundation, 1950), 8.

43. *Kabbalah: The Light of Redemption,* 7.

44. *Kabbalah: The Light of Redemption,* 75.

45. *Kabbalah: The Light of Redemption,* 227–229.

46. *Kabbalah: The Light of Redemption*, 231.

47. *The Omnipotent Light Revealed*, 35–36.

48. Gershom Scholem, review of L. I. Krakovsky, *Kabbalah: The Light of Redemption* (Brooklyn: The Kabbalah Foundation, 1950) in *Jewish Social Studies* 25 (1953), 312.

49. *Kabbalah: The Light of Redemption*, 196–197.

50. *Kabbalah: The Light of Redemption*, 229–230.

51. *Kabbalah: The Light of Redemption*, 226–227.

52. "Key to Paradise" (unpublished manuscript dated 1953, Brooklyn, New York), Introduction, ii.

53. Interviews with Shlomo Krakovsky, February 25, 2004, and August 22, 2004.

54. Interview with Sidney Semel, January 2, 2006.

55. I learned of Krakovsky's role as Gruberger's teacher from my interviews with Shlomo Krakovsky. Gruberger may have learned about Levi Krakovsky from the latter's son Menahem, who was in rabbinical seminary with Gruberger, or from Levi Krakovsky's books. The certificate of incorporation of the National Institute for Research in Kabbalah (registered on July 14, 1965) designates Gruberger as the president, and five other men as members of the corporation: Harry Z. Wulliger, Jacob Flaks, Levi Krakovsky, Eugene Semel, and Yehuda Nussbaum.

56. Interview with Shlomo Krakovsky, August 22, 2004; phone interview with Levi Krakovsky's niece, Joann Weiss, September 1, 2004. Levi Krakovsky's gravestone is set alongside Ashlag's children and disciples, next to Ashlag's grave.

57. Neither Karen Berg nor Michael Berg acknowledges Krakovsky's role in teaching Philip Berg. Interview with Michael Berg, February 9, 2005; interview with Karen Berg, September 2, 2005. In the Kabbalah Centre's collection of the letters from Yehuda Brandwein to Berg, all references to Krakovsky in the original, handwritten letters were omitted from the transcribed version of the letters; see Michael Berg, ed., *Sefer Yedid Nafshi*, 3 vols. [in Hebrew] (Jerusalem: Press of the Kol Yehuda Yeshiva, 1997).

58. Philip Berg, *Education of a Kabbalist* (Tel Aviv, New York, Los Angeles: Kabbalah Centre International, 2000), 149–151. In this history, Berg also discounts the knowledge and ability of Ashlag's sons in regard to transmitting their father's teachings.

59. According to Levi Krakovsky's family, just prior to checking into the hospital for a medical procedure, Krakovsky filled a suitcase with some of his unpublished manuscripts and brought them to his son Shlomo's home for safekeeping. Shlomo learned later that shortly after his father's death, Berg brought his children to visit the elderly widow and pay their respects. He and his children packed up the copies of *Kabbalah: The Light of Redemption* and other writings and carted them away. Interview with Shlomo Krakovsky, February 25, 2004.

CHAPTER 2

1. Elena Lappin, "The Thin Red Line," part one, *The Guardian*, 11 December 2004, http://www.guardian.co.uk/print/0,3858,5082014-103602,00.html (accessed January 6, 2005). Without giving a source for her information, Lappin writes that Max Gruberger worked as a clothes presser. Without giving details, Michael Berg's blog states that Philip Berg came from a family with "a long spiritual tradition of scholars and teachers." See http://blog.kabbalah.com/michael/my-teachers/rav-berg/en/ (accessed March 1, 2006).

2. The ordination certificate is dated 11 Kislev 5712, which is December 10, 1951. I have a photocopy of the original from Ron Csillag, who was given a copy by the Kabbalah Centre for use in his newspaper article.

3. By 1962 he was a millionaire from his thriving insurance and real estate business, Berg told Ron Csillag, "The Kabbalah Centre," *The Canadian Jewish News*, 18 March 1993, 6.

4. Lappin, "The Thin Red Line," part one.

5. The familial relationship is known to me through anecdotal evidence alone. Berg did not mention his first wife and children in his autobiography *Education of a Kabbalist* (Tel Aviv, New York, and Los Angeles: Kabbalah Centre International, 2000). On pp.15–16, he claims that Brandwein was a distant relative whom he met for the first time in 1964 through a series of fortunate coincidences.

6. Certificate of Incorporation of National Institute for Research in Kabbalah, registered July 14, 1965. The Kabbalah Centre provided a copy of this document to me. The incorporation document, which calls for a minimum of six voters for the corporation and includes the six as witnesses and signers, does not include Brandwein's name. (The six voters are Philip S. Gruberger, Harry Z. Wulliger, Jacob Flaks, Levi Krakovsky, Eugene Semel, and Yehuda Nussbaum.)

7. Brandwein describes the yeshiva in Michael Berg, ed., *Sefer Yedid Nafshi,* vol. 1 [in Hebrew] (Jerusalem: Press of the Kol Yehuda Yeshiva, 1997), 221 (Letter 1, dated 2 Tammuz 1964). His reference to the yeshiva as a continuation of Ashlag's Beit Ulpana is found in *Sefer Yedid Nafshi,* vol. 3, 190 (Letter 34, dated 25 Tammuz 1968).

8. The original is in *Sefer Yedid Nafshi,* vol. 3, 354; the abridged transcribed version is in *Sefer Yedid Nafshi,* vol. 2, 333–334 (Letter 20, dated 7 Av 1965).

9. On the page after the title page in *Or Ne'erav,* Philip S. Gruberger is acknowledged as president and Rabbi Yehuda Z. Brandwein as dean of the National Institute for Research in Kabbalah in Brooklyn, with Israeli branches in Tel Aviv, Jerusalem, Beth Shemesh, Ofakim, and Brachya. Problems closing a real estate deal are discussed in *Sefer Yedid Nafshi,* vol. 2, 310, with a fuller version in the original in vol. 3, 353 (Letter 19, dated 28 Tammuz 1965). A speculative venture in medical technology in 1968 is referred to in the original handwritten letters in *Sefer Yedid Nafshi,* vol. 3, 366, 367, 369 (Letter 32), but omitted from the transcription in vol. 3, 147–149.

10. Moshe Cordovero, *Or Ne'erav,* ed. Yehuda Z. Brandwein (Brooklyn, NY: National Institute for Research in Kabbalah, 1965), 3–4.

11. These restrictive opinions may be found in Michael Berg's notes to the letter from Brandwein quoted in the text, *Sefer Yedid Nafshi,* vol. 2, 335–337. I thank Michael Fox for assistance in understanding the intricacies of these texts.

12. *Sefer Yedid Nafshi,* vol. 2, 333. Letter 20, dated 7 Av 1965. This part of the letter is identical in the original (vol. 3, 354) and the transcribed version.

13. Here the reference is in the original and not in the transcribed letter. *Sefer Yedid Nafshi,* vol. 3, 357 (Letter 23, dated 1 Elul 1965).

14. *Sefer Yedid Nafshi,* vol. 3, 118, Letter 28, dated 5 Shevat 1967.

15. These complaints are in the original handwritten letters but are not included in the transcribed letters. For example, see *Sefer Yedid Nafshi,* vol. 3, 336 (Letter 2, dated 3rd night of Hanukkah, 1965); vol. 3, 341 (Letter 7, dated Shushan Purim 1965); vol. 3, 355 (Letter 21, dated 15 Av 1965); vol. 3, 369 (Letter 35, dated 15 Av 1968).

16. These are in the transcribed letters as well as the originals. *Sefer Yedid Nafshi,* vol. 2, 193 (Letter 14, dated 9 Iyyar 1965); vol. 3, 64 (Letter 23, dated 1 Elul 1965).

17. A copy of Brandwein's ordination, and a transcription of it, may be found in *Sefer Yedid Nafshi,* vol. 1, 213–214. I have a photocopy of the original from Ron Csillag, who was given a copy by the Kabbalah Centre for use in his newspaper article.

18. *Sefer Yedid Nafshi,* vol. 3, 190 (Letter 34, dated 25 Tammuz 1968).

19. Looking at the printed record, Berg makes no reference to Brandwein in the prefaces to the books he published in the 1970s; he places great attention on Ashlag, however. In the 1980s, Berg seems to have realized the importance of establishing his genealogy as a scholar, and he does so by citing his years of study with and ordination by Yehuda Brandwein. The basis for Berg's claim that he was designated Brandwein's successor is in the personal conversations between the two, as well as in the implications of the letters in *Sefer Yedid Nafshi.* Michael Berg confirmed this to me via e-mail, January 22, 2007.

20. Robert Wuthnow, *After Heaven: Spirituality in America since the 1950s* (Berkeley: University of California Press, 1998), 59.

21. Jonathan D. Sarna, *American Judaism: A History* (New Haven, CT: Yale University Press, 2004), 277–293. Jack Wertheimer, *A People Divided: Judaism in Contemporary America* (New York: Basic Books, 1993), 3–17. Wertheimer, 202, fn. 57 notes that a 1963 Gallup Poll found that 71 percent of Catholics, 37 percent of Protestants, and 17 percent of Jews reported attending a religious service the previous week.

22. Sarna, *American Judaism*, 318–323.

23. The disproportionate representation of Jews was widely acknowledged, but researchers conducted research on the subject beginning in the 1980s. They estimated that 9 percent of the Church of Scientology, 15 percent of the community of Krishna Consciousness, 6 percent of the Unification Church, and 20 percent of the utopian community established by Bhagwan Shree Rajneesh were Jewish. See J. Gordon Melton and Robert L. Moore, co-authors, *The Cult Experience: Responding to the New Religious Pluralism* (New York: Pilgrim Press, 1982), 30–31; Rodney Stark and William Sims Bainbridge, *The Future of Religion: Secularization, Revival and Cult Formation* (Berkeley: University of California Press, 1985), 398–404; Carl Latkin, R. Hagan, R. Littman, and N. Sundberg, "Who Lives in Utopia? A Brief Report on the Rajneeshpuram Research Project," *Sociological Analysis* 48 (1987), 76.

24. Charles Selengut, "American Jewish Converts to New Religious Movements," *The Jewish Journal of Sociology* 30, no. 2 (1988), 95–109. Wertheimer, *A People Divided*, 202, fn. 57 notes that according to a 1970 Gallup poll, 19 percent of American Jews reported attending a religious service the previous week (60% of Catholics, 38% of Protestants).

25. A good overview of this subject may be found in the entry "Brainwashing (Debate)" by David G. Bromley in *Encyclopedia of Religion*, 2nd ed. (Detroit: Macmillan Reference, 2005), vol. 2, 1030–1036. For a thorough, but dated, overview, see David G. Bromley and James T. Richardson, eds., *The Brainwashing/Deprogramming Controversy: Sociological, Psychological, Legal and Historical Perspectives* (New York and Toronto: Edwin Mellon Press, 1983). A more recent work is Lorne L. Dawson, *Comprehending Cults: The Sociology of New Religious Movements*, 2nd ed. (Don Mills, Ontario: Oxford University Press Canada, 2006).

26. Edgar H. Schein, Inge Schneier, and Curtis H. Becker, *Coercive Persuasion* (New York: W.W. Norton, 1961); Robert Lifton, *Thought Reform and the Psychology of Totalism* (New York: W.W. Norton, 1961).

27. Margaret Thaler Singer with Janja Lalich, *Cults in Our Midst* (San Francisco: Jossey-Bass Publishers, 1995).

28. Bromley, "Brainwashing (Debate)," in *Encyclopedia of Religion*, 2nd ed., 1032. Although some of the most vociferous critics of the new religious movements were clergy, spokesmen for established churches—realizing that limitations on freedom of religion was against their own interests—proved to be the most effective opponents of legislative initiatives that would limit the new religious movements; see J. Gordon Melton, "Perspective: Toward a Definition of 'New Religion,'" *Nova Religio* 8, no. 1 (2004), 81.

29. Some people argue that the ostensibly nonjudgmental academic approach is an escape from the expert's responsibility to call things as they are or, worse, that it enables evil people to use the legitimate identity as "religion" or "spirituality" to engage in fraud, deceit, and manipulation. From their perspective, academics who study new religious movements are "cult apologists."

30. J. Gordon Melton, "An Introduction to New Religions," *The Oxford Handbook of New Religious Movements*, ed. James R. Lewis (Oxford and New York: Oxford University Press, 2004), 22–25. See also Melton, "Perspective: Toward a Definition of 'New Religion,'" 78–81.

31. Melton, "An Introduction to New Religions," 22–23.

32. Eileen Barker, "Perspective: What Are We Studying? A Sociological Case for Keeping the 'Nova,'" *Nova Religio* 8, no. 1 (2004), 88–102.

33. See Boaz Huss, "Ask No Questions: Gershom Scholem and the Study of Contemporary Jewish Mysticism," *Modern Judaism* 25, no. 2 (May 2005), 141–158.

34. Sarna, *American Judaism*, 293–300, 346. Naftali Loewenthal, "Schneerson, Menachem M.," in *Encyclopedia of Religion*, 2nd ed., vol. 2, 8171–8173.

35. Yaakov Ariel, "Hasidism in the Age of Aquarius: The House of Love and Prayer in San Francisco, 1967–1977," *Religion and American Culture* 13, no. 2 (2003), 139–165. Karen Berg informed me that Carlebach was a classmate of her husband, but "they were in two different worlds." She explained that the Bergs were living in Israel for 12 crucial years of Carlebach's activities, and Carlebach's lifestyle was far more radical than theirs. Karen noted that Carlebach was unmarried for many years, but clustered around him were followers who were also living unconventionally. Interview with Karen Berg, September 2, 2005.

36. On the Havurah movement, see Riv- Ellen Prell, *Prayer and Community: The Havurah in American Judaism* (Detroit: Wayne State University Press, 1989). Shaul Magid, "Jewish Renewal Movement," in *Encyclopedia of Religion*, 2nd ed., vol. 7, 4869. One testimony of the absence of Kabbalah is in the book authored by members of the Havurah in Somerville, Massachusetts. The authors did not suggest any English translations of Kabbalah, but easier works written in Hebrew. They noted that the translations and commentaries of Hebrew University scholars had greatly facilitated understanding of kabbalistic texts. They did not suggest any mystical adepts in the United States for guidance, and they regarded academic scholarship as a reliable source of knowledge of Kabbalah. See Richard Siegel, Michael Strassfeld, and Sharon Strassfeld, eds., *The Jewish Catalog: A Do-It-Yourself Kit* (Philadelphia: The Jewish Publication Society, 1973), 231.

37. Christine A. Meilicke, "The Forgotten History of David Meltzer's Journal *Tree*," *Studies in American Jewish Literature* 22 (2003), 52–71. See also her article "Abulafianism among the Counterculture Kabbalists," *Jewish Studies Quarterly* 9 (2002), 71–101; and Harris Lenowitz, "The Appearance of Hebrew Script in Art: Three from the Golden West" (presentation at the 13th annual World Congress of Jewish Studies, Jerusalem, 2001).

38. "The Rav" means "the rabbi"—specifically, the chief rabbi. Berg explained that the shorter name was less cumbersome, and he adopted it in anticipation of his move to Israel in 1971. Comments made by Berg to Ron Csillag, "The Kabbalah Centre," 6. Tova, to whom Berg's first books were dedicated, felt the name Karen was more attractive and had greater connection to Kabbalah (one meaning of the Hebrew word *keren* is "ray of light"); interview with Karen Berg, September 2, 2005.

39. Philip Berg, *Kabbalah for the Layman: A Guide to Cosmic Consciousness* (Jerusalem: Press of the Research Centre of Kabbalah, 1981), 141. There are significant changes in the different printings of *Kabbalah for the Layman*, even though the copyright may have remained the same. The Research Centre of Kabbalah ignored the standard protocol of changing the copyright or noting a revision in the title page when significant changes were made in the book. In the case of the first issue of *Kabbalah for the Layman*, the copyright year is 1981, but the printing year was 1982.

40. Philip Berg, *The Kabbalah Connection: Jewish Festivals as a Path to Pure Awareness* (Jerusalem: Research Centre of Kabbalah Books, 1983), 171.

41. Berg, *Kabbalah For the Layman* (1981 edition), 11.

42. Berg, *The Kabbalah Connection*, 148.

43. Berg, *The Kabbalah Connection*, 145.

44. Berg, *The Kabbalah Connection*, 149.

45. The Certificate of Change of Name was filed on February 19, 1970, after a vote of the majority of the members of the corporation on February 5, 1970. The Kabbalah Centre gave me a copy of this document.

46. It appears that the following publications of the Research Centre of Kabbalah originated with Krakovsky: Yehuda Ashlag, *Ten Luminous Emanations*, vol. 1 (Research Centre of the Kabbalah, 1970)—in some additions and not others, Levi Krakovsky is acknowledge as

translator; Levi Isaac Krakovsky, *Kabbalah: The Light of Redemption* (Research Centre of Kabbalah, 1970). Phillip S. Berg, *Power of the Aleph Beth* (Research Centre of Kabbalah, 1988)
appears to be the same as Levi Krakovsky's manuscript "Kabbalah: Dialogue Between G-d and
the Hebrew Alphabet." In addition, the translation of Moses Luzzatto, *General Principles of the
Kabbalah* (Research Centre of the Kabbalah, 1970) is attributed to "The Research Centre of
Kabbalah," with no credit or mention of Krakovsky. However, there is evidence throughout
Krakovsky's writings that it was his translation. He published two pamphlets on Kabbalah in
which he mentioned his completed translation of Luzzatto's *General Principles of Kabbalah*, in
the hope that an interested reader would support the publication of the manuscript. See p. 2
of Krakovsky's pamphlet called *If eventually—why not now? Oyb nisht yetst, ven?* (self-published
by Krakovsky's own Kabbalah Foundation in Brooklyn, 1938) and p. 8 of *Israel's Survival in
Kabbalah* (no date, but probably issued during the 1940s). Krakovsky also mentions his translation of Luzzatto's book on the book jacket of his 1950 publication of *Kabbalah: The Light of
Redemption*. Berg's right to these works was later contested in court: in 1996, the Estate of Levi
Krakovsky sued Philip Berg and the Kabbalah Centre for plagiarism, but the case was settled,
and the records have been sealed. Berg himself made a veiled reference to the lawsuit in his
Education of a Kabbalist, 151.

   47. See the acknowledgements page in Rabbi Yehuda Ashlag, *An Entrance to the Zohar*, comp.
and ed. Dr. Philip S. Berg (New York and Jerusalem: Research Centre of Kabbalah, 1974), iv–v.

   48. I believe this foundation is connected to the Sangreal Sodality, an entity founded and
fostered by William G. Gray. See http://www.geocities.com/sangreal_sodality/index.htm (accessed May 25, 2006), which explains that Sangreal Sodality promotes "a combination of different approaches to the training ranging from individual study, silent meditation, ritual work, the
keeping of magical records, daily aspirations, and daily work with the Cabalistic Tree of Life."

   49. In the preface to Berg, *The Kabbalah Connection*, 19.

   50. For example, Berg is described as "an ordained Rabbi who holds a doctorate in comparative religions" in the "About the Author" paragraph in Philip S. Berg, *Wheels of a Soul*
(Jerusalem and New York: Research Centre of Kabbalah, 1984), 10. In the 1990s, when critics
of the Kabbalah Centre could find no evidence of this, Berg explained that the title referred to
the advanced rabbinic ordination conferred on him by Brandwein. See Ron Csillag, "The Kabbalah Centre," 6.

   51. Yehuda Ashlag, *Ten Luminous Emanations*, vol. 2 (New York and Jerusalem: Research
Centre of Kabbalah, 1973); Ashlag, *An Entrance to the Zohar*, ed. Philip Berg, vii.

   52. Letter from Karen Silverstein to Mr. Donald Karr on Research Centre of Kabbalah
stationery, dated June 10, 1976. Mr. Karr did not agree to write for the Research Centre of Kabbalah. I thank him for sharing with me copies of his correspondence.

   53. Naomi Levanon, "The Added Value of the Kabbalah" [in Hebrew], *La-Isha*, 14 November 1978 [Israeli women's magazine]. Accessed on the Israeli Kabbalah Centre Web site,
http://www.kabbalah.co.il (May 24, 2005).

   54. Berg, *Kabbalah for the Layman* (1981), 13. Similar comments may be found in *Kabbalah
for the Layman* (1981), 23, 24, 38. This principle is also repeated in an article written by an
Israeli student; see Levanon, "The Added Value of the Kabbalah," 2.

   55. Olav Hammer, "Esotericism in New Religious Movements," in *The Oxford Handbook of
New Religious Movements*, ed. James R. Lewis (Oxford and New York: Oxford University Press,
2004), 446, 450–451. Hammer is unfamiliar with the Kabbalah Centre. For him, Theosophy is
an example of a esoteric religion that has drifted toward democratization.

   56. J. Gordon Melton, "New Age Transformed," published in The Religious Movements
Homepage Project of the University of Virginia, at http://religiousmovements.lib.virginia.edu/
nrms/newage.html (accessed February 9, 2006).

   57. Assaf Inbari, "New Age: The Fall of the Secular State," http://inbari.co.il/en_index.
htm (accessed January 12, 2006). First published in Hebrew in *Haaretz*, September 1999. See

also Inbari, "The Underground of Yearning," available only in Hebrew in *Haaretz,* 17 September 1999, and at http://inbari.co.il/index.htm.

58. Levanon, "The Added Value of the Kabbalah," 4.

59. Levanon, "The Added Value of the Kabbalah," 2.

60. Michael Laitman, now director of the religious movement called Bnei Baruch, does not admit to any past association and study with Philip Berg. See the Bnei Baruch Web site: http://www.kabbalah.info/engkab/abouteng.htm. He has admitted, in interviews [Hebrew], that he studied with Berg; c.f. http://kabbalah.info/hebkab/press_heb/haaretz/haaretz1.htm (accessed September 6, 2006). In his *Kabbalah Lematchil* [Hebrew] (Israel: Bnei Brak, 2005), 543, he does refer to "Kabbalists" that he studied with prior to Baruch Ashlag. I thank Jonatan Meir and Boaz Huss for these references.

61. Interview with Shaul Youdkevitch, March 29, 2006.

62. Interview with Shaul Youdkevitch, March 29, 2006; these points were echoed in my interview with Billy Phillips, March 1, 2006. Bnei Baruch does not currently attribute the same importance to Orthodox religious law.

63. Boaz Huss, "The New Age of Kabbalah: Contemporary Kabbalah, New Age, and Postmodern Spirituality," forthcoming. See also Jonathan Garb, *"The Chosen Will Become Herds": Studies in Twentieth Century Kabbalah* [in Hebrew] (Jerusalem: Shalom Hartman Institute, 2005).

64. Interview with Shaul Youdkevitch, March 29, 2006.

65. Berg, *Kabbalah for the Layman* (1981), 16, 141.

66. Berg, *Kabbalah for the Layman* (1981), 11.

67. Berg, *Kabbalah for the Layman* (1987 edition and copyright), 208–209. The translation of the term *"Kat"* is Berg's (the term is in singular, but Berg translates it into plural form). The title of the book changed slightly in the 1991 edition (copyright date remains 1987), from *Kabbalah for the Layman: A Guide to Cosmic Consciousness* to *Kabbalah for the Layman: A Guide to Expanded Consciousness.*

68. Interview with Billy Phillips, March 1, 2006. Billy was the director of communications at the Kabbalah Centre in Toronto in the early 1990s, and he has remained instrumental in the Kabbalah Centre movement to this day. Eitan Yardeni, interviewed on February 14, 2006, described the Hevre as a "spiritual kibbutz."

69. Private communication with author, January 1, 2006.

70. These concepts are explained more fully in chapter 3. This particular explanation is taken from Eitan Yardeni, Power of Kabbalah III class, March 6, 2006.

71. Interview with Karen Berg, September 2, 2005.

72. Interview with Shaul Youdkevitch, March 30, 2006.

73. Interview with Eitan Yardeni, February 14, 2006; and in Power of Kabbalah III class, May 8, 2006.

74. There are many statements of this sort in the articles on the Kabbalah Centre in http://www.rickross.com, an "anti-cult" Web site. See, for example, Aynat Fishbein, "The Cabal of the Kabbalah Centre Exposed," *Tel Aviv* (September 1994) [originally in Hebrew, translated for the Web site].

75. The spelling of the organization's name—Centre rather than Center—comes from the Israeli and Canadian origins of the name.

76. Interview with Billy Phillips, March 1, 2006. Interview with Shaul Youdkevitch, March 29, 2006. A description of the Toronto Centre may be found in Ron Csillag, "The Kabbalah Centre," 6 and 7. The membership estimate was provided to Csillag by the Centre while he was preparing the article.

77. Private communication with author, January 1, 2006.

78. Interview with Billy Phillips, March 1, 2006. Interview with Shaul Youdkevitch, March 29, 2006. The revision of the books' contents and covers is also evident from a careful examination of the different editions.

79. Berg, *Kabbalah for the Layman* (1981 edition), 141.

80. Berg, *Kabbalah for the Layman* (1991 revised edition, copyright 1987), vol. 1, xxiv. Two more volumes were added to *Kabbalah for the Layman* in 1988, and so all subsequent printings include volume numbers.

81. In my interview with Michael Berg (February 9, 2005), Michael acknowledged the distinction between what Ashlag advocated and what the Kabbalah Centre actually does: "Ashlag urged this, but he didn't actually do it."

82. Berg, *Kabbalah for the Layman* (1991 revised edition, copyright 1987), vol. 1, 141.

83. Much of this information is common knowledge among regular attendees at the Centre.

84. This was issued on March 27, 1990, by Vaad Harabonim of Toronto, the body of Orthodox rabbis of the city.

85. Ron Csillag, "The Kabbalah Centre."

86. The case is Ontario Court of Justice File no. 93-CQ-39877. I have examined many pretrial documents. Rabbi Immanuel Schochet never disputed the facts of the case as laid out by Berg; his claim was that the Canadian court should have no jurisdiction in what was essentially a religious matter. The case never went to trial—Berg let it drop.

87. In addition to the *Canadian Jewish News* article, the most important other publications during the 1990s came from Los Angeles. A small pamphlet, *The Cabal of the Cabbalah Centre Exposed: The Truth about The Kabbalah Centre and Its Guru, Philip S. Berg*, published by the Task Force on Cults and Missionaries [a project of the Jewish community] (Los Angeles, 1995), has circulated throughout the United States and Canada. See also Robert Eshman, "Center of Controversy," *The Jewish Journal* [Los Angeles], 14–20 February 1997. These articles accused Berg of dishonesty regarding his academic credentials (the PhD, or title as "Dr.") and his claims regarding his partnership with Brandwein and his "inheritance" of Ashlag's legacy; his teachings are denounced as violating centuries of Jewish tradition; the Bergs and the Kabbalah Centre staff are accused of emotional and financial exploitation of vulnerable people who come to the Centre for assistance and spiritual guidance. Although the North American Jewish community is quite diverse and by no means united on many issues, its various parts, to this day, voice great scorn for the Kabbalah Centre.

88. Since 1999, when I first began observing the Kabbalah Centre, I have observed that the Kabbalah Centre leaders take great pains to guard Madonna's privacy and name. Madonna takes the initiative in promoting the Kabbalah Centre. In stating this here, I retract my previous published reference to this relationship, which can be found in the entry "Berg, Philip," in *Encyclopedia Judaica*, 2nd ed., vol. 3 (Detriot: Macmillan Reference, 2007), 417–418.

89. For example, see Yehuda Berg, *The Red String Book: The Power of Protection* (Los Angeles: Kabbalah Centre International, 2004), 57–66, 80–81.

90. I thank Lisa Kessler, director of the legal administration of the Kabbalah Centre International, for providing me a copy of the constitution.

91. Interview with Michael Berg, April 13, 2005. He overestimates the Jewish population; Jews constitute .025 percent of the world's population and about 2 percent of the U.S. population.

92. Statement at the Tiferet Institute Forum, December 19, 2006.

CHAPTER 3

1. The Introduction to Kabbalah course has been revised repeatedly since the early 1990s, but the major revision that contained the theme of the "Game of Life" was already in place by the late 1990s. Introduction to Kabbalah has been taught as a series of three courses, each one consisting of at least 10 sessions. I attended Introduction to Kabbalah I in fall 1999, taught by Rabbi Shaul Youdkevitch.

2. Kabbalah I, third lecture Q & A, October 21, 1999, Shaul Youdkevitch.

3. Wouter J. Hanegraaff, *New Age Religion and Western Culture: Esotericism in the Mirror of Secular Thought* (Leiden: E. J. Brill, 1996), 183–188.

4. Berg, *Kabbalah for the Layman* (1981 edition), 70–77. This is Berg's simplification of the narrative that appears in Yehuda Ashlag, *Talmud Eser Ha-Sefirot*.

5. Kabbalah I, second class meeting, October 14, 1999.

6. The concept Bread of Shame appears often in Berg's writings, and it is a cardinal principle of Kabbalah Centre teachings. For example, in *Kabbalah for the Layman* (1981 edition), 13 pages are devoted to the topic: 78–82, 86–87, 89, 116–117, 132–134, 136, and 137. Ashlag also devotes considerable space to this concept, without always mentioning the exact phrase "Bread of Shame" *(nehama dekisufa)* in his essay "Matan Torah" (The Giving of the Torah), found in translation in Yehuda Ashlag, *Kabbalah: A Gift of the Bible* (New York and Jerusalem: Research Centre of Kabbalah, 1984), 34–37. The editor (Berg) notes there that Ashlag also discussed the concept in his volume *Panim Masbirot*, a commentary on Isaac Luria's *Etz Chaim*, first chapter; and in *Talmud Eser Ha-Sefirot* in the section called "An Internal Look," section 1. Boaz Huss informed me that he also found reference to it in Ashlag's *Pticha Le-Hochmat Ha-Kabbalah* (Introduction to the Study of the Kabbalah), section 15, and in one of Ashlag's letters from 1928, published in volume 2 of *Pri Hakham* (Fruit of the Wise).

7. Ashlag's cosmogonic narrative departs from all previous ones in his description of the *tsimtsum* that occurs in malchut and not prior to it. See David Hansel, "The Origin in the Thought of Rabbi Yehuda Halevy Ashlag: Şimşum of God or Şimşum of The World?" *Kabbalah* 7 (2002), 37–46.

8. In Yehuda Berg's *The Power of Kabbalah* (Los Angeles: Kabbalah Centre International, 2004), 228, a summary of the basic principles of Kabbalah presented by the Kabbalah Centre, Rule Number Two, reads "Two basic realities exist: Our 1 percent world of darkness and the 99 percent realm of light!"

9. Private communications with author, May 4, 2006, and June 5, 2006.

10. In *Kabbalah for the Layman* (1981 edition), 79, Berg responds to someone who might ask why human beings must bear the consequences of a voluntary decision made earlier in time. He explains that "what is established by voluntary means on a high level becomes involuntary on successively lower levels." These arguments conveniently ignore the detail that God and the vessels were one and the same in the Endless.

11. Yehuda Berg, *The Power of Kabbalah*, 228–229.

12. Private communication with author, May 4, 2006.

13. Private communication with author, June 5, 2006.

14. Private communication with author, June 20, 2006. The morning prayer she recites is the Hebrew prayer *Modeh/Modah Ani*. Religious Jews recite it upon wakening, and it is taught to young children, girls and boys alike. In its entirety, it reads, "I offer thanks to you, living and eternal King, for you have mercifully restored my soul within me; your faithfulness is great."

15. Private communication with author, June 20, 2006.

16. This is the subject of Philip Berg's book, *Immortality: The Inevitability of Eternal Life* (Tel Aviv, New York, and Los Angeles: Kabbalah Centre International, 2000). It is also the theme of the Kabbalah Centre's celebration of the holiday Shavuot; see the "live streaming connection" for the holiday of Shavuot, 2006, at http://store.kabbalah.com/product_info.php?products_id =725 (accessed July 10, 2006). Also see Yossi Klein Halevi, "Like a Prayer," *The New Republic* 230, no. 17 (May 10, 2004), 18–21.

17. Private communication with author, March 27, 2006.

18. J. Gordon Melton, "A History of the New Age Movement," in *Not Necessarily the New Age: Critical Essays*, ed. Robert Basil (Buffalo, NY: Prometheus Books, 1988), 36. See also Hanegraaff, *New Age Religion and Western Culture*, 324–330. On contemporary Kabbalah as an example of postmodern spirituality, see Boaz Huss, "The New Age of Kabbalah: Contemporary Kabbalah, The New Age" (forthcoming).

19. A summary of New Age concepts and history may be found in Wouter Hanegraaff, "New Age Movement," entry in *Encyclopedia of Religion*, 2nd ed.

20. This early part of the narrative is reconstructed from references to the patriarchs and Moses in Berg's early books (including the glossaries), particularly *Kabbalah for the Layman* and *The Kabbalah Connection*.

21. Berg, *Kabbalah for the Layman* (1st ed., 1981), 22–47, 214–220. Note that Berg omits Brandwein from his chain of kabbalistic tradition. The development of the Ashlag-Brandwein-Berg chain of tradition appeared in print much later, most notably in Berg's *Education of a Kabbalist* (2000).

22. Billy Phillips is responsible for assembling the historical film-lectures, and he has been the presenter at the lectures I have attended. He has also shared his perspective with me through interviews.

23. Berg, *Wheels of a Soul*, 19 (the preface was written by Kenneth R. Clark). In the book's acknowledgments, 10, Berg thanks Holly Clark "for transcribing many of the tapes of lectures I had given on reincarnation."

24. Berg, *Wheels of a Soul*, 44, 26.

25. Scholem, *Major Trends in Jewish Mysticism*, 279–283. See also Rachel Elior, "The Doctrine of Transmigration in *Galya Raza*," in *Essential Papers on Kabbalah*, ed. Lawrence Fine (New York: New York University Press, 1995), 243–269.

26. Berg, *Wheels of a Soul*, 79, 86–87.

27. Berg, *Wheels of a Soul*, 86.

28. Berg, *Wheels of a Soul*, 48, cites *Sha'ar Ha-Gilgulim*, 32.

29. In *Wheels of a Soul*, 102, Berg mentions only that according to *Sha'ar Ha-Gilgulim*, most women are on earth "on a volunteer basis for the benefit of men with whom they may have endured a number of incarnations." The critical role of women at the time of the Golden Calf has since been developed more in the book by Karen Berg, *God Wears Lipstick: Kabbalah for Women* (New York and Los Angeles: Kabbalah Centre International, 2005), 79. Neither Philip Berg nor Karen Berg mentions that, according to Luria, women's souls must serve time after death in Gehinnom for the sins they committed in their lifetimes.

30. Berg, *Wheels of a Soul*, 25.

31. Berg, *Wheels of a Soul*, 62.

32. Berg, *Wheels of a Soul*, 99. In this volume, the word is spelled *tikune*.

33. Berg, *Wheels of a Soul*, 93.

34. Berg, *Wheels of a Soul*, 49–51.

35. Berg, *Wheels of a Soul*, 156, 162–164.

36. Interview with Shaul Youdkevitch, May 10, 2006.

37. Kabbalah Centre Basic Reincarnation course, Lecture 4, February 3, 2000.

38. Yael Yardeni, astrology reading, June 28, 2006.

39. Berg, *Wheels of a Soul*, 150, 107. This was also an important lesson in the Kabbalah Centre Basic Reincarnation course, Lecture 4, February 3, 2000.

40. The basic series of Kabbalah classes is now named "The Power of Kabbalah I, II, and III" (10 sessions per course). When I began studying at the Kabbalah Centre in October 1999, the series was simply "The Introduction to Kabbalah I, II, and III" (still 10 sessions per course). I enrolled in Power of Kabbalah III, taught by Eitan Yardeni, in February 2006.

41. Although Berg praised the religious rebellion, "love movements," and antiwar agitation of the early 1970s as signs of a spiritual awakening, he showed little respect for feminism, writing (in Berg's preface to Ashlag's *Ten Luminous Emanations*, volume 2, xii), "On the lighter side of the coin, we are now experiencing a movement known to most of us as 'Women's Liberation.'" Explicit criticism of feminism is voiced in women-only classes such as "Mind, Body, and Spirit." Jayna Zimmelman attended a coed Kabbalah I class and a women-only course called "Mind, Body, and Spirit" at the San Fernando Valley (in Los Angeles) Kabbalah Centre. I thank her for

full access to her findings and her unpublished research paper from June 2003, "The Powerfully Subordinate: Gender in Theory and Practice at the Kabbalah Learning Centre." Zimmelman found that feminism is blamed for demoralizing and emasculating men to the point of oppression, and problems in the American family such as divorce and drug use are a direct result of feminism's proclamation that women are able to perform men's roles. One of the chief themes in Karen Berg's *God Wears Lipstick: Kabbalah for Women* is the spiritual superiority of women.

42. Berg, *God Wears Lipstick*, 41–46. Yet, no person is purely a giver or a receiver, or purely male or female, I was told by instructor Yehuda Grundman (interview with the author on November 6, 2006).

43. These points were covered in the earlier-mentioned first session (June 6, 2002) of the "Mind, Body, and Spirit" course.

44. Berg, *God Wears Lipstick*, 58–59.

45. Berg, *God Wears Lipstick*, 80.

46. This latter point was suggested to me—and it was taught in the "Mind, Body, and Spirit" course—in response to my question as to why, if women do not need to reincarnate, the Kabbalah Centre teaches them to concern themselves with the tikkun process. I was reminded that each soul is split in two, and because the male side needs fixing, the work of the female is not complete. She comes to this world equipped with a "tikkun package." Interview with Shaul Youdkevitch, May 10, 2006.

47. Berg, *Immortality*, 59. Within the Kabbalah Centre community, Karen is credited and respected for being the practical, result-oriented director.

48. Private communication with author, September 13, 2006.

49. For information on the appearance of this ideology in Modern Jewish Orthodoxy, see Jody Myers and Jane Rachel Litman, "The Secret of Jewish Femininity: Hiddenness, Power, and Physicality in the Theology of Orthodox Women in the Contemporary World," *Gender and Judaism: The Transformation of Tradition*, ed. T. M. Rudavsky (New York: New York University Press, 1995), 51–80. There is no research showing that new religious movements are, in regard to gender roles, inclined more toward or against egalitarian feminism than established religions. This subject has been explored by Susan J. Palmer, "Women's 'Cocoon Work' in New Religious Movements: Sexual Experimentation and Feminine Rites of Passage," *Journal for the Scientific Study of Religion* 32, no. 4 (December 1993), 343–55.

50. Berg, *Wheels of a Soul*, 58–60.

51. Berg, *Wheels of a Soul*, 111.

52. Berg, *Wheels of a Soul*, 60.

53. On the reincarnation into a woman, see *Sha'ar Ha-Gilgulim*, chapter 9. Some of this is paraphrased in Berg's *Wheels of a Soul*, 153. I thank Pinchas Giller for assisting me in the study of the sections of *Sha'ar Ha-Gilgulim* in which this issue is discussed.

54. http://www.becominglikegod.com/?p=ask_michael&s=291 (accessed January 28, 2006).

55. Interview with Shaul Youdkevitch, June 6, 2006.

56. Private communication with this author, May 4, 2006, is the basis of all comments attributed to Jonathan.

57. Richard Kyle, *The New Age Movement in American Culture* (Lanham, MD: University Press of America, 1995), 189.

58. "Astrology," by Alexander Altmann, in *Encyclopaedia Judaica*, vol. 3, 788–795.

59. I thank Martin Leiderman, who teaches in the West Los Angeles Theosophical Society meetings, for pointing out that the Kabbalah Centre teachings on Atlantis were drawn from Helen Blavatsky's writings; see "Atlantis," ch. 24, in *Wheels of a Soul*.

60. Berg, *The Kabbalah Connection*, 130–132; Philip Berg, *Astrology: The Star Connection* (New York and Jerusalem: Research Centre of Kabbalah, 1986), 40.

61. Zohar Study class, Eitan Yardeni, July 19, 2005. I thank Pinchas Giller for assisting me in comparing the Kabbalah Centre material with older kabbalistic sources.

62. See the kabbalistic calendar available from the store on the Kabbalah Centre Web site: http://store.kabbalah.com/product_info.php?products_id=494.

63. Interview with Yael Yardeni, Kabbalah Centre astrologer, December 12, 2005.

64. Astrological reading on June 28, 2006, with Yael Yardeni.

65. Interview with Billy Phillips, March 17, 2006.

66. Private communication with author, June 20, 2006.

67. I thank Ira Robinson for sharing with me his paper presented at the American Academy of Religion conference in 1987, "Kabbalah and Orthodoxy: Some Twentieth Century Interpretations." See also Ira Robinson, "Kabbalah and Science in *Sefer Ha-Berit:* A Modernization Strategy for Orthodox Jews," *Modern Judaism* 9, no. 3 (October 1989), 275–288.

68. James R. Lewis, *Legitimating New Religions* (Piscataway, NJ: Rutgers University Press, 2003).

69. Hanegraaff, *New Age Religion and Western Esotericism*, 62–67. The steps in the argument that follows are neatly summarized in Kyle, *The New Age Movement in American Culture*, 96–99.

70. Kabbalah I class, 1999, and many times thereafter.

71. Berg, *Astrology: The Star Connection*, 44.

72. Berg, *Wheels of a Soul*, 143. This is an accurate quotation, even though it may sound like there is an error in copying it.

73. Berg, *Wheels of the Soul*, 21.

74. Yehuda Berg, *The Power of Kabbalah*, 88.

75. Berg, *Wheels of a Soul*, 122.

76. Berg, *Immortality*, 221–237.

CHAPTER 4

1. Berg, *Kabbalah for the Layman* (1981 edition), 92.

2. Philip [Shraga Feival] Berg, introduction to *Sefer Yedid Nafshi* [in Hebrew], ed. Michael Berg, 47–48.

3. Berg, *Kabbalah for the Layman* (1981 edition), 92.

4. In his preface to *Or Ne'erav*, Brandwein wrote that the Holocaust was a consequence of the Jews removing Kabbalah from the curriculum. He attributes this opinion to Ashlag as well; see Cordovero, *Or Ne'erav*, 3–4. I heard this at the Centre in 1999. An uproar ensued when remarks to this effect by Eitan Yardeni, a senior teacher, were captured on tape and were broadcast by the BBC; see John Sweeny, "Kabbalah Leader's Holocaust 'Slur,'" BBC News, 9 January 2005, http://news.bbc.co.uk/1/hi/world/4158287.stm (accessed December 4, 2005).

5. Private communication with author, May 4, 2006.

6. Private communication with author, September 13, 2006.

7. Berg, *Kabbalah for the Layman* (1981 edition), 102.

8. Berg presents an old kabbalistic theory about Eastern religions. In *The Kabbalah Connection*, 73, he explains that they originated when Abraham gave gifts to Isaac and to the sons of his concubines and sent them to the East (Genesis 25:5–6). The Zohar explains that this means that Abraham gave Isaac a "total system" of right-column energy, left-column energy, and the central column for balancing the two, but lesser gifts to his other sons. Berg explains that Eastern religions were given awareness only of right- and left-column energy (he may be referring to the notion in Chinese religion of the opposing energies of yin and yang).

9. Berg, *Kabbalah for the Layman* (1981 edition), 101.

10. Berg, *Kabbalah for the Layman* (1981 edition), 100–101; the same statement can be found in Berg, *The Kabbalah Connection*, 99.

11. This explanation appears in full in Levanon, "The Added Value of the Kabbalah," *La-Isha*, 3.

12. Berg, *Kabbalah for the Layman* (1981 edition), 125.

13. Chapter 2 deals fully with Berg's views on the principle of noncoercive spirituality. Berg's comment on the uselessness of rituals performed without metaphysical understanding is found in a great many places; this comment is from Berg, *The Kabbalah Connection*, 39, citing the Zohar.

14. Berg, *The Kabbalah Connection*, 149.

15. In 2006, however, advanced registration and payment was requested for attendance at the Los Angeles Kabbalah Centre on Rosh Hashanah and Yom Kippur Connections as well; the explanation for this was that the demand for seats far exceeded the available spots. Recently, the large number of attendees at Sabbath morning Connections as been accommodated by the scheduling of a second, early morning Connection.

16. Upon my request, I received a Shabbat explanation sheet prepared especially for newcomers.

17. Yehuda Berg, ed., *Dialing God: Daily Connection Book* (New York and Los Angeles: Kabbalah Centre International, 2004), 70.

18. Yehuda Ashlag, *A Gift of the Bible* (Jerusalem and New York: Research Centre of Kabbalah, 1984), 41. Ashlag repeats, with variations, a number of quite unfavorable comments about non-Jews; see also 31, 40, 49, 50–51, 54.

19. Ashlag, *A Gift of the Bible*, 50.

20. Berg, *The Kabbalah Connection*, 99–100. See also Berg, *Kabbalah for the Layman* (1981 edition), 98–99.

21. Interview with Michael Berg, April 13, 2005. Of course, Jews were not the only inhabitants of Palestine or Israel at the time; there were also Muslims, Christians, and people of other religious status.

22. Rav S. P. Berg, *Siddur T'filah L'Ani for Shabbat: With Meditations from The Ari Z"L, HaRashash, HaRamchal, Ha'Ba'al Shem Tove, and HaRich*, ed. Rabbi Yehudah [sic] Berg (New York: The Press of the "Yeshivat Kol Yehudah," 1999), 150–151. A Hebrew edition of the prayer book was published earlier, but it omits many of the explanations (such as the one quoted) that may be found in the English.

23. Interview with Billy Phillips, January 8, 2004; private communication with author, January 21, 2005.

24. Interview with Billy Phillips, January 8, 2004; March 1, 2006. The conspiratorial view of world history is most avidly and skillfully promoted by Billy Phillips, an important longtime member of the Kabbalah Centre board of directors. It is a principle theme in his public slide lectures on the history of Kabbalah (I viewed this on September 13, 2005), which have been very well received. Although Philip Berg himself has denounced Jewish leaders for their opposition to the Kabbalah Centre, he has not endorsed this conspiracy theory and takes pains to be nonjudgmental in public. His history of Kabbalah, which includes his explanation for why Kabbalah did not become widely known until the twentieth century, is discussed in chapter 3.

25. Private communication with author, February 14, 2006.

26. Interview with Michael Moskowitz, February 10, 2006.

27. Hanegraaff, *New Age Religion and Western Esotericism*, 324–327.

28. Terry Gross, "Fresh Air from WHYY" Interview with Madonna, NPR, November 23, 2004.

29. Private communication with author, July 26, 2005.

30. I did not write the letter, in order to avoid conflict of interest.

31. Interview with Karen Berg, September 2, 2005. Karen actually referred to Buddhism in her response, not Hinduism, but she meant the latter.

32. Interview with Shaul Youdkevitch, May 10, 2006. Also, see the Web site on the Zohar Project: http://www.kabbalah.com/kabbalah/programs.html#zohar.

33. This is explained in chapter 1. Briefly, according to rabbinic teachings, the covenant made with Noah obliged him and all his descendants—that is, all of humanity—to follow these

seven commandments. Later, a separate covenant was made with Abraham obligating his and Sarah's descendants and proselytes to the greater number of commandments, eventually revealed by God to Moses.

34. Interview with Shaul Youdkevitch, May 10, 2006.

35. Interview with Billy Phillips, January 8, 2004.

36. Interview with Shaul Youdkevitch, May 10, 2006. Private communication with author, September 13, 2006.

37. The desire for a more undiluted Jewish community appears as a frequent reason for a Jew to leave the Kabbalah Centre and join an Orthodox synagogue, according to my interviews with Kabbalah Centre members of the core community and according to the testimonies found in the Jewish media of ex-Kabbalah Centre participants.

38. Interview with Michael Moskowitz, February 10, 2006.

39. Private communication with author, January 1, 2006. A similar point was made in the interview with Michael Moskowitz, February 10, 2006.

40. Interview with Karen Berg, September 2, 2005. This theme is prominent in Kabbalah Centre Hebrew publications that are designed for an Orthodox readership, according to Jonatan Meir, "The Revealed and the Revealed within the Concealed: On the Opposition to the 'Followers' of Rabbi Yehuda Ashlag and the Dissemination of Esoteric Literature," *Kabbalah: Journal for the Study of Jewish Mystical Texts* 16 (2007), forthcoming.

41. Interview with Michael Moskowitz, February 10, 2006. Chapter 6 contains a profile of a proselyte.

42. Interview with Shaul Youdkevitch, May 10, 2006. Private communication with author, September 13, 2006.

43. The word *Sefard*, Spain, is an anagram of *sod* (secret), *peshat* (literal), *remez* (implication), *drash* (homiletical)—the four ways of explicating the Torah. This may be found in the glossary at the back of *The Kabbalah Connection*.

44. This was taught in my Kabbalah I class, and I heard it from Shaul Youdkevitch, May 3, 2006, and May 10, 2006.

45. Interview with Billy Phillips, January 8, 2004. Interview with Karen Berg, September 2, 2005.

46. Private communications with author, May 4, 2006; August 8, 2005; June 5, 2006.

47. Interview with Shaul Youdkevitch, August 21, 2006.

48. Private communication with author, August 21, 2006. This individual was quite definite about the connection between the Kabbalah Centre Zohar edition and the encouragement of scanning. He informed me that he was the first person in Los Angeles to buy the Kabbalah Centre's Zohar, and his scanning practice has been constant since that time.

49. Boaz Huss, "*Sefer ha-Zohar* as a Canonical, Sacred and Holy Text: Changing Perspectives of the Book of Splendor between the Thirteenth and Eighteenth Centuries," *Journal of Jewish Thought and Philosophy* 7 (1998), 295–299.

50. Philip Berg, introduction to *Siddur T'filah L'Ani*, vi.

51. Philip Berg, introduction to *Siddur T'filah L'Ani*, vii.

52. From http://www.kabbalah.com/k/index.php/p=zohar/about/scanning

53. In the Jewish press there have been many complaints about the expense of the Kabbalah Centre Zohar, although I have found that it is actually the cheapest set of the complete Zohar commercially available.

54. In summer 2002, I enrolled in "Healing and Consciousness," a course taught by Chaim Solomon. In my conversations with other students in the course, as well as with people attending the Shabbat morning services, I found that people regarded my question "Do you own a Zohar?" as an insult, responding "Of course!"

55. The practice of keeping books of Zohar or other kabbalistic literature in one's car, office, bedroom, and with children seems to be very widespread. I have interviewed a number of

people who tell me that they keep the Pinchas volume or another Kabbalah Centre publication in their car.

56. Shaul Youdkevitch said this during the connection on July 22, 2006, and he explained it to me on July 27, 2006.

57. Michael Berg speaking at the Tiferet Institute Forum, December 19, 2006; interview with Shaul Youdkevitch, July 27, 2006.

58. Yehuda Berg, introduction to *Siddur T'filah L'Ani*, 12.

59. Private communication with author, July 19, 2006.

60. Private communication with author, September 13, 2006.

61. Joseph Dan, "The Emergence of Mystical Prayer," in *Jewish Mysticism: The Middle Ages*, vol. 2, ed. Joseph Dan (Northvale, NJ: Jason Aronson, 1998), 230; in the same volume, see also Menachem Kallus, "The Theurgy of Prayer in the Lurianic Kabbalah," 62.

62. Pinchas Giller, *Shalom Shar'abi and the Kabbalists of Beit El*.

63. Meir, "Wrestling with the Esoteric," 602–609.

64. Meir, "The Revealed and the Revealed within the Concealed," describes how a number of respected rabbis gave their approval *(haskama)* to the Hebrew prayer book. Rabbi Kadouri— one of the most influential Israeli Kabbalists—later retracted his approval, not because of the contents of the prayer book, but because he learned that it was associated with Philip Berg and the Kabbalah Centre. Kadouri's retraction was publicized many times on the Internet in Hebrew; see, for example, http://www.shofar.net/site/ARDetile.asp?id=4857.

65. The shouting and waving during Kaddish, a distinctive hallmark of Kabbalah Centre Connections for years, has recently been abandoned; see Conclusion below.

66. Yehuda Berg, introduction to *Siddur T'filah L'Ani*, 10.

67. Philip Berg, introduction, *Siddur T'filah L'Ani*, i–iv.

68. There is mention of the red string as an empty practice taken from "the ways of the Amorites" in Tosefta Shabbat, a work composed during the first few centuries of the Common Era. See "Threadbare," by Rabbi Ahron Lopiansky, posted at http://www.aish.com/spirituality/kabbalah101/Threadbare.asp (accessed March 20, 2006).

69. Yehuda Berg, *The Red String Book: The Power of Protection, Technology for the Soul* (New York and Los Angeles: Kabbalah Centre International, 2004), 56.

70. Berg, *The Red String Book*, 58–59.

71. Lappin, "The Thin Red Line," spoke to Israeli military sources who deny that Kabbalah Centre people have wound the red string around the tomb. However, I have seen photographs in the Kabbalah Centre archives that depict Kabbalah Centre "events" at Rachel's tomb. The tomb is wound by yards of red string, with Kabbalah Centre members in attendance and engaged in meditation and celebration.

72. Berg, *The Red String Book*, 64ff.

CHAPTER 5

1. Linda L. Barnes and Susan S. Sered, eds., *Religion and Healing in America* (New York: Oxford University Press, 2005), 3–8.

2. Robert C. Fuller, "Holistic Health Practices," in *Spirituality and the Secular Quest*, ed. Peter H. Van Ness (New York: Herder & Herder, 1996), 242.

3. Philip Berg, *To the Power of One* (New York: Research Centre of Kabbalah, 1991), 215.

4. Berg, *To the Power of One*, 233.

5. Chaim Solomon, "Consciousness and Healing" course, first class session (July 11, 2002).

6. "Is a stumble ever simply just a stumble?" I asked Shaul Youdkevitch (interview, August 18, 2006). No, he answered, and cited a teaching attributed to the Ba'al Shem Tov (the founder of Hasidism) for support. A stumble has been decreed in advance. However, we cannot know whether it was decreed that it *must* occur or whether it was a stumble that could have been avoided had the person acted differently.

7. Chaim Solomon, "Consciousness and Healing" course, first class session (July 11, 2002).

8. See, for example, the biblical explanations for plague. In the first meeting of my "Healing and Consciousness" course (July 11, 2002), my teacher illustrated this point by reference to a story taken from a classical Jewish collection of biblical exegesis. From Adam until Isaac, he told us, there was no sickness whatsoever. People simply died in consequence of their serious evils. Isaac prayed to God to have an "early warning system," and so sickness entered the world. This story, explaining Isaac's blindness, can be found in *Bereishit Rabba*, a collection of elaborations of the book of Genesis composed during the first centuries of the Common Era. Historically, *Bereishit Rabba* was composed centuries prior to the emergence of Kabbalah. The practice of Kabbalah Centre teachers is to identify *all* Jewish religious literature as kabbalistic, and that is how the teacher, Chaim Solomon, identified the story.

9. This is obvious from a cursory examination of the literature. Michael Berg confirmed that in this they are following the advice of their publisher, interview with Michael Berg, July 31, 2006. Since Kabbalah Centre books are published by the Centre's own press, this comment points to the primacy of the organization's outreach mission.

10. Sefirot are explained in greater detail in chapter 1.

11. Chaim Solomon, "Consciousness and Healing" course, second class session (July 25, 2002).

12. Philip Berg, *Astrology: The Star Connection* (New York and Jerusalem: Research Centre of Kabbalah, 1986), 48. The principle of justice is found on pp. 58–59. This book was reissued and revised as *The Star Connection: The Science of Judaic Astrology* (New York: Research Centre of Kabbalah, 1986 copyright, 1992 rev. ed.). The material discussed here appears in both editions.

13. Berg, *Astrology: The Star Connection*, 40.

14. Berg, *Astrology: The Star Connection*, 41.

15. Berg, *To the Power of One*, 220–221.

16. Berg, *The Kabbalah Connection*, 184.

17. The public erasure of the distinction between Jews and the rest of humanity is described in chapter 4.

18. Berg, *To the Power of One*, 139–149; quotation is on p. 148.

19. Berg, *Wheels of a Soul*, 59.

20. Berg, *To the Power of One*, 217.

21. I heard this on September 4, 2004. The Torah portion was *Ki Tavo*.

22. Private communication with author, October 19, 2005.

23. Private communication with author, August 21, 2006.

24. Instructor Elisheva Kelman's teaching to the women, July 22, 2005.

25. Yehuda Berg, Weekly Meditation, August 13–19, 2006.

26. Private communication with author, September 29, 2006.

27. Private communication with author, September 13, 2006.

28. Private communication with author, September 13, 2006.

29. A reader of Berg's books may not realize this when faced with statements such as the following in Berg's *Astrology: The Star Connection*, 41: "Astrology gradually is being recognized as a vehicle of viable, scientific truth encompassing the entire electromagnetic field of our universe. There is growing awareness by scientists that man truly is a responsive element in the cosmos, but the forces that dictate man-inspired events remain largely unseen and unknown."

30. Berg, *To the Power of One*, 124.

31. Berg, *To the Power of One*, 124.

32. Berg, *To the Power of One*, 143, 149.

33. Philip Berg, *Immortality: The Inevitability of Eternal Life* (Tel Aviv, New York, and Los Angeles: Kabbalah Centre International, 2000).

34. One of the frequent charges against Berg lodged by ex-members is that Berg and the teachers advised them to reject medical counsel. I have heard this firsthand in my interview (November 13, 2005) with a person who told of Berg's counsel to her mother, who was suffering from a brain tumor, to forego an advised operation.

35. On augmenting medical treatment with kabbalistic tools, see "The Great Kabbalah Con Exposed," written by cancer patient Tony Donnelly, *The Telegraph* [United Kingdom], 10 January 2005, reprinted on http://www.rickross.com.

36. Interview with Jamie Greene, February 13, 2006; he told me proudly that women in the Hevre give birth at the well-regarded Cedars-Sinai Hospital and do not need to resort to the lower-priced hospitals connected to health maintenance organizations. Interview with Eitan Yardeni, February 14, 2006. Private communication between author and a daughter of a physician who provided free medical care to the Hevre, November 13, 2005.

37. Private communication with author, October 19, 2005.

38. Private communication with author, August 15, 2006.

39. Private communication with author, August 21, 2006.

40. Shaul Youdkevitch, "Health and Healing" video lecture, 2006.

41. Youdkevitch, "Health and Healing" lecture.

42. Interview with Shaul Youdkevitch, August 21, 2006. Private communication with author, September 13, 2006.

43. "Name, Change of," in *Encyclopaedia Judaica*, vol.12, 802. For example, my father's name was changed from Meir to Meir Hayyim when he incurred a potentially fatal childhood disease.

44. Berg, *Wheels of A Soul*, 111–113.

45. Interview with Shaul Youdkevitch, August 18, 2006.

46. Proverbs 10:2 and 11:4; also Babylonian Talmud Baba Batra 10a.

47. Private communication with author, August 4, 2006.

48. Private communication with author, July 19, 2005.

49. Interview with Shaul Youdkevitch, March 29, 2006. Youdkevitch was accused of fraud in November 2005 by the husband of a longtime member of the Tel Aviv Kabbalah Centre who donated money to the Centre, of which Youdkevitch was director, prior to her death from cancer. The charge was never filed because the Israeli court did not find grounds for it. At a news conference held jointly by the Kabbalah Centre and the deceased woman's husband the latter acknowledged that the donations to the Centre had gone for legitimate community concerns. This was reported in *Yediot Aharonot* [Israeli newspaper, in Hebrew], 24 November 2005; see also the online newspaper [in Hebrew], http://www.nfc.co.il/archive/001-D-86627-00.html?tag=11-53-43 Yet the police kept the file open for several months, finally closing the matter on January 30, 2006; see Israeli police documents concluding the investigation on case number 127270/2005.

50. Interview with Billy Phillips, March 1, 2006.

51. Interview with Billy Phillips, March 17, 2006.

52. Private communication with author, January 26, 2006.

53. Chaim Solomon, "Consciousness and Healing" course, second class session (July 25, 2002).

54. Yehuda Berg's commentary in Philip Berg, *Siddur T'filah L'Ani for Weekdays* (New York: Press of the Yeshivat Kol Yehuda, 1999), 32–33.

55. Private interview with the author, June 20, 2006.

56. Yehuda Berg's commentary in Philip Berg, *Siddur T'filah L'Ani for Weekdays*, 96.

57. Private communication with author, September 13, 2006.

58. Interview with Shaul Youdkevitch, August 18, 2006.

59. Chaim Solomon, "Healing and Consciousness" course, second class, July 25, 2002.

60. These are the phrases used in Kabbalah Centre Connections when the prayer leader explains the power of healing that is activated during the third verse in the *Ana Bekoach* prayer, described in the chapter text.

61. "*Ana Bekoach* Meditation" (taped lecture), by Jamie Greene. Teachers recommend to students in the first semester of the Kabbalah series to purchase and use the Kabbalah Centre book *Dialing God: Daily Connection Book*, ed. Yehuda Berg (Kabbalah Centre International, 2004). This is a collection of meditations and prayers considered essential on a daily basis. It contains a number of the healing meditations described below.

62. There are some meditations taken from kabbalistic astrology that may not be part of the RaSHaSH tradition, such as the two Hebrew letters assigned to each month.

63. Berg, *The Kabbalah Connection*, 114.

64. Berg, *The Kabbalah Connection*, 114–119.

65. This is the mode of healing called "change of place" because the person is changing his or her position on the sefirotic Tree of Life.

66. Berg, *The Kabbalah Connection*, 119; and see the discussions of Binah in Rav P.S. Berg, *Days of Power*, part 1 (New York and Los Angeles: Kabbalah Centre International, 2005), 72–85, 144–150.

67. Private communication with author, September 13, 2006.

68. For a history of the use of these names and their appearance in Kabbalah Centre teachings, see Boaz Huss, "All You Need Is LAV: Madonna and Postmodern Kabbalah," *The Jewish Quarterly Review* 95, no. 4 (Fall 2005), 611–624. Philip Berg's explanation can be found in his introduction to *Siddur T'filah L'Ani for Shabbat*, iii.

69. This is on the Kabbalah Centre Web site at http://www.kabbalah.com/k/index.php/p=life/tools/72names (accessed August 28, 2006).

70. Yehuda Berg, *The 72 Names of God: Technology for the Soul* (New York and Los Angeles: Kabbalah Centre International, 2003). I thank Joel Hecker for the information that one of Yehuda Berg's sources was the volume called *Ve-Herev Pifiyot*, written by Yeshaya Yaakov Halevi (d. 1801).

71. Yehuda Berg's commentary in Philip Berg, *Siddur Tefilah L'Ani for Shabbat*, 288.

72. Yehuda Berg, *The 72 Names of God*, 59.

73. Interview with Shaul Youdkevitch, August 18, 2006, and e-mail correspondence August 30, 2006. Actually, *mem hey shin* equals 345 (40 + 5 + 300), and this is one less than *resh tsadi vav nun*, which is 346 (200 + 90 + 6 + 50). The two letter combinations are considered equivalent even though there is a difference of one, in accordance with the principle that when a few letters create a word, a new entity is created as well.

74. On this phenomenon, see Susan Sered, "Healing as Resistance: Reflections upon New Forms of American Jewish Healing," in *Religion and Healing in America*, ed. Linda L. Barnes and Susan S Sered, 231–252.

75. Philip Berg, *Siddur T'filah L'Ani for Shabbat*, 338. The phrase in the prayer, "Please God, heal him, please" is adapted from Moses's prayer on behalf of Miriam's health (Numbers 12:13). The *Misheberach* for women acknowledges the different number of organs tradition ascribes to women ("may He send complete healing to her 252 organs and her 365 sinews") and uses the original Hebrew of the prayer.

76. Yehuda Berg, commentary in Philip Berg, *Siddur T'filah L'ani for Weekdays*,129.

77. This is on the Kabbalah Centre Web site at http://store.kabbalah.com/product_info.php?cPath=143&vcats=143&products_id=296

78. "*Ana Bekoach* Meditation" (taped lecture), by Jamie Greene.

79. "*Ana Bekoach* Meditation" (taped lecture), by Jamie Greene. It is generally taught that the *ideal* time to engage in kabbalistic meditation is between midnight and 4 A.M., and morning meditations are additional to the nocturnal ones.

80. Interview with Shaul Youdkevitch, March 29, 2006.

81. Interview with Shaul Youdkevitch, March 29, 2006.

82. Many of the people I interviewed mentioned mikveh immersion as a regular ritual in their lives. I first learned of it in my Kabbalah I class, 1999; private communication with author, August 21, 2006, about the early years of the Los Angeles community who—before there was a separate Kabbalah Centre building and mikveh—faced the hostility of the Orthodox men at the Los Angeles Mikveh who objected to their study of Kabbalah; interview with Michael Moskowitz, February 10, 2006.

83. This history of water is found on a Kabbalah Centre Web site: http://www.kabbalah water.com.

84. Interview with Michael Berg, April 13, 2005. A former member of the Kabbalah Centre, who has since started his own kabbalistic synagogue and study center in the neighborhood of the Kabbalah Centre in Los Angeles, claims to have learned from the Rav the passage in Lurianic writings containing the "recipe" of blessings and meditations and to have prepared some. I have not been able to learn the exact source in kabbalistic literature or the formula. I have heard a number of anecdotes from Centre members about the years (1993–1998) in which Berg experimented with creating Kabbalah water; private communications with author, March 25, 2006; July 19, 2006; September 13, 2006.

85. Private communication with author, September 13, 2006.

86. Youdkevitch, "Health and Healing" lecture gives a detailed description of the "science" of water. Kabbalah water has also been mentioned by the prayer leaders many times in passing at Shabbat and holiday Connections. It is quite acceptable, and even recommended, to drink Kabbalah water during the Connections.

87. Masaru Emoto, *Messages from Water* (Leiden: Hado Publishing, 1999); *The Hidden Messages in Water* (Hillsboro, OR: Beyond Words Publishing, 2004); and many more. See his Web site: http://www.hado.net

88. Both of these men were mentioned as authorities in the Youdkevitch, "Health and Healing" lecture. Emoto is far better known, and his name has been mentioned to me several times by Kabbalah Centre members.

89. Much has been written on the subject. See Robert L. Park, *Voodoo Science: The Road from Foolishness to Fraud* (New York: Oxford University Press, 2000). See also Martin Gardner, *Science: Good, Bad, and Bogus* (Amherst, NY: Prometheus, 1981, 1989) and *Weird Water and Fuzzy Logic* (Amherst, NY: Prometheus, 1996); and Michael W. Friedlander, *At the Fringes of Science* (Boulder, CO: Westview Press, 1996).

90. Stephen Lower was on the faculty of the chemistry department at Simon Fraser University in Vancouver, Canada, from 1965 to 1999. His Web site on Aqua Scams may be found at http://www.chem1.com/CQ/ (accessed October 5, 2006).

91. Steven I. Weiss, "Florida Lawmaker in Flap Over 'Holy Water,'" *The Forward*, 15 July 2005. The water, named "Celestial Drops," was not officially identified as Kabbalah water, but it was suggested to the secretary of state by Abraham Hardoon of the West Boca Kabbalah Learning Centre, and it was described with identical language.

92. I have heard this account many times, the first being at the Kabbalah I class, 1999.

93. Private communication with author, September 13, 2006.

94. Private communication with author, September 13, 2006.

95. Private communication with author, September 23, 2006.

96. Interview with Philippe van den Bossche, director of development, The Kabbalah Centre Charitable Foundation, September 12, 2006.

97. Quotation from the Spirituality for Kids Web site, http://www.spiritualityforkids.org/curriculum.htm (accessed November 4, 2006) and interview with Heath Grant, October 27, 2006.

98. Observation at the SFK class at Challengers Boys and Girls Club, October 26, 2006, and conversation with the teacher, Holly.

99. Interview with Philippe van den Bossche, September 12, 2006; interview with Heath Grant, October 27, 2006; interview with Michelle Raymond, SFK Global organizer. On the connections between Raising Malawi, the Malawi government, and community-based organizations in Malawi, see George Ntonya, "Madonna's Visit to Benefit Malawi's Orphans," *The Malawi Nation*, 6 September 2006, http://www.nationmalawi.com (accessed September 10, 2006).

100. Interview with Osnat Youdkevitch, October 25, 2006.

101. Yehuda Berg's Daily Meditations, Weekly Meditation for July 30–August 5, 2006.

102. Heath Grant, PhD, formerly professor in the Department of Law, Police Science and Criminal Justice Administration at John Jay College of Criminal Justice, is now director of global research and training for Spirituality for Kids; interview with Heath Grant, October 27, 2006.

CHAPTER 6

1. Discussion with Syd Kessler, Board member of the Toronto Kabbalah Centre and marketing expert, September 23, 2006. Kessler estimates that the Kabbalah Centre's rate of retention is only 6 percent.

2. The original version of the hundredth-monkey effect is attributed to Lyall Watson, *Lifetide* (New York: Simon and Schuster, 1979), and it was further popularized by Ken Keyes, Jr., *The Hundredth Monkey* (Coos Bay, OR: Vision Books, 1982). For a scientific analysis of Lyall Watson's research, see Ron Amundson, "The Hundredth Monkey Phenomenon," *Skeptical Inquirer* 9 (Summer 1985), 348–356; Boyce Rensberger, "Spud-Dunking Monkey Theory Debunked," *Washington Post*, 6 July 1985. For full references showing the spread of these ideas within popular (particularly New Age) culture, see http://www.uhh.hawaii.edu/~ronald/HMP.htm (accessed October 22, 2006).

3. "Blessed [*Baruch*] are you, Lord our God, King of the universe, who creates the fruit of the vine."

Bibliography

Altmann, Alexander. "Astrology." In *Encyclopaedia Judaica*. Vol. 3, 788–795. Jerusalem and New York: Macmillan, 1972.

Amundson, Ron. "The Hundredth Monkey Phenomenon." *Skeptical Inquirer* 9 (Summer 1985): 348–356.

Angel, Marc. *The Rhythms of Jewish Living: A Sephardic Exploration of the Basic Teachings of Judaism*. Northvale, NJ: Jason Aronson, 1997.

Ariel, Yaakov. "Hasidism in the Age of Aquarius: The House of Love and Prayer in San Francisco, 1967–1977." *Religion and American Culture* 13, no. 2 (2003): 139–165.

Ashlag, Yehuda. *An Entrance to the Zohar*, comp. and ed. Philip S. Berg. New York and Jerusalem: Research Centre of Kabbalah, 1974.

———. *Etz Chaim*, with the commentaries *Panim Me'irot and Panim Masbirot* [in Hebrew]. Jerusalem: Research Centre for the Study of Kabbalah, 1978.

———. *A Gift of the Bible*. Jerusalem and New York: Research Centre of Kabbalah, 1984.

———. *Pri Hacham* [in Hebrew]. Bnei Brak: A.Y. Ashlag, 1985.

———. *Talmud Eser Ha-Sefirot Me-Haari Zal, im Shnei Biurim Maspikim Lemathilim, Hanikrain or Penimit . . . Histaklut Penimit*. Brooklyn, NY: The Kabbalah Foundation, 1943.

———. *Ten Luminous Emanations*, vol. 1. New York and Jerusalem: Research Centre of Kabbalah, 1970.

———. *Ten Luminous Emanations*, vol. 2. New York and Jerusalem: Research Centre of Kabbalah, 1973.

Barker, Eileen. *The Making of a Moonie: Choice or Brainwashing?* Oxford: Basil Blackwell, 1984.

———. "Perspective: What Are We Studying? A Sociological Case for Keeping the 'Nova.'" *Nova Religio* 8, no. 1 (2004), 88–102.

Barnes, Linda L., and Susan S. Sered, eds. *Religion and Healing in America*. New York: Oxford University Press, 2005.

Berenbaum, Michael and Fred Skolnick, eds. *Encyclopedia Judaica*, 2nd ed. Detroit: Macmillan Reference, 2007.

Berg, Karen. *God Wears Lipstick: Kabbalah for Women*. New York and Los Angeles: Kabbalah Centre International, 2005.

Berg, Michael, ed. *Sefer Yedid Nafshi*, 3 vols. [in Hebrew]. Jerusalem: Press of the Kol Yehuda Yeshiva, 1997.

Berg, Philip. *Astrology: The Star Connection*. New York and Jerusalem: Research Centre of Kabbalah, 1986. Revised as *The Star Connection: The Science of Judaic Astrology*. New York: Research Centre of Kabbalah, 1986 copyright, 1992 rev. ed.

———. *Education of a Kabbalist*. Tel Aviv, New York, and Los Angeles: Kabbalah Centre International, 2000.

———. *Immortality: The Inevitability of Eternal Life*. Tel Aviv, New York, and Los Angeles: Kabbalah Centre International, 2000.

———. *The Kabbalah Connection: Jewish Festivals as a Path to Pure Awareness*. Jerusalem: Research Centre of Kabbalah Books, 1983.

———. *Kabbalah for the Layman: A Guide to Cosmic Consciousness*. Jerusalem: Press of the Research Centre of Kabbalah, 1981. Also 1987, 1991.

———. *Power of Aleph Beth*, 2 vols. Jerusalem and New York: Research Centre of Kabbalah Press, 1988.

———. *The Star Connection: The Science of Judaic Astrology*. New York: Research Centre of Kabbalah, 1986 copyright, 1992 rev. ed.

———. *To the Power of One*. New York: Research Centre of Kabbalah, 1991.

———. *Wheels of a Soul*. Jerusalem and New York: Research Centre of Kabbalah, 1984.

——— [Berg, Rav P.S.]. *Days of Power*, part 1. New York and Los Angeles: Kabbalah Centre International, 2005, pp. 72–85, 144–150.

——— [Berg, S.P.]. *Siddur T'filah L'Ani for Shabbat: With Meditations from The Ari Z"L, HaRashash, HaRamchal, Ha'Ba'al Shem Tove, and HaRich*, ed. Yehudah Berg. New York: Press of the Yeshivat Kol Yehudah, 1999.

——— [Berg, S. P]. *Siddur T'filah L'Ani for Weekdays*. New York: Press of the Yeshivat Kol Yehudah, 1999.

Berg, Yehuda, ed. *Dialing God: Daily Connection Book*. New York and Los Angeles: Kabbalah Centre International, 2004.

———. *The Power of Kabbalah*. Los Angeles: Kabbalah Centre International, 2004.

———. *The Red String Book: The Power of Protection, Technology for the Soul*. New York and Los Angeles: Kabbalah Centre International, 2004.

———. *The 72 Names of God: Technology for the Soul*. New York and Los Angeles: Kabbalah Centre International, 2003.

Bnei Baruch World Center for Kabbalah Studies. http://www.kabbalah.info.

Bromley, David G. "Brainwashing (Debate)." In *Encyclopedia of Religion*, 2nd ed., vol. 2, 1030–1036. Detroit: Macmillan Reference, 2005.

Bromley, David G., and James T. Richardson, eds. *The Brainwashing/Deprogramming Controversy: Sociological, Psychological, Legal and Historical Perspectives*. New York and Toronto: Edwin Mellon Press, 1983.

The Cabal of the Cabbalah Centre Exposed: The Truth about The Kabbalah Centre and Its Guru, Philip S. Berg. Los Angeles: Task Force on Cults and Missionaries, 1995.

Cohen, Mark, and Yedidah Cohen, eds., *In the Shadow of the Ladder: Introductions to Kabbalah by Rabbi Yehudah Lev Ashlag*. Safed, Israel: Nehorah Press, 2002.

Cohn-Sherbok, Lavinia, and Dan Sherbok. *A Short Introduction to Judaism*. London: Oneworld Publishing, Ltd., 1997.

Cordovero, Moshe. *Or Ne'erav*, ed. Yehuda Z. Brandwein [in Hebrew]. Brooklyn, NY: National Institute for Research in Kabbalah, 1965.

Coudert, Allison, and Jeffrey S. Shoulson, eds. *Hebraica Veritas? Christian Hebraists, Jews, and the Study of Judaism in Early Modern Europe*. Philadelphia: University of Pennsylvania Press, 2004.

Csillag, Ron. "The Kabbalah Centre." *The Canadian Jewish News*, March 18, 1993.

Dan, Joseph. "The Emergence of Mystical Prayer." In *Jewish Mysticism: The Middle Ages*, vol. 2, ed. Joseph Dan. Northvale, NJ: Jason Aronson, 1998.

Dan, Joseph, and Ronald Kiener. *The Early Kabbalah*. Ramsey, NJ: Paulist Press, 1986.

Dawson, Lorne L. *Comprehending Cults: The Sociology of New Religious Movements*, 2nd ed. Don Mills, Ontario: Oxford University Press Canada, 2006.

Donnelly, Tony. "The Great Kabbalah Con Exposed." *The Telegraph* [United Kingdom], 10 January 2005, reprinted at http://www.rickross.com.

Dynner, Glenn. *Men of Silk: The Hasidic Conquest of Polish Society.* New York and London: Oxford University Press, 2006.

Elior, Rachel. "The Doctrine of Transmigration in Galya Raza." In *Essential Papers on Kabbalah*, ed. Lawrence Fine. New York: New York University Press, 1995.

Emoto, Masaru. *Messages from Water.* Leiden: Hado Publishing, 1999.

———. *The Hidden Messages in Water.* Hillsboro, OR: Beyond Words Publishing, 2004.

Eshman, Robert. "Center of Controversy." *The Jewish Journal* [Los Angeles], 14–20 February 1997.

Faivre, Antoine. "Esotericism." In *Encyclopedia of Religion*, 2nd ed., vol. 4, 2842–2845. Detroit: Macmillan Reference, 2007.

Fine, Lawrence. *Physician of the Soul, Healer of the Cosmos: Isaac Luria and His Kabbalistic Fellowship.* Stanford: Stanford University Press, 2003.

Fishbein, Aynat. "The Cabal of the Kabbalah Centre Exposed" [in Hebrew]. *Tel Aviv*, September 1994.

Friedlander, Michael W. *At the Fringes of Science.* Boulder, CO: Westview Press, 1996.

Fuller, Robert C. "Holistic Health Practices." In *Spirituality and the Secular Quest*, ed. Peter H. Van Ness, 242. New York: Herder & Herder, 1996.

Garb, Jonathan. *"The Chosen Will Become Herds": Studies in Twentieth Century Kabbalah* [in Hebrew]. Jerusalem: Shalom Hartman Institute, 2005.

Gardner, Martin. *Science: Good, Bad, and Bogus.* Amherst, NY: Prometheus, 1981, 1989.

———. *Weird Water and Fuzzy Logic.* Amherst, NY: Prometheus, 1996.

Giller, Pinchas. *Shalom Shar'abi and the Kabbalists of Beit El.* New York and London: Oxford University Press, in press.

Gottlieb, Avraham Mordecai. *Ha-Sulam: Biographies of Rabbi Yehuda Lev Ashlag and Rabbi Baruch Ashlag and their Pupils* [in Hebrew]. Jerusalem: Or Baruch Shalom, 1997.

Green, Arthur. *Ehyeh: A Kabbalah for Tomorrow.* Woodstock, VT: Jewish Lights, 2003.

Gross, Terry. "Fresh Air from WHYY" Interview with Madonna. NPR, 23 November 2004.

Halevi, Yossi Klein. "Like a Prayer." *The New Republic* 230, no. 17 (10 May 2004): 18–21.

Hammer, Olav. "Esotericism in New Religious Movements." In *The Oxford Handbook of New Religious Movements*, ed. James R. Lewis, 445–465. Oxford and New York: Oxford University Press, 2004.

Hanegraaff, Wouter J. *New Age Religion and Western Culture: Esotericism in the Mirror of Secular Thought.* Leiden: E. J. Brill, 1996.

———. "New Age Movement." In *Encyclopedia of Religion*, 2nd ed., vol. 10, 6495–6500. Detriot: Macmillan Reference, 2005.

Hansel, David. "The Origin in the Thought of Rabbi Yehuda Halevy Ashlag: Ṣimṣum of God or Ṣimṣum of the World?" *Kabbalah: Journal for the Study of Jewish Mystical Texts* 7 (2002): 37–46.

Huss, Boaz. "All You Need Is LAV: Madonna and Postmodern Kabbalah." *The Jewish Quarterly Review* 95 (Fall 2005): 611–624.

———. "'Altruistic Communism': The Modernistic Kabbalah of Rabbi Ashlag" [in Hebrew]. *Iyunim Bitkumat Israel* 16 (2006): 115–116.

———. "Ask No Questions: Gershom Scholem and the Study of Contemporary Jewish Mysticism." *Modern Judaism* 25, no. 2 (May 2005): 141–158.

———. "The Construction of Jewish Mysticism and the Politics of Teaching It." Unpublished paper, presented at the 14th Annual World Congress of Jewish Studies, Jerusalem, 2005.

———. "The New Age of Kabbalah: Contemporary Kabbalah, New Age, and Postmodern Spirituality." Forthcoming.

————. "*Sefer ha-Zohar* as a Canonical, Sacred and Holy Text: Changing Perspectives of the Book of Splendor between the Thirteenth and Eighteenth Centuries." *Journal of Jewish Thought and Philosophy* 7 (1998): 257–307.

Idel, Moshe. "On the History of the Interdiction against the Study of Kabbalah before the Age of Forty" [in Hebrew], *AJS Review* 5 (1980), 1–15.

————. *Kabbalah: New Perspectives.* New Haven, CT: Yale University Press, 1988.

————. "Perceptions of Kabbalah in the Second Half of the 18th Century," *Journal of Jewish Thought & Philosophy* 1 (1991), 55–114.

————. " 'One from a Town, Two from a Clan'—The Diffusion of Lurianic Kabbala and Sabbateanism: A Re-Examination." *Jewish History* 7 (1993): 79–104.

————. "Perceptions of Kabbalah in the Second Half of the 18th Century." *Journal of Jewish Thought and Philosophy* 1 (1991): 55–114.

Inbari, Assaf. "New Age: The Fall of the Secular State" [in Hebrew]. In *Haaretz,* September 1999. Available in English at http://inbari.co.il/en_index.htm (accessed on January 12, 2006).

————. "The Underground of Yearning" [in Hebrew]. In *Haaretz,* 17 September 1999.

Jones, Lindsay, ed. *Encyclopedia of Religion,* 2nd ed., 15 vols. Detroit: Macmillan Reference, 2005.

Kallus, Menachem. "The Theurgy of Prayer in the Lurianic Kabbalah." In *Jewish Mysticism: The Middle Ages,* vol. 2, ed. Joseph Dan. Northvale, NJ: Jason Aronson, 1998.

Katz, Steven T. *Jewish Ideas and Concepts.* New York: Schocken Books, 1977.

————. "Language, Epistemology and Mysticism." In *Mysticism and Philosophical Analysis,* ed. Steven T. Katz. New York and London: Oxford University Press, 1978.

Keyes, Jr., Ken. *The Hundredth Monkey.* Coos Bay, OR: Vision Books, 1982.

Krakovsky, Levi Isaac. *If eventually—Why Not Now? Oyb nisht yetst, ven?* Brooklyn: Kabbalah Foundation, 1938.

————. *Israel's Survival in Kabbalah.* n.p., n.d.

————. *Kabbalah: The Light of Redemption.* Brooklyn, NY: The Kabbalah Foundation, 1950.

————. "Kabbalah: Dialogue Between G-d and the Hebrew Alphabet." Unpublished manuscript, n.d.

————. "Key to Paradise." Unpublished Manuscript, 1953.

————. *The Omnipotent Light Revealed: The Luminous Tegument to Unite Mankind into One Loving Brotherhood.* Hollywood, CA: Kabbalah Culture Society of America, 1939.

Kyle, Richard. *The New Age Movement in American Culture.* Lanham, MD: University Press of America, 1995.

Laitman, Michael. *Kabbalah Lematchil* [in Hebrew]. Israel: Bnei Baruch, 2005.

Lappin, Elena. "The Thin Red Line," part one. *Guardian,* 11 December 2004, http://www.guardian.co.uk/print/0,3858,5082014-103602,00.html (accessed January 6, 2005).

Latkin, Carl, R. Hagan, R. Littman, and N. Sundberg, "Who Lives in Utopia? A Brief Report on the Rajneeshpuram Research Project." *Sociological Analysis* 48 (1987): 73–81.

Lenowitz, Harris. "The Appearance of Hebrew Script in Art: Three from the Golden West." Unpublished paper, presented at the 13th Annual World Congress of Jewish Studies, Jerusalem, 2001.

Levanon, Naomi. "The Added Value of the Kabbalah" [in Hebrew]. *La-Isha* [Israeli women's magazine], November 14, 1978. Accessed on the Israeli Kabbalah Centre Web site, http://www.kabbalah.co.il (May 24, 2005).

Lewis, James R. *Legitimating New Religions.* Piscataway, NJ: Rutgers University Press, 2003.

Liebes, Yehudah. *Studies in the Zohar.* Albany: State University of New York Press, 1993.

Lifton, Robert. *Thought Reform and the Psychology of Totalism.* New York: W.W. Norton, 1961.

Loewenthal, Naftali. "Schneerson, Menachem M." In *Encyclopedia of Religion,* 2nd ed., vol. 12, 8171–8173. Detroit: Macmillan Reference, 2005.

Lopiansky, Ahron. "Threadbare." http://www.aish.com/spirituality/kabbalah101/Threadbare (accessed March 20, 2006).

Lower, Stephen. Web site on Aqua Scams, http://www.chem1.com/CQ.

Luzzatto, R. M. *General Principles of the Kabbalah.* New York: Press of the Research Centre of Kabbalah, 1970.

Magid, Shaul. "Jewish Renewal Movement." In *Encyclopedia of Religion,* 2nd ed., 4869. Detroit: Macmillan Reference, 2005.

Meilicke, Christine A. "Abulafianism among the Counterculture Kabbalists." *Jewish Studies Quarterly* 9 (2002): 71–101.

———. "The Forgotten History of David Meltzer's Journal *Tree.*" *Studies in American Jewish Literature* 22 (2003): 52–71.

Meir, Jonatan. "The Revealed and the Revealed within the Concealed: On the Opposition to the 'Followers' of Rabbi Yehuda Ashlag and the Dissemination of Esoteric Literature" [in Hebrew]. *Kabbalah: Journal for the Study of Jewish Mystical Texts* 16 (2007), forthcoming.

———. "Wrestling with the Esoteric: Hillel Zeitlin, Yehudah Ashlag, and Kabbalah in the Land of Israel" [in Hebrew]. In *Be'er Rivkah: Festschrift in Honor of Professor Rivka Hurvitz,* ed. Efraim Meir and Haviva Padia, 585–647. Beer Sheva: Ben Gurion University Press, 2006.

Melton, J. Gordon. "A History of the New Age Movement." In *Not Necessarily the New Age: Critical Essays,* ed. Robert Basil. Buffalo, NY: Prometheus Books, 1988.

———. "An Introduction to New Religions." In *The Oxford Handbook of New Religious Movements,* ed. James R. Lewis, 16–35. Oxford and New York: Oxford University Press, 2004.

———. "New Age Transformed." The Religious Movements Homepage Project of the University of Virginia, http://religiousmovements.lib.virginia.edu/nrms/newage.html (accessed February 9, 2006).

———. "Perspective: Toward a Definition of 'New Religion.'" *Nova Religio* 8, no. 1 (2004): 73–85.

Melton, J. Gordon, and Robert L. Moore. *The Cult Experience: Responding to the New Religious Pluralism.* New York: Pilgrim Press, 1982.

Myers, Jody. "Berg, Philip." In *Encyclopedia Judaica,* 2nd ed., vol. 3, 417–418. Detroit: Macmillan Reference, 2007.

Myers, Jody, and Jane Rachel Litman. "The Secret of Jewish Femininity: Hiddenness, Power, and Physicality in the Theology of Orthodox Women in the Contemporary World." In *Gender and Judaism: The Transformation of Tradition,* 51–80, ed. T. M. Rudavsky. New York: New York University Press, 1995.

Ntonya, George. "Madonna's Visit to Benefit Malawi's Orphans." *The Malawi Nation,* September 6, 2006, http://www.nationmalawi.com (accessed September 6, 2006).

Odenheimer, Micah. "Latter-day Luminary." In *Haaretz,* 16 December 2004. Translated at www.haaretz.com/hasen/objects/pages/PrintArticleEn.jhtml?itemNo=515439 (accessed December 18, 2004).

Palmer, Susan J. "Women's 'Cocoon Work' in New Religious Movements: Sexual Experimentation and Feminine Rites of Passage." *Journal for the Scientific Study of Religion* 32, no. 4 (December 1993): 343–355.

Park, Robert L. *Voodoo Science: The Road from Foolishness to Fraud.* New York: Oxford University Press, 2000.

Prell, Riv- Ellen. *Prayer and Community: The Havurah in American Judaism.* Detroit: Wayne State University Press, 1989.

Rensberger, Boyce. "Spud-Dunking Monkey Theory Debunked." *Washington Post,* July 6, 1985.

Richardson, James T. "Sociology and the New Religions: 'Brainwashing,' the Courts, and Religious Freedom." In *Witness for Sociology: Reflexive Essays on Sociologists in Court,* ed. P. Jenkins and S. Kroll-Smith, 115–137. New York: Praeger, 1997.

Rick A. Ross Institute for the Study of Destructive Cults, Controversial Groups, and Movements. http://www.rickross.com.

Robinson, Ira. "Kabbalah and Orthodoxy: Some Twentieth Century Interpretations." Unpublished paper presented at the American Academy of Religion conference, 1987.

———. "Kabbalah and Science in *Sefer Ha-Berit*: A Modernization Strategy for Orthodox Jews." *Modern Judaism* 9, no. 3 (October 1989): 275–288.

Sarna, Jonathan D. *American Judaism: A History.* New Haven, CT: Yale University Press, 2004.

Schein, Edgar H., Inge Schneier, and Curtis H. Becker. *Coercive Persuasion.* New York: W.W. Norton, 1961.

Scholem, Gershom. *Kabbalah.* Jerusalem: Keter Publishing House, 1974.

———. *Major Trends in Jewish Mysticism.* New York: Schocken Books, 1946.

———. Review of L.I. Krakowsky, *Kabbalah: The Light of Redemption. Jewish Social Studies* 25 (1953): 312.

———. *Sabbatai Sevi.* Princeton, NJ: Princeton University Press, 1976.

Selengut, Charles. "American Jewish Converts to New Religious Movements." *The Jewish Journal of Sociology* 30, no. 2 (1988): 95–109.

Sered, Susan. "Healing as Resistance: Reflections upon New Forms of American Jewish Healing." In *Religion and Healing in America*, ed. Linda L. Barnes and Susan S. Sered, 231–252. New York: Oxford University Press, 2005.

Siegel, Richard, Michael Strassfeld, and Sharon Strassfeld, eds. *The Jewish Catalog: A Do-It-Yourself Kit.* Philadelphia: The Jewish Publication Society, 1973.

Singer, Margaret Thaler, with Janja Lalich. *Cults in Our Midst.* San Francisco: Jossey-Bass Publishers, 1995.

Spirituality for Kids Web site. http://www.spiritualityforkids.org.

Stace, Walter T. *The Teachings of the Mystics.* New York: New American Library, 1960.

Stark, Rodney, and William Sims Bainbridge. *The Future of Religion: Secularization, Revival and Cult Formation.* Berkeley: University of California Press, 1985.

Sweeny, John. "Kabbalah Leader's Holocaust 'Slur.'" BBC News, 9 January 2005, http://news.bbc.co.uk/1/hi/world/4158287.stm (accessed December 4, 2005).

Underhill, Evelyn. *Mysticism.* London: Methuen & Co., 1911.

Watson, Lyall. *Lifetide.* New York: Simon and Schuster, 1979.

Weiner, Herbert. *9½ Mystics: The Kabbalah Today.* New York: Collier Books, 1969.

Weiss, Steven I. "Florida Lawmaker in Flap Over 'Holy Water.'" *The Forward*, July 15, 2005.

Wertheimer, Jack. *A People Divided: Judaism in Contemporary America.* New York: Basic Books, 1993.

Wijnhoven, Jochanan H. A. "The *Zohar* and the Proselyte." In *Texts and Responses: Studies Presented to N. Glatzer*, ed. Michael Fishbane, 120–140. Leiden: Brill, 1975.

Wuthnow, Robert. *After Heaven: Spirituality in America since the 1950s.* Berkeley: University of California Press, 1998.

Zimmelman, Janya. "The Powerfully Subordinate: Gender in Theory and Practice at the Kabbalah Learning Centre." Unpublished paper.

The Zohar Project. http://www.kabbalah.com/kabbalah/programs.htm/#zohar.

Index

About the Author

JODY MYERS is Professor of Religious Studies at California State University, Northridge and author of *Seeking Zion: Modernity and Messianic Activism in the Writings of Tsevi Hirsch Kalischer*, and many other journal articles and book chapters.